The History of Menshevism

Leopold H. Haimson, *General Editor*

HOOVER INSTITUTION PUBLICATIONS

The Russian Revolution of 1905

The Russian

THE WORKERS' MOVEMENT

THE HOOVER INSTITUTION
on War, Revolution,
and Peace

Solomon M. Schwarz

Revolution of 1905

AND THE FORMATION OF BOLSHEVISM
AND MENSHEVISM

Translated by GERTRUDE VAKAR

 THE UNIVERSITY OF CHICAGO PRESS

CHICAGO AND LONDON

This volume is one of a series arising from the
work of the INTER-UNIVERSITY PROJECT ON THE
HISTORY OF THE MENSHEVIK MOVEMENT

Library of Congress Catalog Card Number: 66–20582

THE UNIVERSITY OF CHICAGO PRESS, CHICAGO & LONDON
The University of Toronto Press, Toronto 5, Canada

© *1967 by The University of Chicago*
All rights reserved. Published 1967

Printed in the United States of America

Preface

In tracing any extended historical process the dramatic culmination of which left so vivid an imprint on men's minds as the Russian Revolution of 1917, it is tempting—especially from the distance of a half-century—to lose sight of the actual complexity of the chain of events that it encompassed in an effort to find in the process, just as in the ideas and feelings of the men who were active in it, an essential coherence and consistency from its very inception to its ultimate conclusion. Such temptations arise, of course, in the conduct of any historical study, as the historian, faced by the "booming, buzzing confusion," the density and ultimate irreducibility of particular events, is impelled to abstract from them in order to establish the connections, the explicit or implicit relations of cause and effect, between one event and another, on which all historical narrative ultimately depends. But the impulse to find a logic and a pattern in the meandering course of history has been felt especially strongly by students of the development of Bolshevism and Menshevism, partly because these two wings of Russian Social-Democracy were themselves impelled, from the very first, to seek clear, explicit ideological and historical grounds for the differences that were pulling them apart.

That such stresses on continuity vastly oversimplify the actual process by which Bolshevism and Menshevism assumed their separate identities is evident if only from the fact that many of the men who were, or became, prominent in the two factions shifted their allegiance from one to the other until well after the October revolution. Actually, the development of both Bolshevism and Menshevism occurred as the result of a complex process in which the changing character and behavior of each faction profoundly influenced the other; this process unfolded in the setting of changing environments in both Russia and Western Europe, and it encompassed the appearance on the historical stage of at least three political generations, the members of which were characterized in many respects by quite distinctive intellectual and emotional makeups and social backgrounds.

Yet even when all this is conceded, it remains true that the Revolution of 1905—the period with which this volume is concerned—constituted a most significant landmark in the development of Bolshevism and Menshevism. In the crucible of this revolution, the masses of the Russian working class came dramatically and explosively to political life—on a nation-wide scale —and in the face of this unleashed and largely uncontrollable mass movement, most of the contradictions and tensions that had beset the development of Russian Social-Democracy from its inception were brought dramatically to the surface.[1] Both Bolsheviks and Mensheviks were now compelled to articulate and act out—and eventually to reconsider—many of the often unspoken assumptions that they had entertained about their self-appointed roles as spokesmen of the Russian workers. In the process, the differences between them gradually emerged from the shadows of submerged attitudes and half-understood doctrinal and organizational differences and led eventually to significant realignments in the ranks of Russian Social-Democracy.

Solomon Schwarz is singularly well equipped to grasp some of the more significant dimensions of this phase in the self-definition of Bolshevism and Menshevism because of the variety of perspectives that he has been able to project on it from his own life experience. A Bolshevik agitator in 1905 who in his later years (when he became one of the leading Menshevik spokesmen on labor affairs) joined hands with some of the very Menshevik labor leaders with whom he had argued and fought during Russia's First

---

[1] Some of these early tensions and contradictions in the early development of Russian Social-Democracy, particularly as they affected the relations between intelligentsia and workers, are examined in Allan Wildman's volume in this series, "The Making of a Worker's Revolution: Russian Social-Democracy, 1891–1903" (to be published by the University of Chicago Press in 1967).

Revolution, he has brought to his study a unique capacity to relive the ideas and feelings that were experienced at the time by the members of both factions of Russian Social-Democracy. The very theme that he has elected to emphasize in his discussion of 1905—the attitudes displayed by the two factions of the RSDRP (*Rossiiskaia Sotsial-Demokraticheskaia Rabochaia Partiia*) toward the various contemporary manifestations of the Russian labor movement—is the one that underlay his own gradual disillusionment with Bolshevism and ultimate switch to the Menshevik faction. The personal insights that he sheds on the nature of this transition are especially valuable because they are largely applicable to other Social-Democratic *praktiki*[2] (such as Bienstock, Dubois, Kefali, Romanov) who during the same years, and under similar psychological pressures, made the same political journey.

In this monograph, and in his interviews with the Inter-University Project on the History of the Menshevik Movement at Columbia University, Schwarz also sheds considerable light on the sources of this group's original allegiance to Bolshevism. He emphasizes that what originally drew so many in what has come to be called the generation of 1905 to Lenin and the Bolsheviks was basically the fact that, of the two rival factions in the RSDRP, it seemed the more radical, the more decisive, the more "revolutionary." By comparison, the Mensheviks appeared too moderate, too abstract. "I would say that the most dedicated, the most active young Social Democrats became Bolsheviks," Schwarz observes in one of his interviews. "We couldn't understand the Mensheviks' tactics. And therefore it seemed natural to us to become Bolsheviks."[3] What was puzzling and disconcerting about the Mensheviks' views, as the Revolution of 1905 began, was not merely the abstract character—often bordering on fantasy—of their tactical plans for rousing "bourgeois" society to political activism "without antagonizing it" (such as the so-called *Iskra* plan for the zemstvo campaign). Unintelligible to many of the intelligentsia's youth and the working class who were then attracted to Social-

---

[2] The term *praktiki* has been applied to those in Social-Democracy who actually sought to organize and run the activities of the Party, particularly in the labor movement. Their differences of outlook and attitudes with Party theorists and publicists were often profound.

[3] Protocols of interviews with Solomon M. Schwarz (Archives of the Menshevik Project, Columbia University), p. 43.

Democracy was the basic Menshevik assumption that the Party should act as the chief agent of the revolution, indeed exercise hegemony in the process of its becoming, and yet virtuously refrain from participating in the new government that would be established once the success of the revolution had been insured. As against these shades of Talmudic complexity and caution in the Mensheviks' strategy and tactics at the beginning of the Revolution, there was the attraction of the far more radical and easily understandable Bolshevik conception of a dictatorship of the proletariat and peasantry and the figure of Lenin as the personification of the revolutionary will embodied in it. Schwarz and others of his generation have noted the importance of the personal factor in the equation—the intellectual and moral sway that Lenin had managed to win by 1905, through his writings and personal legend, over the minds and hearts of many young Social-Democrats. He seemed at the time to many of them a heroic figure, to whom one could turn for guidance about the most delicate moral issues—this not merely because of the quality of his intellect and will but also because of his seeming personal selflessness and dedication to the revolutionary cause.

It was with this unquestioning sense of allegiance to Bolshevism and to the person of Lenin as the true embodiments of the revolutionary spirit of Russian Social-Democracy that Schwarz and many other young Social-Democratic *praktiki* plunged into the intoxicating turbulence of the Revolution of 1905. As Schwarz properly emphasizes in his study, what drew them gradually away from Bolshevism was the attitude that the Bolshevik leaders, and especially the *komitetchiki*—the entrenched members of the Bolshevik-controlled Party Committees—displayed from the opening days of the revolution toward the workers' strivings for *samodeiatel'nost'*—for independent activity and organization.

In Schwarz's own case, and it was by no means unique, clashes with the local Party leadership arose almost from the moment of his arrival in St. Petersburg in September, 1905. The close contacts into which he and other young Social-Democratic *praktiki* were thrown with the now unleashed workers' movement made such clashes inescapable and gave them an explosive character. As a member of the College of Agitators, and later as the *otvetstvennyi agitator* in charge of one of the six district organizations operating under the direction of the Petersburg Party Committee, Schwarz found himself drawn more and more closely to the side of the workers he was supposed to proselytize and increasingly antagonized by the Bolshevik Committeemen's suspicion of all "spontaneous" manifestations of the workers' movement.

Schwarz has given in this monograph a description of the first personal crisis that he underwent in his gradual estrangement from the Bolshevik leadership: the conflict that arose during the days leading up to the October general strike when the pressure of the Petersburg workers to join the Railroad Workers' Union in such a strike ran into the opposition of the Petersburg Party Committee to any action that might interfere with the careful "planning and organization of an armed uprising." In this instance, Schwarz's eventual response and that of other young Bolshevik members of the Petersburg College of Agitators was to adopt an ambiguous slogan ("Hail the organization of a general strike!") which in fact yielded to the workers' demands without formally breaching party discipline. But this was only the first of a series of conflicts from which Schwarz and other young Social-Democratic *praktiki* drew the conviction that the Bolshevik Committeemen were incapable of appreciating the "potential of the workers' movement." Such conflicts arose in the course of the Revolution over the workers' urge to promote their economic interests (partly through the establishment of independent trade unions) and especially over the position the Party should adopt toward the institution of the soviets—the very embodiment in 1905 of the conception of workers' revolutionary self-government.

Yet these conflicts notwithstanding, the parting of the ways for this group of young Social-Democrats with Bolshevism did not take place swiftly or painlessly. In Schwarz's case, the break occurred early in the summer of 1906—following a clash with Lenin at one of the regional conferences of the Bolshevik faction over the Bolsheviks' decision to boycott the elections to the First Duma. In the case of other young Social-Democratic *praktiki* who eventually followed the same course, it took place even later.

To understand the slow pace of this political realignment within the Social-Democratic generation of 1905, it is important to stress once again the appeal that the Leninist conception of the dictatorship of the proletariat and peasantry continued to hold for them well after the revolutionary wave had begun to recede. This persistent appeal of a radical program for a group whose members in 1905 were in their early twenties or even younger is hardly surprising. After all, even in the Menshevik camp in the revolutionary turmoil of October and November, 1905, older and more experienced figures such as Dan and Martynov had been drawn to an equally radical, if theoretically different, conception of proletarian dictatorship. As for the Menshevik rank and file, it may well be argued that at least during these months their differences with Bolshevism had narrowed down, as had the tensions within Bolshevism itself, almost entirely to the issue that Schwarz has properly placed at the foreground of his study of 1905: the nature of the Party's relationship to the workers' movement.

It was only after the Stolypin coup d'etat of June, 1907, when it had become amply clear that Russia had entered a period of relative political stability, that the disagreements of this group of young Social-Democratic *praktiki* with the Bolshevik leadership over its attitude toward the labor movement became connected in their own minds with broader differences over political perspectives and goals. During this period of stagnation for the revolutionary movement, which was to extend until the revival of labor unrest in the spring of 1912, the attention of the young *praktiki* who had left Bolshevism after the Revolution of 1905 turned more and more single-mindedly, as had that of the Menshevik labor leaders whose ranks they now rejoined, to the objective of building the institutional framework for the emergence on Russian soil of a mass labor movement of the Western type—legal trade unions, workers' societies of self-improvement and mutual aid, workers' insurance funds—through which the workers might not only win tangible improvements in the conditions of their daily life but also gain the organizational experience and maturity that would enable them to play a central role in Russia's future development.

By the end of the decade, as the Party appeared to be dissipating its energies in futile and often sordid factional discord, many of these Social-Democratic *praktiki* came to regard the pursuit of revolutionary politics per se as a distraction from the major task of building a Europeanized labor movement in Russia. To the extent that this attitude was rationalized in political terms, it was

reflected, particularly in 1909–10 (the low ebb of the revolutionary movement), in the view that the old underground party—
beset by moral decomposition as well as by the presence at all
levels of its organization of agents of the secret police—was
doomed, and that a new workers' party would have to be rebuilt
from the ground up, largely through the agency of the organs of
the open labor movement. This view was often combined with a
now more faithful and literal interpretation of the old Social-
Democratic conception of the bourgeois revolution—with the
insistence that the Social-Democrats would have to collaborate
with liberal elements in society in building in Russia a modern,
"bourgeois" political and legal order of the Western type before
moving on to the pursuit of more radical socialist objectives.

For many of those who shared it, this new orientation was reinforced by a sense of personal revulsion against the degradation
of life in the underground, by an urge to resume a more normal,
more immediately fruitful pattern of existence: to complete one's
education, to assume a useful professional role, and to join in the
efforts to build a new Russia even within the restrictive cast of
the existing political system. Given the government's repressions
of the organs of the open labor movement, which grew in intensity
as the war approached, and the seeming inability of liberal society
to combat them, this was a most difficult and frustrating course to
maintain.

Schwarz himself had resumed his academic studies in 1907,
even while continuing his Party work among Petersburg workers,
but he was arrested in the summer of that year, sentenced to three
years of administrative exile, and finally permitted in 1909 to
emigrate to Germany, where he completed studies leading to a
doctorate of law.

He returned to Russia in the summer of 1911, intent on the
pursuit of a professional and scholarly career, but within a year
was again diverted from it by his passionate concern with the
Russian labor movement. In Moscow in the second half of 1912, he
drafted the statutes for new printers' and metalworkers' unions in
an effort to revive and gain legal recognition for the then almost
extinct local trade union movement. In St. Petersburg where he
was allowed to move after the amnesty of 1913, he assumed, in
collaboration with his friend Baturskii, the editorship of the

journal *Strakhovanie rabochykh* (*Workers' Insurance*) and became one of the most prominent figures in the workers' insurance
movement that the Mensheviks had launched in the wake of the
legislation passed on the subject at the end of the Third Duma.
Although Schwarz also became engaged in other activities (he
acted briefly as one of the editors of *Metallist*, the journal of the
metalworkers' union), the establishment of a workers' insurance
system, supported by the workers' own dues and largely independent of both government and employers, remained his major
interest, in this period and in later years. It was while he was engaged in drafting a pamphlet outlining a model statute for factory
insurance funds that Schwarz was arrested again, in November,
1913, "for Social-Democratic convictions and contacts with the
labor movement," and compelled to resume his exile in Germany,
where he remained until the outbreak of the First World War.

This second arrest and exile was typical of the vicissitudes that
Menshevik labor leaders underwent in the immediate prewar
period. They found themselves hopelessly squeezed between two
sets of pressures: police repressions that did not discriminate
between genuine revolutionary activities and the efforts to establish a legalized, economically oriented, and basically reformist
labor movement, and a rising wave of labor unrest that—partly
because it could find no other channels for its expression—
assumed, as the war approached, an increasingly desperate and
explosive character. The Mensheviks vehemently condemned what
they considered to be the erratic violence of the strike movement
of the period and its "adventurist" exploitation by the Bolsheviks;
they argued desperately that it was endangering the survival of
the organs of the open labor movement and dissipating the
workers' energies without securing for them any tangible gains.
But in the absence of any viable alternatives, their laments only
contributed to the process of their own estrangement from the
masses of the Russian working class and to the success of the
struggle on which the Bolsheviks had now embarked to win
control of the organs of the open labor movement. To touch only
on the aspects of this struggle which bore directly on Schwarz's
own experience, the Bolsheviks, by the end of 1913, when he was
forced once again to go into exile, had won firm control of the
Petersburg Metalworkers' Union and expelled the two Menshevik

representatives on the editorial board of its organ, *Metallist;* and they had won a majority among the workers' representatives on the insurance boards of the city and province of Petersburg—the very organs on which Schwarz had focused his vision of the emergence of a Europeanized labor movement on Russian soil.

By this time, little was left of the unquestioning worship with which Schwarz and other young Social-Democratic *praktiki* had greeted in 1905 all manifestations of the "spontaneous" workers' movement. It seemed, to a degree, as if the tables had been reversed. For it was the Bolsheviks who were now riding the crest of "elemental" labor unrest, and the Mensheviks who now deplored its lack of organization and control. This reversal was of considerable significance for the future, for it reinforced in Schwarz and other Menshevik labor leaders a sense of disgust with the vagaries of revolutionary politics that they later were never able to shake off.

The suicidal character of the government's policies toward labor problems which had so greatly contributed to this state of affairs was reflected even more tangibly in Schwarz's experience of the war years. On his return to Russia, via Scandinavia, shortly after the outbreak of hostilities, Schwarz, and many other Menshevik leaders of the labor movement, rallied to the Defensist camp in Russian Social-Democracy, which considered that until the war was brought to a halt there was no alternative to joining with other elements in society to defend Russia against German imperialism. Yet despite his position on the war issue, he was forced to spend most of the war years in administrative exile. It was only in the summer of 1916 that he was allowed to settle in Moscow, where he had been invited to serve as the secretary of the workers' group attached to the local War Industrial Committee. Indefatigably, Schwarz sought to use this springboard to revive the open labor movement in the old capital. He attempted to strengthen the authority of the workers' group by inducing the *vyborshchiki,* the worker electors who had selected it, to establish representative workers' organizations at their local factories. He launched a number of "campaigns" to rouse the workers' initiative and draw it into legal channels: to add workers' representatives to the insurance board of Moscow province, to secure improvements in municipal regulations on rent control, to establish mediation boards on which workers would be represented for the peaceful settlement of labor disputes. But these efforts to give the workers of the city and province of Moscow a sense of participation in, and responsibility for, public affairs were once again cut short by the authorities. Schwarz was arrested at the end of the summer of 1916, sentenced once more to administrative exile, and then drafted into the militia; he was unable to return to public service until after February, 1917.

The outbreak of Russia's second revolution drew Schwarz back to the center of the Russian labor scene—but this time into positions of official responsibility. As deputy chairman of the Division of Labor of the Petersburg Soviet and its representative in the Labor Division of the Ministry of Trade and Industry, it was his charge during the early months of the Revolution to try to contain the growing restlessness of the Russian working class so as to keep the economy of the country functioning. It had always been an article of faith for the Menshevik *praktiki* that if only the workers' initiative could be given proper organizational expression the Russian labor movement would display growing maturity and responsibility. In accord with this principle, Schwarz sought to establish mediation machinery for the settlement of labor disputes in the Petersburg Soviet and at the end of April, 1917, drafted the legislation establishing the *fabzavkomy*, the workers' factory committees which were soon to provide the first stepping stones in the Bolsheviks' drive for power. In May, 1917, following the Mensheviks' reluctant agreement to join with the representatives of "bourgeois" parties in the first coalition ministry, he was appointed head of the Division of Social Insurance of the newly established Ministry of Labor and, during the increasingly desperate months of the summer and fall of 1917, was entirely absorbed in the effort to draw up, and win approval for, the establishment in Russia of a comprehensive insurance system.

By this time, two mutually reinforcing orientations, which had already emerged among Menshevik *praktiki* in the prewar period, had become strikingly manifest among most Menshevik leaders. The first of these was an involvement in public responsibilities— in running and perfecting public institutions—which by the spring of 1917, when the Menshevik party agreed to share in the responsibilities of power, almost completely diverted the attention and energy of its ablest members from the political struggle, on the outcome of which the survival of these institutions would obviously depend. With this ever growing absorption in public responsibilities went a hardening of the conviction, particularly among Menshevik *praktiki* of Schwarz's stamp, that Russia's governmental machinery and institutions could not possibly be kept functioning without the co-operation of the groups in Russian society represented in the provisional government by its non-Socialist ministers. However compelling both these attitudes may have appeared in the context of the war emergency, they had the inevitable effect of crippling the Mensheviks' struggle with the Bolsheviks for the support of the working class. Its energies almost entirely invested in the effort to keep the administration of the country running, its pressures for changes in public policy stymied, more often than not, by its non-Socialist partners in the provisional government, the Menshevik party found itself increasingly cut off from the masses of the Russian workers, and let their political leadership fall from its hands almost by default.

Schwarz could only sit by helplessly as the *fabzavkomy* that he had helped establish, and eventually the Petersburg Soviet, gradually fell under Bolshevik control. By September, 1917, he clearly saw the writing on the wall. "We had the sense," he recounts, "that the ground was slipping under our feet, that a great social enterprise was coming to naught." But there was nothing he felt he could do. On the night of the Bolshevik seizure of power in Petrograd, he recalls, he spent his time editing, for his old journal *Workers' Insurance,* "an article on the struggle against tuberculosis. Such is the irony of fate!"[4]

So ended a political journey, on which in 1905—when Schwarz had joined his fate to that of the Russian workers' movement—he had embarked with such faith and such high hopes.

Although first to appear, *The Russian Revolution of 1905* is intended as the second volume in a new English-language series on the history of Menshevism, which the Inter-University Project on the History of the Menshevik Movement is publishing with the

---

[4] Protocols of interviews with Solomon M. Schwarz (Archives of the Menshevik Project, Columbia University), p. 144.

University of Chicago Press, under the sponsorship of the Hoover Institution.[5] The project was launched in the fall of 1959, with the support of the Ford Foundation, by an ad hoc committee of specialists in Russian history who were teaching at American universities, in collaboration with representatives of the then already fast dwindling Menshevik émigré community in the United States. (The subsequent work of the project was also supported by grants from the Rockefeller and Atran foundations, the Hoover Institution, and the American Council of Learned Societies.)

The American scholars on the committee were impelled to embark on this unusual collaborative effort by the sense that this was one of the most urgent responsibilities that American scholarship could assume at this time toward the study of the background and eventual course of the Russian Revolution. This sense of urgency was in part drawn from the fact that despite the prominence of the historical role of the Menshevik Party, some of the most basic data concerning it were preserved only in scattered, fragmented, and often perishable records or, indeed, solely in the memories of a few aging survivors. Just as important as the task of assembling and preserving the factual record was the need to provide a suitable medium through which those survivors might—with the benefit of a half-century's perspective—most profitably re-examine their views about those aspects of the Party's history in which they had been most directly involved.

The pursuit of these two objectives since 1959 has culminated in the following:

1. The establishment at Columbia University of a permanent archive on the history of Menshevism, in which have been deposited an extensive collection of documents and newspapers of the Menshevik Party, records of interviews conducted by associates of the Project with survivors of the Party, and transcripts of seminar discussions of various of the Project's studies at which an effort was made—through the confrontation of conflicting viewpoints—to explore in some depth the motives underlying the politi-

---

[5] In the first volume—Allan Wildman's "The Making of a Workers' Revolution: Russian Social Democracy, 1891–1903"—the reader will find, as I have already indicated, a study of the genesis, during the formative years of Russian Social-Democracy, of some of the conflicts that subsequently affected the development of Bolshevism and Menshevism.

cal course adopted by the various factions represented in Menshevism over the past half-century.

2. The preparation, and distribution in multilith form, of accounts by Mensheviks residing in the United States and Western Europe of events in the Party's history in which they were participants. To date, seventeen of these studies have been deposited by the Project in major American and European libraries.

3. The preparation for publication of memoirs, bibliographies, and documentary and monographic studies by Menshevik associates of the Project as well as participating American scholars. Those volumes that are to appear in English are being published by the University of Chicago Press; others will appear in a Russian-language series sponsored by the Hoover Institution.

It has been noted that the contributions of the Project's Menshevik associates have been intended not only to reconstruct certain crucial factual aspects of the development of early twentieth-century Russia but also to provide a proper vehicle for the expression of the views and values of a group in Russian political and cultural life whose collective voice was largely muffled in the aftermath of the October Revolution. In most cases, this twofold objective could best be served by encouraging contributors to write about periods and events in the history of the Menshevik Party in which they were most closely involved. Yet even though most of the Project's studies thus bore a partly memoiristic character, every effort was made to induce their authors to draw exhaustively and carefully on all the printed and unprinted sources available on the subjects they discuss. It was hoped that by following this rule, the source materials examined would refresh and sharpen each author's recollection of his own experience, and at the same time that this experience would fill out and illuminate the often fragmentary records available.

These were the hopes with which, some seven years ago, the Inter-University Project on the History of the Menshevik Movement embarked on its work. Solomon Schwarz's *Russian Revolution of 1905* constitutes, we believe, a worthy example of their fulfillment.

Leopold H. Haimson

Contents

The Basic Conception
of the Revolution

THIS book does not attempt to cover the vast subject of Social-Democracy and the mass labor movement during the First Russian Revolution. It is, rather, a study of the interaction of these two movements, with the main stress on the development of Russian Social-Democracy just after its emergence as a factor of consequence on the political scene, when it began to divide into the two parts that in time crystallized, not as two variants of Social-Democracy, but as Social-Democracy, on the one hand, and, on the other, the authoritarian labor movement that later assumed the name of Communism.

In the early days this fundamental divergence was still far in the future. Despite their differences, both the Bolshevik and the Menshevik wings of the Russian Social-Democratic Labor Party (*Rossiiskaia Sotsial-Demokraticheskaia Rabochaia Partiia*, or RSDRP) sincerely considered themselves parts of a single party with a common ideology and program. Common, too, was their basic conception of the revolution—until the revolution began.

From the founding of the Liberation of Labor Group (1883), Russian Social-Democracy had consistently distinguished between the *bourgeois-democratic* and the more distant *socialist* revolution. The first was to result in the fall of autocracy and the conquest of political freedom and was to establish favor-

1

able conditions for rapid economic development along capitalist lines. The second presupposed a further growth of the working class, as well as the development of its consciousness and organization, which could be promoted on a large scale only *after* the bourgeois revolution. As G. V. Plekhanov wrote in his famous pamphlet *Socialism and the Political Struggle* (1883), the first systematic exposition of the views of the Liberation of Labor Group:

> To tie together two such essentially different matters as the overthrow of absolutism and a socialist revolution, to engage in revolutionary struggle in the hope that these two moments in social evolution will *coincide* in the history of our country, *means to retard the arrival of both*. But it does depend on us to *shorten the interval* between these two moments. We must follow the example of the German Communists who, in the words of the Manifesto, marched "side by side with the bourgeoisie insofar as it was revolutionary in its struggle against absolute monarchy" but at the same time never for a moment ceased to foster in the workers' minds the clearest possible realization of the fact that the interests of the bourgeoisie and of the proletariat were mutually antagonistic. In acting thus, the German Communists wanted "the German bourgeois revolution to serve merely as a prologue immediately preceding a popular revolution."
>
> The present situation of bourgeois societies and the impact of international relations on the social evolution of every civilized country permit us to hope that the social emancipation of the Russian working class will follow very shortly after the fall of absolutism.[1]

In formulating so sharply the conception of two revolutions, the Liberation of Labor Group wished to dissociate itself from the Populists, who disapproved of political struggle and preached a "revolution by the people" that would bypass the capitalist phase and establish socialism in Russia through the development of the village commune.[2]

---

[1] G. V. Plekhanov, *Sotsializm i politicheskaia bor'ba*, in *Sochineniia*, II (Moscow, 1923), 86.

[2] See Solomon M. Schwarz, "Populism and Early Russian Marxism on Ways of Economic Development of Russia (the 1880's and 1890's)," in *Continuity and Change in Russian and Soviet Thought*, ed. Ernest J. Simmons (Cambridge, Mass.: Harvard University Press, 1955).

Although Plekhanov and his circle, like most other Western and Russian Social-Democrats of the time, conceived of the social (that is, the "workers' ") revolution as relatively close, the imprudent phrase about the bourgeois revolution as a "prologue immediately preceding a popular revolution" was definitely not meant to suggest an uninterrupted transition from one to the other. A "historically short" period of time was expected to elapse between the two.

These views of the Liberation of Labor Group were also embodied in two drafts of its program, both written by Plekhanov. The first, entitled "Program of the Social-Democratic Group 'Liberation of Labor'" (1884), states that it is the "task of today's liberation movement" to create "free political institutions" and that socialists "must try to make it possible for the working class to participate actively and fruitfully in Russia's future political life." Only thus will the "political self-education of the working class," which is a precondition of its economic emancipation, become possible.[3]

The second draft, published in 1888,[4] states even more explic-

---

[3] Plekhanov, *Sochineniia*, II, 353–56.

[4] *Ibid.*, pp. 400–404. Here this draft is called "Vtoroi proekt programmy russkikh sotsialdemokratov," and a note states, "first printed as an appendix to the pamphlet *Chego khotiat sotsialdemokraty?* [by J. Guesde and P. Lafargue], Geneva, 1888; composed in 1887." But in an appendix to P. B. Axelrod's pamphlet *K voprosu o sovremennykh zadachakh i taktike russkikh sotsialdemokratov* (Geneva, 1898; reprinted in the periodical *Rabotnik*, 1899, No. 5/6), the same draft appears with the comment, "This program was published in 1885." The discrepancy stems from the fact that the draft was made in 1885, hectographed, and sent for discussion to the embryonic Social-Democratic groups in Russia. The 1887/88 draft is the 1885 draft amended (hence it is called the second). The original 1885 draft never appeared in print. B. I. Nicolaevsky found (and copied) it in 1918 in the archives of the Department of Police, dossier No. 100 for 1886 "po rozyskam v S.Peterburge."—See Nicolaevsky's article "Pervyi s"ezd RSDRP i ego sovremennye kommunisticheskie istoriki," *Sotsialisticheskii Vestnik*, May, 1959, pp. 96–97.

Soviet historians apparently remain unaware of the original 1885 draft, which may still be lying in police archives, and continue to believe that Plekhanov called the 1887/88 draft the second because the first was the program of the Liberation of Labor Group. See, for example, Iu. Z. Polevoi, *Zarozhdenie marksizma v Rossii. 1883–1894 g.g.* (Moscow: Akademiia nauk SSSR, 1959), p. 211.

The note in Axelrod's pamphlet that the draft appended to it is the 1885 draft is mistaken. This draft is identical with the 1887/88 draft except for two words, both probably copying errors (*krest'iane* in the draft in Axelrod's pamphlet, *krest'ianstvo* in the other; *terroristicheskie fakty* in Axelrod instead of *terroristicheskie deistviia*. At the time, the word *fakty*, by the way, was used more often than *akty* in this connection).

Comparison of Nicolaevsky's copy of the 1885 draft with the "second draft" shows that all but four of the corrections made in the original draft are purely

itly that "the goal of the Labor Party's struggle against absolutism is to win democratic institutions." This is only the immediate goal; its attainment will permit the introduction of universal suffrage, compulsory free secular education for all, inviolability of the person, freedom of conscience, speech, the press, assembly and association, and other democratic civil rights. Then the workers' party will press for economic improvements, still within the framework of the socialist program-minimum (to borrow from a later terminology), that is, attainable in a bourgeois society. However, "Russian Social-Democrats, like those of other countries, aspire to the complete emancipation of labor from the yoke of capital. This emancipation can be achieved by transferring all products and means of production to public ownership," which in turn can be done only through a "communist revolution" ("communist," "socialist," and "social-democratic" were often used interchangeably in those days). The program relegates this revolution to an indefinite future date.

In the last quarter of the nineteenth century, all Marxist socialist parties in Europe distinguished between demands realizable in a bourgeois society (the "socialist program-minimum," as these demands came to be called in the nineties) and the "ultimate aims" of the working class (the "socialist program-maximum"). But almost everywhere in Europe a bourgeois structure of state and society had already become established, and the battle for the "socialist program-minimum" could be waged openly. Next on the agenda was the social revolution.[5] In Russia,

---

stylistic. The part about bourgeois and socialist revolutions that I have quoted is identical in both drafts. The first draft not being readily available, it may be useful to indicate here the four corrections that are more than stylistic. Two of them tone down the text: (1) the addition in the "second draft" of the words *v obshchem* to the phrase *interesy truda diametral'no protivopolozhny interesam èksploatatorov;* (2) the addition of *bednykh* before *detei* in the proposed demand that children (in schools) be supplied with food, clothing, and textbooks. One amendment seems, on the contrary, to sharpen the text: *glavneishaia* instead of *sushchestvenneishaia* (*opora absoliutizma zakliuchaetsia v politicheskom bezrazlichii i otstalosti krest'ianstva*). The fourth change is the omission of the following paragraph, which amplified the first paragraph of the original draft, on the transition to socialism: "Modern technological advances in civilized societies not only provide the *material possibility* for this kind of organization but make it *imperative* and inevitable for resolving the contradictions that hamper the peaceful all-sided development of these societies."

5 For the Western socialist parties the question was not one of bourgeois versus socialist revolution but of realizing the program-minimum (without revolution) and

however, a bourgeois-democratic revolution was still to be achieved. A clear distinction between the political, or bourgeois, and the socialist revolutions was therefore an imperative necessity, and in the first half of the nineties the young leaders of Russian Social-Democracy readily adopted the conception of two revolutions developed by the Liberation of Labor Group.

Lenin's first sizable work, *Who Are the "Friends of the People" and How Do They Fight the Social-Democrats?* upheld the notion of "[the working class] struggling side by side with radical democracy against absolutism and the reactionary classes and institutions" but stressed that the worker needed democracy "merely [!] to clear the way to victory over the chief enemy of the laboring people, capital, which is an institution of a purely democratic nature."[6] Lenin concluded with the prediction that "the Russian worker, having risen up at the head of all the democratic elements, will overthrow absolutism and lead the proletariat (side by side with the proletariat of all other countries) along the straight road of open political struggle to a victorious communist revolution."[7]

This was later interpreted as an indication that, unlike the Liberation of Labor Group, Lenin believed in a direct transition from the bourgeois-democratic to the socialist revolution.[8] There

---

the program-maximum (through a socialist revolution), and even this distinction began to be drawn in clear-cut form relatively late. The Italian party was the first to use the terms "program-maximum" and "program-minimum" in its program adopted at the Genoa Congress in 1892, which was clearly divided into two parts. Contrary to popular belief, the terms do not appear in the Erfurt program of German Social-Democracy (1891). The programs of the German, Austrian, Italian, French, Belgian, and Swiss socialist parties (from 1875 to 1904) are given in full in I. V. Chernyshev, *Pamiatnaia knizhka marksista* (Petersburg, 1906), pp. 179–228.

6 V. I. Lenin, *Chto takoe "druz'ia naroda" i kak oni voiuiut protiv sotsialdemo-kratov?* in *Sochineniia* (4th ed.), I, 273.

7 *Ibid.*, p. 282.

8 See, for example, N. Sergievskii, "Plekhanov i gruppa Blagoeva," *Proletarskaia Revoliutsiia*, 1928, No. 8 (79), pp. 141–42, and especially A. S. Martynov, *Kak Lenin borolsia za pererostanie revoliutsii i protiv tsentrizma* (Moscow, 1932), pp. 6–7. The wish to prove that from the beginning of his political career Lenin favored the idea of the bourgeois revolution "growing over" into a socialist revolution engendered a spate of literature in the late twenties. Most important are K. Popov, "Ob istoricheskikh usloviiakh pererastaniia burzhuazno-demokraticheskoi revoliutsii v proletarskuiu," *Bol'shevik*, 1928, Nos. 21/22 and 23/24; D. Kardashev, "Problema pererastaniia burzhuazno-demokraticheskoi revoliutsii v sotsialisticheskuiu v svete leninskoi teorii 'amerikanskogo' i 'prusskogo' puti razvitiia Rossii," *Proletarskaia Revoliutsiia*, 1929, Nos. 2/3 (85/86) and 5 (88); Ia. Rezvushkin, "O pererostanii burzhuazno-demokraticheskoi revoliutsii v sotsialisticheskuiu," *Prole-*

are no grounds for such an interpretation. During the nineties, Lenin repeatedly expressed his complete agreement with the conception Plekhanov had presented in *Socialism and the Political Struggle*. I shall give just one example. Arguing with *Rabochaia Mysl'*, the organ of the extreme Economists, Lenin wrote in 1899:

> Why must the overthrow of autocracy be the first objective of the Russian working class? Because under autocracy the working class cannot really deploy its struggle, cannot conquer any firm positions in the economic or the political sphere, cannot build up stable mass organizations, unfurl the banner of social revolution before all the laboring masses, and teach them to fight for it. Only with political freedom does the decisive struggle of the whole working class against the bourgeois class become possible, and the final goal of this struggle is that the proletariat conquer political power and organize a socialist society. . . . But the Russian Social-Democrats have never regarded the seizure of power as the first objective of the Russian workers. The Russian Social-Democrats have always said that only with political freedom and a broad mass struggle can the Russian working class evolve organizations for the final victory of socialism.[9]

These ideas were so much taken for granted that no one thought of raising the conception of two revolutions as an issue when the RSDRP discussed its program at the Party Congress of 1903. The Party split at that Congress, but Bolsheviks and Mensheviks alike continued for a long time to accept as an axiom the necessity for both a bourgeois and a socialist revolution. Only the conclusions they drew from this axiom when the revolutionary wind began to blow would reveal their radically different understanding of the tasks of Social-Democracy and of its relation to the masses.

The overthrow of autocracy, which had been the Social-Democrats' goal since the nineties but which they had placed in

tarskaia Revoliutsiia, 1928, Nos. 10 (81) and 11/12 (82/83); and the report on three sessions devoted to the subject, of the Nauchno-Istoricheskaia Gruppa Instituta Lenina in December, 1928, and January, 1929, *Proletarskaia Revoliutsiia*, 1929, No. 5 (88).

[9] Lenin, "Popiatnoe napravlenie v russkoi sotsialdemokratii," in *Sochineniia*, IV, 243–44. See also "Protest russkikh sotsialdemokratov" (1899), in *Sochineniia*, II, 163.

some fairly remote future, suddenly became a distinct possibility in the latter half of 1904. The political atmosphere became tense, as the war with Japan revealed Russia's military weakness, and a revolution and a provisional government seemed very near. The Social-Democratic leaders had to decide what the role of their party and that of the working class should be in the imminent *bourgeois* revolution.

Martov formulated the basic tactical stand of Social-Democracy in the lead article of the Menshevik *Iskra* of December 1/14, 1904:

> Under the leadership of Social-Democracy, the Russian proletariat will save the bourgeois revolution from all attempts to wreck it by "timely compromises." Impressing the bourgeois opposition with its strong influence over the *popular masses,* its solidarity, and the *independence* of its political stand, the conscious proletariat is rallying to itself and to its political activity all the social elements *not yet* satisfied at this time; [it is] subordinating them to its own leadership, and thus advancing the progress of bourgeois "reform". . . . The social forces destined to play an active role in the coming "reconstruction" are only beginning to enter the political arena; the drama of the bourgeois revolution is only beginning to unfold; the peasantry is [as yet] barely heard, the millions of sectarians are silent, the voices of the nationalities oppressed by tsarism are weak. Only a truly revolutionary program can bring unity and order to the process of awakening these elemental forces. And this program, which can only be a program of *comprehensive, well-rounded, and consistent development of the bourgeois revolution,* will be supplied by the socialist proletariat. In the name of this program, it will push all of bourgeois society forward in its struggle with tsarism; in its name, it will split that society whenever some group of it, having obtained the satisfaction of its *private* interests through some "timely compromise," adopts a policy that goes counter to the *common* interests of bourgeois development.[10]

As such, this formulation could have united the two wings of the Party, but it did not touch on the question of Social-Democracy's participation in the government that was to supersede autocracy during the revolution. As soon as this issue was raised,

---

[10] "Rabochii klass i burzhuaznaia revoliutsiia," *Iskra,* No. 79. *Ukazatel' zagranichnykh sotsialdemokraticheskikh periodicheskikh izdanii, 1883–1905 g.g.,* ed. Iu. K[amenev] (Paris, 1913), attributes this article to L. Martov.

a deep rift became apparent. A. S. Martynov formulated the Mensheviks' stand in *Two Dictatorships* (*Dve diktatury*), written practically on the eve of Bloody Sunday (January 9, 1905, the acknowledged "beginning of the revolution").[11] A theoretical analysis of the proletarian dictatorship in the future socialist revolution and a retrospective consideration of the "dictatorship of sans-culottes," the Jacobin petty-bourgeois dictatorship of 1792–95 in France, impelled Martynov to the following conclusions concerning Russia:

> We are on the eve of the political self-liberation of Russian bourgeois society, on the eve of a bourgeois revolution. Anyone who takes stock of the conditions involved in bringing about a revolutionary dictatorship will see that to advise Social-Democracy to prepare for revolutionary dictatorship or even for a "temporary seizure of power" in *that* kind of revolution is to advise it to prepare for its own bankruptcy and to discredit the socialist flag in the eyes of the proletariat for a very long time. . . . It means, moreover, betraying the true business of the revolution, for in *attracting* the proletariat onto the road of fantastic adventures we *distract* it from its real revolutionary task. . . .
>
> We must always remember that until the socialist revolution Social-Democracy is and must remain *the party of the extreme opposition,* unlike all the other parties, which in one way or another, to a greater or lesser extent, can count on joining in the government of a bourgeois society.[12]

In *Two Dictatorships* this view was expressed dogmatically. After January 9, in several articles in *Iskra* under the overall title "Revolutionary Prospects,"[13] Martynov developed it in the light of the new Russian experience:

> The recent grandiose events may seem out of harmony with the fact that we are going through a bourgeois revolution. Has not the tremendous explosion of the proletarian movement drowned out the faint voices of our grumbling [*frondiruiushchaia*] liberal democracy? Do not the timorous movements of our bourgeoisie look pitiful next to the mighty movement of the Russian proletariat in

---

[11] The appearance of A. S. Martynov's *Dve diktatury* was announced in *Iskra,* No. 84 on January 18, 1905 (O.S.)—the first issue to come out after January 9. This was of course only a coincidence.

[12] A. Martynov, *Dve diktatury* (2d ed.; Petrograd: Kniga, 1917), pp. 73–74.

[13] *Iskra,* Nos. 90, 93, and 95, March 3, 17, and 31, 1905 (O.S.).

revolt? Do not the liberal-democratic banquets of the recently ended political "thaw" pale before the vivid, tempestuous January events? All this is undoubtedly true; yet it does not at all contradict the fact that the present Russian revolution is a bourgeois revolution. [*Iskra,* No. 90.]

In the setting of a surging labor movement, the bourgeois character of the revolution would be bound to encourage the growth of a bourgeois-democratic revolutionary movement free of the liberals' tendency to seek compromises with tsarism and eager for a political rapprochement with Social-Democracy. But

> this "alliance" of the conscious proletariat with revolutionary bourgeois democracy will not only fail to reduce the class antagonism between them but may even contribute to it in certain respects. To some extent this is already noticeable. The more actively bourgeois democracy participates in the common revolutionary struggle, the harder it will try, in return for revolutionary co-operation, to free the proletariat from the influence of Social-Democracy, that is, from the influence of its own class ideology.
>
> These two facts—the inevitable revolutionary collaboration of the proletariat with bourgeois democracy and its inevitable struggle with [bourgeois democracy] for its political independence—must determine the line of our tactics in the immediate future. [*Iskra,* No. 90.]

"Collaborating" in the revolution did not mean, however, that the allies should form a joint provisional government. As the party of the working class, Social-Democracy was to press for the satisfaction of the workers' demands to the utmost extent possible in a bourgeois revolution—that is, try to put through the socialist program-minimum—without participating in the provisional government ("without contracting official responsibilities vis-à-vis bourgeois society as a whole"). It should "remain in the opposition, exerting pressure on the government from without." Martynov turned to the French Revolution to bolster his argument:

> After the uprising of August 10, 1792, the Paris Commune on its own initiative established a "Committee of Public Safety"; on its own initiative, it armed the people and purged the administration of "suspect" elements, of "enemies of the people." It took these revolutionary measures not because it had been given the appropriate authority (the Gironde was in power) but because it was a *de*

facto power, because it had taken part in the victorious uprising. This right, the right of victorious revolution, our proletariat, too, will retain after a successful uprising, but only if it remains a *de facto* power, if its independent class party does not become disorganized, if it does not dissolve in revolutionary democracy. [*Iskra*, No. 95.]

Martynov seems to have been dimly aware that such a course of action would result in one of two alternatives: either the bourgeois-democratic revolutionary government would try to extend its base to the right, and its relations with Social-Democracy would deteriorate, or Social-Democracy would have a share in government—perhaps the decisive share. Social-Democracy's forced participation in government struck Martynov as an almost tragic prospect:

> But if the inner dialectic of revolution, regardless of our will . . . carries us to power while conditions in our country are not yet ripe for Social-Democracy, we should not retreat. We should set ourselves the goal of shattering the narrow national confines of the revolution and pushing the West onto the road of revolution, just as France, a hundred years ago, pushed the East onto that road.
>
> A party striving for the dictatorship of the proletariat has no right to covet the trappings of power, which promise only to sever its ties with the proletariat; and if it does find itself in power, it has no right to evade carrying out its socialist obligations to the full. Either Millerandism or Marxism! [*Iskra*, No. 95.]

In other words, the bourgeois character of the revolution would oblige the provisional government to build a bourgeois state with all its social contradictions; therefore Social-Democracy could not be part of that government and remain true to itself. But if the inadequacy of all the bourgeois parties *forced* Social-Democracy to participate in the government or to form a Social-Democratic government, it could escape bankruptcy only if it managed to go far beyond the bourgeois revolution. This in turn would be possible only if the Russian revolution spread to the West.

These views were expressed still more definitely in Martov's article "The Workers' Party and the 'Seizure of Power' as Our Proximal Task" in *Iskra*, No. 93 (March 17 [O.S.]). Arguing with the Bolshevik *Vpered* and with Parvus and Trotsky (who were associated with the Mensheviks but had put forward a theory of their own; see Appendix 1), Martov insisted that Social-Democracy must remain outside the government to be able to influence "the course of the revolution" all the more:

> Were it true that it is *indispensable* for the triumph of a democratic republic, for the triumph of the revolution, that socialists take the helm of the "ship of state," then the revolutionary party of the proletariat would have to renounce its political independence and exclaim with the Montagne, *périsse notre nom pourvu que la liberté soit sauvée!* ("Let our name perish, so long as liberty is saved!"). In reality, however, no such conflict is possible; as the revolutionary opposition, the proletariat, if it follows the revolutionary, that is, the "intelligent Marxist," tactic, can and must become the lever in the development of the bourgeois revolution; but if Social-Democracy becomes the ruling party and thus inevitably ties its hands as far as organizing the class struggle of the proletariat is concerned, it will, on the contrary, weaken its influence on the course of the revolution.

Yet one must fulfil one's obligations. "Should all the strong bourgeois-revolutionary parties wither without having bloomed . . . the proletariat will not be able to turn its back on political power. And it is equally evident that once having come to power in the course of the social struggle, it cannot restrict its use to the limits of a bourgeois revolution":

> If [*the proletariat*] *as a class comes to power,* it cannot but lead the revolution on, it cannot fail to strive for *Revolution in Permanenz,* for an outright struggle with all of bourgeois society. Concretely, this means either a repetition of the Paris Commune or the beginning of a socialist revolution "in the West" and its spread to Russia. And it will be our *obligation* to strive for the second.

Joining in the provisional government without setting oneself such tasks would mean "the dissolution of the proletariat's class struggle in the amorphous 'democratic' movement." "Either-or! Either the tritest Jauresism or the negation of the bourgeois character of the revolution!"

This conception was further developed at the "First All-Russian Conference of Party Workers," in reality a Menshevik conference held in April/May, 1905, in Geneva as a counterpart to the simultaneous Bolshevik "Third Congress" in London. Its resolution "On Conquering Power and on Participating in the Provisional Government"[14] stressed that defeating tsarism would be only the first phase of the revolution. The next phase would bring the problem of participating in the provisional revolutionary government. In regulating the struggle between the classes, a provisional government carrying out its tasks in accordance with the "bourgeois character of the revolution" would be obliged "not only to further the development of the revolution but also to combat those of its factors that threaten the foundations of the capitalist system."

> This being so, Social-Democracy must endeavor to preserve throughout the revolution a position that will best enable it to further the revolution, that will not hamstring it in combating the inconsistent and selfish policies of the bourgeois parties, and that will keep it from dissolving in bourgeois democracy.
>
> Therefore Social-Democracy must not aim at seizing or sharing power in the provisional government but must remain the party of the extreme revolutionary opposition.

The framers of the resolution must have realized that a party playing a decisive role in the revolution could not altogether refrain from taking part in the emerging organs of government. They added:

> Of course this tactic by no means excludes the expediency of partial, episodic seizures of power and of forming revolutionary communes in this or that city or district, purely to further the spread of the uprising and the disorganization of the government.

Necessary as this addition was, it clashed with the rest of the resolution. Years later, a prominent member of the Menshevik Conference, F. I. Dan, justly remarked:

> This paragraph indicates neither the extent of "partial" nor the duration of the admissible "episodes"; it bypasses the question of the possible expediency of "purely furthering the spread of the revolution" and taking a more central part in "seizing power," as well as the question of when, under what conditions, and how the Party should withdraw from the "revolutionary communes" organ-

---

[14] *Pervaia obshcherusskaia konferentsiia partiinykh rabotnikov,* a separate supplement to *Iskra,* No. 100, May 15 (O.S.), pp. 23–24.

ized with its assistance. It does, in fact, knock a hole in the logic of the resolution.[15]

On the basic issue of participating in the central government, the resolution of the Menshevik Conference also admitted of an exception:

> Only in one case should Social-Democracy try on its own initiative to gain power and to keep it . . . as long as possible—namely, if the revolution spreads to the advanced countries of Western Europe, where conditions are more or less ripe for the realization of socialism. In that case the historically limited bounds of the Russian revolution could considerably expand and it would become possible to set out on the road of socialist reforms.

As in Martynov's and Martov's writings before the Conference, the conception of the Russian revolution as bourgeois is practically effaced here by the idea of its setting off a socialist revolution in the West, which in turn would change the character of the Russian revolution.

From the distance of a half-century, one is struck by the dogmatism of these arguments. International Social-Democracy has long since abandoned—in fact, if not in principle—the mechanical opposition of bourgeois to socialist revolution, of program-minimum to program-maximum. Hence the argument that Social-Democracy would be untrue to itself if it joined in the government of a bourgeois revolution without immediately pressing for socialism has also lost its meaning. Yet behind the Mensheviks' dogmatic arguments about participating in the organs of government in a bourgeois revolution, their overriding concern can be clearly seen—to insure the political independence of the young labor movement. This basic orientation, in contrast to the Bolsheviks' mistrust of "spontaneity" in the labor movement and to their belief in the firm leadership of an organization of rigidly disciplined "professional revolutionaries," may explain why two outstanding Social-Democratic publicists, Parvus and Trotsky, who strongly disagreed with the Mensheviks' stand on participa-

---

15 F. I. Dan, *Proiskhozhdenie bol'shevizma. K istorii demokraticheskikh i sotsialisticheskikh idei v Rossii posle osvobozhdeniia krest'ian* (New York: Novaia Demokratiia, 1946), p. 371.

tion in government, nevertheless continued to collaborate with the Mensheviks throughout 1905.

The views expressed in the resolution of the Menshevik Conference in May were almost unanimously accepted in Menshevik circles until the "Days of Freedom," the short period that followed the October general strike and the Manifesto of October 17. Among the Menshevik writings during the intervening months, Martynov's article "Struggling with Marxist Conscience" (*Iskra*, Nos. 102 and 103, June 15 and 21 [O.S.]) deserves special notice. It was a reply to Lenin's attempt to prove that the Menshevik tactic of non-participation in a bourgeois revolutionary government ran counter to the tactic Marx and Engels had recommended in revolutionary crises. Martynov lucidly argued that Menshevism was, on the contrary, continuing the tradition of *orthodox* Marxism—an argument that carried great weight in the intraparty disputes of the time.[16]

The October events reshuffled all the cards. *Iskra* closed (its last issue, No. 112, came out on October 8/21) and was replaced by the Menshevik *Nachalo* (first issue, November 13/26), pub-

---

[16] Martynov first raised the question in *Dve diktatury*, and Plekhanov took it up in "K voprosu o zakhvate vlasti. Nebol'shaia istoricheskaia spravka," *Iskra*, No. 96, April 5/18, 1905, reprinted in Plekhanov, *Sochineniia*, XIII (1926), 203–11. Lenin criticized this argument at great length in his speech at the Third Congress about Social-Democracy's participation in the provisional government (*Sochineniia*, VIII, 350–63). Martynov's reply to this was the article mentioned in my text. It makes several references to Engels and, as the conclusive argument, quotes Engels' letter to Turati in 1894 warning against mistakes in the event of a republican overturn in Italy, which seemed likely at the time: "If the movement proves truly national, our people will not remain in the shadow, will not wait for a special summons. . . . But in that case one must be on guard, and it will be our duty to let everyone know that we are participating as an independent party—in alliance with radicals and republicans but quite distinct from them; that from the moment of victory our paths diverge; that from that day on we shall form *a new opposition* to the new government, though not a reactionary one but a progressive opposition of the extreme left, which will lead to new victories. . . . It is possible that after the joint victory we shall be offered some place in the new government—but always in the *minority*. *This presents the gravest danger*. After February, 1848, the French democratic socialists made a mistake in accepting these obligations. As a minority in the government, they voluntarily took a share of the responsibility for all the basenesses and treacheries committed against the working class by the majority of pure republicans; meanwhile, *their being in the government completely paralyzed the revolutionary activity of the working class which they claimed to represent*." Martynov also "reminds the reader" of "Lenin's own statement that Russian Social-Democrats must not indulge in the pernicious illusion that they might turn out to be in the majority in our future provisional government." (See the quotation from Lenin's *Sochineniia* [VIII, 262–63], p. 20 below.)

lished legally in Petersburg in coalition with Parvus and Trotsky by the former editors of *Iskra* (except for Axelrod and Plekhanov, who were still in Switzerland). Parvus' influence was particularly strong. The programmatic lead article of No. 1, signed "The Editors," bore the unmistakable imprint of his personal views.[17]

How the shift in the Mensheviks' stand came about has never been fully explained. The published memoirs and correspondence tell us little about it. It may have been partly due to the influence of Trotsky, who had been in Petersburg since mid-October and was an important figure in the Soviet of Workers' Deputies; but the real causes, of course, lay much deeper. Martov, whom the new line had greatly disturbed, wrote in 1909 in his *History of Russian Social-Democracy* of "mitigating circumstances" that explained the "aberration in the Mensheviks' political vision." He saw them not so much in the "oscillations and betrayals" of the liberals during the Days of Freedom—these were not unexpected —as in the disappearance of liberalism from the political scene as a factor contending for influence over the masses:

> The amazing ineptness of the liberal party, which without a fight surrendered to the "left" all its positions in the *popular* movement, could indeed create the illusion that two camps, the government's and the socialist, were in direct confrontation in the political arena, with helpless little groups of bourgeois ideologues merely floundering between them.
>
> This illusion could not but fatally affect the traditional view of the historical meaning and the social content of the ongoing crisis.[18]

Dan in his last book stresses another aspect of the isolation of the proletariat noted by Martov. He links the temporary but profound deviation of Menshevism to the fact that after October 17 the interest of the masses, including the advanced industrial proletariat, had begun to shift from political to economic problems and that the workers naturally applied in their economic struggle the same *fait accompli* methods (*iavochnym poriadkom*, that is, without legal sanction) that had succeeded so well in the

---

[17] L. Martov, *Istoriia rossiiskoi sotsialdemokratii* (2d ed.; Moscow-Petrograd: Kniga, 1923), pp. 162, 166. Parvus diverged far less than Trotsky from the official Menshevik conception. See Appendix 1 for the differences between Parvus' and Trotsky's conceptions.

[18] Martov, *Istoriia rossiiskoi sotsialdemokratii*, p. 166.

political struggle and that the Social-Democrats themselves had taught them. As a result, the economic struggle too was assuming an "anarcho-syndicalist" character of "direct action." The Mensheviks foresaw the danger of the complete isolation of "the proletariat" from all the other forces of the "liberation movement" and hence of its defeat. But, says Dan, they were psychologically more receptive than the Bolsheviks to the trend represented by Parvus and Trotsky: first, because of their traditional orientation in favor of "spontaneity" and organized independent activity in the labor movement; second, because of their stress on "class," that is, socialist, objectives and thus their conviction that if the power to govern were prematurely thrust into the proletariat's hands it must still be used for *socialist* reforms of social relations.[19]

Dan remarks that the Mensheviks' "susceptibility" was evidenced in *Nachalo* in "the 'Trotskyite' notes that began to resound more and more loudly" in the articles of the former editors of *Iskra*—in the first place, in those of Martynov and Dan himself —"with the manifest approval of a large number of Mensheviks, especially of Menshevik workers." The newspaper's general editorial line was also becoming increasingly "Trotskyite." *Nachalo* now "treated the obvious and constantly growing isolation of the proletariat less as a source and omen of its defeat than as a golden opportunity to hasten its socialist liberation."[20]

Several Menshevik leaders—Martov in Petersburg, Axelrod and Plekhanov abroad—resisted the turn toward Trotsky's views that Menshevism made in November/December.[21] By January the situation changed, and at the Party Congress in Stockholm in the spring of 1906, Menshevism again emerged as a united movement, with Axelrod, Plekhanov, and Dan at its head.

That the coming revolution would be a bourgeois revolution and would not exceed these limits was unquestioningly accepted

---

[19] Dan, *op. cit.*, p. 383.

[20] *Ibid.*, p. 384. Very few articles in *Nachalo* were signed, and it is impossible now to tell which were written by Dan and which by Martynov. But it can be stated with certainty that the paper as a whole developed a definite "Parvus-Trotsky" flavor.

[21] Dan relates (*loc. cit.*) that all three opposed the Trotskyite trends in Menshevism and continued to maintain the original Menshevik conception of the revolution, to insist that the bourgeoisie was the only possible heir to power and that the proletariat's "isolation" would be fatal to both the proletariat and the

by the Bolshevik leaders as well. Lenin constantly reverted to this idea with an aggressiveness suggesting some inner conflicts. In late December, 194—that is, shortly before Bloody Sunday—he wrote in the lead article, "Autocracy and the Proletariat," of *Vpered*, No. 1:

It is one of our most widespread and tenacious illusions in Russia that . . . the coming revolution . . . is not a bourgeois revolution. To the Russian *intelligent*, from the most moderate Liberationist to the most extreme Socialist Revolutionary, it always seems that to acknowledge our revolution as bourgeois is to tarnish, diminish, debase it. The conscious Russian proletarian sees in this acknowledgment the only correct way to define the situation from a class point of view. For the proletarian, the struggle for political freedom and a democratic republic in a bourgeois society is only one of the necessary stages in the struggle for the social revolution that will overthrow the bourgeois order. Strictly distinguishing the essentially different stages, soberly studying the conditions that bring them about, does not at all mean shelving the ultimate aim . . . [or] slowing down one's progress. . . . *Only disillusionment and wobblings await those . . . who want to be socialists and yet are afraid to call the coming revolution in Russia a bourgeois revolution.*[22]

In a lead article in *Vpered* in April, 1905, "The Revolutionary Democratic Dictatorship of the Proletariat and Peasantry," Lenin warned once more against "confusing the democratic and the socialist overturn—the struggle for a republic (including our entire program-minimum) and the struggle for socialism":

In trying to aim at an immediate socialist overturn, Social-Democracy would only disgrace itself. Such hazy ideas of our "Socialist Revolutionaries" are just what Social-Democracy has always fought. That is why it has always stressed the bourgeois character of the revolution looming before Russia; that is why it has demanded strict separation of the democratic program-minimum and the socialist program-maximum.[23]

---

revolution. Martov, according to Dan, was so unhappy about his disagreement with a large number of the Mensheviks that he decided not to attend the Stockholm Congress and in general became far less active in the Party.

[22] Lenin, "Samoderzhavie i proletariat," *Sochineniia*, VIII, 8 (italics added).

[23] Lenin, "Revoliutsionaia demokraticheskaia diktatura proletariata i krest'ianstva," in *Sochineniia*, VIII, 267 (italics added).

Lenin would defend these ideas still more positively after the Third Congress.[24] But what should be the stand of Social-Democracy on participating in the provisional government of such a revolution? Lenin and his organ *Vpered* evaded this question entirely for a long time. Only in March, and then speaking only of a democratic dictatorship of the proletariat and peasantry (without using the words "provisional government") did a lead article exhort the proletariat, in strangely vague terms:

> Now is just the time for the proletariat to put itself at the head of the people for the revolutionary realization of its program-minimum, which must become the banner of all of Russian democracy. The proletariat will carry out [the complete program-minimum] and thus lay the foundation for the future socialist struggle. *We reject as utopian, as unconscious provocation, all attempts to saddle the proletariat with the task, unrealizable in the present socioeconomic conditions, of immediately carrying out the maximal program, that is, immediately creating a socialist order.*[25]

The author strongly disagreed with the "cowards . . . timorously looking to see if there isn't some liberal general or magistrate around to whom one could delegate the revolution and deferentially step aside," and ended with a touch of braggadocio:

> No! You step aside, you generals and magistrates, professors and capitalists! The proletariat is setting out to build your bourgeois revolution for you, and it will build it in a way that will make it easiest to rebuild on socialist lines when the longed-for hour comes.

Another month passed before Lenin took up Martynov's challenge directly in a long article, "Social-Democracy and the Provi-

---

[24] In *Dve taktiki sotsialdemokratii v demokraticheskoi revoliutsii*, written in June–July, 1905, Lenin said: "The degree of Russia's economic development (an objective condition) and the degree of consciousness and organization of the broad proletarian masses (a subjective condition inseparably linked with the objective one) make the immediate complete liberation of the working class impossible. *Only the most ignorant people can disregard the bourgeois character of the ongoing democratic overturn;* only the most naïve optimists can forget how little the mass of workers still knows about the aims of socialism and the methods of realizing it. Yet we all feel sure that the job of liberating the workers can be done by the workers themselves. Unless the masses are conscious and organized, unless they are prepared and trained in an open struggle with the entire bourgeoisie, a socialist revolution is out of the question." (Lenin, *Sochineniia*, IX, 14 [italics added].)

[25] "Bankrotstvo politseiskogo rezhima," *Vpered*, No. 10, March 15 (N.S.), 1905 (italics added).

sional Revolutionary Government," in *Vpered*, Nos. 13 and 14 (April 5 and 12 [N.S.]), and in the lead article in No. 14, which I have already quoted (p. 17).[26] In these articles Lenin categorically insisted on the bourgeois character of the Russian revolution. But he had to find a way out of the theoretical difficulties in which that insistence involved him. He found it in counterposing the bourgeoisie proper and the urban and especially the rural petty bourgeoisie (that is, mainly the peasantry):

> To speak of a democratic overturn and stop at the bald and simple counterposition of "proletariat" and "bourgeoisie" is the greatest inanity, for *this* overturn marks that period in the development of society when its bulk . . . the extremely vast petty-bourgeois, peasant stratum, stands in fact between the proletariat and the bourgeoisie. Precisely because the democratic overturn has not yet been accomplished, this gigantic stratum has far more common interests with the "proletariat" in the matter of establishing political forms than does the "bourgeoisie" in the true and narrow sense of that word.[27]

---

[26] The latter opens with the statement that "the question of Social-Democracy's participation in the provisional revolutionary government has been put on the order of the day not so much by the course of events as by the theoretical speculations of Social-Democrats of a certain bent"—and points to Martynov by name. Nevertheless, Lenin adds, the question has aroused great interest and should be discussed. (Lenin, *Sochineniia*, VIII, 264.) Lenin's speech "Ob uchastii sotsialdemokratii vo vremennom revoliutsionnom pravitel'stve" at the Third Congress began with a similar remark: "At first glance it may seem strange that such a question should have arisen. It may seem that Social-Democracy is doing splendidly and that the likelihood of its participation in a provisional revolutionary government is very great. Actually this is not so. It would be quixotic to discuss this question from the point of view of immediate practical realization. But the question has been forced upon us not so much by the actual state of affairs as by literary polemics. One must always keep in mind that this question was first raised by Martynov, before January 9." (*Sochineniia*, VIII, 350.)

Mikha Tskhakaia expressed his agreement with Lenin (*Tretii s"ezd RSDRP. Aprel'-mai 1905 goda. Protokoly* [Moscow: Institute of Marxism-Leninism, 1959], p. 203), as did B. V. Avilov (p. 208). The following disagreed: L. B. Krasin (p. 198: "The question has not been forced on us by our opponents" but by "the entire course of the Russian revolution"), N. V. Romanov (p. 202), and A. V. Lunacharskii (p. 205: "I mainly want to refute only those who say that the differences of opinion on the question of the provisional government are caused by faction quarrels. The differences are more substantial than that and would exist even without factional quarrels").

[27] Lenin, *Sochineniia*, VIII, 254–55. Lenin returned to this idea many times, especially clearly in the article "K otsenke russkoi revoliutsii," written in the spring of 1908 for the Polish *Przeglad Socjaldemokratyczny*: "The victory of a bourgeois revolution is impossible in our country *as a victory of the bourgeoisie*. Paradoxical as it sounds, this is a fact. The preponderantly peasant population, its dreadful oppression by the semifeudal big landownership, the strength and

The petty bourgeoisie was quickly becoming "revolutionized"; only in collaboration with it, after the establishment of a "revolutionary democratic dictatorship of the lower classes," of a "revolutionary dictatorship of the proletariat and peasantry," could the working class win the socialist program-minimum. At the same time, to think of setting up a socialist dictatorship would be a dangerous illusion:

> This cannot be, because only a revolutionary dictatorship supported by a colossal majority of the people can be at all lasting (not in the absolute sense, of course, but relatively). And right now the Russian proletariat forms a minority of the population. . . . It can become a colossal, overwhelming majority only by uniting with the mass of those who are partly proletarian and partly small proprietors, that is, the mass of the petty-bourgeois urban and rural poor. And that kind of social basis for the . . . revolutionary-democratic dictatorship will of course be reflected in the composition of the revolutionary government; it will inevitably result in the participation or even the predominance in it of a motley assortment of representatives of revolutionary democracy. . . . They cannot become Social-Democrats instantly, without going through various revolutionary trials—not only because they are so backward (the revolution enlightens, we repeat, with fabulous rapidity), but because their class situation is not proletarian and because the objective logic of historical development faces them at the moment with the tasks of a democratic, not socialist, overturn.[28]

Like the Mensheviks, the Bolsheviks were not generally ready as yet to accept the idea of Social-Democracy's participation in a provisional revolutionary government. At the Bolshevik so-called Third Congress in April, the very discussion of the question met with some obstacles. Lenin had prepared a draft of the agenda, the second item on which was "the participation of Social-Democracy in the provisional revolutionary government."[29] But

consciousness of the proletariat already organized into a socialist party—all these circumstances give *our* bourgeois revolution a *special* character. This peculiarity does not eliminate the bourgeois character of the revolution. . . . This peculiarity only makes for the counterrevolutionary character of our bourgeoisie and [creates] the need for a dictatorship of the proletariat and peasantry in *this kind* of revolution. (*Sochineniia*, XV, 41.)

[28] Lenin, *Sochineniia*, VIII, 262–63.
[29] *Leninskii Sbornik*, V (1926), 224.

when the Congress, on the second day, began working out its agenda, Lenin, Bogdanov, and Litvinov submitted a draft in which this item did not appear;[30] and despite Kamenev's protest,[31] the Congress did not include it.[32] Yet the eleventh session opened with Lenin's report "On the Participation of Social-Democracy in the Provisional Revolutionary Government."[33] From the protocols of the Congress it is impossible to tell how this happened.

Lenin had drafted a resolution on the subject, which was circulated among the delegates.[34] But at the end of his report he submitted another, markedly different draft. The original draft had stressed

> . . . that more and more representatives of various bourgeois and petty-bourgeois layers of the population, the peasantry, etc., are now advancing revolutionary-democratic slogans which naturally and inevitably flow from the basic needs of the popular masses, and the satisfaction of which—impossible under autocracy—is absolutely required by the objective development of Russia's whole socioeconomic life; [and] . . . that international revolutionary Social-Democracy has always recognized the need for the proletariat's most energetic support of the bourgeoisie in its struggle with the reactionary classes and institutions on the condition of the proletarian party's complete independence and of a severely critical attitude on its part toward its temporary allies.

The text that Lenin submitted (and that the Congress adopted with minor changes in wording as shown below)[35] made no reference to revolutionized "bourgeois and petty-bourgeois layers" or to the need for the proletariat to support them in their fight with reaction. Instead, something new appeared in the "motivational" part of the resolution: "The democratic overturn in

---

[30] *Tretii s"ezd RSDRP . . . 1905 . . .*, p. 61.

[31] *Ibid.*, p. 62.

[32] *Ibid.*, pp. 66–67.

[33] *Ibid.*, p. 185. Curiously enough, the literature now describes Lenin's speech as the high point of the Third Congress. See, for example, the article by D. Kardashev cited in n. 8 above.

[34] At the top of the sheet on which the draft was written there was the inscription, "Please pass on to whoever wishes to read it and return to the Bureau by dinner" (*Leninskii Sbornik*, V, 250). This draft of the resolution was first published in 1926, in *Leninskii Sbornik*, V, 250–51, and an addition to it in 1931, in *Leninskii Sbornik*, XVI, 104. See also Lenin, *Sochineniia*, VIII, 347–49.

[35] *Tretii s"ezd RSDRP . . . 1905 . . .*, pp. 451–52.

Russia, given [the Russian] socioeconomic order, will strengthen, not weaken, the dominance of the bourgeoisie; at a certain point [the bourgeoisie], stopping at nothing, will inevitably attempt to take away from the Russian proletariat as great a part as possible of the conquests of the revolutionary period." The main part of the resolution was changed accordingly. Lenin's preliminary draft had declared it "possible" for Social-Democracy to participate in the provisional revolutionary government "in order to wage a ruthless struggle *together with revolutionary bourgeois democracy* against all counterrevolutionary attempts and in order to defend the independent interests of the working class" (italics added). The resolution adopted by the Congress declared it "admissible" for Social-Democracy to participate in the provisional government "in order to wage a ruthless struggle against all counterrevolutionary attempts and to defend the independent interests of the working class." The words "together with revolutionary bourgeois democracy" had been removed.[36]

---

[36] Dan notes correctly in *Proiskhozhdenie bol'shevizma* . . . (cited in n. 15 above) that "a big breach was made in the Bolshevik conceptions by the last point of the resolution: 'Regardless of whether it will be possible for Social-Democracy to participate in the provisional government, [we] should propagandize, in the broadest strata of the proletariat, the idea that it is imperative for an armed proletariat led by Social-Democracy to exert constant pressure on the provisional government, so as to protect, reinforce, and broaden the conquests of the revolution.' Social-Democracy's action from above, through a dictatorial provisional government based on 'military might, the armed masses, uprisings,' is replaced here by 'pressure' on the provisional government from below, by armed proletarian masses led by Social-Democracy. If this differed from the Menshevik conception of the time, it was only in its stress on 'armed' (p. 374)."

It should be noted that neither Lenin's preliminary draft nor the resolution adopted by the Congress mention dictatorship of the proletariat and peasantry. When Martov later reproached the Bolsheviks for consistently avoiding the formula in their resolutions, Lenin answered in the article "Tsel' bor'by proletariata v nashei revoliutsii," *Sotsialdemokrat,* Nos. 3 and 4, March 9 and 21, 1909 (O.S.): "The Bolsheviks themselves did *not once* include in their drafts of resolutions or in their resolutions the expression or the formula: dictatorship of the proletariat and peasantry. Nevertheless, up to now *not a single person* ever thought of denying that *all* the Bolshevik drafts and resolutions of 1905–7 are *wholly* built on the idea of a dictatorship of the proletariat and peasantry." (*Sochineniia,* XV, 338.)

"Built on"—then why is it nowhere expressed openly? Referring to a resolution of the Third Congress, Lenin attempted in the same article to justify this somewhat surprising reticence: "The Bolsheviks themselves, in their official resolution, at a purely Bolshevik congress, *did not include* anything like the formula: dictatorship of the proletariat and peasantry but spoke *only* of the admissibility of participating in the provisional government and of 'calling' the proletariat 'to play a decisive role' (the resolution on armed uprising). The formula 'a revolutionary-democratic dictatorship of the proletariat and peasantry,' given in the Bolshevik press before the

Throughout these waverings, the strict distinction between the bourgeois and the socialist overturn and the view of the Russian revolution as bourgeois stood unchanged. The bourgeois revolution was to clear the way for the free development of bourgeois society and enable the working class to struggle openly for the eventual socialist revolution. In the already quoted article "Social-Democracy and the Provisional Revolutionary Government" (April, 1905), Lenin had advised "the revolutionary Social-Democrat" to build dreams "on the eve of the revolution":

> He will dream, it is his duty to dream if he isn't a hopeless Philistine, that after the tremendous experience of Europe, after the unprecedented surge of energy of the working class in Russia, we shall succeed in raising as never before the beacon of revolutionary light before the ignorant, downtrodden masses; that we shall succeed . . . in realizing with unparalleled fulness all the democratic reforms, our entire program-minimum; that we shall succeed in making the Russian revolution *a movement not of a few months but of many years,* so that it may lead not merely to minor concessions on the part of the powers that be but to [their] complete overthrow. And if this succeeds, then—then the revolutionary conflagration will set Europe on fire; the European worker languishing amid bourgeois reaction will rise in turn and show us "how it is done"; the revolutionary surge will revert to influence Russia and *turn an era of a few revolutionary years into an era of several revolutionary decades.*[37]

This was the most optimistic forecast of the developments a dreamer could dream. In the lead article of *Vpered,* No. 14, after describing the proletariat's ascent from a bourgeois to a socialist revolution, Lenin had written: "This picture is by and large correct in the long run . . . *over the span of a century.*"[38]

Third Congress, was repeated in the pamphlet *Dve taktiki* after that Congress, and no one thought of accusing the Bolsheviks of discrepancies between their comments and their resolutions. It did not occur to a single person to demand that the resolutions of a party of the masses, engaged in political struggle, coincide word for word with Marxian formulas defining the class content of a victorious revolution." (*Ibid.,* p. 332.) Yet one would assume that resolutions were the proper place for "Marxian formulas" rather than articles and pamphlets addressed to the masses. And if such a formula repeatedly figured in popular writings, its *systematic* exclusion from resolutions is all the more puzzling.

[37] Lenin, *Sochineniia,* VIII, 259 (italics added).

[38] *Ibid.,* p. 270 (italics added).

After the Third Congress, Lenin developed doubts. The idea of an *immediate* transition from a democratic to a socialist revolution began to appear with increasing frequency in his writings. In June/July, 1905, he wrote in *Two Tactics of Social-Democracy in the Democratic Revolution:*

> The complete victory of the present revolution will be the end of the democratic overturn and the beginning of the decisive struggle for a socialist overturn. The realization of the demands of today's peasantry, the total rout of reaction, the conquest of a democratic republic, will mark the end of the revolutionary mood of the bourgeoisie and even the petty bourgeoisie—and the beginning of the proletariat's real struggle for socialism. The more complete the democratic overturn, the sooner, the more broadly, clearly, [and] decisively will this new struggle unfold. The slogan of "democratic" dictatorship expresses both the historically limited character of the present revolution and the need for a new struggle, on the basis of the new order, for the complete deliverance of the working class from all oppression and all exploitation. . . .[39]

Two months later (in an article on the attitude to the peasantry!) Lenin wrote still more definitely: "From the democratic revolution we shall *at once* begin to go on . . . to a socialist revolution We are for continuous revolution. We shall not stop halfway."[40]

This is indicative of Lenin's uncertainty in the early summer of 1905. The above quotation is, to speak in conventional terms, his farthest swing "to the left." Within a month—again in an article on the attitude to the peasantry—he wrote in a quite different tone:

> A decisive victory of the democratic revolution is possible only in the form of a revolutionary-democratic dictatorship of the proletariat and peasantry. But the sooner and more fully this victory comes about, the sooner and more deeply will new contradictions, and a new struggle, develop on the battleground of a fully democratic bourgeois order. The more completely we execute the bourgeois overturn, the more closely shall we find ourselves face to face with the tasks of the socialist overturn, the sharper will be the

---

[39] Lenin, *Dve taktiki sotsialdemokratii v demokraticheskoi revoliutsii*, in *Sochineniia*, IX, 109.

[40] *Ibid.*, p. 213 (italics added) ("Otnoshenie sotsialdemokratii k krest'ianstvu," *Proletarii*, No. 16, September 1/14, 1905).

proletariat's struggle against the very foundations of bourgeois society.

Social-Democracy must wage an unflagging struggle against all deviations from this way of putting the proletariat's revolutionary-democratic and socialist tasks. It is absurd to ignore the democratic, that is, the basically bourgeois, character of the present revolution . . . absurd to confuse the tasks and conditions of a democratic and a socialist revolution, which are disparate both in their character and in the social forces participating in them.[41]

During his farthest swing to the left, when he wrote of moving "at once" from a bourgeois to a socialist revolution, Lenin, curiously enough, did not connect the transition with a socialist revolution in the West. Possibly this was a mere oversight; since the spring, his writings had more and more frequently related a successful Russian revolution to a socialist revolution in Europe. His early article "The Revolutionary-Democratic Dictatorship of the Proletariat and Peasantry," from which I have already quoted, had ended with the prediction: "We shall make the Russian revolution the prologue to the European socialist revolution."[42] He had elaborated this idea right after the Third Congress (the resolutions of the Congress themselves do not reflect it) in his *Communication about the Third Congress of the RSDRP:*

By being victorious in the impending democratic revolution we shall make an enormous stride toward our socialist goal, we shall free all Europe from the heavy yoke of a reactionary military state and help our brothers, the conscious workers of the whole world, who have languished so long under bourgeois reaction and are now spiritually reviving at the sight of the revolutionary successes in Russia, to advance more resolutely and boldly toward socialism. And with the aid of the socialist proletariat of Europe we shall be able not only to defend the democratic republic but also to move toward socialism in seven-league strides.[43]

Lenin expressed his thoughts on the interdependence of the Russian and the Western revolutions most clearly in his unpub-

---

[41] *Ibid.*, pp. 281–82 ("Sotsializm i krest'ianstvo," *Proletarii*, No. 20, September 27/October 10, 1905).

[42] Lenin, *Sochineniia*, VIII, 274. On the Russian revolution as "prologue" to a socialist overturn in Europe, see also Vol. IX, p. 380 ("Obostrenie polozheniia v Rossii," *Proletarii*, No. 23, October 18/31, 1905).

[43] Lenin, *Sochineniia*, VIII, 405.

lished theses "The Stages, the Direction, and the Prospects of the Revolution," written in late 1905 or early 1906.[44] In these theses, Lenin divides the development of the revolution into six "stages" or "periods," beginning with the rise of the labor movement in the late nineties. The events of 1905 are the third stage in this scheme:

> The labor movement develops into a regular *revolution;* the liberal bourgeoisie has already been consolidated into a constitutional-democratic party and is thinking of stopping the revolution by reaching an agreement with tsarism; but the *radical* elements of the bourgeoisie and petty bourgeoisie are inclined to form an alliance with the proletariat to *continue* the revolution: 1905 (especially the end).

A victorious democratic revolution and a "revolutionary-democratic dictatorship of the proletariat and peasantry" are the expected fourth stage. In the fifth, counterrevolution raises its head:

> The liberal bourgeoisie, marking time in the third stage, passive in the fourth, becomes counterrevolutionary and organizes to take the conquests of the revolution away from the proletariat. The prosperous part of the peasantry, and a goodly segment of its middle part, also "get wise," calm down, [and] turn toward counterrevolution in order to knock the power out of the hands of the proletariat and the poor peasants who sympathize with the proletariat.

The transition to a socialist revolution is the sixth and last stage:

> On the basis of the relationships formed during the fifth period, a new crisis and a new struggle develop, with the proletariat now fighting to preserve the democratic conquests for the sake of the socialist overturn. This struggle is almost hopeless for the Russian proletariat, and its defeat is as inevitable as the defeat of the German revolutionary party in 1848–50, or the defeat of the French proletariat in 1871, *unless the European socialist proletariat* comes to the aid of the Russian proletariat.
>
> To sum up, at this stage the liberal bourgeoisie and the prosperous (plus part of the middle) peasantry organize a counterrevolution. The Russian proletariat *plus* the European proletariat organize a revolution.

---

[44] Lenin, "Étapy, napravlenie i perspektivy revoliutsii," *Sochineniia,* X, 73–74, The theses were not published until 1926, in Volume V of *Leninskii Sbornik.*

Under these conditions the Russian proletariat can win a second victory. The matter is no longer hopeless. The second victory will be a *socialist overturn in Europe*.

The European workers will show us "how it is done"; together with them, we shall then effect a socialist overturn.

Although he avoided explicit public commitment on these premises, this is how Lenin, in early 1906, visualized the process by which the Russian bourgeois-democratic revolution would "grow over" (to use an expression that became popular much later) into a socialist revolution. However, this was by no means his final stand, as later developments proved. He soon returned to his original conception and in the main stuck to it until the Revolution of 1917.[45]

The turn toward the West in the Mensheviks' orientation in 1905 somewhat blunted the disagreements between them and the Bolsheviks on the development of the revolution. On the basic issue, however—that of the grouping of the social forces in the Russian revolution—their views continued to diverge quite radically. And the Bosheviks were right in stressing, far more than the

---

[45] Of great interest for understanding Lenin's basic orientation from 1905 to the Revolution of 1917 is the foreword he wrote in 1907 for the second edition of *Razvitie kapitalizma v Rossii*. (I believe it has never before been cited in connection with the question we are discussing.) It was the first clear formulation of the theory, which Lenin elaborated during the following years, of the possible agrarian development of Russia along "Prussian" or "American" lines: "Either the old gentry economy, tied with a thousand threads to serfdom, is preserved, slowly changing into a purely capitalistic, 'Junker' economy . . . or the revolution breaks up the old gentry economy, destroying all remnants of serfdom—first of all, large landownership. The final transition from *otrabotki* to capitalism is based on the free development of a small peasant economy, which will receive a powerful impetus from the expropriation of landlords' holdings in favor of the peasantry. The whole agrarian system becomes capitalistic, for the more completely the vestiges of serfdom are abolished, the faster the peasantry develops. In other words, either the preservation of the majority of landed estates and of the main foundations of the old 'superstructure' . . . or the abolition of landed estates and of all the main corresponding foundations of the old 'superstructure'; the neutralization of the unstable and counterrevolutionary bourgeoisie, with the proletariat and peasant masses playing the foremost role; and the speediest and freest development of productive forces on a capitalistic basis, with the position of the working and peasant masses the best conceivable under the conditions of commodity production. Hence—the most favorable conditions for the further realization by the working class of its true and basic objective, socialist reconstruction." (*Sochineniia*, III, 10–11.) One outcome is predicated on the victory of counterrevolution; the other, on the complete victory of the democratic revolution and the development of capitalism.

Mensheviks did, the role of the peasantry in the bourgeois-democratic revolution. Yet their plans for bringing about a proletarian-peasant dictatorship assigned a very modest role to the peasantry, and even the workers were to be represented by a centralized party of "professional revolutionaries." The dictatorship of the proletariat was in fact to be a dictatorship of the Social-Democratic Party. Throughout their gropings on the question of participating in the provisional government in a bourgeois revolution, the Mensheviks were basically concerned with fostering the proletariat's political independence. The Bolshevik slogan of a revolutionary-democratic dictatorship of the proletariat and peasantry in fact concealed a meaning unclear at the time even to many of its proponents. In practice, the chief inferences for the labor movement that the Bolsheviks drew from their formula were the ideas of "firm" leadership from above and iron "discipline" on the lower levels. These divergences in their basic orientations were at the bottom of all the disputes about tactics between Bolsheviks and Mensheviks in 1905.

CHAPTER I

On the Eve of 1905

F UNDAMENTALLY, Bolshevism stressed the initiative of an active minority; Menshevism, the activization of the masses. One might say, therefore, that Bolshevism inherited some of the traditions of *Narodnaia Volia,* and Menshevism, some of the traditions of the Go-to-the-People Movement and of Lavrism. In its sociopsychological content, if not in its theoretical conceptions, Menshevism could be viewed as a proletarian variant of Populism. In keeping with these basic emphases, the central idea of Bolshevism was leadership; that of Menshevism, service. Bolshevism logically developed dictatorial conceptions and practices; Menshevism remained thoroughly democratic. A historical accident gave the two tendencies their names: a slight Leninist majority (*bol'shinstvo,* as against *men'shinstvo,* "minority") when the Second Party Congress voted on the editorial board of the Party organ.[1]

---

[1] Originally, there were 43 delegates with 51 votes at the Congress, and Lenin did not have a majority. His formulation, supported by Plekhanov, of the controversial Article 1 of the Party Rules received only 23 votes, and Martov's, which received 28, was accepted. That there was as yet no clear-cut division is obvious from the fact that Egorov (E. J. Levin), the delegate from *Iuzhnyi Rabochii,* for example, and the Petersburg *Rabochedelka* Bruker (L. P. Makhnovets), sister of Akimov (V. P. Makhnovets), voted for Lenin's formula, and such a staunch Leninist as Rusov (B. M. Knuniants), for Martov's. See *Vtoroi s"ezd RSDRP. Iiul'-avgust 1903 goda. Protokoly* (Moscow: Gospolitizdat, 1959), p. 279. When two delegates of the Union of Russian Social-Democrats Abroad and five delegates of the Bund, who usually sided with the future Mensheviks, left the Congress, the Leninists gained a small majority, and then only thanks to the support of Plekhanov, who broke with Lenin soon after the Congress. The division into a Majority and a Minority became a more acute issue during the several ballots

Actually, as we shall see, the label "Bolshevik" would have fitted the Mensheviks better, and vice versa.

At the time of the First Russian Revolution even the leaders of the Social-Democratic movement understood the basic distinction between the two only dimly. For the rank-and-file, Bolshevism was simply a more radical, and Menshevism a more cautious, variant of European Social-Democracy on Russian soil. Understandably, Bolshevism had a greater appeal to young people, in particular to the university students who were drawn into the movement just before 1905. Many who later became prominent Menshevik party workers passed through a Bolshevik phase at this time, for example, the future contributors to the Menshevik *Sotsialisticheskii Vestnik* G. Ia. Aronson, G. O. Binshtok (G. Osipov), V. S. Voitinskii, Iu. P. Denicke, A. E. Dubois, M. S. Kefali, and B. I. Nicolaevsky. I myself was no exception.

The great revolutionary surge of 1905 faced Social-Democracy with complex problems. It was in their attempts to solve them that Bolshevism and Menshevism crystallized as two factions dedicated to opposite principles. For a long time, however, Bolshevism still remained, and considered itself, a branch of Social-Democracy. Years would pass before it came to realize its basic differences with Social-Democracy and openly moved away from it, leaving Menshevism its only voice in Russia.

By 1905 the leaders on both sides were only beginning to perceive that they had come to a parting of the ways. From the Second Congress until almost the end of 1904 their arguments turned mostly on matters of organization, with the Bolsheviks accusing the Mensheviks of "opportunism,"[2] and the latter accus-

---

on how the new editorial board of *Iskra* should be elected. Lenin's group prevailed, with 22, 24, and 25 votes, every time with several abstentions. From that time on, the Party was divided into Bolsheviks and Mensheviks.

But the clean break was still far away, as witness the results of the elections of the three editors of *Iskra*, by secret ballot, in which the Bolsheviks alone voted— the Mensheviks had refused to take part in the elections: Plekhanov, 23 votes; Martov, 22 (he did not accept); and Lenin, 20. See *Vtoroi s"ezd RSDRP . . . 1903 . . .*, pp. 374–75.

[2] In the foreword to *Shag vpered, dva shaga nazad. Krizis v nashei partii*, completed in May, 1904, in which he analyzed the struggle at the Second Congress and critically analyzed the Mensheviks' activities after the Congress, Lenin wrote: "Both analyses, which represent nine-tenths of my pamphlet [this 'pamphlet' occupies over two hundred pages in Lenin's *Sochineniia.*—S. S.] lead to the conclusion that 'the Majority' is the revolutionary, and 'the Minority' the opportunistic, wing

ing the former of "creating a state of siege."[3] Even in P. B. Axelrod's articles "The Unification of Social-Democracy and its Tasks" (*Iskra,* Nos. 55 and 57, December 15, 1903, and January 15, 1904), which put the question of the role of Social-Democracy in Russia on a historicophilosophical plane (and greatly influenced the evolution of Menshevism), Bolshevism was treated mainly from an organizational point of view, as "center fetishism" and "an organizational utopia of a theocratic nature."[4]

---

of our Party; the differences that at present divide the two wings boil down mainly to questions of organization, not of program or tactics; the new philosophy, which is the clearer in the new *Iskra* the more it tries to strengthen its position and the freer that position becomes from squabbles over co-optation, is opportunism in organizational matters." (Lenin, *Sochineniia* [4th ed.], VII, 188.)

[3] Martov deals with this question in his pamphlet *Bor'ba s "osadnym polozheniem" v RSDRP (Otvet na pis'mo t. Lenina)* (Geneva, 1904). It was a reply to Lenin's leaflet "Pochemu ia vyshel iz redaktsii 'Iskry'? (Pis'mo v redaktsiiu 'Iskry')" (*Sochineniia,* VII, 102–8).

[4] Martov wrote later that in these articles Axelrod had shown that, paradoxically, "behind the tutelage of the impeccably 'orthodox' socialists over the labor movement and their efforts to immunize it, through organizational measures, against the bacillus of opportunism there lurked the struggle of the extreme wing of the democratic (Jacobin) intelligentsia against the class independence of the proletariat—the desire to dissolve the proletariat's movement in the people's general revolutionary movement, directed against tsarism and essentially petty-bourgeois, which the ideologues of Bolshevism, relying on the personal authority of leaders and the iron hand of a conspiratorial organization, hoped to channel toward socialist aspirations." (L. Martov, *Istoriia rossiiskoi sotsialdemokratii* [2d ed.; Moscow-Petrograd: Kniga, 1923], p. 88.)

During the polemics sparked by Axelrod's articles, the Bolsheviks stressed the need for extreme centralization "as a weapon against the danger of opportunism lying in wait for the labor movement. In this newspaper literature, there could be discerned more and more sharply the idea of the need for dictatorial guidance of the Party by leaders whom the proletariat trusted absolutely. Lenin himself expressed this idea in his letter to the editors of *Iskra* in which he reduced his falling-out with Plekhanov and the Mensheviks to his opponents' failure to see the need of handing to a suitable person the 'conductor's baton,' without which one cannot create an orchestra out of a multitude of musicians playing diverse parts. The idea of personal dictatorship was more sharply formulated in a letter, published in *Iskra,* from representatives of three Ural committees, arguing that the proletariat would be ready for its coming class dictatorship over society only when it had itself gone through the school of iron discipline under the leadership of the dictators who would bring that class dictatorship about. The same tendency permeates also the long political pamphlet (*One Step Forward, Two Steps Backward*) in which Lenin settled accounts with his critics. Here, the organizational centralism and the dictatorship of the Party centers are proclaimed the basic guaranty of the labor movement's immunization against the poison of opportunism. To reproaches of corrupting Social-Democracy and reviving Jacobinism, Lenin replied that a Jacobin linked to the proletarian masses was exactly what the present-day revolutionary Social-Democrat was.

"The dispute over organization between the two parts of Russian Social-Democracy attracted the attention of Western European socialists as well. Karl

Behind the mutual accusations, deep political differences lay hidden. Their not being fully conscious may have lent all the more passion to the disputes, which looked like mere intraparty squabbles to outsiders and to the less sophisticated members of the two movements. The political differences came into the open only in late 1904, when the Mensheviks sought to organize the active intervention of the laboring masses in the political turmoil that had broken out among large segments of Russian society and found expression in the widely attended meetings of the intelligentsia and the resolutions adopted by zemstvo assemblies and municipal dumas.

The Zemstvo and Banquet Campaigns of 1904

The harsh repression of all revolutionary and liberal trends by the minister of the interior, V. K. Plehve, and the unrest over Russia's defeats in the unpopular war with Japan led up to a political crisis. On July 15/28 Plehve was killed by Egor Sazonov on the orders of the Fighting Organization of the Party of Socialist Revolutionaries. The country received the news with immense satisfaction. Even such a sober historian as P. N. Miliukov could write, forty years later, "Everybody rejoiced at his assassination."[5] The perturbed government did not appoint Plehve's successor for six weeks. Finally, on August 26/September 8 Prince Sviatopolk-Mirskii was made minister of the interior—an appointment supposed to usher in an "era of trust" between the government and "society." Addressing his staff, Mirskii spoke of his "profound conviction that the fruitfulness of administrative work is based on a sincerely benevolent and genuinely trustful

Kautsky and Rosa Luxemburg spoke of the danger of dictatorial and ultracentralistic tendencies in a Social-Democratic party directing a labor movement. Rosa Luxemburg's mordant criticism, demonstrating the Blanquist bent of Lenin's policy, provoked strong irritation in Bolshevik circles." (*Ibid.*, pp. 89–90.)

Lenin's above-mentioned letter to *Iskra* was printed in *Iskra*, No. 53, November 25, 1903 (see also Lenin, *Sochineniia*, VII, 98–101); the letter from the Ural committees, in *Iskra*, No. 63, April 1, 1904; Kautsky's letter about the dissent in the RSDRP, in *Iskra*, No. 66, May 15, 1904; and Rosa Luxemburg's article "Organizatsionnye voprosy russkoi sotsialdemokratii," in *Iskra*, No. 69, July 10. Kautsky's letter led to a further exchange of letters between him and Axelrod; see *Iskra*, No. 68, June 25, 1904.

[5] Miliukov, *Vospominaniia (1859–1917)* (New York: Chekhov Publishing House, 1955), I, 224.

attitude to community and class [*soslovnye*] institutions and the population in general."[6] A series of liberal gestures followed. Three *Narodovol'tsy* serving life sentences, one of them Vera Figner, were released after some twenty years in Schlüsselburg Fortress. Writers and public figures, in particular liberal members of the zemstvos, were returned from administrative exile.[7] The *uezd* [subdivision of a province] zemstvos were holding their conventions at the time and responded with messages to the minister of the interior, which expressed, usually in the most loyal terms, many of the demands that preoccupied Russian society.

The zemstvos obtained permission from the minister to hold a congress in Petersburg in November. At the last moment they were forced to call their congress (November 6–8) a "private conference," but it remained a "zemstvo congress" in the public mind. In October the Council of the Union of Liberation, which had many ties with liberal zemstvo members, drafted a plan which considerably influenced the zemstvo "campaign." It proposed (to quote the condensed paraphrase of the text that has been left to us):

1. To take the most active part in the coming congress of zemstvo and municipal leaders and make every effort to steer it toward stating constitutional demands openly.

2. November 20 being the fortieth anniversary of the Judicial Statutes, to have our members organize banquets on that day in Petersburg, Moscow, and as many other cities as possible, at which must be adopted constitutional and democratic resolutions much more decisive in tone than could be expected from a congress of zemstvo and municipal leaders.

3. Through our zemstvo members, to raise at as many of the coming *uezd* and province conventions as possible the question of introducing a constitutional order in Russia and of the need to convoke to this end representatives of the people on a broad democratic basis.

4. To begin to agitate for the formation of unions of lawyers, engineers, professors, writers, and others in the liberal professions;

---

[6] Sviatopolk-Mirskii's speech is given in full in I. P. Belokonskii, "K istorii zemskogo dvizheniia v Rossii," in *Istoricheskii sbornik* (Petersburg, 1907), p. 26. This collection was published instead of the November and December issues of the journal *Byloe,* closed by the censor.

[7] *Ibid.,* p. 27.

for having them organize conventions and elect permanent bureaus; and for having these bureaus unite among themselves as well
as with the bureaus of zemstvo and municipal leaders into a single
union of unions.[8]

The author of this summary adds parenthetically: "This union of
unions was to establish organizational ties with the central agencies of the political parties of the left, work out a common
platform, and become in a sense a preparliament."

Note that the plan suggests merely "constitutional and democratic resolutions much more decisive in tone" and "representatives of the people on a broad democratic basis." The Council of
the Union of Liberation itself did not yet venture to include the
issues of a constituent assembly and universal, direct, equal, and
secret suffrage in its outline for the zemstvo campaign. However,
the demand for universal suffrage (but not for a constituent
assembly) was by that time widely, though far from unanimously, approved in Liberationist circles; it was included in the
draft of a constitution worked out by a group of Liberationists in
October, 1904, although even here franchise was demanded only
for males.[9]

At the zemstvo congress, Liberationists did move to demand a
constituent assembly, but this received few votes.[10] The congress
approved a demand for "proper participation of the people's
representatives, as a special elected body, in legislation, in drawing up the state budget, and in controlling the legality of the
administration's actions," but the nature of the participation of
the people's representatives was not defined, and nothing was
said about electing them by universal, equal, and direct suffrage
and secret ballot (the famous "four-tailer" [chetyrekhkhvostka]).
The congress merely approved the demand for equal personal,
civil, and political rights. At the banquets that began soon after-

---

[8] This paraphrase of the original text is presented in the editors' note to
Belokonskii's article, in *Istoricheskii sbornik*, p. 29.

[9] *Osnovnoi gosudarstvennyi zakon Rossiiskoi Imperii. Proekt russkoi konsti-
tutsii, vyrabotannyi gruppoi chlenov 'Soiuza Osvobozhdeniia'* (Paris: Osvobozhdenie, 1905), p. 19.

[10] Belokonskii, "K istorii zemskogo dvizheniia v Rossii," p. 34. See also *Zemskii
s"ezd 6 i sl. noiabria 1904 g. Kratkii otchet* (Paris: Osvobozhdenie, 1905), pp.
12–13.

ward, Liberationist orators sheepishly explained that "political equality" meant the "four-tailer."[11]

At the zemstvo conventions of November and December and at the banquets intended mainly to unite the intelligentsia, the demands for a constituent assembly and universal suffrage often met with stiff opposition; still, in many places they gradually gained ground.[12] The more radical elements usually proposed them under the influence of Social-Democrats. The zemstvo conventions had already begun to interest Social-Democrats in October, but it was difficult to influence them directly, because of their social composition. In most cases they could be influenced only at second hand. After the November congress, many people began to take a lively interest in zemstvo conventions and in the meetings of the intelligentsia initiated by the Union of Liberation, which soon became much more than group meetings of the liberal professions. In many cities Social-Democracy saw the need for active intervention in this social movement, which was so rapidly gathering momentum.

This movement presented an opportunity for a display of activity by the working class. Moreover, if the Social-Democrats ignored it, the masses might be caught up in it without them. Martov wrote of this quite frankly in early November:

> At a time when a wide field of overt, legalized, or at least tolerated activity is slowly opening up for the political self-expression of various classes, or groups within classes, we should be displaying the naïveté of self-conceited conspirators if we tried to persuade the broad masses of the population which are more or less under our influence not to occupy the positions opened for them by the relaxation of police tutelage. . . . It would be a mistake to let the working masses seek and find new political leaders. . . . It would be political narrowness not to try and exert our influence over the course and the outcome of this introduction of the prole-

---

[11] N. Cherevanin, "Dvizhenie intelligentsii (Ot 'ėpokhi doveriia' kn. Sviatopolka-Mirskogo do kontsa perioda obshchestvennogo pod" ema)," in *Obshchestvennoe dvizhenie v Rossii v nachale XX-go veka*, ed. L. Martov, P. Maslov, and A. Potresov (Petersburg, 1910), Vol. II, Pt. 2, pp. 148–49.

[12] There is an interesting analysis of many data about these meetings in Cherevanin's study, pp. 149–63 (cited in n. 11). Much material is quoted in Belokonskii, "K istorii zemskogo dvizheniia v Rossii," pp. 33–52.

tariat into the oppositional sociopolitical activity of the liberal democratic bourgeoisie.

It may not be superfluous to point out that such "non-intervention" tactics, with all their fateful consequences (perhaps up to the creation of a new labor party, which would be formed without us when the proletariat has had the experience of collaborating and—upon being disappointed—of breaking with the bourgeoisie)—that such tactics would be unavoidable for us if those tendencies, conspiratorial indeed, came to prevail in our Party for which the ground has been laid by all the so-called Leninism and which exclude a priori the Party's combining secret "underground" work with the complex task of directing such civic activities of the masses as are at all overt.[13]

In November, too, the policy-making center of Menshevism, the editorial board of *Iskra*, formulated the tasks of Social-Democracy in face of the increasingly spirited zemstvo conventions and meetings of the intelligentsia. In a "Letter to the Party Organizations" *Iskra* outlined a vast plan for agitation and organization, which came to be known as the zemstvo campaign.[14]

Iskra's "Zemstvo Campaign" and Its Critique

Iskra's letter set off heated arguments in the Party and played a marked role in the development of Social-Democratic thinking in the crucial months preceding the revolution. I shall quote excerpts from its first part (the second dealt mainly with technical problems of organization):

It can be said with certainty that Russia has never been so close to a constitution as now. Of course, it would be vain to prophesy the exact date and hour when Russia's transformation into a constitutional state will at last come about. But the day is fast approaching; that much is certain. There is no need to tell you, of course, how far from indifferent it is for the future development of Russia, and for the Russian working class, and for the destinies of our Party, whether this overturn is accomplished with the active and conscious intervention of our proletariat under the banner of Social-Democ-

---

13 L. M., "Na ocheredi," *Iskra*, November 5/18, 1905.

14 *Iskra's* November "Pis'mo k partiinym organizatsiiam" was distributed in the form of a leaflet ("Tol'ko dlia chlenov partii") and later reprinted in the section *Dokumenty i materialy* in the second edition (and the third, but not in later ones) of Lenin, *Sochineniia*, VII, 410–16.

racy or while we remain entirely passive. Of course, the matter must not be confined to a mere bestowal from above of a measly constitution; we must see to it that this gift, like the convocation of the French Estates General in the past, does not serve as a dampener for the seething opposition but as a beginning of the revolution. But the earlier we intervene in the course of events, the sooner we can count on such a revolutionary development of events, for the earlier we intervene the better are our chances—on the one hand—of strengthening our own organization and our ties with the working masses and [on the other] of preventing the most *moderate* elements of the liberal opposition from consolidating their positions, from getting firmly organized in alliance with reaction to combat the "extremist" parties, that is, everything that goes beyond a census constitution.

The letter specified what Social-Democracy should do forthwith to counteract the zemstvo's bid for a "census constitution," that is, a constitution restricting the electoral rights of the great mass of the population:

> Even the more extreme elements of the zemstvo will demand a census constitution—most likely representation of the zemstvos and the [city] dumas. This is clear enough from the proclamation of the "Liberationists," which does not mention universal suffrage by as much as a single word. . . . It is necessary to explain to the workers right now the true, narrowly liberal sense of the demands which will be heard at zemstvo conventions to "let the voice of the land be heard," or to call "grass-roots representatives" to take part in governing the state, or to form a "central zemstvo," a *zemskii sobor,* and so forth. We must see to it that to all these slogans masking a desire for a limited monarchy and a census constitution the workers firmly and steadfastly oppose their own demands: a nationwide constituent assembly and universal, equal, direct, and secret suffrage.

These *political* demands were to be stated with complete clarity. But the fact that the zemstvos were fighting autocracy, however timidly, also imposed on Social-Democracy a complex *tactical* task:

> In dealing with liberal zemstvos and dumas we are dealing with enemies of our enemy, though they do not, do not wish to, or cannot go as far in their struggle with him as the interests of the proletariat require; still, in officially speaking up against absolutism

and confronting it with demands aimed at its annihilation, they are in fact our allies (in a very relative sense, to be sure), even if [they are] insufficiently resolute in their actions and insufficiently democratic in their aspirations. The facts and manifestations of this indecisiveness and halfheartedness furnish concrete material for graphically describing the social nature and the sociopolitical tendencies of the bourgeois factions and for illustrating the inimical opposition of the interests of the classes they represent, on the one hand, and the proletariat's interests, on the other. And it certainly is our duty to use this material to the fullest, in accord with the principles of our program. But within the limits of fighting absolutism, especially in the present phase, our attitude to the liberal bourgeoisie is defined by the task of infusing it with a bit more courage and moving it to join in the demands that the proletariat, led by Social-Democracy, will put forward. But we should be making a fatal mistake if we set ourselves the goal of *forcing* the zemstvos or other organs of the bourgeois opposition, through energetic measures of *intimidation* and under the influence of *panic*, to give us *now* a formal promise to present our demands to the government. Such a tactic would compromise Social-Democracy because it would turn our whole political campaign into a lever for reaction.

Finally, the letter touched upon the value of the campaign in preparing the working class to play its own influential role in the political life of the country:

> In carrying out the proposed "plan" . . . we must remember that we are taking the first steps on a new road of political action, the road of planned intervention of the working masses in civic life, with the direct aim of opposing them to the bourgeois opposition as an autonomous force with opposite class interests, yet offering it conditions for a joint energetic struggle against the common enemy.

The task was indeed complex, and somewhat contradictory: to *support* the zemstvo opposition, yet to *oppose* the masses to the bourgeois opposition "as an autonomous force with opposite class interests." Axelrod, who had developed the plan, brought out its dual nature very clearly in his speech at the Party's ("Unification") Congress in Stockholm in the spring of 1906:

> Organs of zemstvo and municipal self-government, various legal civic organizations and meetings, the legal press, and all overt

manifestations of the oppositional tendencies of the bourgeoisie were utilized as instruments, toe holds, and material, not only in the interests of the general democratic movement, not only to expand and intensify the rise of the new revolutionary wave against the class-and-bureaucratic order, but also for the *sociopolitical* education of the workers in the proletarian-class sense and for their unification under the flag of Social-Democracy into an independent political organization. In mobilizing the working masses for the political arena controlled and managed by the ideologues and organizations representing non-proletarian classes, in bringing the masses into direct contact with the socially influential elements of these classes, both in order to reach some agreements with them for stronger joint attacks against the common enemy and in order to make the workers see that their interests were in principle antagonistic to the economic foundations of the bourgeois order, we [planned to] turn a social arena previously inaccessible to us into a political grade school for the masses, in which they would gain experience and exercise their forces for a purely proletarian class struggle and for uniting into a political organization of a type approaching that of the wholly proletarian parties of the West.[15]

As if fearing that his idea might be misconstrued as a one-sided "utilization" of the zemstvo and other meetings, Axelrod again and again returned to the dual nature of the campaign:

Yes, I repeat and emphasize: our task consisted in mobilizing the working masses politically not only as social opponents of the bourgeois classes but also as a force ready to enter on certain conditions into a coalition with other groups and parties fighting the old regime to mount a joint attack against the government.[16]

The Mensheviks living abroad were at first rather opposed to the plan. Axelrod told of arguments in Geneva, then the ideological center of the Russian emigration:

A good many comrades, especially abroad, reacted to our plan with strong, very mordant censure and reproaches toward its authors. And it cannot be said that the Mensheviks disagreed with the Bolsheviks in this case. In Geneva, for instance, ten evenings were devoted to impassioned debates [at the Menshevik club.—S. S.] about the letter of the editors of the CO [Central Organ] to the

[15] *Chetvertyi (Ob"edinitel'nyi) s"ezd RSDRP. Aprel' (aprel'-mai) 1906 goda. Protokoly* (Moscow: Gospolitizdat, 1959), p. 258.
[16] *Ibid.*, p. 260.

Party organizations. . . . And almost until the end of these debates, virtually the majority of Mensheviks agreed with the Bolsheviks on one point, namely, that by adjusting the Party's tactics at the time of the first widespread rise of oppositional sentiments among the bourgeoisie, while a great lull still prevailed among the working masses . . . we would deprive the proletariat of all political independence and turn it from the vanguard of the revolution into a political tail of the liberal bourgeoisie.[17]

P. A. Garvi, who escaped from Iakutsk in the fall of 1903 and a year later in Geneva joined the *kruzhok ot"ezzhaiushchikh* ("circle of those about to leave") conducted by Axelrod (many members of which soon made their mark in Russia), tells us that *Iskra's* plan was "minutely discussed from all angles" in this circle "and on the whole met with no objections."[18] At the Menshevik club, however, the debates took a stormier turn:

All the Menshevik leaders spoke in defense of the plan—Martov, Plekhanov, Dan—and the former *Rabochedelets* Martynov joined them. A small but persistent group of comrades headed by A. K. Ermanskii, whom S. Iu. Semkovskii supported with particular energy, resolutely objected to the plan and passionately defended its negative stand. . . . But Ermanskii's and Semkovskii's objections had no success. . . . Axelrod is mistaken in asserting that virtually "the majority" of Mensheviks spoke against the plan for the zemstvo campaign.[19]

The attitude of the Menshevik Petersburg Group is described by S. Somov, who returned from abroad in the fall of 1904. A former *Rabochedelets* only half reconciled with Menshevism, he nevertheless played an important role in the Group in 1905. He writes that it tried

to react very vigorously to the general movement of opposition, the liberal movement in the zemstvos and at banquets. The Petersburg groups [this is clearly a misprint; the author no doubt wrote "the Petersburg Group." —S. S.] discussed more than once the question of having Party-affiliated workers participate in the banquets. Indeed, in connection with the writers' banquet in December, a special meeting of the more outstanding Party-affiliated workers of

---

[17] *Ibid.*, pp. 258–59.
[18] Garvi, *Vospominaniia sotsialdemokrata* (New York, 1946), p. 414.
[19] *Ibid.*, pp. 414–16.

all Petersburg was called, which after long and heated debate defined both its attitude to the banquets and its tactics in relation to them. The majority of the meeting viewed participation in the banquets from the standpoint of the need for class self-determination and demarcation of liberals from Social-Democrats; hence it recommended that workers attend banquets for pedagogical reasons. At these banquets the Social-Democrats were first of all to bring out vividly the class basis of Social-Democracy and thus to compel the other oppositional parties to reveal their non-proletarian character. The banquets were to give workers a chance to become thoroughly aware of the chasm that divided them in principle from all the other oppositional trends. Hence all the speeches prepared for the banquets were sharply critical of both the principles and the tactics of the liberal opposition and ridiculed the feeble banquet resolutions and petition projects.[20]

This was quite a deviation from *Iskra*'s plan. Little was left of the "support" to be given any movement opposing autocracy—an important point of the Party program adopted at the Second Congress. I shall return to this when we examine how the plan for the "zemstvo campaign" was actually carried out. First let us see how the top Bolshevik leaders reacted to *Iskra*'s letter.

Possibly as early as November 20 (N.S.) Lenin published a pamphlet, *The Zemstvo Campaign and* Iskra's *Plan*.[21] (He did not yet have his own paper—*Vpered* appeared on January 4, 1905 [N.S.].) In this pamphlet Lenin criticized the letter's general conception of the Social-Democrats' relation to the liberals. The question had been discussed at the Second Congress, and two resolutions had been adopted—Plekhanov's, which Lenin had indorsed, and A. N. Potresov's (Starover's) to which he had objected, mildly at the Congress[22] and very strongly later, in *One Step Forward, Two Steps Backward*.[23] Both resolutions started

---

[20] Somov, "Iz istorii sotsialdemokraticheskogo dvizheniia v Peterburge v 1905 godu (Lichnye vospominaniia)," *Byloe* (Petersburg), April, 1907, pp. 29–30.

[21] *Zemskaia kampaniia i plan "Iskry."* Lenin wrote from Geneva to A. A. Bogdanov in Russia on November 21 (N.S.): "An analysis and demolition by Lenin of this [the *Iskra* editors'] letter has appeared here." (*Sochineniia*, XXXIV, 230.)— Another clue helpful in determining the publication date of Lenin's pamphlet is that Parvus had read it and wrote Lenin a long letter about it from Munich on December 2 (N.S.). This letter is given in Parvus' book *Rossiia i revoliutsiia* (Petersburg: Glagolev, 1906), pp. 177–81.

[22] *Vtoroi s"ezd RSDRP . . . 1903 . . .*, p. 403.

[23] Lenin, *Shag vpered, dva shaga nazad*, in *Sochineniia*, VII, 303–8.

with the proposition that Social-Democracy "supports any oppositional and revolutionary movement directed against the present
social and political order in Russia." Plekhanov's resolution
stressed, however, that "on the other hand, [the Social-Democratic Party] is duty-bound to expose to the proletariat the
narrowness and inadequacy of the liberation movement of the
bourgeoisie wherever this narrowness manifests itself"; it recommended—and this was the only inference for practical politics!—
that all party workers "draw the workers' attention . . . to the
antirevolutionary and antiproletarian character of the movement that finds expression in Mr. P. Struve's *Osvobozhdenie.*"
Potresov's resolution stressed that the Party

> does not refuse to enter, and if need be will enter, through the
> intermediary of its central agencies, into a temporary agreement
> with liberal and liberal-democratic movements, but only on condi-
> tion, first, that these movements clearly and unequivocally declare
> that in their struggle with the autocratic government they are
> definitely ranging themselves on the side of Russian Social-Democ-
> racy; second, that they do not advance in their programs any
> demands contrary to the interests of the working class and democ-
> racy in general . . . ; and third, that they make universal, equal,
> direct and secret suffrage their battle cry.[24]

In his criticism of *Iskra's* plan, Lenin condemned Potresov's
resolution and gave a new interpretation of Plekhanov's. Certainly one should support the liberal opposition, he said, but "how
can we instil courage in the liberal democrats otherwise than
through ruthless analysis and devastating criticism of their halfheartedness in matters involving democracy?"[25] If everything
came down to *ruthless* struggle and *devastating* criticism, no
possibility of "support" was left. Lenin denounced the whole idea
of trying to influence this "ally" directly and positively:

> The hotter the fight, the closer . . . the decisive battle, the more
> we must direct our attention and our influence at our real enemy,
> not at the ally whom we *know* to be conditional, problematic,
> unreliable, and halfhearted. It would not be sensible to ignore this
> ally, and it would be senseless to aim at intimidating and frighten-

24 *Vtoroi s"ezd RSDRP* . . . *1903* . . . , p. 402.
25 Lenin, *Sochineniia,* VII, 465.

ing him—but all this is so obvious that it is strange even to talk about it. But the main focus and the guiding thread of our agitation must be, not influence over this ally, but preparation for the decisive battle with the enemy.[26]

If it came to the question of where to demonstrate, "we would point to the buildings where the police work of persecuting the labor movement is done . . . the buildings of police, gendarmerie, censorship . . . the places where political 'criminals' are incarcerated"[27]—and not to those where zemstvo meetings are in progress.[28]

In practice, this meant reducing the workers' part to acts of "exposure"—*with the zemstvo as principal target*—or else deliberately keeping them out of the zemstvo and banquet campaigns and diverting their energy into some other channel. Perhaps it was precisely because Lenin was not yet ready to accept the first alternative (since it was not sensible to ignore this ally and senseless to frighten him) that he spoke so warmly in favor of demonstrations in front of police, gendarmerie, and censorship buildings but on no account in front of zemstvo conferences.

In a second "Letter to the Party Organizations," the editors of *Iskra* replied that following Lenin's advice not to address demands to liberals but only to the government would in fact put the embattled proletariat in the position of "laborer for the bourgeois revolution" while letting the bourgeoisie negotiate with the autocratic regime reeling under the proletariat's onslaught.[29] *Iskra*'s plan was altogether different:

The working class, through its advanced stratum, must express its collective political will to the social elements engaged along with it in the present political struggle but occupying more prominent and advantageous positions because of historical conditions. If the proletariat addresses its political demands to *them,* and reinforces these demands with vigorous, truly revolutionary action, [they will

---

[26] *Ibid.,* p. 470.

[27] *Ibid.,* p. 481.

[28] *Ibid.,* p. 476.

[29] This letter was published in December, 1904, as a leaflet ("Tol'ko dlia chlenov partii") and has never been reprinted anywhere, I believe. I used the copy in B. I. Nicolaevsky's private collection. Since it is inaccessible to most of my readers, I will quote from it at greater length than I should have done otherwise.

view it] as the most resolute enemy of their enemy, ready to support them in their struggle with tsarism if they in turn support its demands or, rather, include them in their program of action. Any wavering in the ranks of non-proletarian "society" when faced with such demands, every attempt of its representatives to evade "talks" with the organized proletariat or to get rid of it by dubious promises, will furnish rich material for agitation to us and for political education to the proletariat. Any such wavering will be used by the proletariat for further pressure calculated to strengthen in our society the position of the extreme democratic elements of the bourgeoisie at the expense of its moderate elements and thus to give these democratic elements a stake in the success of the proletarian struggle. Either immediate practical success (if the bourgeois opposition gives in to our demands) or failure (if it . . . rejects them) will be used by us for further agitation, always aimed at strengthening the proletariat's revolutionizing influence over the entire opposition—the bourgeoisie or certain parts of it—and, as this influence grows, at molding the proletariat into an independent fighting force.

This, however, did not mean giving up other forms of struggle:

Iskra not only does not suggest giving up either the angriest demonstrations in front of prisons and police stations or the organized protests by the reserves and self-defense squads against police-led anti-Semitic thugs—it not only does not advise neglecting any of these forms of the proletariat's class action, but it also is inclined to think that the peaceful demonstrations around zemstvos which it advocates will not always prove entirely "peaceful," since the demonstrators will have to reckon with the entire belligerent police as well as with peaceable zemstvo members. Therefore, in preparing every such peaceful demonstration, one must also think of organizing effective resistance to possible interference by the servants of autocracy and a resolute protest against the "police stations" and "censorship departments," which will try to prevent the "peaceful" demonstration by workers.

What was happening to the actual correlation of forces was, so far, "a movement from absolutism to a 'dock-tailed constitution' " —a situation that could and must be changed:

It can be changed only by tactics of the proletarian party that are aimed at, and will achieve, direct, immediate pressure on the bourgeois opposition and—whether by an outright split between its moderate and radical elements or the threat of a split—will induce it, or considerable parts of it, to join in genuinely democratic demands. This goal cannot be reached unless we try to establish direct contact between the revolutionary-minded proletarian masses and the bourgeois opposition in the political foreground. And only after reaching this goal shall we accomplish our main task, the one that distinguishes us from bourgeois revolutionaries, the task of forming *an independent labor party in the course of the social struggle*. For such a party can be formed only if the proletariat takes an active part in all the manifestations of political life; by socialist propaganda alone, or the proletariat's collisions with "police stations" alone, we cannot help the proletariat emerge from its present state of a politically amorphous mass, imbued with revolutionary feeling and class instinct but still devoid of true class consciousness.

The basic ideas of *Iskra*'s letter were "in the air" and had begun to be applied, in a simpler form, even before the letter became widely known. Martov wrote later that locally

the Bolsheviks, too, approved the ideas of the *Iskra* editors' letter at first. In Saratov, Odessa, and other cities, the Bolsheviks organized workers' appearances at civic meetings where liberals and democrats composed addresses to the authorities. It was only under the influence of Lenin's pamphlet that the Bolshevik organizations withdrew from this movement. The Mensheviks, on the contrary, involved the advanced [workers] in the "zemstvo" and "banquet" movements wherever they could.[30]

---

[30] Martov, *Istoriia rossiiskoi sotsialdemokratii*, p. 100. Before Lenin's pamphlet, the Bolsheviks in Petersburg were inclined to accept *Iskra*'s plan. In "Protokoly Zasedanii Peterburgskogo Komiteta RSDRP (noiabr'-dekabr' 1904 goda)," *Proletarskaia Revoliutsiia*, 1925, No. 1, pp. 85–116, there is a speech by P. P. (P. P. Rumiantsev, at the time the most influential Bolshevik in the Petersburg Committee) during a discussion of the Central Committee's report on *Iskra*'s zemstvo campaign plan (the CC fully supported the plan): "Generally speaking, we concur in the CC's proposal. As to concrete action, our general position is this: Every opportunity for concrete action should be used. . . . I have just had a chance to acquaint myself with *Iskra*'s leaflet on the subject. In this political campaign we shall act hand in hand, if our tactics prove to be the same. I am interested in the CC's attitude to this leaflet. The impression I got from the leaflet is that we should direct our attention at the liberals and put pressure on them" (pp. 92–93). The protocols are badly written and parts of Rumiantsev's speech are unclear, but it leaves no doubt about the basically positive reaction of the Petersburg Bolsheviks, for whom Rumiantsev spoke.

At the same time, the literature does not mention a single practical application of Lenin's idea of demonstrations against the police during the campaign.

The argument, however, concerned far more important matters than the proper place to hold demonstrations. Martov writes:

> With a conspirator's flair, Lenin detected in the Mensheviks' proposals the signs of their tendency to lead the movement out of the confines of the underground, which knows no other militant actions than street demonstrations and more or less demonstrative political strikes, and to open up for it, in the new political ambience of the beginning collapse of absolutism, new vistas for action by the working masses side by side with the other social classes rising against tsarism.

For Lenin, Martov continues,

> the true role of the working class was to leave it to the liberals to knock on the door of absolutism demanding reforms and to continue its own militant actions, for instance against "police stations," increasing their intensity and revolutionary character until they and the natural course of events had paved the way for the decisive blow.[31]

The conflict between the two factions of Social-Democracy was coming out of the purely organizational sphere. Two conceptions were taking shape:

> . . . on one side, an attempt to train the labor movement, under the backward Russian sociopolitical conditions, in the European methods of independent political action whenever a conflict in propertied society posed problems of national import and gradually to mold the blindly churning proletarian masses into a stable political force capable of deliberate action at the moment of the revolutionary crisis; on the other side, the concentration of all Party forces on training these agitated masses for combat, so as to throw them into the decisive battle when the political circumstances were ripe.
>
> One tactic visualized the forthcoming gradual disintegration of tsarism and the advance toward power of the opposition-minded propertied classes as a series of stages propitious to the proletariat's self-determination as a class and its transformation into a force capable of carrying the beginning revolution to extreme democratic

---

[31] Martov, *Istoriia rossiiskoi sotsialdemokratii*, pp. 97–98.

limits. The other gambled, on the contrary, on the lack of organization and the relative helplessness of the non-proletarian classes as the factor that must permit the extreme revolutionary Party, supported by the aroused masses that had been organized in the school of combat, to achieve its political aims at one blow. All the dissensions concerning tactics that developed between Mensheviks and Bolsheviks in the period 1905–7 were contained in embryo in this dispute about tactics.[32]

The campaign set off by *Iskra*'s letter sometimes took unexpected turns. Let me cite a few examples from reports published in *Iskra* on the intervention of workers in zemstvo and other gatherings in Kharkov, Odessa, Petersburg, Ekaterinodar, Kiev, Saratov, Rostov-on-the-Don, and Chernigov.

The Kharkov organization was the first to act, at a meeting of the Kharkov Society of Jurists on November 6, the very day the zemstvo congress opened in Petersburg. The chairman, Professor N. A. Gredeskul, wanted the members to vote without preliminary discussion on a message of greetings to Sviatopolk-Mirskii, drawn up by the Council of Attorneys, with diffidently expressed wishes for reforms—whereupon the meeting turned into a violent demonstration against both the liberals and the government. This was not, however, entirely the chairman's fault—it suited the plans of the local Social-Democratic committee, which had carefully prepared for the meeting. "An excellent opportunity was offered to express openly our attitude to that orgy of liberalism in which the utter political immorality of the 'leaders' of so-called society appears so clearly," *Iskra*'s correspondent wrote.[33] This is quite close to the ideas of the Petersburg Mensheviks described by Somov in a passage I have quoted: it was the *basic purpose* of the campaign to show the workers the *chasm* that divided them from the rest of the opposition; and the *basic theme* of speeches, to *ridicule* "the *feeble* banquet resolutions and petition projects."

Iskra's Ekaterinodar correspondent wrote of an impressive demonstration at the municipal duma on November 10:

> The local workers welcomed the idea of demonstrating. The conscious workers are in general chafing at their inaction at such an important moment in history as this and readily agree to any

---

[32] *Ibid.*, p. 99.
[33] *Iskra*, No. 79, December 1, 1904.

undertaking whose usefulness they can see, minimizing the question of the safety of the enterprise. An important factor in this case was the knowledge that the proposed demonstration was another new step in developing the forms of political struggle and that the possibility of future and wider use of similar tactics depended on the measure of its success.[34]

The demonstration itself is described as follows: "At a suitable moment, a group of workers appeared before the table of the town council members, and one of the group began a speech." The mayor tried to stop him, but lost his head when the workers resisted; the speech was concluded amid the hushed attention of the audience with these words:

> You and we represent opposite social classes, but we can be united by hatred of the same enemy, the autocratic order. We can be allies in our political struggle. For this, however, you must abandon the former road of meekness; you must boldly, openly, join in our demand: Down with autocracy! Hail to a constituent assembly elected by the entire people! Hail to universal, direct, equal, and secret suffrage!

After the speech, proclamations of the Kuban Committee of the RSDRP were scattered in the hall; the next day the Committee issued a leaflet (in one thousand copies) describing the meeting and giving the Social-Democratic speech in full.

Stormy events occurred in Odessa.[35] On November 18, in the municipal duma building, there was a meeting of the Society for Safeguarding Public Health, attended by "about two thousand people, among them a lot of workers." Participants had already brought up demands for a constituent assembly and universal suffrage, and the Social-Democrats' speeches were enthusiastically received. After the meeting there was a very successful street demonstration. Two days later the fortieth anniversary of the Judicial Statutes was celebrated in the district court building. Several thousand attended. After a paper on the statutes had been read, the occasion turned into a true popular meeting and ended with a street march. This time Cossacks were thrown against the

---

[34] *Ibid.*
[35] *Ibid.*

crowd, and there were many wounded. A huge banquet of the local intelligentsia was going on at the time at the Hall of the Nobility. It was invaded by workers, in whose name a Social-Democrat made a speech in the vein of the Ekaterinodar address.

However, the "coalitional" note (as Axelrod called it in his speech at the Stockholm Congress) was sounded somewhat tentatively and doubtfully in the Social-Democrats' appeals—perhaps because it did not elicit enough response from the liberal and democratic intelligentsia, which often took a leery view of workers' and Social-Democrats' performances. As a result, what chiefly remained in the workers' minds from their participation in the campaign was that the liberals' spinelessness had been "unmasked."

In this setting, Lenin's stand on the zemstvo campaign underwent a radical change. He never admitted it in so many words, and more surprisingly, the fact has never before been mentioned in print so far as I know, but in the second half of December he definitely did a *volte-face*. In the article "On Good Demonstrations by Proletarians and Bad Ratiocinations of Certain *Intelligenty*" in *Vpered*, No. 1, December 22/January 4, he castigated the Ekaterinodar demonstration but praised the experiments at Kharkov and, in particular, at Odessa.[36] No longer did he so much as mention gathering in front of police stations. He said: "Shouldn't we organize workers' demonstrations also at zemstvo meetings and in connection with zemstvo meetings? Of course we should."[37]

For all its shortcomings, the campaign had notable consequences. It would be an exaggeration to say that the shift to the left in the demands formulated at zemstvo and other meetings was entirely due to Social-Democrats; but their organized action in alerting the masses to these meetings undoubtedly contributed to it. The ideas stressed in *Iskra*'s letter—universal suffrage and a constituent assembly—began to prevail at meetings and banquets. Another consequence, perhaps equally important, was the

---

[36] Lenin, "O khoroshikh demonstratsiiakh proletariev i plokhikh rassuzhdeniiakh nekotorykh intelligentov," in *Sochineniia*, VIII, 13–18.
[37] *Ibid.*, p. 17.

political education of the advanced elements of the working class; in this campaign they received their first and often bitter lessons in the political art of partial collaboration with a partial ally against a common enemy.

All this stopped almost completely after a ukase of the emperor to the Senate and an "announcement" by the government, both of December 12, 1904.[38] The ukase reminded the Senate of the necessity to "preserve the immutability of the fundamental laws of the empire," yet directed it to begin work on several reforms—a partial concession to the moderate opposition. The "announcement" was frankly aggressive and entirely reactionary in spirit:

> In certain cities of the empire there has occurred a number of noisy gatherings, which have declared the need to present to the government various demands, inadmissible in view of the immutable principles of our governmental system consecrated by the fundamental laws of the empire; and street demonstrations by large mobs have been organized, at which the police and the authorities were openly resisted. . . . [Those who demand] radical changes in the fundamental principles, hallowed by centuries, of the life of the Russian state are unwittingly serving not the motherland but its enemies. . . . Any disturbance of order and peace and any gatherings of an antigovernmental nature must and will be stopped by all the legal means at the authorities' disposal, and those guilty of such infractions, especially persons in government service, will be legally prosecuted. It is the duty of zemstvo and municipal boards and of institutions and societies of any kind not to overstep the limits of their competence and not to touch upon subjects which they have no legal authorization to discuss; chairmen of public meetings are liable to prosecution on the basis of existing laws for allowing [the meetings] to discuss general questions concerning the state, which are not within their competence.

The "era of trust" was over. An atmosphere of nervous tension developed at the zemstvo and other meetings, and their frequency declined. The intraparty arguments about the zemstvo campaign also receded into the background. In the masses the

---

[38] Both documents are in Belokonskii, "K istorii zemskogo dvizheniia v Rossii," pp. 53–55.

tide of discontent was rising high. Bloody Sunday—January 9, 1905—resounded like a tocsin across the land.

The Social-Democratic Organizations on the Eve of the First Russian Revolution

Looking back on the events of 1904–5 and trying to understand their political significance, one is amazed by a paradoxical fact: the Social-Democrats were a considerable force in the country's political life; they were listened to, not only by a great many workers, but also by sizable groups of the intelligentsia and of so-called cultured society; yet the Social-Democratic Party taken as an organized whole, as the sum total of Social-Democratic organizations, was extremely weak. The weakness of its bonds with the working masses is especially surprising. The contrast between its ideological influence and its poor organization was, if possible, intensified in the last eighteen months preceding the revolution. At the Second Congress the Party had in fact split in two. Each side attempted to form a homogeneous whole, and acute dissension developed between them. The Bolsheviks were increasingly bent on making Social-Democracy a closed organization of conspirators, of professional revolutionaries keeping an iron hand on any show of activity by the masses and themselves submitting to authoritarian guidance from above—in short, a "party of the new type," to borrow from later terminology. The Mensheviks were trying to solve a problem virtually insoluble in the Russian underground—to link the Party with the masses not only ideologically but also by close organizational bonds and to apply the democratic principle within the Party.

When two opposing tendencies in an underground party become to all intents and purposes two separate organizations, the advantage lies with the conspiratorial and centralistic faction. Well aware of this, Lenin put all his energy into making the Bolshevik faction a virtually *autonomous* ultracentralist entity. He had to engage in a fierce struggle not only with Mensheviks but also with the "conciliationists" in his own camp intent on preserving party unity. When the Central Committee of the Party, elected at the Second Congress and consisting solely of

Bolsheviks, turned toward "reconciliation" to allay the crisis and assuage the feelings of the lower-echelon party workers, publishing a "declaration" about possible and desirable ways to insure unity,[39] Lenin rebelled against the Central Committee. According to official history, he convoked in Geneva the so-called Conference of Twenty-two Bolsheviks, mainly for the purpose of calling a third Party congress as soon as possible. The Conference drafted a plan for the creation of a *Bolshevik center* to direct the struggle for a congress which would secure the Bolshevik's undivided dominance over the Party (under the flag of unity, of course, though not of united Social-Democracy but of united "revolutionary" Social-Democracy). This was never made public, it is true, but subsequent events, such as the formation soon afterward of the Bureau of the Committees of the Majority (BCM), make it perfectly clear that planning such a center was the main purpose of the Conference.[40]

This book does not aim to survey the state of the Party organizations in the entire country. To clarify the evolution of Menshevik and Bolshevik tactical and political views about the mass movement, it will suffice to examine in some detail the Petersburg organization, whose role in the ideological development of the Party was outstanding, and to take a quick look at one or two other large centers of the movement. The situation in the provinces was no better, and in most cases worse, than in Petersburg, except in the areas where the so-called national organizations—the Bund, the Polish and the Latvian organizations—were active, and in the Caucasus, where the RSDRP had exercised an important influence, both politically and organizationally, well before 1905. In the main, the ideological development of the "national" Social-Democratic parties went its own ways and does not concern us here; in the Caucasus, except in relation

---

[39] This declaration, known in Bolshevik literature as "Iiul'skaia deklaratsiia TsK," appeared in *Iskra*, No. 72, August 12/25, 1904.

[40] "The Conference of Twenty-two Bolsheviks took place, under Lenin's leadership, in Geneva in August (N.S.), 1904. Nineteen people took part in it; three more later joined in its decisions" (Lenin, *Sochineniia*, VII, 520, n. 96). The Conference approved the address "K partii" Lenin had written (*ibid.*, pp. 420–27). For details about the Conference and the origins of the Bureau of the Committees of the Majority, see Appendix 3.

to the peasant movement, the Party developed along the same lines as the RSDRP generally.

In the latter half of 1904 the Petersburg organization was in very poor shape. Weakened by arrests and still more by internal strife, it was badly out of touch with the masses. In December it split formally, and until the Stockholm Congress in the spring 1906, two organizations of the RSDRP existed side by side, one Menshevik and the other Bolshevik.

The break came when the disastrous demonstration of November 28, 1904 had revealed the ineptitude of the Petersburg Committee, in which the Bolsheviks had an overwhelming majority. Several important, predominantly Menshevik factory sectors (raiony, into which cities were divided for Social-Democratic work) now rebelled against it.[41] The committee of the Vasil'ev-Ostrov sector officially informed the Petersburg Committee of its "complete lack of confidence"; the Narva sector expressed in a resolution its "disinclination to continue working under the leadership of the [Petersburg] Committee" and suggested that the Central Committee investigate the matter.[42] In all, four of the organization's six sectors—Vasil'ev-Ostrov, Narva, Neva, and Petersburg (Peterburgskaia Storona)—declared their solidarity with the Mensheviks; only the City (Gorodskoi) and the Vyborg sectors remained loyal to the Bolsheviks.[43] In mid-December the rebel sectors united around the Menshevik Petersburg Group of the CC of the RSDRP (called simply Petersburg Group of the RSDRP from the spring of 1905).[44]

There are several inside reports on the state of the Petersburg organization after the schism and the relative influence in it of Bolsheviks and Mensheviks. Zemliachka, an active member of the Bureau of the Committees of the Majority, who had recently come to Petersburg, wrote Lenin and Krupskaia in Geneva on December 19:

---

[41] See Appendix 2.

[42] "K raskolu partii," Proletarskaia Revoliutsiia, 1924, No. 11 (34), pp. 60–61.

[43] See the letter from Petersburg (author unknown) to Iurii (probably Kamenev) of December 22, 1904, Proletarskaia Revoliutsiia, 1925, No. 3 (38), pp. 22–23.

[44] Another Menshevik Group was formed in Petersburg in late 1904. It was more conciliatory toward the Bolsheviks (see A. L. Sokolovskaia, "Neskol'ko strochek vospominanii," Krasnaia Letopis', 1923, VII, 23–29). In the spring of 1905 it merged with the main Menshevik organization.

You have no idea how critical the situation in Russia is just now. No end of Mensheviks have flocked into Russia. The Central Committee has managed to turn many people against us. There are not enough forces to carry on the fight and consolidate positions. Demands for people are coming in from all over. It is imperative to make a tour of the committees immediately. There is no one who can go. I am neglecting the Bureau and am absorbed in local work, things here couldn't be worse. We need people. Everybody is asking. There's no one to work with. . . .[45]

On January 7, 1905, she wrote them again:

We are running the risk of losing one city after another for lack of people. Every day I get heaps of letters from various places, imploring [us] to send people, Bolsheviks. Just now I got a confused letter from Ekaterinoslav, they write that unless we send people and money at once we shall lose Ekaterinoslav. But there are no people: one after another are retiring, and no new ones arrive. Meanwhile the Mensheviks have consolidated their positions everywhere. They would be easy as can be to drive out, if only we had people. The Bureau is a fiction since we're all busy with local affairs. . . .[46]

A still somberer picture—and not only of Petersburg— emerges from M. M. Litvinov's letter to Lenin and Krupskaia of December 12, written immediately upon his return to Riga from the Conference of the Northern Committees in Petersburg, where he had stayed about two weeks:

The trouble is that she [Zemliachka] does not in the least realize in what a critical and sorry situation we are. The periphery, if not everywhere against us, is hardly anywhere for us. The bulk of the party workers still think that we are a bunch of disorganizers without any kind of backing, that since the reconciliation [of the Central Committee and the Mensheviks.—S. S.] the attitude of the committees has changed, that all our efforts are but the death throes of the Bolsheviks. No conferences (least of all secret ones), no agitation, will change this widespread view. I repeat, our situation is utterly shaky and precarious. We can get out of it only by (1) immediately calling a congress (not later than February) and (2) immediately starting a newspaper.

---

[45] "Perepiska N. Lenina i N. K. Krupskoi s Peterburgskoi organizatsiei," *Proletarskaia Revoliutsiia*, 1925, No. 3 (38), p. 21.
[46] *Ibid.*, p. 35.

Without the speediest fulfilment of these two conditions we are going to certain ruin, and with giant steps too. . . . Petersburg we shall probably have to lose. Swarms of Mensheviks have arrived there. . . . We too ought to mobilize our forces for Petersburg, but where do we get them. We've decided to transfer Aleksei [A. I. Rykov.—S. S.], even at the cost of losing Moscow. Losing Petersburg would be the worst blow for us. . . .[47]

Another reliable source is a long written report of the Petersburg Committee to the Third Congress, not intended for publication:

The January events caught the Petersburg Committee in an extremely sorry state. Its ties with the working masses had been utterly disorganized by the Mensheviks. We managed to preserve them, with great effort, only in the City sector (this sector has always held to the Bolshevik viewpoint), on Vasil'ev-Ostrov, and in the Vyborg sector. In late December the printing press of the Petersburg Committee was discovered. By that time the Petersburg Committee consisted of a secretary (through him the Committee communicated with the head of the press and with the finances commission), a chief writer and editor [otvetstvennyi literator], a chief organizer, an agitator (he was also the student organizer), and four organizers. There was not a single worker among the members of the Committee. The strike at the Putilov plant caught the Committee unprepared. Several mimeographs were hurriedly set up. The printing group displayed incredible energy at that time. . . . Before January 9, the workers' feelings toward the Committee were extremely hostile. Our agitators were beaten up, our leaflets destroyed, the first five hundred rubles sent to the Putilov strikers were accepted grudgingly. Nonetheless agitation went on wherever possible. The Committee decided not to declare itself categorically against the march to the Winter Palace before January 9. It was decided not to unfurl our banners in the square in front of the Winter Palace until a suitable moment and not to agitate until the mood could be definitely gauged. It was decided to send teams consisting of an agitator, a standard-bearer, and a core group to defend them to the outskirts of the city. The agitator was instructed to start speaking when he saw that the mood was right (collisions with troops were expected); at the same time the banner was to be

---

[47] "Perepiska N. Lenina i N. K. Krupskoi s M. M. Litvinovym," *Proletarskaia Revoliutsiia*, 1925, No. 2 (37), pp. 78–79.

raised, thus creating a kind of open meeting. It did prove possible to organize such meetings in many parts of Petersburg, but they had a haphazard and disorderly quality.[48]

It would be a mistake to infer from these Bolshevik accounts that all was well with the Mensheviks' party work. The latter was tolerable only in comparison. A remarkable account of it is given by S. Somov (I. A. Peskin). (His past lends a polemical tinge to his reminiscences, but he sincerely tried to be objective, and was a keen observer.) He writes:

After the demonstration [of November 28] four of the six sectors passed resolutions in which they noted the inertia and ineptitude of the Committee and refused to recognize it henceforward as their leading organization; in the remaining sectors, opinion was about equally divided for and against the Committee. Disaffected *intelligenty* began to hold meetings, too, which also made decisions to act on their own, independently of the Committee; and finally from among them a small group emerged that decided to assume the functions and tasks of the Committee. It became the center of the *Menshevik* movement in Petersburg. . . .

The new group, which was later named the Petersburg Group of the Central Committee of the RSDRP, first had to obtain the Committee's permission to exist, which it managed to do after some friction. Within a few months of its establishment, it had concentrated in its hands virtually all the Social-Democratic work in Petersburg; during those months the Petersburg Committee led a precarious existence.

How did things stand with respect to the influence and organization of Social-Democracy in Petersburg at that time? The central Group began by trying to inform itself about the state of Social-Democratic work in the various sectors. A very sad picture emerged. Well-functioning organizations were to be found only in the Narva sector, on Peterburgskaia Storona, and partly on Vasil'ev-Ostrov, and even these organizations left a good deal to be desired. In the Narva sector, with its thirty thousand workers, for example, the whole Social-Democratic organization consisted of six or seven circles of workers of the Putilov and the Railroad Car Construction plants (five to six workers in each circle); and the work was con-

---

[48] *Tretii s"ezd RSDRP. Aprel'-mai 1905 goda. Protokoly* (Moscow: Gospolitizdat, 1959), pp. 544–45.

ducted according to old-fashioned methods, with long courses in political economy and primitive culture.

True, there was also a sector organization of representatives of the circles, but what it did is hard to determine. Factory life found no echo at all in the circles. The diffuse unrest . . . that was finding expression in the powerfully developing Gapon movement, in which the yearning of the working masses for broad organization and class unity was so clearly displayed, was ignored as Zubatovism. Moreover, most of the workers belonging to our circles were very young men, just out of apprenticeship and with no influence whatsoever in their factory milieu.[49]

The last remark dovetails with the observations of others that older workers, trained in the movements of the late nineties or the first years of the new century, now kept away from party organizations. P. A. Garvi, who had worked in Odessa from 1900 to 1902, had been in prison, escaped from exile, spent a short time abroad, and returned illegally to Russia in December, 1904, to become a member of the Kiev Committee, writes in his memoirs:

A strange dearth of people in the organization, a remoteness from the working masses and their daily interests, a meager organizational life in comparison with the recent past—that is what struck me in Kiev, suggesting melancholy comparisons with the past, with the ebullient life of the Odessa organization of the 1901–2 period. There was the Kiev Committee; there were sector committees; in the sectors, there were propagandists conducting propaganda circles. Usually leaflets were distributed through the circles. That was about all.

Getting ahead of myself, I will say that during all of 1905—in Kiev, and in Rostov, and in Moscow—I invariably came up against one and the same phenomenon. In the Party organizations were gathered mostly callow youths, hotheaded and resolute but weakly linked to the working masses and uninfluential in the factories. The old Social-Democrats among the workers—the real vanguard of advanced workers formed in the period of propagandism and of so-called Economism—these old workers for the most part stood aside. In Kiev, and in Rostov, and in Moscow, and right up to the October strike, I—and not only I—had to resort to more or less artificial methods to draw the "oldsters" into active party work. We arranged

---

[49] S. Somov, "Iz istorii sotsialdemokraticheskogo dvizheniia v Peterburge . . . ," pp. 24–25.

special meetings and evening parties with them, we reasoned with them, but they went into party work reluctantly and looked upon our organizations and our working methods with mistrust.[50]

This was the sad aftermath of *Iskra's* earlier campaign against Economism and in favor of political propaganda, which had diverted the Party from the everyday problems of the worker's life. Probably in a still greater measure, it was a natural reaction of the more mature workers to the intraparty conflict, which they tended to see as an inexcusable quarrel between cliques of the intelligentsia. All this partly explains the lack of contact, painfully manifest during the "January days," between the Party and the turbulently rising mass movement.

Social-Democracy and the Gapon Movement

The name of the priest Georgii Gapon is inseparable from the march of Petersburg workers to the Winter Palace on January 9/22, 1905, to present a petition to the tsar. Hundreds of thousands, almost all the factory workers of the capital, many accompanied by their parents, wives, and children, streamed to the palace from all directions, carrying church gonfalons and the tsar's portraits, only to be stopped by troops and fired upon, in many cases without warning. Many hundreds were killed or wounded (the first reports spoke of thousands).[51] The day has gone down in history as Bloody Sunday. The Russian Revolution had begun.

There is a vast literature on "January 9" and on the events that preceded and followed it. In this book I can touch upon

---

[50] Garvi, *Vospominaniia sotsialdemokrata*, pp. 440–41.

[51] As often happens, the first reports were exaggerated. A Bolshevik historian wrote later: "Taking into account that single cases of killing continued through January 10, 11, and 12, one can put the approximate number of wounded at from 450 to 800 and of killed at from 150 to 200, that is, a total of 800 to 1,000 victims; at most, including those who died from wounds and all injured during those days, at 1,500, with the number of deaths perhaps about 500 at most.

"At any rate the 5,000 or more mentioned during the first days was obviously wrong, as also, most likely, was the government's figure of 429; 1,000 is apparently the approximately correct figure. Our newspapers estimated the number of killed at 976, the Organizational Committee of the Technological Institute at 1,216. There is no question that not only the public but even such responsible organs as *Vpered* and *Iskra* greatly exaggerated the number of killed and wounded." (V. Nevskii, *Rabochee dvizhenie v ianvarskie dni 1905 goda* [Moscow: Vsesoiuznoe Obshchestvo Politkatorzhan, 1930], pp. 124–25.)

them only insofar as is necessary to clarify the role of Social-Democracy during those momentous days. The Social-Democrats' attitude to the Gapon movement, which was launched almost two years before the tragic Sunday, has never been the subject of a special study. It is usually associated with their attitude toward the movement initiated by the Moscow Okhrana at the turn of the century under the leadership of S. V. Zubatov. Yet the Zubatov and Gapon movements, though connected historically and to a degree psychologically, differed in many respects and confronted Social-Democracy with different sets of problems. If the first was a police maneuver against the revolutionary labor movement, the second, although an offshoot of the first, was in a sense a police maneuver against both the revolutionary labor and Zubatov movements. The chronological bounds of this book confine me to the interrelation of Social-Democracy and the Gapon movement, but since much may remain unclear to readers unfamiliar with the Zubatov epopee, two appendixes outline the differences between the two as well as the Social-Democrats' attitude toward the latter (see Appendixes 4 and 5).

Because of its nature, the Gapon movement was of little interest to the Social-Democrats until the second half of 1904. An Okhrana "inquiry" of early summer characterizes Gapon's Assembly of Russian Factory Workers of Petersburg as "a friendly social element" having "a very beneficial influence on the working masses" and enlisting sympathy "among reasonable and honest Russian workers." Friendly, reasonable, honest, beneficial, from the Okhrana viewpoint, of course—and especially pleasing to the Okhrana in that it was free of the Zubatovite demagogy that in the end so alarmed the authorities. Furthermore, the Gapon movement was quite small. It had only one tearoom–reading room, on Vyborgskaia Storona, until late May, 1904, when another was opened in the Narva sector. A third was opened in August, 1904, on Vasil'ev-Ostrov. These minor organizations attracted apolitical and even frankly antirevolutionary workers whose influence in the factories was almost nil. (For details, see Appendix 4.) The situation began to change only when Plehve's assassination had electrified the country. An all-city meeting of the Gapon societies in September, 1904, was so successful that even its organizers were surprised. Gapon locals began to mushroom. By the end of the year, they covered all of Petersburg. The working masses seeking an outlet for their newly awakened social energies were flocking into them, and the Gapon organizations, born as a mongrel police offspring of the labor movement, were turning into far-flung, somewhat diffuse labor organizations reflecting the restive, semirevolutionary mood of the workers.

If it was only natural that the Social-Democrats had paid no attention to the Gapon movement before it began to mutate, only the poor state of the Party organization in Petersburg can explain the fact that even the Mensheviks, who at that time were closer to the masses than the Bolsheviks, continued to ignore it until the very end of 1904, almost up to the "January days." As active a member of the Petersburg Group as Somov learned of the scope of the Gapon movement almost by accident. The Menshevik Group, which was just beginning to function as a separate body, had appointed him organizer of the Neva sector (the best sector of the Petersburg organization), and he decided to arrange a meeting of the more prominent Party-affiliated workers in his sector to discuss future work:

> The meeting was scheduled for a Sunday morning at the flat of a middle-aged worker of the Obukhov plant. I came to the meeting about ten o'clock and had to wait until about two while the workers slowly assembled. However, my time wasn't wasted. The hostess, a weaver, turned out to be bright, experienced, remarkably mature and sensible, a veteran of more than one phase or our Party life. She spoke superbly, in pure literary language, and had a good grasp of tactical questions; later I learned that she was known in her milieu by the nickname Kursistka ["student"]. She met me with something like mistrust, or perhaps a kind of touching pity. . . . We soon drifted into a conversation about our Social-Democratic work, and she told me frankly that in her opinion the best workers did not, and would not, come to us; that the results of our work were so negligible that for their sake no sensible man, even a man inclined to self-sacrifice, would run the risk of being arrested and leaving his family to hunger and cold. "I remember you used to have circles and a good many followers," she said. "Where are they now? In our whole sector you now have perhaps a dozen workers, yet you continue to talk of big plans, to call to political struggle. But it really comes down to dull regular studies in circles and to giving us once in a while a book that isn't too bad. No, better go to

the Gapon organizations, thousands of people go there, people believe in them and put their hope in them. Never mind if they set themselves small goals at present, this cannot last long, and it may depend partly on you to broaden the work over there. Though it is just as well not to scare people off from the start with too drastic and unrealistic demands."

To my shame I must confess that I first heard from her of the wide influence of the Gapon organizations. Until then, the disdainfully uttered word "Zubatovism" that we applied to them completely blocked in us all concern about a clearer definition of our attitude to the immense proletarian movement hidden behind that name.[52]

This conversation apparently took place on December 26, a fortnight before Bloody Sunday—too late for revising the Petersburg Group's tactics and affecting significantly the swiftly moving events. Somov notes that the Putilov strike on January 3, which activated the Gapon movement, also came as a surprise to the Social-Democrats:

> Before that, rumors had begun to reach us through workers that Gapon meetings were attracting multitudes of workers, that workers were making bold, fervent speeches there. . . . All this news induced us to observe the Gapon movement more attentively, but at the same time we persisted in advising workers as well as *intelligenty* not to speak at Gapon meetings, because the Zubatovite origin of Gaponism blinded us to all that was healthy and promising in that movement. . . . Thus the January days caught us *completely unprepared,* and that is why we made no joint decision of any kind about them. Our organization was simply not functioning as a whole during those days, every sector acting on its own account and at its own discretion.[53]

In the Neva sector the Social-Democrats (Mensheviks) played a more noticeable role. Several members of the organization, *intelligenty* and workers, met in the evening of January 3 and decided "to make the rounds of the factories the next morning and try to bring them to a halt," then visit a meeting at the Gapon

---

[52] Somov, "Iz istorii sotsialdemokraticheskogo dvizheniia v Peterburge . . . ," p. 26. Somov's reminiscences are a particularly valuable source for the Social-Democratic movement in Petersburg in late 1904 and the first half of 1905.

[53] *Ibid.,* p. 31.

local and try to give it a more political tone. Somov has left a striking account of the Gapon meeting:

> . . . Even now I still remember the tremendous impression this meeting made on me and my comrades. A kind of mystic, religious ecstasy reigned throughout the meeting; thousands of people stood shoulder to shoulder for hours in a dreadful crush and heat, avidly listening to the artless, amazingly powerful, simple, and passionate speeches of the exhausted orators, their fellow workers. In content all the speeches were poor, repeating in every key the phrases, "We cannot endure any more," "Better death than this kind of life," and so on. But all of it was said with such striking, moving sincerity, so from the very depths of the tortured human soul, that the same phrase uttered for the hundredth time brought tears to the eyes.
> . . . This unusual mystic setting quite overwhelmed us, and when our first speaker took the floor, very unwillingly and merely obeying our previous decision, his speech, undoubtedly much pithier and on the whole very good, though much less "extreme" than had been agreed on, sounded strangely remote and weak, like an echo from a different, distant world. . . .
> . . . Afterward the same simple but powerful speeches poured forth again; as one crowd left, another replaced it; new, still bigger meetings opened at the door, in the courtyard. The mood kept mounting, and finally we could not resist it either, we gave in to the general mood, and instead of criticizing Gaponism as before, our speakers began to come out with appeals to struggle, vivid descriptions of the workers' impossible situation and the need to put an end to it, exhortations to the broadest struggle in all areas. In short, from us, too, speeches poured, richer in content than the Gaponites' speeches, but their tone, their mood, were already different, induced entirely by that heaving crowd. From then on, the influence of the Social-Democratic speakers grew, the crowd eagerly listened to them, without in the least understanding what distinguished them from Gaponites. Many actually called them "Gapon Social-Democrats," convinced that the Gapon local maintained special officials called Social-Democrats. They could see, besides, that the Social-Democrats were fairly well-informed, "intellectual" Gapon officials, and so workers of individual factories turned to them when they needed to draw up separate demands for their factories. In this way, in addition to the general public meetings, there began more or less secret meetings of maturer workers of every factory, at

which Social-Democrats helped the workers to draw up lists of the special demands of their factories.[54]

Thus, literally in a few hours, close collaboration developed in the Neva sector between Social-Democrats (Mensheviks) and Gapon people, especially in supplying speakers for the outdoor meetings:

> At the Gapon local in the Neva sector meetings were going on all day, from 8:00 or 9:00 A.M. to 10:00 or 11:00 P.M. Every hour one crowd succeeded another. In addition, despite the bitter cold, grandiose meetings went on all the time in the huge yard. We had to work every day to the point of total exhaustion. The Social-Democrats in fact did most of the speaking. Once or twice a journalist whom I did not know [spoke], and once a Socialist Revolutionary spoke in the yard, but by and large the whole burden of ceaseless agitation had to be carried by a few Social-Democrats and one or two Gapon workmen. The latter were at first openly hostile to the Social-Democrats' "competition." Later, however, when they saw that no conflict resulted, that we were following the same line as they, and finally when they decided not to keep silent about politics, they even became somewhat dependent on us since they felt pretty helpless in the field of political agitation.
> . . . All the time we worked very harmoniously together, sharing even such functions as distributing subsidies to strikers, checking who was in real need, and so on.[55]

On a smaller scale, the same thing was happening in other sectors. Everywhere the initiative came from the local party workers, without guidance from the Petersburg Group (or the Central Group, as it was called in the organization). "The Group met to determine its tactics only two days before January 9,"[56] and its attitude to the innovations in the Neva sector was by no means unanimous:

> In the Petersburg Central Group itself, voices were raised to the effect that collaboration with Gapon was a betrayal of Social-Democratic principles. In their opinion it was the duty of Social-

---

[54] *Ibid.*, pp. 33–34.
[55] *Ibid.*, pp. 36–37.
[56] *Ibid.*, p. 31.

Democrats to combat Gapon and his plans in the firmest way. Most of the Group, however, fully realized the worldwide significance of the unfolding events and advocated all-out participation in them.[57]

The same day, January 7, at Gapon's wish, the Social-Democrats (Mensheviks) held a conference with him in the Neva sector. It lasted from 9:00 P.M. until 2:00 A.M. Besides Gapon, "six or seven of his more outstanding workers from various sectors were present, and on the Social-Democrats' side, one worker and three *intelligenty*"—one of them Somov, representing the Petersburg Group. By that time everything was preordained and could not possibly be changed in any important way. Gapon was optimistic. He thought that a fatal outcome, though possible, was unlikely. Somov writes:

> We did not conceal from Gapon our more pessimistic view; we told him that we foresaw a bloody turn to the movement, and evidently we succeeded in shaking his optimism somewhat. The next morning, after some more talk with Social-Democrats who had stayed overnight with him at the same apartment, Gapon wrote his famous letter to Prince Sviatopolk-Mirskii.[58]

The ideas that Somov had eloquently defended, and the Petersburg group approved, at its meeting of January 7 were not unanimously shared by the Menshevik factory workers. On January 8, the day after the conference with Gapon, the Neva sector committee called two meetings of Social-Democratic workers, "whose number had markedly increased during those days," to discuss participation in the march on January 9. The organizers ran into unexpected resistance:

> The workers, especially those of the Obukhov plant, on the whole disapproved of the Gapon movement and strongly insisted that Social-Democrats ought to refuse to participate in it in any way. It was shameful and unworthy of Social-Democrats, they said, to

---

[57] *Ibid.*, p. 40.

[58] *Ibid.*, pp. 37–40. At this writing, one of the Mensheviks who attended this conference, Ludwig G. Gerb (known in France by the pseudonym Gerby) is still living. He was the author of the long article in *Iskra*, No. 86, "Sobytiia v Peterburge 9–11 ianvaria (Ot chlena mestnoi gruppy pri TsK)," in which the Mensheviks' meeting with Gapon was first publicly mentioned. Except in unimportant details, Gerb's story corroborates Somov's.

march to the Winter Palace in a religious procession led by a priest, to beg for compassion and pity for workers, especially as it would end only in shooting and beatings. Only after long debate did we manage to convince them that our taking or not taking part in the demonstration could not have any effect on its being carried out but that we had no right to turn our backs on this first mass action of the Petersburg proletariat and should combat the negative traits of the Gapon movement by taking part in it and trying to broaden its aims.[59]

These doubts were reflected in the leaflets issued by the Petersburg Group. On January 4 an appeal "To the Workers of the Putilov Plant," who had gone on strike the day before, was still uncompromisingly anti-Gapon.[60] Even the leaflet on the eve of the march covertly argued against Gapon's petition:

> The tsar is not our friend, he is an enemy of the workers, he does not wish them well. And we must not *beg* him for anything. The tsarist government will yield only to force. Voluntarily the tsar will not give up power, give rights to the people. And we must not debase the dignity of the people by entreaties. The tsar must bow to the majesty of the people. We must demand, yes demand, our rights.[61]

If the Petersburg Mensheviks, who were closer to the masses and less bound by dogma than the Bolsheviks, took so long to see that the Gapon movement was turning into a potentially revolutionary mass movement, what could be expected of the Bolsheviks? In their camp, things were even worse. S. Gusev, who arrived from Geneva at the very end of December, if not in early January, and took over as secretary and leader of the Petersburg

---

[59] *Ibid.*, p. 40.

[60] *1905 god v Peterburge*, Vol. I: *Sotsialdemokraticheskie listovki* (Leningrad-Moscow: Gosizdat, 1925), pp. 10–12. This appeal began: "The general animation of Russian life has also affected the so-called Assembly of Factory Workers. As you know, this society was founded by servants of the government to divert the credulous and less conscious workers from the real Social-Democratic struggle for their interests. And so long as the government was strong, the society was its faithful ally. Now it, too, has raised its head; relying on the government's weakness, it has dared to talk of a strike and to present insignificant demands. But we Social-Democrats know very well that the dismissal of a foreman or the reinstatement of four workers cannot radically improve the life of the working class and that we must advance more substantial demands as we begin the struggle. . . ."

[61] *Ibid.*, p. 21.

Committee (and also as secretary of the Bureau of the Committees of the Majority), wrote Lenin on January 5 about "cursed Gapon":

> This Father Gapon is most certainly a Zubatovite of the purest water. Though there is no direct evidence for it, the fact alone that they do not arrest and deport him for his speeches (while Novikov, the Baku mayor, has been asked to leave Petersburg for his talks at banquets) speaks more eloquently than any evidence. Moreover, Father Gapon misses no opportunity to discredit S-D's in one way or another. Then, too, the assemblies in question are organized on the initiative of the Russian Assembly, which has opened eleven locals in Peter. . . . [A surprising confusion of Gapon's Assembly of Russian Factory Workers with the well-known Russian Assembly, an organization of reactionary high society.—S. S.] . . . Exposing and fighting Gapon will be the basis of the agitation we are hurriedly preparing. We have to move all our forces into action, even if we have to squander them all on the strike, for the situation obligates us to save the honor of Social-Democracy.[62]

The next morning Gusev added a postscript: "Gapon's personality is not quite clear. Probably a naïve idealist of whom everyone is taking advantage, especially the reactionary clique, I think."[63] This was only a passing doubt, which did not affect Gusev's or the Petersburg Committee's stand. On January 30 Gusev wrote Lenin:

> The workers are also a bit confused (again, under the influence of the Mensheviks' antirevolutionary preachings) about the [proper] attitude to Gapon. Your article in No. 4 depicts the government's role very justly, but you are too lenient with Gapon. *He is a shady character.* I have written you this several times, and the more I think the more suspicious he seems. One cannot call him a mere crank, he was a Zubatovite and worked with Zubatovites *knowing* what they are and *what* they want.[64]

On the day Gusev wrote to Geneva about "cursed Gapon"—January 5/18, 1905—Krupskaia in Geneva was writing to the Petersburg Committee:

---

[62] "Perepiska N. Lenina i N. K. Krupskoi s S. I. Gusevym," *Proletarskaia Revoliutsiia*, 1925, No. 2(37), pp. 23–24.

[63] *Ibid.*, p. 25.

[64] *Ibid.*, p. 36.

But where are the proclamations with which the Committee promised to deluge the city? We aren't getting them. Nor any reports. We learned from foreign papers that the Putilov plant was on strike. Do we have connections there? Will it really be impossible to get information about the strike? Only it has to come quickly. Make every effort to arrange for workers themselves to write reports.[65]

Nevskii, quoting this letter, adds:

One of the greatest proletarian movements was beginning, already its spearhead—the Putilov workers—was fighting capitalists, but the center abroad learned of these clashes from foreign papers, because the Bolshevik Committee in Petersburg had to devote itself entirely to fighting the conciliationist Menshevik organizations.[66]

"Had to" is of course tendentious, but the Petersburg Committee was indeed so engrossed in fighting the Mensheviks that it could hardly think of anything else. Farther on, no longer blaming the wicked Mensheviks, Nevskii writes about "the remoteness of our organization from the broad masses and its ignorance of the life and interests of these masses":

Indeed, a vast strike movement was in progress, some unknown tremendous wave was rising, but the Bolshevik Committee was living its own segregated life; having once and for all appraised the Gapon movement as Zubatovite, it was not even able to sense that the strike at the Putilov plant was no common strike but a movement linked by the closest ties to all the Gapon locals, to the whole mighty strike movement of the entire Petersburg proletariat.[67]

January 5 was also the day the Petersburg Committee responded to events with a leaflet, "To All the Workers of the Putilov Plant." It did not even allude to the Gapon organizations, let alone to the fact that they were directing the strike[68]—nor did the leaflet of January 7, which stated some general demands in connection with the by then almost general strike.[69] Only on January 8, in reply to an appeal of "the Putilov Workers' Assembly" (!) "to gather together on Sunday to go to the Winter Palace and present a petition to the tsar," did the Committee's

---

[65] Nevskii, *Rabochee dvizhenie v ianvarskie dni . . .*, p. 85.
[66] *Ibid.*
[67] *Ibid.*, p. 157.
[68] *1905 god v Peterburge*, I, 12–14.
[69] *Ibid.*, pp. 14–15.

leaflet "To All Petersburg Workers" guardedly advise them not to go:

> The Petersburg Committee salutes the workers who have understood the need for political freedom. But the Petersburg workers must realize that the demands which are now being put forward mean the end of autocracy, no less. . . . Consequently, it is futile to address these demands to the tsar. . . .
>
> No, comrades, one cannot expect freedom to come from the tsar, who only recently, in the last manifesto, firmly declared that he had no intention to renounce autocracy. Even if the tsar does promise reforms, he and his functionaries will deceive us. Freedom isn't bought at so cheap a price as one petition, even if presented by a priest in the workers' name. Freedom is bought with blood, freedom is conquered arms in hand, in fierce battles. Not by begging the tsar, nor even by demanding anything of him, not by groveling before the sworn enemy, but by throwing him off the throne and ousting the whole monarchist gang with him—only in this way can freedom be won. Much workers' and peasants' blood has already been shed in our Russia for the sake of freedom, but only when all the Russian workers rise and attack autocracy, only then will the dawn of freedom shine. The workers' liberation can be achieved only by the workers themselves; you will never get freedom from priests and tsars, no matter how long you wait.[70]

As if it had suddenly struck them that under the circumstances their arguments were beside the point, the authors added: "On Sunday, in front of the Winter Palace, if they let you get there, you will see that you cannot expect anything from the tsar. And then you will realize. . . ."

The situation in the Petersburg Committee is also described by one of its members, N. V. Doroshenko, the organizer of the City sector (until January, the propagandist of the Vasil'ev-Ostrov and the Petersburg sectors). Though written twenty years later, his story seems to be basically correct. He too notes the Petersburg Committee's ignorance of the developing movement:

> Until the last days of December, I and my close comrades had had no occasion to visit a single local of the Gapon society. More than that, I do not recall a single conversation with organized workers of

---

[70] *Ibid.*, pp. 16–17.

the Vasil'ev-Ostrov and the Petersburg sectors about any of our people's having visited the said locals.[71]

In early January the party workers of the Petersburg Committee began to take notice of the Gapon movement:

> The workers, most of whom were unquestionably under Gapon's influence, did not at that time regard Social-Democracy as their own party. More than that, it seemed to them that the clear-cut, unambiguous line of Social-Democracy hampered them in accomplishing what Gapon was urging them on to. At one of the secret committee rendezvous at which all of us party workers congregated, S. I. Gusev informed us of the steps taken by the Committee and relayed its directive enjoining us to penetrate into the factories to the locals of the Gapon society and *oppose* to Gapon's demands the program-minimum of the Party, *exposing* the hopelessness and absurdity of the project of marching to the palace.[72]

Doroshenko himself tried to carry out the assignment of opposing and exposing at a meeting of the Gapon local in the City sector on January 7 but was stopped by shouts of "Enough, go away, don't interfere," and so on. "It was made impossible for me to continue my speech and I had to leave the hall."[73]

From this meeting Doroshenko went to a conference of the Petersburg Committee:

> The overall impression was that the conference somehow did not believe that the march to the palace would materialize. The idea was that the government would take steps to nip Gapon's intentions in the bud. Hence, there was at any rate no certainty that mass slaughter would be allowed to occur.[74]

It can be inferred from Doroshenko's account (he does not say so outright) that the Petersburg Committee decided to have members of the organization participate in the march after all:

> To carry out the measures planned by the Petersburg Committee, the committee of the City sector chose as the gathering point for

---

[71] N. Doroshenko, "Rol' sotsialdemokraticheskoi bol'shevistskoi organizatsii v ianvarskie dni 1905 goda," *Krasnaia Letopis'*, 1925, III, 211.

[72] *Ibid.*, p. 212 (italics added).

[73] *Ibid.*, pp. 213–14.

[74] *Ibid.*, p. 214.

January 9 the corner of Sadovaia and Chernyshev Alley, where the subsector organizers were to come in the morning with their organized circles.[75] [That is, the workers connected with the organization were to march not with their factories but in a separate group?! —S. S.]

However, "only a small group, some fifteen workers, no more," appeared at the rendezvous. In the face of all this, the title of Doroshenko's article, "The Role of the Social-Democratic Bolshevik Organization in the Events of January, 1905," sounds ironical.

Lenin and the paper *Vpered* did not quite share the relentless anti-Gapon attitude of the Petersburg Committee and its spokesman, Gusev, who wrote Lenin on January 30, "You are too lenient with Gapon." *Vpered* first took up the events connected with the Gapon movement in its issue No. 3, January 11/24:

> The strike that began January 3 at the Putilov plant is growing into one of the most majestic manifestations of the labor movement. . . . The legal "Russian Society of Factory Workers" is taking part in it, and the strike is moving into the next, higher phase.
>
> The legal workers' society has been the object of special attention from Zubatovites. But lo! the Zubatovite movement is outgrowing its bounds. Started by the police in the interests of the police, to bolster autocracy, to corrupt the political consciousness of the workers, this movement is turning against autocracy, becoming an explosion of the proletarian class struggle.
>
> The Social-Democrats pointed out long ago the inevitability of just such results from our Zubatovism. The legalization of the labor movement, they said, is sure to be useful to us Social-Democrats. It will draw into the movement certain particularly backward strata of workers; it will help to rouse those whom a socialist agitator would not soon, if ever, arouse. And once drawn into the movement, [once] interested in the problem of their destinies, the workers will go on. The legal labor movement will be only a new, broader base for the Social-Democratic labor movement.[76]

This is a reference to Lenin's well-known remarks in *What Is To Be Done?* (*Chto delat'?*) about Zubatovite attempts to legalize the labor movement.[77]

---

[75] *Ibid.*, p. 215.
[76] Lenin, *Sochineniia*, VIII, 71–72.
[77] Quoted in Appendix 5, pp. 287–88.

The views expressed in this article, closer to those of the Petersburg Mensheviks than to the intransigeance of the Petersburg Committee, were recorded before January 9. In the next issue of *Vpered* (No. 4, January 18/31), in the article "The First Steps," these ideas were elaborated:

> The legal Zubatovite workers' society founded with the assistance of the government in order to corrupt the proletariat by systematic monarchist propaganda has been of no little service in organizing the movement in its lower stages and expanding it. What has happened is what the Social-Democrats pointed to long ago when they told the Zubatovites that the revolutionary instinct of the working class and its spirit of solidarity would prevail over any petty police stratagems. The most backward workers will be drawn into the movement by the Zubatovites, and after that, the tsarist government itself will take care of prodding the workers on; capitalist exploitation itself will make them shift from peaceable— and hypocritical through and through—Zubatovism to revolutionary Social-Democracy.[78]

Vpered, No. 4, also contained "letters from Petersburg Social-Democrats," obviously compiled from real letters and foreign newspaper correspondents' reports:

> For a long time we could not be sure what kind of person this priest was; at first (before the strike) his behavior made us think that we were dealing with a Zubatovite of the new school, but since the beginning of the strike this view has had to be abandoned. It seems to me that he is some sort of naïve idealist. [Recall the postscript to Gusev's letter of January 5.—S. S.] Looking at the priest as we did before, it is quite impossible to explain his conduct at yesterday's meeting: he said that on Sunday all the striking workers would go to the palace to present to Nicholas their petition about the urgent needs of the workers.

After a detailed report on workers' meetings in Gapon locals during the last days preceding January 9, *Vpered*'s correspondent (or imaginary correspondent) continued:

> Our people, who at first regarded the whole movement as purely Zubatovite, can now see that it has to be reckoned with in any case and are trying to influence the priest, trying to guide him at least a little. [In Gusev's real letters to Geneva there is not a word of all

---

[78] Lenin, *Sochineniia*, VIII, 94–95.

this; quite the contrary, what they said excluded "trying to influence the priest."—S. S.] Sad as it is to admit it, the Social-Democrats have been pushed aside by this downright elemental movement. But leaflets continue to be issued—a very good one, to the workers of the Putilov plant, came out January 5. Tomorrow another is due. [These leaflets have been discussed above, and they cannot possibly be called "very good" if their authors wished to "influence the priest."—S. S.]

Commenting on these letters, *Vpered* asked, "Who is the priest Gapon: an *agent provocateur* or a Christian socialist?" and answered that much in his past suggested the former. But, wrote Lenin,

> one cannot entirely exclude the thought that the priest Gapon may have been a sincere Christian socialist and that Bloody Sunday pushed him onto a wholly revolutionary path. We are inclined to assume this, especially as Gapon's letters written after the slaughter of January 9, where he says "We have no tsar," his appeal to fight for freedom, and so on—all these facts speak for his integrity and sincerity.[79]

Lenin concluded:

> Be that as it may, the Social-Democrats' tactics toward this new leader took shape by themselves: a cautious, wait-and-see, mistrustful attitude to the Zubatovite was imperative. Imperative, in any case, was energetic participation in the strike movement (even if it had been initiated by a Zubatovite) and energetic promotion of Social-Democratic views and slogans. Our comrades of the Petersburg Committee of the RSDRP also followed these tactics, as can be seen from the above letters.

This was an attempt to veil the differences that had arisen in January between the editors of *Vpered* and "our comrades of the Petersburg Committee" and to correct history slightly, for political and pedagogical reasons.

Later Soviet writings and official history have likewise been contradictory in their treatment of Gapon and the January events. In the twenties the trend was o follow the tactics of Lenin and of *Vpered*, to conceal the passivity and confusion of the Petersburg Committee and build up the impression that the Bolsheviks had

---

[79] *Ibid.*, p. 86.

collaborated with Gapon in some way. An example is V. Nevskii's book-length study, from which I have quoted. His method of glossing over the Bolsheviks' remoteness from events is to say "Social-Democrats" when describing the Mensheviks' activity in order to give the impression that the activity was Bolshevik or at least partly Bolshevik:

> It would of course be a mistake to assume that the Social-Democrats took no part in the movement. On the contrary, despite differences of opinion, they tried during those great moments to act in common and to take the movement in hand in one way or another, at least in some places.
>
> In the sectors where the illegal S-D organization was strong and the workers were most conscious, if the Social-Democrats did not manage to take the movement in hand they at least achieved one thing: they were reckoned with, and as the movement was becoming more and more a mass movement, Social-Democrats gained access to the crowd independently of the Gapon organization; people consulted the Social-Democrats directly, approached them and invited them to meetings.
>
> This was the case especially in two sectors where the Social-Democrats were strong—the Neva and the Vasil'ev-Ostrov.[80]

The same tendency can be discerned in the description of how the "Social-Democrats'" conference with Gapon came about:

> The Social-Democrats' active attitude to the events, their attempts, however weak, to gain control of the movement at least in some sectors, forced Gapon to reckon with the Social-Democrats.
>
> Gapon proposed to arrange a joint conference with Social-Democrats.
>
> Such a conference was arranged on Friday evening, that is, January 7, in the Neva sector.[81]

---

[80] Nevskii, *Rabochee dvizhenie v ianvarskie dni* . . . , p. 94.

[81] *Ibid.*, p. 96. In notes to his correspondence with Lenin and Krupskaia (*Proletarskaia Revoliutsiia*, 1925, No. 2[37]), Gusev tells of an attempt to meet Gapon, giving the date categorically as January 7 (the day of Gapon's meeting with the Mensheviks): "The very evening I spoke with Comrade Shelgunov [who told Gusev that Gapon had visited him in prison and 'talked in a purely Zubatovite vein.'—S. S.] I was supposed to meet Gapon at Rutenberg's apartment, at the decision of the PC [Petersburg Committee] and despite my protests, to try and reach an agreement with him and get him into our organization's hands. I considered the attempt completely hopeless and therefore protested against the PC's decision. Gapon did not come to the rendezvous. I had only a long talk with

Later it becomes evident that the conference was with Mensheviks, but this does not change the author's account of the Bolsheviks' "active attitude":

> Whatever we may think of these negotiations of the Menshevik Social-Democrats with Gapon, one fact is certain: the Social-Democrats did strive to influence events, and the correspondent of the Socialist Revolutionaries was, of course, wrong when he wrote the following on this subject in his paper: "Gapon approached the revolutionary organizations. The Social-Democrats met him with mistrust. The Socialist Revolutionaries promised him their co-operation."[82]

The reader is bound to assume that the Bolsheviks in Petersburg followed virtually the same policy as the Mensheviks, or at least the one Lenin advocated in *Vpered*. In the thirties all this was scrapped. The *Short Course* [*Kratkii kurs*] revived, in a sharpened and vulgarized form, the ideas of the Petersburg Committee: Gapon was simply an *agent provocateur;* it was his "plan" to help the Okhrana by provoking the shooting of workers and "drowning the labor movement in blood."[83]

Rutenberg, who turned out to be a [former] classmate of mine at the Technological Institute (in 1896). Rutenberg kept fanatically praising Gapon's genius and revolutionary spirit. In view of his fanaticism I didn't say much" (p. 71).

This was written twenty years later. In earlier documents, even in Gusev's voluminous correspondence with Lenin, there is not a word about any of this. However, Doroshenko says in his reminiscences (also written twenty years after these events) that at a conference of the Petersburg Committee on January 7, "if memory does not fail me, Comrade Gusev reported on his meeting with Gapon. This meeting did not result in any definite, concerted course of action either" ("Rol' sotsialdemokraticheskoi bol'shevistskoi organizatsii . . . ," p. 214).

[82] Nevskii, *Rabochee dvizhenie v ianvarskie dni . . . ,* p. 97. Nevskii also says: "The Bolsheviks did not lag behind the Mensheviks and, besides making speeches, tried together with the Mensheviks on Vasil'ev-Ostrov to prepare for armed struggle as well" (p. 95).

No preparations for armed struggle were made during those days. Nevskii no doubt had in mind a primitive barricade and a raid on a secondhand weapons shop improvised on January 9 by a student Social-Democrat in a fit of revolutionary zeal. See a correspondent's long report in *Iskra*, No. 85, and D. Gimer's article "9 ianvaria 1905 goda v S.Peterburge. Vospominaniia," *Byloe*, 1925, No. 1 (29), pp. 1–14. It was to this event that the following lines of the Petersburg Committee's report to the Third Congress referred: "On Vasil'ev-Ostrov a crowd, having ransacked a used metals shop, armed itself with old sabers. The impression was pitiful." (*Tretii s"ezd RSDRP . . . 1905 . . . ,* p. 545.)

[83] *Istoriia Vsesoiuznoi Kommunisticheskoi Partii (bol'shevikov). Kratkii kurs* (Moscow, 1938), pp. 54–55.

CHAPTER 2

The Shidlovskii Commission

JANUARY 9 put the revolutionary organizations squarely face to face with the mass labor movement and the unexpected forms it was taking. The new facts had to be assessed and the proper inferences drawn, but history did not leave time for careful reorientation. Adjustments had to be made on the go, partly by feel, and this gave a pronounced tinge of empiricism to the Social-Democrats' tactics in the early months of 1905.

Not quite three weeks after Bloody Sunday, the Petersburg workers were asked to elect representatives—not the "factory elders" of the unnatural and unpopular law of June 10, 1903, but democratically elected representatives of the city's workers—to take part in what came to be known as Senator Shidlovskii's Commission. The Commission was to "determine without delay the causes of workers' discontent in Petersburg and its suburbs and devise means of eliminating them in the future." Governmental commissions had studied the "labor problem" before, but never yet had they included workers' elected representatives. Now the government, not without hesitation, decided to attempt this experiment.

To understand the social significance of this novelty and the public's reaction to it—in particular, the reaction of the revolutionary organizations—we must first see how the Shidlovskii Commission came into being.

The Origins of the Shidlovskii Commission

In government circles the events of January 9 made less of a stir than is generally assumed. The tsar, as we can see from his diary, was somewhat upset on Bloody Sunday but had quite recovered his calm by Monday, and life in the palace went on in its usual placid way.[1] At the bureaucratic pinnacles the events merely sharpened the long-standing rivalry in regard to the "labor problem" between the Ministry of the Interior and the Ministry of Finances, which directed industrial policies (the Ministry of Commerce and Industry did not yet exist). Their rivalry was basically a struggle between the bureaucratic-legalistic and police traditions. The Ministry of Finances tried to keep labor policy within existing laws, modifying them only insofar as this could not be helped and safeguarding employers' interests as much as possible. The Ministry of the Interior was less concerned with the economic welfare of employers than with fighting the revolutionary movement and the revolutionary organizations' influence over the masses. Having found that repression and provocation alone could not stem the revolutionary movement, the political police at the turn of the century had begun to promote workers' organizations under its own auspices and led by its own agents. Both of the rival trends showed up clearly after January 9.

The chief spokesman for the bureaucratic-legalistic tradition was Minister of Finances V. N. Kokovtsov; for the police tradition, General D. F. Trepov. Trepov's position was the stronger, be-

---

[1] In *Dnevnik imperatora Nikolaia II* (Berlin: Slovo, 1923), p. 194, we read: "*January 9, Sunday.* A painful day! There have been serious disorders in Petersburg because workmen wanted to come up to the Winter Palace. Troops had to open fire in several places in the city; there were many killed and wounded. God, how painful and sad! Mama arrived from town, straight to Mass. I lunched with all [the others]. Went for a walk with Misha. Mama stayed overnight."

But already on the next day: "Received a deputation from Ural Cossacks, who brought caviar. Tea at Mama's. For co-ordinated action in stopping the disorders in Petersburg have decided to appoint M.Gen. Trepov governor general of the city and the province. In the evening, had a conference on this subject with him, Mirskii, and Gesse. Dibich (on duty) to dinner." And on Tuesday, January 11: "After lunch received Rear Admiral Nebogatov, appointed commander of an auxiliary division of the Pacific squadron. Went for a walk. It was a cold, gray day. Spent the evening all together. I read aloud."

cause of his personal influence over the tsar, who trusted him implicitly. A ukase of January 11 created the office of governor general of Petersburg, with extensive powers and the right to report directly to the tsar, and Trepov was appointed to the post on the same day.[2] His policy immediately upon taking office is described in Kokovtsov's memoirs:

As governor general of Petersburg, General Trepov . . . energetically promoted the idea that it was necessary for the emperor personally to influence the workers . . . to pacify them by telling them directly that he had their interests at heart and was taking them under his personal protection. . . . In revolutionary circles the thought of involving the emperor has been ascribed to me, but that is entirely inaccurate since I did not share it and did not go beyond announcing in the emperor's name that the labor problem was close to his heart and that he had directed the government to take at once all the necessary measures to meet the justified needs of the workers. But during my . . . reports the emperor more than once expressed his definite approval of Trepov's idea [that] he ought to make a personal attempt to restore calm among the workers and to this end summon [their] representatives. . . . My objections displeased the emperor. He was obviously under Trepov's influence and said to me repeatedly, though very tactfully, that he hoped he might have a good influence on the workers' representatives, if only it proved possible to elect reasonable people.[3]

The rivalry of the two traditions finds distinct if muted expression in Kokovtsov's reports to the tsar of January 11, 16, and

[2] Since 1896 Trepov had been chief of the Moscow police and the right hand of the Moscow governor general, Grand Duke Sergei Aleksandrovich. He sponsored the Zubatov experiment in Moscow, which he understood much more primitively than Zubatov. Trepov was a doughty, ruthless police general, formed in the traditions of the Horse Guards. He owed his appointment as governor general of Petersburg to Minister of the Court Baron Frederiks, a former commanding officer and a fervent devotee of the Horse Guards. Having left his post as Moscow chief of police on January 1—in connection with the Grand Duke's leaving his to become commander of the Moscow Military District—Trepov came to Petersburg to ask to be transferred to the army in the Far East and was thus on hand to be made governor general of Petersburg and virtual dictator. For details, see Count S. Iu. Witte, *Vospominaniia. Tsarstvovanie Nikolaia II* (Moscow-Petrograd: Gosizdat, 1923), I, 282–89.

[3] Count V. N. Kokovtsov, *Iz moego proshlogo. Vospominaniia, 1903–1919* (Paris: Illiustrirovannaia Rossiia, 1933), I, 55–56.

19, published in Soviet times.[4] On January 11, while deprecating the Ministry of the Interior's policy, on which he largely blames the events of January 9,[5] he is still seeking a workable compromise with Trepov:

> My conscience and an honest appraisal of the present events lead me to the one conclusion that peace can be brought to the capital, and the inevitable spreading of the unrest to other parts of your empire prevented, only by the august word of Your Imperial Majesty.
>
> . . . .
>
> That word must be an imperious word. At such moments as this, when the streets of the capital have been stained with blood, the voice of a minister or even of all the ministers together will not be heard by the people. This word must belong only to Your Imperial Majesty, and before your voice the heads raised in rebellion cannot fail to bow. The word of reason must resound in the name, or at least on the order, of Your Majesty. The workers will believe your word that it is not in the alluring promises of their ringleaders but only in your benevolence that the working people will find the source of all good and solicitude.

Kokovtsov then remarks that he has discussed the matter with Sviatopolk-Mirskii and with Trepov and that both have authorized him to tell the tsar "that they fully share my view"; and he begs the tsar:

> If these thoughts are honored with your approval, allow me to draft an address at your command to the factory workers of the capital, upon agreement with the governor general, and to communicate it, for information, to other [industrial] regions of the empire.

A characteristic idea in Kokovtsov's report was held in common by bureaucratic and police circles, and the tsar, too, found it

---

[4] *Krasnyi Arkhiv*, XI/XII (1925, IV/V), 4–19. Kokovtsov's report of January 14, to which he refers in the report of January 16, has not been preserved.

[5] Having pointed out that the main task was to end the disorders, Kokovtsov wrote: "I do not see how they can be ended through police action alone. Nor do I expect this from suppressing the unrest by force of arms. The police did not manage to prevent the flare-up; for many months it remained a passive spectator of the growth and strengthening of a criminal organization authorized at first by the minister of the interior himself. Military force, though of course inevitable in times of trouble and under the obligation to restore order, leaves new discontent in society; and in the lower strata of the population and in those who fall accidental victims of the military operations, there merely develops new irritation, which does not bring the moment of calm any closer."

especially appealing—the idea of the "guilt" of the workers who had marched to the Winter Palace on January 9 and of the need for them to "repent their error."[6] It was mainly to induce this repentance that an "imperious word" from the tsar was supposed to be important.

The tsar wrote in the margin of Kokovtsov's report, "I share your thoughts"; and on January 15, "at His Imperial Majesty's sovereign command" and over the signatures of the minister of finances and the Petersburg governor general, the following "announcement"[7] was issued:

> The peaceful course of public life in St. Petersburg has in the past few days been disrupted by the cessation of work in factories and plants. Having left their work, to their own and their employers' obvious loss, the workers have presented a number of demands concerning the relations between them and factory owners. This movement has been utilized by ill-intentioned persons who have chosen the workers as tools for their own designs and, by deceptive unattainable promises, lured the working people onto a false path.

The workers' guilt and the need for repentance were not mentioned; but then, of course, the announcement said nothing about the government's guilt either. It stressed, on the contrary, that "the government has always been concerned with their [the workers'] needs, as it is concerned now, ready to listen to their just desires and to satisfy them insofar as is feasible"; that "their needs are close to the heart of the emperor, as are the needs of all his faithful subjects"; that "His Majesty has recently, at his

---

[6] The following lines of Kokovtsov's report of January 11 are worth quoting: "However great may be the guilt of your subjects, the factory workers of the capital, who have started trouble at a trying time of military reverses, it is my profound conviction that not all and not even the majority have raised their hand against the peace of the capital. Their ignorance and weakness have been taken advantage of by others, who have pushed the working masses to crime for their own selfish ends. With alluring promises of a quick improvement of their lot and deceitful assurances that the government itself was on the side of the labor movement, organizing it to combat capitalists, the leaders of the movement now rampant have aroused a huge mass of workers who did not realize where they were going and still less comprehend the absurd pretensions with which they imagined they had the right to trouble you.

"Your Majesty, I do not want to believe that a Russian is incapable of repenting his error. It is merely necessary to explain his error to him, to tell him that his hand is being guided by an alien evil will [which] has chosen him as a blind tool for carrying out designs that have nothing to do with improving the life of the workers."

[7] *Novoe Vremia* (St. Petersburg), January 15, 1905.

personal desire, deigned to order that the question of workers' insurance be worked out, with a view to providing for them in the event of accident or illness . . ."; and that, "concurrently with this, the Ministry of Finances is about to begin work on a law further reducing working hours and on such measures as would enable the working people to discuss and make known their needs in legitimate ways."

Somewhat unexpectedly the announcement also promised the workers "the government's protection of themselves, their families, and the inviolability of their home and hearth"—in the context, however, of safeguarding the notorious "right to work":

> The government will shield those who are willing and ready to work from the criminal attempts upon their freedom to work by ill-intentioned persons loudly appealing to liberty but understanding it only as their own right to bar from work, by coercion, those of their own comrades who are prepared to return to peaceful labor.

The entire document is a vivid illustration of how little the ruling bureaucracy understood the events and the temper of the working masses.

If to the minister of finances it seemed most important, and on the whole feasible and sufficient, to steer the "labor problem" back into bureaucratic commissions, General Trepov had more ambitious visions. He was taken with the idea of arranging some sort of demonstration by the workers themselves, to offset the one of January 9.

On January 12, the day after he became governor general, Trepov had received three workers of the Putilov plant, sent to him by Sviatopolk-Mirskii with a note saying that they had taken no part in the disturbances and were perfectly reliable. "They beg very much to be heard, and they say that most of the workers at the Putilov plant have come to their senses and would like to start working."[8] It may have been his talk with these men that gave Trepov the idea of a workers' deputation to the tsar. Within a few days, he had organized it. With the help of the police and the management of a few large factories, he rounded up a "deputation" of thirty-four men, which the tsar received, in his presence,

---

[8] *Krasnyi Arkhiv*, XX (1927, I), 241.

on the nineteenth. According to the official bulletin, the emperor favored the deputation with "gracious words."[9] The first draft of the speech, written by Trepov,[10] had been both more aggressive and more demagogical than the version actually used. Trepov had written (in the tsar's name): "When the blood of my subjects was shed in the streets of Petersburg, my heart also bled with grief for the unfortunate, mostly innocent victims of the current disorders. The guilt for them lies with the traitors and criminals who have misled you and whom, to your undoing, you believed." The tsar (or his counselors at the court) changed this to an outright reproof for "having let traitors and enemies of the motherland lead you into error and delusion" (not a word about the tsar's bleeding heart). Altogether, the final version of the speech is remarkable for its dryness and its complete disregard of the workingman's psychology:

> I know that the workman's life is not easy. Much needs to be improved and put in order, but have patience. You yourselves understand, in conscience, that one must be fair to your employers too, and take into account industrial conditions. But to come in a mutinous crowd to apprise me of your needs—that is criminal.
>
> In my concern for the working people I shall see to it that everything possible is done to improve their lot and that they shall henceforward be assured of legitimate ways to make known their pressing needs.
>
> I believe in the honorable feelings of the working people and in their unshakable devotion to me, and therefore I forgive them their guilt.

One can imagine the feelings of outrage this speech aroused among workers. Even Witte condemns Trepov's maneuver (to be sure, he did not count him among his friends):

> . . . When Trepov became governor general, he conceived the excellent idea of dispelling the ghastly impression made on the workers January 9. But in keeping with his policeman's notions, this is what he thought up.
>
> Having found out from manufacturers the names of some thor-

---

[9] *Novoe Vremia*, January 20, 1905.
[10] This draft, in Trepov's hand, was found in archives. It is printed in *Krasnyi Arkhiv*, XX (1927, I), 241–42.

oughly dependable workers, who could even be used as informers in the most important political matters, he suddenly took about a dozen such men [actually, there were thirty-four], drove them to Tsarskoe Selo, and introduced them to the emperor as deputies from Petersburg workers. . . . Of course this kind of demonstration did not impress the workers in the slightest, and at some factories the representatives who had traveled to Tsarskoe Selo were greeted in such a manner that they had to leave.[11]

Meanwhile the partisans of the bureaucratic-legalistic approach had not been idle. On January 16, reporting to the tsar on labor troubles in the country, Kokovtsov had said, with a touch of irony unusual in such documents, that "the labor problem and the movement to which it has given rise, for all their seriousness, are, I am deeply convinced, much less menacing than certain other phenomena of our domestic life—which of course it is hardly up to the minister of finances to report to Your Majesty."[12]

Later in the report the polemical note resounded again: "At the present time any vacillation is undesirable, and all the more so the exclusion of this [the labor] problem from the competence of the departments whose province it is by law; the creation of any kind of extraordinary special agencies for its solution is especially inadmissible." So much for what ought not be done. But what ought to be done? Kokovtsov was "deeply convinced" that there was "only one way to the satisfactory solution of the labor problem: the development of measures benevolent toward the workers and yet firm and consistent, by granting sufficient latitude in this matter to the department intrusted with the care of our industry's needs." This department, upon consultation with the factory owners of the capital (consultation with workers was not mentioned) would "attempt" to satisfy

those of the ascertained needs that prove justified and can be satisfied on the basis of laws now in force, without introducing any upheavals into the situation of our manufacturing industries. . . . But apart from the needs that can and must be satisfied on the basis of laws now in force, the workers undoubtedly have other needs, whose satisfaction presupposes enacting a new law.

---

11 Witte, *Vospominaniia. Tsarstvovanie Nikolaia II*, I, 285.
12 *Krasnyi Arkhiv*, XI/XII, 8–10.

He, Kokovtsov, would shortly submit to the emperor a special report on the subject, with the request to have it presented to the Committee of Ministers for consideration.

Kokovtsov's ideas found indirect support from a man whose outlook had little in common with his, let alone with Trepov's. The next day, January 17, the tsar received the minister of agriculture and state domains, State Secretary A. S. Ermolov, a "liberal" minister of the Sviatopolk-Mirskii type, who believed that the way out of the troublesome situation was to "convoke representatives of the Russian land." Far from blaming the workers for their march to the Winter Palace, he saw the government's behavior during those days as a string of fatal blunders, and insisted that the tsar express to the people his "deep regret for what has happened," promise to "investigate and satisfy the legitimate requests and desires of the workers," and "above all . . . show sympathy for the innocent victims of the catastrophe," besides, of course, attending to the workers' main grievances immediately.[13] This unusual speech seemed to impress the em-

---

[13] "Zapiska A. S. Ermolova," quoted in my text, and another note by him, dated January 31, 1905, are printed in *Krasnyi Arkhiv*, VIII (1925, I), 49–69. Ermolov's report of January 17 shows how deeply the January events had shaken Russian society and even some of the top bureaucrats: "Your Majesty, you can rely only on the people, but for this the people must be able to believe in you and continue to see in you its defender, yet look what happened January 9. A multitude of workers from all over Petersburg [wanted to] gather before the palace of Your Majesty, without nefarious intentions, not in order to overturn the throne, not even to present to you any demands of a political nature—of the demands expressed in their petitions at the instigation of various revolutionaries the great mass of workers did not know, nor did they understand them; they were guided by one thought alone—they were going to their tsar, to lay at the foot of the throne a loyal statement of their vital needs, to pour out to you all the bitter hardship of their lot. Representatives of this mass had previously approached your ministers, but no one received them, no one listened, although at the same time meetings of factory owners were being arranged and their opinions listened to and taken into account. . . . The crowd was met with volleys of fire, dispersed with weapons. Perhaps, for the preservation of external order, it was impossible to act otherwise—I am not speaking of that, but the fact is that among this defenseless crowd there were many hundreds of victims who did not even understand why they were being killed. . . .

"I do not know if it would have been possible for Your Majesty to come out to this crowd, but I think that its statements should have been heard and considered earlier, and perhaps it would have been possible for Your Majesty to announce beforehand that you would deign to receive a deputation from the workers, that you would order the investigation and satisfaction of their legitimate wishes, dismissing what could not have originated from workers, such as the demand for separation of church and state and similar phrases obviously inspired by others. Unfortunately, no such preventive measures were taken, and the fatal events did occur. But it is necessary that Your Majesty address his sovereign word to the

peror, who said that he had "already decided to address a proclamation or manifesto to the people . . . and as soon as order is
restored, at least outwardly . . . to receive a deputation from
workers and to address them directly"; he also said that he had
"decided to come to the aid of the victims of the catastrophe." (As
we have seen, this did not prevent him, two days later, from
treating the "deputation" with marked coolness and plainly
speaking of the "guilt" of the marchers.) The tsar instructed
Ermolov to "go straight from here to the chairman of the Committee of Ministers" (Witte) and relay to him the tsar's "will" that
he "immediately convene a conference of all the ministers and
department heads of the State Council to discuss such measures
of state import as are called for by the recent events."

Ermolov did drive straight from the palace to Witte, and a
somewhat chaotic conference took place the next day, January 18,
at 1:00 P.M.[14] After a preliminary vote on the need to issue a
manifesto in the emperor's name (fourteen to nine in favor), a
text, probably prepared by Witte,[15] was approved, with some
modifications; but as the tsar was to receive the workers' "deputation" the next day, it was decided to meet again on the twentieth
for a final discussion of the draft. This second conference apparently never took place. At any rate, no manifesto was issued.

---

people, in one form or another; it is necessary that the population hear directly
from you of your deep regret for what has happened, an expression of Your
Majesty's will to investigate and satisfy the legitimate requests and desires of the
workers, but above all there is need to show sympathy for the innocent victims of
the catastrophe. Not all of the many victims were leaders and revolutionaries—
there was the crowd, there were women and children, some were only accidentally
on the scene. It is necessary that Your Majesty come to their aid. If some were
guilty and deserved their fate, still their families and children too are innocent
victims, and it is imperative that Your Majesty treat them with equal kindness. All
sorts of young ladies, students, are going around in Petersburg collecting donations
for the victims. I know that they have already called on several members of the
State Council. They have not yet approached me, but if they do come to me I shall
consider myself duty-bound to give as much as I can, and I shall give, without
inquiring where the money will go—really to help the innocent victims of the
catastrophe or for more agitation. When I am asked for help in the name of the
victims, I shall consider that I have no right to refuse; but it is necessary, Your
Majesty, that not we but you come to their aid; only then will the people separate
you from the true culprits for what happened January 9." (Here the tsar inter-
rupted Ermolov with the words, "I have already decided to address a proclamation
or manifesto to the people. . . .")

[14] About this conference only the rough notes of the minister of public
education, V. G. Glazov, have been preserved. They are printed in *Krasnyi Arkhiv*,
XI/XII (1925, IV/V), 28–37.

[15] The original draft of the manifesto and all the accepted corrections are
printed in an appendix to V. G. Glazov's notes.

Meanwhile events continued to develop on two planes. On the nineteenth the tsar received the "deputation" arranged by Trepov, but in the morning of the same day, Kokovtsov had made a long report tracing the history of the disagreements between the Ministry of Finances and the Ministry of the Interior over the labor problem and submitting some "preliminary propositions" concerning labor legislation for the tsar's "gracious consideration," "thereupon to be subjected to exhaustive discussion by the appropriate departments and interested persons." The tsar approved, and Kokovtsov's proposal was discussed at the January 28 and 31 meetings of the Committee of Ministers, with the result that a "commission to discuss measures for improving the living and working conditions of workers in the industrial enterprises of the empire"—under the chairmanship of the minister of finances —was appointed.[16]

We need not go into the work of the so-called Kokovtsov Commission here; I shall return to it only in connection with the general topic of workers' representation in governmental commissions. The Kokovtsov Commission was eclipsed by another. Right after the tsar's reception of the "deputation," and in view of the bad impression it had made on the Petersburg workers, the idea arose to appoint a special commission in the tsar's name to determine the causes of unrest and the means of removing them and to include in it elected representatives of workers; this was the so-called Shidlovskii Commission. The source of the idea remains obscure. Kokovtsov, writing twenty years later and using no documents, ascribed it to Witte.[17] Witte, writing in the period 1907–12, when the events of 1905 were still fresh in memory, has this to say: "Who recommended him [Shidlovskii] for the job I do not know—I merely received a note from the emperor, informing me that he wanted to set up a special commission and was appointing Shidlovskii its chairman." Witte also mentions that Shidlovskii "was to work under Trepov's direction."[18] All this rather suggests Trepov as the originator. The idea certainly

[16] The special journal of the Committee of Ministers for January 28 and 31 is printed in the Tsentrarkhiv collection of materials, *Rabochii vopros v komissii V. N. Kokovtsova*, with a foreword by B. A. Romanov (Moscow: Voprosy Truda, 1946), pp. 18–28. Kokovtsov's January 19 report to the tsar is in the same collection, pp. 1–18.

[17] Kokovtsov, *Iz moego proshlogo* . . . , p. 58.

[18] Witte, *Vospominaniia. Tsarstvovanie Nikolaia II*, pp. 301–2.

reflected the assumptions underlying Trepov's policies. This is also how public opinion was inclined to see it at the time. It is hardly surprising that there was a certain wariness on the workers' part and that the revolutionary organizations were unsure of the attitude to take toward the elections of workers to the Commission.

An Attempt To Break with the Past: Elected Workers' Representatives

The "sovereign command" creating a special commission under the chairmanship of State Council member Senator N. V. Shidlovskii was signed Saturday January 29 and announced in all Petersburg factories during the night of January 30–31. Besides representatives of the relevant departments, it was to include elected representatives of manufacturers and of workers. The inclusion of the latter was a novelty—not an about-face in the government's policies but *an experiment,* not to be taken to mean that the traditional practices had been abandoned in principle.[19] The number of deputies and the electoral procedures were to be

---

[19] The traditional way of handling labor problems in commissions is exemplified in the account of a conference of the Committee of Ministers on December 24, 1904, when it was resolved to form a commission to study state insurance for workers, under the chairmanship of the deputy minister of finances (the so-called Timiriazev Commission). This decision was ratified by the tsar on January 17, 1905, less than two weeks before he decided to set up the Shidlovskii Commission. Besides government officials, the Timiriazev Commission was to include a generous number of representatives of the industrialists. The conference of the Committee of Ministers of December 24 discussed "the desirability of inviting to work in the Commission . . . persons of the working class from whom one might expect useful information and explanations illuminating the matter from all sides"—without elections but merely at the chairman's invitation. Even this cautious proposal was turned down. It was merely stated in general terms that the chairman had the right to "invite to the sessions of the Commission persons knowledgeable in the topics under discussion." ("Izvlechenie iz zhurnala Komiteta Ministrov 24 dekabria 1904 goda," *Novoe Vremia,* January 23, 1905.)

When the ministers discussed the Kokovtsov Commission on January 31, they felt uncomfortable about barring workers' elected representatives: the Shidlovskii Commission, which included them, had just been announced to the people. But they did bar them just the same. According to the special journal not intended for publication, they explained their decision by the difficulty of getting competent representatives from "the working-class millions" and by the fact that most workers were unable to understand complex bills. And feeling "obliged to renounce the idea of workers' representatives . . . the Committee [of Ministers] considers it awkward explicitly to include . . . representatives of industry in view of the unpleasant impression which might be created by the thought that the two interested

determined by the chairman of the Commission. The rules were sent out to the factories on February 7.[20]

In the literature on the subject there is a tendency, largely traceable to Iu. Milonov,[21] to assume that the rules were based on the law of June 10, 1903, concerning elections of factory elders, but that is a mistake: the 1903 rules were incomparably worse than those governing the elections to the Shidlovskii Commission. The one point on which they agreed was the minimal age of the representatives, with the slight difference that by Shidlovskii's rules they had to be at least twenty-five years old and by the 1903 rules the minimal age—which could not be less than twenty-five—was decided separately for every factory by its management and approved by the governor. In almost every respect Shidlovskii's rules, for all their defects, were a big step forward from the terms offered the workers in 1903.

Only factories employing at least one hundred workers could hold elections to the Commission. Apprentices were excluded. Workers could participate regardless of sex and age, but the rules explicitly barred "foremen and their assistants" from taking part in the elections—and hence from attending the assemblies of workers at which the elections were held. Dictated partly by demagogical and partly by police considerations, this rule harked back to the Zubatov-Gapon practices.[22]

---

parties are inequitably represented." The Committee emphasized that it did not mean to close access to the Commission "to individuals or even to groups" representing industry that the Commission might find it useful to bring in; but the draft of the decisions simply empowered the chairman of the Kokovtsov Commission to invite "anyone who might be expected to give useful information." (*Rabochii vopros v komissii V. N. Kokovtsova*, pp. 31–33.)

Since this clashed with the "sovereign command" about the Shidlovskii Commission, it was probably no accident that the journal of the Committee of Ministers for January 28 and 31 awaited the tsar's signature until February 20, when the fiasco of the Shidlovskii Commission had become clear.

[20] *Novoe Vremia*, February 8, 1905.

[21] From his introduction to *1905. Professional'noe dvizhenie*, compiled by A. Kats and Iu. Milonov, in *Materialy i dokumenty*, pod obshchei redaktsiei M. N. Pokrovskogo (Moscow, 1926), p. 19. The 1903 rules were incorporated in "Ustav promyshlennosti," *Svod zakonov*, Vol. XII, Part II, pp. 1561[10]–1561[18].

[22] The statute of the Zubatovite Moscow Mutual-Aid Society of Textile Workers barred "employees, foremen, and the latter's assistants" from active membership (Kats and Milonov, *1905. Professional'noe dvizhenie*, p. 88). The statute of the Gapon Assembly of Russian Factory Workers of St. Petersburg barred "employees and foremen," but "foremen's assistants and so-called elders of shops can be active members" (*ibid.*, p. 93.)

The elections were to be a two-stage operation: each factory was to elect electors, on the basis of one elector from factories employing 100 to 500 workers, two electors from factories with 500 to 1,000 workers, and one additional elector for every 500 workers over 1,000. The chosen electors had to be male, not less than twenty-five years of age, and employed at the given factory not less than one year. (And they had to be working there at the time of the elections! Anyone discharged, let alone arrested, was automatically excluded.) As to procedure, the workers were given great freedom: elections were to be held "in the manner the workers themselves will choose." It was taken for granted that they would be held at workers' assemblies (voting without holding a general assembly of the voters was not yet known in Russia at the time). To maintain order, the workers were to choose one or several chairmen at each assembly. No managerial personnel was to be present. That no police and no factory inspectors were to be present was not mentioned—police attendance was unthinkable under the circumstances, and there seem to have been no factory inspectors at any of the assemblies.

Elections at the factories were scheduled for February 13, and the chosen electors were to assemble a few days later to elect deputies to the Commission. For these second elections the electors were to be divided into nine groups, "by the type of production [characteristic] of the enterprises from which they had been elected." The number of deputies from each group approximately corresponded to the number of workers in the given industry— from as few as two deputies each from the chemical and the explosives industry to seventeen from the metalworkers—and added up to a total of fifty. This division into groups annoyed the workers and was largely ignored.

The Elections of Electors: The Workers' Demands

The Petersburg workers learned of the Shidlovskii Commission on Monday morning January 31. The announcement of elections to a commission "to determine without delay the causes of workers' discontent" was interpreted at many factories as an invitation to hold elections "without delay." Curiously enough, in the sector in which the Putilov plant was located even the police understood it in this way. The plant, seething since late December, was in the throes of another conflict between labor and management. The newspapers carried the following item:

> On January 31 the police proposed to the large number of workers gathered in front of the Putilov plant to elect deputies then and there to take part in a special commission formed by sovereign command to determine the causes of workers' discontent. . . . The workers pointed out that they had already chosen representatives for talks with the factory management and that they could not hold new elections for lack of suitable premises, the factory being closed.[23]

At many other factories, however, the workers did hold premature elections. At the Sampsoniev cotton and textile mill and the Neva thread factory elections took place as early as February 1.[24] Along the Schlüsselburg road (in the so-called Neva sector) elections were held almost everywhere before February 6: at the Neva shipyards, the Aleksandrovskoe cast-iron foundry, and the Spasskii and Petrovskii textile mills, to name only some of the biggest. The great Obukhov plant did not vote as early. No elections were held on Vasil'ev-Ostrov and Vyborgskaia Storona. The Putilov plant voted on February 6.[25] These spontaneous elections ceased when the election rules were published and the date set; the workers concentrated on preparing for February 13.

It is indicative of the atmosphere of smoldering or open conflict prevailing in many factories at the time that, while preparing for the elections to the Commission, the workers also discussed demands to be presented to the management. As soon as the Commission was announced, they began to present demands to Senator Shidlovskii as well. Spokesmen for the Chesher mills came to see him on February 1. "Wishing to present [their] needs to the Commission truthfully and in their full scope," they addressed to Shidlovskii the following "petition":

> 1. To open the eleven locals of Petersburg workers closed at the decision of police authorities.

---

[23] *Russkie Vedomosti* (Moscow), February 1, 1905 (a report by telephone from Petersburg).

[24] *Novoe Vremia*, February 6, 1905.

[25] *Novoe Vremia*, February 7, 1905.

2. To allow elections of workers at the locals on the basis (*a*) of two representatives from every factory employing more than 500 workers; (*b*) of one from every factory employing less than 500; (*c*) of one representative for every 1,000 workers from factories employing 2,000 or more; and (*d*) of one from each local.

3. To grant the workers the right to hold free elections and to intrust the defense of their interests not only to workers but also to other persons they might elect to the Commission.

Only under the conditions we have indicated will the workers' elected representatives be true spokesmen for the needs of the working class, and only then can the agreement that is to be reached bring peace and order into the relations of workers and employers.

Any other method of electing workers' representatives will impel us to refuse to participate in the Commission. Then the Commission will consist of officials and manufacturers or at best include some workers agreeable to factory owners, whom the latter will call to the Commission at their discretion. But such random representation of workers is not only incapable of determining their needs but will also provoke even greater unrest in the working class.[26]

On February 2, a deputation from the St. Petersburg Railroad-Car Construction plant brought a very similar statement (not a petition but a statement of "what in our opinion is necessary").[27] Here, too, the demand to reopen the eleven closed locals was foremost, but the first two items of the Chesher petition were elaborated in much more detail:

I. To open immediately the eleven locals of Petersburg workers closed at the decision of the authorities and to allow the workers to open new locals as the need arises and to assemble in the locals, for only then can the following be assured: (1) elections of workers' representatives free of police and managerial pressure; (2) continuous exchanges of views between representatives and workers and keeping the workers up to date on the work of the Commission; (3) only through locals will it be possible to have factories with an insignificant number of workers, and different shops of large factories, represented in the Commission; (4) the possibility

---

[26] *Nashi Dni* (St. Petersburg), February 2, 1905.

[27] *Nashi Dni*, February 5, 1905. After its third point, the railroad-car workers' statement differed from the Chesherites' only in formulation. That the former visited Shidlovskii on February 2 (*Nashi Dni* gives no date) is mentioned in the article "K istorii rabochikh vyborov v komissiiu Shidlovskogo," in *Istoriia Proletariata SSSR*, 1935, II, where both statements are given in full (pp. 192–94).

for workers' deputies to discuss among themselves all the questions arising in the Commission, since this possibility is already granted the factory owners and officials participating in the Commission.

II. Authorization to publish without any omissions the decisions and debates of the assemblies.

III. Full freedom of speech at the assemblies and personal immunity for all the participants in the assemblies. Release of arrested comrades taken after January 1, 1905.

On February 3, Putilov workers came to Shidlovskii with a statement closely resembling those of the Chesher and the rail-road-car workers.[28] All this suggested someone's guiding hand. From materials published in Soviet times it transpires that a Petersburg lawyer, È. S. Margulies, played a part in this matter. A communication dated February 8 from the Petersburg city governor to the chief of the Petersburg gendarmerie,[29] and a report of the same date from the chief of the Petersburg Division of the Okhrana to the governor general[30] both indicate that on February 1 and 2 workers from various factories had visited Margulies; that on February 2 he gave workers a draft he had made of an address to Shidlovskii; that he was arrested during the night of February 2; and that in the search of his quarters many copies of the draft were found.[31] It is known that another Petersburg lawyer, G. S. Nosar', also had a hand in the workers' demands. The Chesher deputies who had seen Shidlovskii on February 1 had already been to see the minister of finances on January 31, the very day the Commission was announced, and he had sent them to Shidlovskii. They had consulted Nosar', whose connection with the Chesher mills had begun soon after January

[28] *Putilovets v trekh revoliutsiiakh* (Vol. III of *Istoriia zavodov*), compiled and prepared for publication by S. B. Okun', foreword by I. I. Gaz, introduction by N. N. Popov (Leningrad: Gosizdat, 1933), pp. 100–101.

[29] "K istorii rabochikh vyborov v komissiiu Shidlovskogo," pp. 179–80.

[30] *Putilovets v trekh revoliutsiiakh*, pp. 98–99.

[31] Margulies did not belong to any political party. In 1906 he unsuccessfully tried to form a party of his own (the "Radical Party"). Soviet publications some-times refer to him as a "Gaponite" (see, for example, Kats and Milonov, *1905. Professional'noe dvizhenie*, pp. 21, 143, where the Putilov workers' statement to Shidlovskii is also described as a statement by Gaponites, with no mention of Putilovites). There is no reason to think that Margulies was connected with Gapon and no hint of this in the two police documents cited. Apparently Margulies acted on his own in this matter. Being a Mason, he may have consulted some of the "brothers."

9, when the striking workers had come to him for legal advice in their dispute with the management. Nosar' was apparently the author of the Chesher workers' petition. He himself wrote Shidlovskii (among whose papers the letter was found) asking that the eleven locals be reopened "on my personal responsibility."[32] Nosar' took a very active part in the electoral campaign at the Chesher mills, and when the weavers P. A. Khrustalev and A. S. Korotkov were elected on February 13, he advised them to meet with other electors to map out their future moves. Such a conference, attended by about fifteen electors from the textile and metal workers, took place in a private home at the station Udel'naia of the Finnish Railroad. At Nosar's own suggestion, it was decided to smuggle him into the official assembly of electors; Khrustalev passed on to him his own mandate and identification papers. As "Khrustalev," Nosar' attended the electors' assemblies and, it is said, even presided at the one of seven groups on February 16.[33]

But let us return to the statements presented to Shidlovskii in early February. The ideas they expressed were in the air in the working-class quarters of Petersburg. Other factories besides the ones I have mentioned also sent such statements to Shidlovskii. Indeed, among the deputations was one from the Zubatovite Association of Machine-Shop Workers, which existed in Petersburg independently of the Gapon Assembly and was headed by M. A. Ushakov, a worker at the printing office of the Mint. In substance, the "Ushakovites'" statement differed little from the others, except that it did not mention the locals, which during the last weeks of their existence had not been at all to the Ushakovites' taste (nor, of course, did it ask that workers be given the right to elect outsiders to represent them). Consequently, the demand that the elections be held at the locals was also absent—in fact, the necessity to hold them at individual factories was stressed. But the Ushakovites' demands did include the guarantee of free elections (they even asked that if the elected workers were in

[32] This is recounted by Nevskii in "Vybory v komissiiu senatora Shidlovskogo," *Arkhiv Istorii Truda v Rossii*, 1922, Book 3, pp. 89–90.

[33] V. Perazich, "Tekstil'shchiki v komissii Shidlovskogo," *Krasnaia Letopis'*, 1930, No. 6(39), pp. 51–53. The article draws on archival data and on the interrogation of several former electors to the Shidlovskii Commission. Nosar' was a leftist Liberationist who joined the Mensheviks in the latter half of 1905 and who, under the name of Khrustalev-Nosar', played a big role in the first Soviet of Workers' Deputies.

prison they be freed for the duration of their participation in the Commission) and freedom of action for the workers' representatives in the Commission.[34]

All these lists essentially repeated and elaborated the petition of January 9 to the tsar. The Petersburg Social-Democrats had played a certain part in drafting that petition. They would play an even greater role in the elections to the Shidlovskii Commission, but at this stage, in the first week of February—the time of the spontaneous elections and of the deputations to Shidlovskii— they had little direct influence on events. There are no indications, either in the contemporary press or in memoirs and documents published later, that even a single petition to Shidlovskii during that week had been composed at the instigation, or with the assistance, of either Mensheviks or Bolsheviks. The reasons for this will become clear when we discuss the Menshevik and Bolshevik tactics and attitudes toward the Shidlovskii Commission.

The petitions had a certain effect on the election rules, which on the whole seem to have provoked no discontent, except for the

---

[34] The Ushakovites expressed the following wishes to Shidlovskii: "(1) that the elections be held at the factories; (2) that they be held outside of working hours; (3) that no one save workers be present at these assemblies (especially undesirable is the presence of police officers and members of the plant management); (4) that any worker may be elected, regardless of age, length of employment in the factory, and political reliability (if workers who are in prison are elected, they must be freed for the duration of their participation in the Commission); (5) that the electoral assemblies have the right to discuss freely any matters touching on the causes of workers' discontent and the means of eliminating them in the future; (6) that the number of workers' representatives in the Commission be not less than the number of industrialists' representatives." In addition, "(1) workers' representatives must be able to vote in the Commission rather than [appear only in] an advisory capacity; (2) workers' representatives must have the right to express freely all the needs of the workers without exception, as they understand them, and to indicate measures for their satisfaction, whatever these measures may be; (3) workers shall not be called to account in any way for opinions expressed in the Commission; (4) to enable the workers to be thoroughly conversant with all issues discussed in the Commission, it is necessary that the latter's sessions be given publicity and that the press have the right to discuss freely everything that goes on in the Commission; (5) workers must have precise information on the deliberations of the Commission and especially on the views of their representatives; for this, stenographic accounts must be distributed to workers after every meeting, free of charge and as soon as possible; (6) while the Commission is active, the workers must be given the possibility of discussing freely in their assemblies the issues that interest them and of giving instructions to their representatives." (D. Kol'tsov, "Rabochie v 1905– 1907 gg.," in Obshchestvennoe dvizhenie v Rossii v nachale XX veka, ed. L. Martov, P. Maslov, and A. Potresov, Vol. II, Part 1, [Petersburg, 1909], pp. 196–97.)

rule about the deputies' minimal age and the prohibition against electing women. The first was apparently ignored: many factories automatically re-elected the electors they had chosen during the informal elections in early February, when nothing was known about any age limit, and the press does not mention any complications on this score; evidently the authorities closed their eyes to the fact that some of the electors may have been under twenty-five. The great majority undoubtedly met the age requirement. The question involving women was more difficult. Several had been elected earlier. The newspapers noted, for instance, that there was one woman among the eleven electors of the Sampsoniev mills[35] and that three had been elected at the Russian-American rubber works[36] and one at the Kersten factory.[37] However, a much larger number of electors had generally been chosen than Shidlovskii's rules allowed, and the official elections on February 13 produced no women. The prohibition was resented, but apparently all the workers were anxious not to provide formal grounds for having their deputies rejected and, by and large, strictly followed the rules.

Two other rules were criticized in the press: the requirement that electors be elected from among the workers of the given factory and the two-stage form of the elections. The barring of "outsiders" apparently corresponded to the wishes of the majority of workers. The two-stage elections did not cause noticeable discontent either. At a few giant factories the workers had already resorted to this method in electing electors. Thus, at the Obukhov plant on February 13, thirty workers were first chosen at separate shops and then chose nine electors from among themselves; at the Neva shipyards twelve electors were chosen by fifty workers who had been elected by the shops.[38]

The elections of February 13 were the first basically free elections ever held in Russia by workers. They aroused enormous

---

[35] *Novoe Vremia*, February 6, 1905.

[36] *Istoriia Proletariata SSSR*, 1935, II, 163.

[37] Perazich, "Tekstil'shchiki v komissii Shidlovskogo," p. 48. Shidlovskii received a protest "Ot vsekh zhenshchin-rabotnits fabrik i manufaktur g. Peterburga" against the prohibition of electing women. Though anonymous, the statement was taken seriously by the press, and it probably reflected the feelings of many women workers quite accurately. For its text, as preserved in archives, see *Istoriia Proletariata SSSR*, 1935, II, 195. It is also mentioned in Perazich's article, pp. 48–49.

[38] *Novoe Vremia*, February 14, 1905.

interest among workers not only in Petersburg but also in other industrial centers,[39] and they were carried out on the whole in exemplary order. According to the first newspaper reports, on February 16, 208 factories with a total of 145,250 workers had voted, and 372 electors had been elected.[40] At this count, results had not yet come in from fifty smaller plants with a total of about 15,500 workers, so that altogether about 160,000 workers had taken part in the elections. Later more complete data came to light in the archives, setting the number of chosen electors at 417, of which 188 had come from the fourth group (metals), 55 from the first (textiles), 54 from the second (paper and paper goods, printing, and so on), 45 from the seventh (food processing), and 75 from the remaining five groups.[41] The earnestness of the workers' approach to the elections, the widespread interest in them, the spirit of independence that reigned at the electors' assembly made it a kind of first parliament of the Petersburg workers. But its days were already numbered.

The Mensheviks and the Elections to the Shidlovskii Commission

The announcement about the Shidlovskii Commission and the inclusion in it of representatives elected by the workers themselves caught the Social-Democratic organizations unprepared— not only the Bolsheviks (of whom we shall speak later) but also the Mensheviks, who had had a chance, during the weeks just preceding January 9, to take a closer look at the mass movement

---

[39] In Kharkov, at a meeting of the Artisans' Mutual-Aid Society on January 30 (!), "with a large attendance of workers and the general public . . . a telegram passed on by the chief of police was discussed, about electing deputies from the society to Petersburg, to the Shidlovskii Commission to determine the causes of workers' discontent and devise measures for eliminating these causes. Some members proposed that deputies be elected right away, but the meeting, mindful of Russian realities, agreed with those members who 'out of prudence' found it undesirable, in view of the numerous audience, to name persons whom the workers trusted and elected instead a special commission to elect deputies, intrusting it also with drawing up the 'demands' of the workers." (*Russkie Vedomosti*, February 16, 1905.) In Kiev, workers demanded "the right to send a deputation to the Shidlovskii Commission to take part in considering all-Russian labor problems." (Kol'tsov, "Rabochie v 1905–1907 gg.," p. 200.) Martov mentions a similar demand by Odessa workers in his article in *Iskra*, No. 88, February 17/March 2, 1905.

[40] *Novoe Vremia*, February 16, 1905.

[41] *Istoriia Proletariata SSSR*, 1935, II, 166.

unleashed by the Gapon Assembly of Workers. At the time there was a widespread feeling, among the democratic and liberal intelligentsia as well as in revolutionary circles, that January 9, in conjunction with the bad news from the Russo-Japanese front, marked "the beginning of the revolution"—not only in a histori-cal, but in the most immediate, sense, that is, that the fall of autocracy was perhaps a matter of a few months. Under the circumstances, people tended to regard a new governmental com-mission, even if it did include workers, as just another futile gesture on the part of a tottering regime. This is how the Men-shevik *Iskra*, too, at first evaluated the Shidlovskii Commission. In an unsigned editorial, "An Episode of the Revolution," written a few days after the imminent appointment of the Commission became known, we read:

> At difficult moments in its history, the autocracy has more than once resorted to similar commissions, in which many promised and long-needed reforms were buried. . . . Will Senator Shidlovskii's Commission have a different fate? Of course not.
>
> The Commission has been invented to give an outlet to the workers' acute discontent and to lull them with prospects of im-provement. But the government is, in addition, pursuing another goal, no less important for it. January 9 was a day of terror for the government. It became obvious that even legal and tame workers' unions inevitably develop political aspirations. The Commission is meant to turn the workers back into the channel of economics—to convince them that autocracy can satisfy their economic demands and that it is consequently not in their interests to seek the liquida-tion of the present political system.[42]

The author of the article was not impressed even with the planned elections of workers ("After January 9, the workers can-not be satisfied with playing at elections"), nor with the promises of personal immunity for the deputies:

> So far, Senator Shidlovskii has promised the workers only one thing—the immunity of their deputies. But even supposing that Mr. Trepov will agree to keep Mr. Shidlovskii's word, we shall have a

---

[42] *Iskra*, No. 87, February 10/23, 1905. In the collection *Iskra za dva goda* (Petersburg, 1906), D. Kol'tsov is named as author of this article, but in *Ukazatel' zagranichnykh sotsialdemokraticheskikh periodicheskikh izdanii, 1883–1905*, ed. Iu. K[amenev] (Paris, 1913), it is ascribed to A. Martynov.

few rare specimens, a score or so of workers freely promenading in Petersburg in spite of having made radical speeches in a certain Commission (if they will make them), while their comrades, for similar speeches, or for criticizing their behavior in the Commission (if they hear of it) will be thrown into prison or deported.

What, then, was to be done? The author replied:

Social-Democracy's task was foreshadowed in its conduct on January 9. At that time, although convinced that not pleas but demands must be directed to the government [and] that all pleas were useless, it went nonetheless at the head of the workers so as to influence the consciousness of the masses immediately, on the spot, with the example of the awesome events that were taking place. So now, although convinced ahead of time of the impotence and futility of the Shidlovskii Commission, it must exploit this instance of the government's confusion for its agitation; [it must] demand, and agitate for, free elections of workers' deputies, publicity of debates, full freedom of speech at the assemblies where deputies will be elected and in the Commission itself, and so forth. . . . But it goes without saying that the Party must not stop there in its agitation. It must see to it that the mandate of the deputies . . . includes the obligation to announce in the Commission—and one must try to make the necessity for such an announcement clear to them—that the causes of the workers' discontent cannot be removed, or the Commission work fruitfully, under the present political conditions and that the workers therefore insist on the convocation of a constituent assembly. Only with this kind of agitation can it be hoped that the episode of January 29 will strongly stimulate the developing revolution.

Apparently the Menshevik organization in Petersburg fully shared this conception. Somov notes that, unlike the great mass of workers, the more conscious ones were skeptical about the "experiment" of electing deputies to the Commision[43] and that in

---

[43] The metalworkers "viewed the Commission from the beginning as an adroit move to deflect the workers' attention from important problems . . . to petty factory needs. They expected no practical results from the Commission, any more than from all the other commissions active at the time in all departments. . . . The backward workers of many Petersburg factories had a different attitude. There was ceaseless talk among them about demands that should be presented to the Commission, of petitions to address to it. They sincerely believed that in the guise of the Commission an organ had been created where one could send spokesmen to convey needs. By and large, the Shidlovskii Commission elicited great excitement among

the Petersburg Group boycottist tendencies were quite strong
during the first days:

> At first the Social-Democrats were inclined to advocate absten-
> tion, boycott of the elections to Shidlovskii's Commission. They
> wanted to begin by demanding that conditions be provided to
> make proper elections of deputies possible. [That is, they evidently
> did not plan an *outright boycott,* with an appeal to the workers to
> shun the elections, but a *conditional boycott:* to shun the elections
> *if* the conditions on which the workers would participate were not
> met.—S. S.]
>
> In particular, they demanded personal immunity, freedom of
> assembly, and full publicity for the Commission's meetings. They
> advised the workers not to take part in the elections unless these
> conditions were met. But it soon turned out that although there
> were no workers' assemblies open [to the public] it was still
> possible to agitate fairly extensively and . . . that no reasonably
> successful boycott could be carried out in any case. Moreover, the
> elections to the Commission offered such a splendid setting for
> political agitation that many thought it absurd to destroy it from
> the start. In view of all this, as soon as the rules . . . were
> published, the Social-Democrats decided to begin an intensive
> electoral campaign and, circumventing certain electoral restrictions,
> to carry out elections of electors everywhere—and if necessary [!]
> also those of deputies—but afterward to refuse either to elect
> deputies or to take part in the Commission unless a number of
> general democratic demands covering all civil rights, and summed
> up in the basic demand for a constituent assembly, were satisfied.
> As we know, they succeeded in carrying out the whole campaign
> according to this plan.[44]

An error in Somov's narrative must be pointed out. He writes
that the Social-Democrats decided to begin an intensive electoral
campaign as soon as the election rules were published. In reality
the decision was taken as soon as the announcement about the

---

workers, and at the time workers animatedly discussed problems connected with it
everywhere—at home, at work, in taverns, in the street—eagerly attended mass
meetings, joined circles, attended the legal meetings of various unions, and everywhere asked insistent questions about their tactic in this Commission." (S. Somov
[I. A. Peskin], "Iz istorii sotsialdemokraticheskogo dvizheniia v Peterburge v 1905
godu [Lichnye vospominaniia]," *Byloe,* April and May, 1907; the passage quoted
is in the April issue, pp. 44–45.)

[44] *Ibid.,* p. 45.

forthcoming Shidlovskii Commission was published on January 31. The first leaflet outlining the plan was issued immediately, and a second, elaborating the plan, after the publication of the rules. This is clear from the Petersburg Group's summation of the campaign in *Iskra*, No. 92, March 10/23. Both leaflets may be found in the collection of Petersburg Social-Democratic leaflets, including Menshevik ones, published by Istpart in 1925. The editors themselves say of the first that it appeared "at the beginning of February," and this is borne out by its text, which states that "nothing as yet is known of the method" by which workers would elect deputies.[45] But—

> leaving aside the question of the Commission as such and of our participation in it until its nature, its tasks, and the extent of its rights are made known to us—we must now determine our attitude toward the elections to the Commission. To vote or not to vote? That, comrades, is the question we must answer. Yes, let us vote! But for this we must have conditions under which our elections will not be a hollow comedy and our representatives can truly speak of our needs and in our name.

After the experience of January 9, the Mensheviks' entire conception of their tactics was such that they could not have chosen *outright boycott of the elections* to the Shidlovskii Commission; and the tactic of the Petersburg Group did in fact require *active positive participation in the elections*, while firmly *rejecting positive participation in the Commission*. Somov frankly says that the Group had decided to advise the electors "to elect deputies to the Commission, but only in order to have them appear at its first meeting, state their main civic demands, and— upon receiving an *undoubtedly negative* answer to the effect that the Commission had not been empowered to discuss these questions—refuse to participate further in the Commission and leave."[46]

In substance, this was a call for a boycott—not of the elections but of the Commission—though the term was avoided in the arguments of the time, perhaps being reserved for the tactic of shunning the elections. The arguments in many ways prefigured

---

[45] *1905 god v Peterburge*, Vol. I: *Sotsialdemokraticheskie listovki* (Leningrad-Moscow: Gosizdat, 1925), p. 84.

[46] Somov, "Iz istorii sotsialdemokraticheskogo dvizheniia . . . ," *Byloe*, April, 1907, p. 52 (italics added).

those about the elections to the Duma a year later. But in the case of the Duma there was plenty of time to thresh out the attitude to take and the tactics to follow; with the Shidlovskii Commission, everything had to be decided in a few days—and this in itself assured the victory of the qualified boycott policy.

It is true that the editors of *Iskra,* after defending this approach on February 10, had second thoughts almost at once. A week later, in Number 88, February 17 (O.S.), another editorial, "What Shall We Do with the Shidlovskii Commission?" posed the question differently and explored it in greater depth. It came too late to affect the tactics of the Petersburg Mensheviks toward the Commission, but its influence was to prove all the stronger when the Mensheviks drew their conclusions from the experience of the Commission and planned their next moves. The article, which markedly affected the ideological evolution of Menshevism in 1905, maintained that any gain strengthening the organization, the class unity, the fighting readiness, of workers was a true gain for their class:

> From this point of view, the decree appointing Senator Shidlovskii's Commission is a major proletarian victory—no matter what motives inspired its authors to make this "concession." But it stands to reason that this new conquest can display its real content only to the extent that the proletariat *consciously* exploits the opportunities offered by the new "reform" to the cause of its development as a class.

The author of the article[47] argued against the *"negative stand"* of those who held that "the workers must refuse to participate in this Commission and repeat that they demand a nationwide constituent assembly." This demand must of course be made, but it should not mean refusing *"direct participation in the Commission"*:

> The struggle of the working class for a constituent assembly will be the more energetic and conscious the more firmly established in its mind is the program of those social demands that must become objects of struggle in the constituent assembly and in the legislative mechanism of free Russia. And if the *struggle* within the Shidlovskii Commission and *around* it can help the proletarian masses to espouse these social demands, if it can stimulate the workers to

---

[47] According to *Iskra za dva goda,* Martov was the author of this article.

organize in the name of these demands, then we have a weighty argument against the negative stand recommended by the said comrades.

The workers' representatives in the Commission must become mouthpieces of the whole working class—not only of the Petersburg workers:

> The deputies of the Petersburg proletariat must from the very beginning appear in the role of representatives of all Russian proletarians, and the whole Russian proletariat must make them its representatives, while insisting that deputies from other cities also be admitted to the Commission.
>
> Drawing on the collective declarations of many thousands of workers all over Russia and sending far and wide its reports on its work in the Commission, the workers' deputation will be an enormous force in organizing the masses and influencing their consciousness. It will become the national tribune to whom workers of all branches of industry and all regions of Russia will turn to recount their needs and at the same time the agitational center that can set the slogans for the ongoing struggle of the whole country's proletarians. And if Social-Democracy succeeds in exercising a strong influence over the work of the deputies, the Party can steer the economic struggle of the Russian proletariat in the proper direction.
>
> This is the goal that conscious workers must set themselves in the face of the new tsarist "concession." Whether the goal is reached, whether they succeed in winning for themselves an *organizing political center* [italics added] depends, of course, on many conditions—not least on the stamina, energy, and consistency of the conscious workers. But whether the goal is reached or not, *moving toward it must bring considerable results in organizing and educating the working class.*

Iskra's article was, however, far ahead of the tactics the Mensheviks actually used. Martov in one of his later works noted the discrepancy:

> The Mensheviks joyfully seized the opportunity to organize the broad working masses and establish close contact with them on the basis of the elections to the Commission. That is why they spoke against "boycott" [that is, against outright refusal to participate in the elections.—S. S.] from the very first, pointing out to the masses the need to conduct well-organized elections of deputies and to fight for the right to conduct these elections freely and indepen-

dently of any pressures from the authorities and the owners. *Iskra,* published abroad, went farther and insisted that the experiment with the Commission gave Social-Democracy a convenient chance not only for wide agitation but also for inaugurating lasting organizational unity among the workers. The paper pointed out that the network of "deputies" would make it possible to introduce an organizing factor into the economic struggle and to advance the cause of trade unions.[48]

That was the core of the difference: for the Mensheviks involved in active party work in Russia, the main point was to "create a platform for agitation," to use an expression we shall meet presently in the Petersburg Group's summation of the campaign. For the ideological leadership, however, there already arose, in conjunction with the great extension of agitation, the question of "lasting organizational unity among the workers." Martov writes:

> *Iskra's* tendency ran counter to the prevailing mood not only among the "Bolshevist" but also among the "Menshevist" workers, as well as among most of the people active in the Party. A [wholesale] emphasis on political agitation prevailed among them—the view that every new fact of civic life should be put to use for ever wider and deeper agitation against the collapsing regime. The task of consolidating the gains of the mass movement organizationally was ignored by some and time and again sacrificed by others in favor of the agitational task. In this respect the Mensheviks were ahead of the Bolsheviks in only one way—a very important one, it is true: not trying to simplify the task of political agitation, they sensed more readily than the Bolsheviks the vital nerve of the spontaneous processes springing up among the masses and easily saw the concrete forms that agitation could take in connection with new facts. Hence the Petersburg Menshevik Group . . . quickly oriented itself in the situation and, having rejected the idea of boycotting the elections to the Shidlovskii Commission, successfully flung to the masses the directive of organized negotiations with the Senator about the conditions for the election of Commission members and for the Commission's functioning.[49]

The editors of *Iskra* did not yet find it possible to criticize the line of the Petersburg Group openly. When the campaign ended

---

[48] L. Martov, "Sotsialdemokratiia v 1905–1907 godakh," in *Obshchestvennoe dvizhenie v Rossii v nachale XX veka* (Petersburg, 1914), III, 545.
[49] *Ibid.*

in the disbandment of the Commission, which most of the Petersburg workers regarded as a victory due to their bold campaign,
Iskra printed a rather elated lead article, "After Two Months":

> Their [the Petersburg workers'] brilliantly conducted revolutionary
> campaign against the phony experiment with the Shidlovskii Com-
> mission, culminating in the suicidal closing of that Commission, has
> demonstrated to autocracy that the Petersburg proletariat—after
> January 9—will not rise to the bait of "heartfelt solicitude," and so
> on.[50]

Only a cautious editorial comment on the article expressed *Iskra's*
critical view of the Petersburg tactics:

> We had proposed—in *Iskra*, No. 88—a differently planned cam-
> paign in regard to the notorious Commission, calculated for a
> longer period, to allow the proletariat of *all Russia* to experience its
> revolutionizing impact. We believed that the tactic we were propos-
> ing to the comrades could postpone the moment—inevitable in an
> autocracy—when the workers would sharply break with this at-
> tempt at reform and thus unite the whole Russian proletariat
> around the "electors" guided by Social-Democracy. If this had
> succeeded, we should have hastened the emergence of the *nation-
> wide mass organization* which we must have for a planned, decisive
> attack and for which the foundation has now been laid in Peters-
> burg.

That the Petersburg party workers were far from sharing this
conception can be seen from a long letter, published in *Iskra*, in
which the Petersburg Group summarized the campaign:

> Our campaign in connection with the Shidlovskii Commission
> was entirely successful. I would say that it went off brilliantly,
> considering the novelty of the enterprise, the exceptional historical
> moment, and the local political conditions. The final political result
> of the campaign—the electors' refusal to elect deputies—we can
> ascribe with justifiable pride to our work. The first problem we
> faced was that of a slogan. What should we tell the masses? To
> elect or not to elect? In order to create an agitational platform for
> ourselves, we answered yes, but on certain conditions.
> A directive not to elect would have meant not a boycott of the
> Shidlovskii Commission but cutting ourselves off from the masses,

---

[50] *Iskra*, No. 91, March 6/19, 1905. This article was also written by Martov.

for they would not have followed us, our influence being so weak. Apart from that consideration, we never issue this kind of directive, even when we are sure the masses will take it. The main thing in such political combinations as the Shidlovskii Commission is to create a platform for agitation.[51]

The Bolsheviks and the Elections to the Shidlovskii Commission

The question of how to react to the Shidlovskii Commission appeared in a different light to the Bolsheviks. The Petersburg Committee favored an outright appeal to the workers to boycott the elections and gave up the idea only because it was forced to. Later writings misrepresent the matter, but the numerous published documents and materials leave no room for doubt.

From the protocols of the sessions of the Petersburg Committee for February, 1905,[52] we can see that the Committee looked into the matter only on Wednesday February 2, when the Petersburg proletariat was already churning at the prospect of electing representatives to the Commission and several factories had actually held premature spontaneous elections. At its meeting of February 2, the Committee minutely discussed the declaration of the Bureau of the Committees of the Majority about a third party congress; then it discussed organizing students (in connection with a strike at the universities); and only after that did the Committee's secretary, S. I. Gusev, report on the forthcoming elections to the Shidlovskii Commission.[53] "The most consistent

---

[51] "Komissiia Shidlovskogo i sotsialdemokratiia (Ot mestnoi gruppy TsK)," *Iskra*, No. 92, March 10/23, 1905.

[52] *Proletarskaia Revoliutsiia*, December, 1924, pp. 10–50.

[53] The Petersburg Committee's lack of interest is even more surprising than its late awareness of the Shidlovskii Commission; only the last half-page of the protocols of three and a half pages is given over to a sketchy discussion of it. Gusev's comments on the protocols are still more astonishing: "In the affair of the Shidlovskii Commission the Petersburg Committee had in a way a 'lucky break': the announcement about the Commission first appeared in *Novoe Vremia* on the very day a conference of the Petersburg Committee was scheduled (in the other papers it appeared the next day). Thus the Petersburg Committee could react immediately, while the trail was hot, to this attempt to deceive the workers (it was extremely difficult then to convoke special meetings). . . . The meeting of February 2 was scheduled for twelve noon, and in the morning of the same day I saw in *Novoe Vremia* a solemn announcement in the tsar's name about the creation of Senator Shidlovskii's Commission to discuss workers' needs. Before the Committee's

line of action, from the Social-Democratic viewpoint, would be to boycott these commissions [Gusev was speaking of Shidlovskii's, Kokovtsov's, and other commissions] . . . but we wouldn't be able to bring it off. It remains, then, to work out our tactics in this particular case."[54] Several decisions were taken, almost duplicating those of the Menshevik Group. But the forced nature of the approval, when the real preference was to have the workers boycott the elections, could be felt throughout. The view that the elections should have been boycotted in principle was hotly defended at the Bolsheviks' so-called Third Party Congress when it convened in London in May.

The subject of the Petersburg campaign was brought up by Filippov (P. P. Rumiantsev), reporting "On the Attitude to the Government's Policy on the Eve of the Overturn." (Incidentally, in February he himself had been a member of the Petersburg Committee.) The part of his report that interests us is missing from the published protocols, but we learn from the speech of Leskov (N. Romanov) that Filippov gave only a cursory description of the Petersburg Committee's tactics toward the Shidlovskii Commission. Leskov himself spoke of them with some frustration:

> I agree with the tactics of the PC only relatively, inasmuch as the PC missed the right moment to launch a campaign against any kind of participation of workers in the Commission. The PC started to agitate when the workers had already elected some of the electors. Hence it was forced to agitate for taking part in the elections but refusing to take part in the Commission's work. When

---

meeting I had time to talk the matter over with P. P. Rumiantsev; we quickly reached an agreement and presented our proposal jointly." (*Ibid.*, p. 13.)

But the announcement in the tsar's name had been displayed in all factories on January 31. What Gusev read in *Novoe Vremia* was a report that on February 1 the machine-shop workers of the Putilov plant had "expressed the wish to begin electing deputies at once, to present petitions to the chairman of the newly organized commission to determine workers' needs, State Council member Senator Shidlovskii," but that the management of the plant had insisted that they postpone the elections until Sunday February 6, "when lists of workers and ballot boxes will have been prepared." The workers refused and went on strike. Apparently it was only this news item that alerted the Petersburg Committee to the Shidlovskii Commission. Could there be more telling proof of its lack of contact with the masses?

[54] *Ibid.*, p. 11.

we agitate for participating in commissions or in elections [of representatives] to them we are blurring the workers' consciousness, keeping up the hope that something can be gained by peaceful agreement with the government. . . .

It is therefore imperative to say categorically in our resolution that workers must refuse commissions proposed by the government and to hold up the opposite, revolutionary method of realizing their demands.[55]

Some members of the Third Congress agreed with Leskov (the delegate from Moscow, Sergeev [A. I. Rykov] took an especially uncompromising boycottist stand); others approved the Petersburg Committee's tactics. Answering the critics, Filippov said:

There was no disagreement that the Commission should be boycotted. But merely issuing leaflets about boycott, though in keeping with the general principle of our tactics, would have resulted in elections without the Committee's participation. The voters were undecided, they thought that the Commission might produce something useful for the workers—the government also engages in agitation, you know.

The workers' eagerness to take part in the elections was unmistakable. We had either to stay away from any pre-election agitation or prove the spuriousness and deceptiveness of the government's policy. And this could be done only by joining in the elections, getting conscious workers elected as electors, and facing the Commission with demands which certainly would not be honored. . . .

. . . .

. . . Of course, if the Petersburg workers had been politically mature, it would have been possible to recommend boycott from the first.[56]

In February Lenin's *Vpered*, published abroad, had reacted to the announced Commission in an article, "A Commission of Government Hocus-Pocus,"[57] which argued that only the workers' lack of consciousness forced the Social-Democrats to participate in the elections:

---

[55] *Tretii s"ezd RSDRP. Polnyi tekst protokolov* (Geneva: Central Committee of the RSDRP, 1905), p. 151.

[56] *Ibid.*, pp. 156, 160.

[57] "Komissiia gosudarstvennykh fokusov," *Vpered*, No. 8, February 15/28, 1905. According to the *Ukazatel' zagranichnykh sotsialdemodraticheskikh periodicheskikh izdanii . . .*, Voinov (Lunacharskii) was the author of this article.

How do we Social-Democrats, the conscious vanguard of the working class, regard the notorious Commission of Senator Shidlovskii? In our eyes it is no more than a commission of government hocus-pocus. . . . A vile, cheap Zubatov-Witte farce.

If the Russian working class were already consciously arrayed under the banner of Social-Democracy, it would—as the natural leader of the whole oppressed Russian people—in reply to the government's plan to dupe it behind a hypocritical, fawning mask, drive its mighty fist in the face of the monarchist killers and swindlers and smash it to smithereens together with the mask. But there still are some workers who will not take our, the Social-Democrats', word for it and who are asking themselves, "Suppose the Shidlovskii Commission turns out to be good for something?" Do you want to put it to the test, comrade non-Social-Democratic workers?

The article advised the workers to press for "the right of workers to gather in open assemblies to discuss their needs freely, the right to hear anyone there whom the workers deem it necessary to hear, [and] guaranteed complete personal immunity for all participants in workers' assemblies"; and to persist in demanding that representatives be elected "by all men and women workers on the basis of direct secret suffrage," that the representatives' "right and obligation to inform their constituents of everything going on in the Commission" be recognized, and that workers of all the industrial centers be included in the elections. Then, somewhat surprisingly, the article took the position that the Commission could "become a weapon in the hands of the proletariat":

> The government has landed in a situation that is awful for it, though funny from the outside. It had extended a gracious hand to the Petersburg workers, expecting them to kiss it gratefully. The workers . . . have clasped the lordly fingers so hard that they cannot be pulled back. They have looked the canny diplomats straight in the eye, sternly and seriously. And Mr. Shidlovskii is afraid, cold sweat covers his brow. He regrets that the hand had been so imprudently extended.
>
> Squeeze it harder, that outstretched hand, since you have chosen to respond to the diplomacy of the lord-magistrates. . . .

This contradictory article reflected the Bolsheviks' contradictory attitude to the Shidlovskii Commission.

All this left its mark on the leaflets issued by the Petersburg Committee on the eve of the elections of electors. One, of February 12—the first Bolshevik leaflet on the Commission—listed the terms "on which it is possible to participate in the Shidlovskii Commission" (note the interesting detail: participate in the Commission, not just in the elections!). The terms repeated the political demands already formulated in many workers' declarations, with the added demand of direct elections ("wherever the workers consider this possible"), but characteristically omitted the opening of the "eleven locals."[58]

A second leaflet, undated but evidently issued simultaneously, explained the events and the recommended tactics:

> Not only officials will sit in the Shidlovskii Commission; representatives of factory owners and workers are also being invited. In other words, the government wants to falsify the record; it wants to cover its infamous acts with the names of your representatives. When the Commission makes its decisions, which have already been worked out in advance by officials and factory owners, the government will say that the workers have agreed to these decisions through their representatives. Comrades! Do not let yourselves be deluded, do not fall into the trap the government has set for you. But how should the workers deal with the Shidlovskii Commission? The answer is clear: simply refusing to vote would of course be best. But if the majority of the workers do decide to vote, then, to avoid a split, one must take part in the elections and try to send to the Commission really devoted working people of our own, properly elected, who will carry out the workers' instructions. . . . And if the workers' representatives see that they are being muzzled in the Commission or that their demands are going to be declined, they must all leave the Commission, declaring that the decisions are a fake. . . .[59]

Letters from Petersburg printed in the Geneva *Vpered* show how the lower-echelon party workers reacted to these tactics. The first letter about the campaign described a meeting of the First

---

[58] *Listovki Peterburgskikh bol'shevikov. 1902–1917*, Vol. I: *1902–1907* (Leningrad: Ogiz, 1939), pp. 197–98. In the previously mentioned 1925 collection of 1905 leaflets (see n. 45), this leaflet is printed on pp. 99–100.

[59] *Listovki Peterburgskikh bol'shevikov . . .*, p. 199. This leaflet is missing from the 1925 collection (see n. 45).

factory subcommittee of the City sector on February 3, the day after the Petersburg Committee had made its decisions.[60] The meeting resolved to put forward the proposed political demands (including that of direct elections):

> Unless these demands are satisfied, it is imperative to agitate for boycotting the elections (unanimous). The committee is of course sure that these minimal demands cannot be satisfied under autocracy, but they have to be presented in order to underscore once again to the workers that autocracy is in principle incompatible with the basic claims of the proletariat (unanimous).

The same letter related that at a conference of organizers of the City sector several people pointed out (after the chief organizer of the sector, a member of the Petersburg Committee, had spoken on the decision of the PC) that "boycott of the Commission has already begun at certain factories, on the same grounds as the Committee had thought of provoking it, so that the Committee's assumption that boycott at the first stage was impossible has not been borne out."

Vpered's correspondents wrote that the leaders of the Bolshevik organization had convinced the party workers that it made sense to refrain from "straight boycott"—that this was, in fact, the best way to abort the Commission. Another letter, in the same issue of *Vpered* but apparently of a later date, said that "we have definitely decided to participate in the elections but at the same time to demand immunity of deputies, freedom of assembly, press, and so on, in everything concerning the Commission. And in the event of non-fulfilment of these demands to scuttle the Commission." The last communication from Petersburg about the elections actually called the campaign a "campaign against the Shidlovskii Commission."[61]

But these boycottist undertones did not greatly affect the concrete moves of the Bolsheviks. Often their campaign differed little from that of the Mensheviks. In Gusev's letters to Lenin, the main source of *Vpered*'s coverage of the Petersburg events, this actual, if largely superficial, similarity is obscured by the writer's crude

---

[60] *Vpered*, No. 9, February 23/March 8, 1905.
[61] *Vpered*, No. 10, March 2/15, 1905.

distortion of the Menshevik stand and exaggeration of the Bolsheviks' role in the campaign. In the first half of February (the exact date was not given) Gusev wrote Lenin:

> With respect to the Shidlovskii Commission it has been definitely decided to go through with the elections but to demand immunity for the deputies, freedom of assembly, freedom of the press in all questions concerning the Commission, publicity of meetings. In the event of non-fulfilment of these demands (or even of a part of them), to scuttle the Commission, complete boycott, a general strike with political and economic demands, an appeal to the whole population, and so on. [As will be shown, the Petersburg Committee soon abandoned the idea of a general strike.—S. S.]
> . . . Here again the Mensheviks got snarled up: they began by preaching total boycott, non-participation in the elections, and now, seeing the failure of this plan, they don't quite know what to do and are hopelessly floundering. I am sure, insofar as one can be sure of the future, that on the affair of the Shidlovskii Commission we shall show them how one can act and, I am almost sure, settle the hash of the whole miserable [Petersburg Menshevik] Group.[62]

After the campaign Gusev again wrote Lenin:

> Hurray! The PC can be proud: its whole plan, all its resolutions, all the tactics it had worked out, even the details—all has gone through brilliantly. I have already written you about the first [stage of the] elections. Even from the incomplete information I gave you, one can see how great was the PC's influence during the elections. . . .
> And where was the Minority? Where were they whose independent activity so captivated . . . even the old fox [literally, "wolf" (volk)] Lenin that he started shouting that the PC had let Petersburg slip through its fingers, that we had become old maids, etc.? Where were they whom the old fox—who still hasn't learned that not one word in the new Rabochee Delo [that is, the Menshevik Iskra.—S. S.] can be trusted, that everything in it, from the first letter to the last, is full of sham, deceit, falsehood, fabrications, etc.—advised us to follow, opening the doors wide, letting in any and all comers, etc.? That is shrouded in mystery. . . .[63]

---

62 "Perepiska N. Lenina i N. K. Krupskoi s S. I. Gusevym," foreword and notes by S. Gusev, Proletarskaia Revoliustsiia, February, 1925, p. 46. The Mensheviks are similarly described in the letter from Petersburg in Vpered, No. 10, March 2/15.
63 Ibid., p. 47.

We can infer from Gusev's letter that Lenin had been irritated by his bragging. But outwardly—that is, on the pages of *Vpered*—no sign of this appeared. The letter against which Gusev is arguing here, in a rather superior tone, remained unpublished. Only Lenin's reply to Gusev is known. He turned the matter into a joke:

> Quite a going-over you gave the "old fox," he had to scratch just from reading you! But No. 11 [the number of Gusev's next letter.— S. S.] showed that you are after all too much of an optimist if you hope to get the better of the Peter Mensheviks so easily.[64]

In reality the elections passed in a very different mood. Listening to Social-Democratic speakers, the workers couldn't even tell Mensheviks and Bolsheviks apart—they all seemed to them just Social-Democrats. Even the Bolshevik historian V. I. Nevskii implicitly recognized this in an account of the elections that he published early in the Soviet period:

> Now at one, now at another factory the workers abandoned work, returned to their machines a few days later only to stop the factory again the next day or even within a few hours; pressure from a foreman, the arrest of elected comrades, the arrest of deputies to the Commission—all this excited the masses, which, while trusting nobody, attentively listened nonetheless to the Social-Democrats. In late January and early February, in connection with the Shidlovskii Commission, there was a continuous series of strikes linked to the great movement of January 9. . . .
>
> Under such conditions and circumstances the elections to the Shidlovskii Commission took place. In addition to their preparatory work, the Social-Democrats did a great deal during the elections themselves: the Bolshevik Committee alone sent more than sixty agitators to electoral meetings at factories; the Mensheviks also supplied many agitators. The agitators spoke at the meetings and of course made use of the right to speak with utter frankness, which the workers had won. The organizers had seen to it that the plants were deluged with proclamations about the demands the Bolshevik S-D Committee and the Menshevik S-D Group had worked out. As a rule, the workers adopted these demands. . . .[65]

---

[64] Lenin, *Sochineniia* (4th ed.), XXXIV, 258.

[65] V. I. Nevskii, "Vybory v komissiiu senatora Shidlovskogo," *Arkhiv Istorii Truda v Rossii*, 1922, Book 3, p. 87.

The Menshevik party worker Somov also wrote that "there were at first no major disagreements between Bolsheviks and Mensheviks."[66] The major disagreements came later. We shall discuss them at the end of this chapter, as well as the Bolshevik tactics during the last phase of the movement connected with the Shidlovskii Commission.

The Assemblies of Electors:
The End of the Shidlovskii Commission

According to the rules, the deputies to the Shidlovskii Commission were to be elected separately by the nine industrial groups, not at a general assembly of electors. The list of buildings at which the electors were to meet has been found in archives: those of the first group, at the Nobel *narodnyi dom* on N'iushtadt Street; of the second, at a school on the corner of Grecheskii Pereulok, No. 1/8; of the third, at the Railroad-Car Construction plant on the Moscow highway; of the fourth, at the municipal auction hall on Meshchanskaia Street; of the remaining five groups, at various factories.[67] The time was "Friday February 18 at 3:00 P.M." No preliminary assemblies were planned either of groups or of all the electors together between February 13, the day of the election of electors, and February 18—but the workers changed that. Nevskii writes:

> The workers of Petersburg were in turmoil. On February 14, 15, 16, and 17 many large plants again went on strike—the Spassko-Petrovskii mills, the Alekseev box factory, the Frank mirror factory, the Chesher mills, the Pipe factory, the repair shops of the Warsaw Railroad, the New cotton mills, the Pal' factory, the Aleksandrovskoe plant, the Rozenkrants plant, the Old-Sampsoniev mills, the Great-Okhta mills, the Phoenix factory, and a multitude of small ones. And during those days some factories now resumed work, now stopped once more, and in some places workers did not work on February 17 because it was the fortieth day after January 9 and the whole factory attended a prayer service for the killed.[68]

---

[66] Somov, "Iz istorii sotsialdemokraticheskogo dvizheniia . . . ," *Byloe*, May, 1907, p. 161.

[67] *Istoriia Proletariata SSSR*, 1935, II, 163.

[68] V. I. Nevskii, "Vybory v komissiiu senatora Shidlovskogo," *Arkhiv Istorii Truda v Rossii*, 1922, Book 3, p. 88.

Senator Shidlovskii had to give in. Two assemblies of electors were convoked for February 16: one, for seven groups (all save the fourth and the ninth), at Countess Panina's *narodnyi dom;* the other at the Nobel *narodnyi dom,* for the fourth group (metal-workers, the most numerous, comprising nearly half of the electors). (Why the ninth group, the explosives industry, with ten electors, seems to have been overlooked remains unclear.) According to the Petersburg Menshevik Group's report to *Iskra,* "the total of approximately four hundred electors was made up, roughly, of 20 per cent organized Social-Democrats, 40 per cent politically radicalized workers, 30 or 35 per cent 'Economist' workers, and a small proportion of backward elements."[69] These data are often quoted in the literature (with or without reference to *Iskra*). Another account has been preserved in the archives. In a personal letter of March 3, sent "via agent," a Petersburg citizen wrote to Kursk that he had attended, at a private home, a lecture on the labor movement by the writer Tan (V. G. Bogoraz):

> According to Tan, who had attended all the assemblies of electors, among the 400 men there were 180 Gaponites, about 80 Social-Democrats, and 80 "Economists" (that is, workers whose demands were purely economic); the rest were uncommitted.[70]

This does not clash with *Iskra*'s figures but complements them, since it underscores the immense proportion of former active members of the Gapon Assembly among the electors. It hardly could have been otherwise. (The "Economists" and the uncommitted may also have included a good many workers formerly connected with the Gapon movement in one way or another.)

The electors who met at twelve noon at Countess Panina's *narodnyi dom* first broke up into groups and discussed such questions as freedom of the press, assembly, unions, and strikes, state insurance of workers, the release of arrested deputies, im-

---

[69] *Iskra,* No. 92, March 10/23, 1905.

[70] *Istoriia Proletariata SSSR,* 1935, II, 163. A letter from Petersburg in *Iskra,* No. 90, March 3/16, says that fifty of the electors who gathered at Countess Panina's *narodnyi dom* turned out to be "Zubatovites." They met separately, elected a chairman, and decided to ask the others for a hearing and forgiveness. In view of their sincere repentance, they were forgiven and admitted to the general assembly. *Iskra*'s correspondent places this at the assembly of February 18, but it is more likely that it happened on February 16 or 17.

provement of the peasants' lot, the eight-hour working day, pay raises for workers, and so on. Each group also unanimously resolved to ask for the reopening of the eleven locals.[71] At 4:00 P.M. all seven groups came together and composed a long message to Shidlovskii, interesting both in what it included and what it left out:

> We, the electors of seven groups, came to the preliminary assembly and, having discussed the organization of work in the Commission, have reached these conclusions:
> 1. That the method of elections proposed by you deprives us of the possibility to gather together, to discuss our needs, and to pick out worthy candidates for deputies. Only if the eleven locals are opened, and we become free to assemble, can we work out and discuss all our demands, general as well as specific, in consultation with workers of different factories. It is in their locals that our deputies must report on the work of the Commission to the comrades who have elected them. Therefore our first and main demand is to open immediately the eleven factory locals.
> 2. The working procedures you propose for the Commission do not guarantee that our needs will be truly and fully presented there. Our demands are neither exaggerated nor arbitrary; they have not been inspired by agitators or by foreign millions. We want our demands to be judged by all Russia; let everyone know what the workers want and what the persons concerned will not let them have. For this we must demand (a) that all deputies be present at the Commission's meetings and not called in a few at a time for questioning; (b) that deputies be granted full freedom of speech at the Commission's sessions; (c) that the sessions of the Commission be public, that is, reported in the papers without any censorship.
> 3. The working procedures proposed by you do not guarantee the personal immunity of our comrade deputies. In your announcements you have declared that deputies will not be punished for "pertinent communications" at the Commission's meetings. But you did not explain what you consider pertinent communications. By demanding full freedom of speech for the deputies at the Commission's meetings we mean the abolition of any and all limitations on freedom of opinion. Our deputies must not be called to account for any of their statements in the Commission, and this must be guaranteed by you. We shall believe that our deputies will not face

---

[71] *Novoe Vremia*, February 17, 1905.

prison terms only when you have demanded that the proper authorities release all our comrades arrested since January 1 of the current year for defending our interests (a list of these persons is inclosed) and when our comrades really are released.

4. The method of election proposed by you deprives workers of small factories of representation in the Commission. . . . We want them, too, to state their needs to the Commission, and therefore we demand additional elections from small workshops, on the basis of one deputy from each of the eleven factory locals.

All our demands concerning the method of election and the work of the Commission you are able to fulfil personally. You have been given enormous powers. If the government sincerely and earnestly wishes to change the workers' situation and to satisfy their vital needs, we shall receive a favorable answer to our demands. We shall wait until twelve noon on February 18, when the second assembly is scheduled. If we do not receive from you a favorable affirmative answer to all our demands by the opening time of the assembly, we shall refuse to elect deputies. We have had many lessons in the past. Within the limits outlined by you the deputies cannot work freely in the Commission, and therefore we shall refuse to become deputies.[72]

Two points in this resolution deserve special notice. First, it featured the reopening of the "eleven locals." This demand had long since ceased to connote a revival of the Gapon organization. In the last two weeks before January 9 the locals had been turning into genuine labor centers, which was precisely why they were closed the day after Bloody Sunday. Since then the demand to reopen them had come to mean a demand for freedom to organize in a familiar and already legalized form—of course, without the restrictions of the original statute of the Gapon Assembly. During the electoral campaign the reopening of the locals became the focal demand of the whole Petersburg proletariat, and only the Bolshevik Petersburg Committee closed its eyes to this. It did not actively oppose the demand but passed it over in silence. The two leaflets it issued on the eve of the elections of electors dealt only with general political demands and the immunity of deputies, as did the resolution of the Petersburg Committee proposed on February 11 at a meeting of the

---

[72] *Russkie Vedomosti,* February 17, 1905 (a report by telephone from Petersburg).

Petersburg Union of Engineers (by Gusev, of course under an alias).[73] As the reader will see, this resolution played a certain role at the electors' assembly of February 16.

Second, the political demands boiled down, in fact, to the guaranteed freedom of action of the workers' deputies in the Commission. This was skilfully tied in with "the release of all our comrades arrested since January 1 . . . (*a list of these persons is inclosed*)." This self-restraint made it somewhat difficult for Shidlovskii to refuse the electors' demands. Possibly it also, empirically, pointed the way to the tactics proposed by *Iskra* a few days later, in its No. 88, in the article cited earlier (pp. 100 f.). The resolution of the seven groups was sent to Shidlovskii on the day of the assembly.

The fourth group (of metalworkers), assembled at the Nobel *narodnyi dom*, also on February 16, decided first of all to send four spokesmen to Shidlovskii with a demand to convoke a general meeting of all electors. ("In view of the necessity for all the deputies *together* to discuss in advance the needs of the workers and to reach an agreement about them, we, the deputies of the fourth group, declare that we cannot begin elections of deputies to the Commission until all the groups are given a chance to assemble together."[74]) The assembly sent for the factory inspector of the precinct to have him take this declaration to Shidlovskii. He arrived about 6:00 P.M. and agreed to act as mediator between the workers and Shidlovskii, to whom he went together with the deputies. Shidlovskii authorized a general meeting of electors to be held on Thursday February 17 at noon.[75] Before the inspector arrived, the assembly had discussed the situation of the working class and adopted a resolution identical with the one proposed by Gusev at the Union of Engineers on February 11.[76]

At noon on February 17 the electors of all nine groups gathered at Countess Panina's *narodnyi dom*. The newspaper *Russkie Vedomosti* reported:

---

[73] This resolution is given in the Kats and Milonov collection, *1905. Professional'noe dvizhenie*, p. 140.

[74] Kol'tsov, "Rabochie v 1905–1907 gg.," p. 199.

[75] *Novoe Vremia*, February 17, 1905.

[76] *Istoriia Proletariata SSSR*, 1935, II, 198; *Arkhiv Istorii Truda v Rossii*, 1922, Book 3, p. 88.

As on the sixteenth, the assembly broke up into groups, which conferred in separate rooms. By one o'clock the meeting moved to the large auditorium. . . . The assembly began discussing the general program. The first group (textiles) announced that its demands were purely economic and offered a proposal that the question of women's labor be discussed, which received no support from the other groups. The group that received no support ostentatiously left the meeting and conferred separately. Several speeches on the labor problem followed. . . . Then the assembly took up the subject of the Commission. . . . The fourth and the ninth groups indorsed the resolutions of yesterday's assembly, after making a few additions. In its final form, the assembly's resolution reads:

"We, the electors of nine groups, gathered in general assembly, have resolved to indorse the resolutions of the seven groups, adding the following demands:

"(1) guaranteed personal immunity of all workers freely discussing their needs;

"(2) guaranteed inviolability of workers' homes.

"We expect an answer to all our demands by twelve noon on February 18 at Countess Panina's *dom*. . . . In the event of an unfavorable answer . . . a general strike beginning in the morning of February 19 has been proposed. Adopted by the assembly unanimously with the exception of the representatives of the workers of the printing office of the Mint."[77]

The idea of topping off the electoral campaign with a general strike had a double purpose. If the conditions the workers had set for participating in the Commission were refused, it was to be a sign of protest, and if the deputies did enter the Commission, a sign of solidarity with them and of support of their demands in the Commission.

The idea had been suggested by the Mensheviks. The letter of the Petersburg Group in *Iskra*, No. 92, quoted earlier, explained the origin of the plan:

Along with the question of our policy toward the Shidlovskii Commission, the question of our attitude to strikes kept coming up. You know that the workers are in continuous turmoil. Now one, now another factory is on strike. It strikes one day, two days, sometimes more, then resumes work. A few days later it is on strike again. We had to unify this movement, channel it into one stream, give a

---

[77] *Russkie Vedomosti*, February 18, 1905.

normal outlet to this energy. Therefore we gave the directive for all the workers to leave work on the opening day of the Commission, as a sign of their solidarity with the deputies, who were to make a political demonstration in the Commission on the very first day.

The assumption was that the tension would reach its peak on that day. The Mensheviks had even prepared a kind of political manifesto, with details of motives, to be read in the Commission in the name of the deputies.[78] But events moved more swiftly than anyone had expected. In answer to the electors' resolutions of February 16 and 17, Shidlovskii said:

> 1. Workers will not be prosecuted for any frank statements relative to their situation as workers that they may make in the Commission.
> 2. All workers' deputies will sit in the Commission together with its other members. . . .
> 3. I shall take the necessary measures to have the needs of workers in small industrial enterprises discussed in the Commission.
>
> As to all the other requests of the electors, they are beyond the Commission's competence and hence require no answer on my part.[79]

On February 18 the electors came to Countess Panina's *narodnyi dom* and found Shidlovskii's reply on its locked door. Later they gathered at the various buildings assigned to the nine

---

[78] It was printed in *Iskra*, No. 94, March 25/April 7, 1905, as "a declaration proposed by the Petersburg Group of the RSDRP and adopted by the majority of the electors." It is reprinted with the same comment in the Kats and Milonov collection, *1905. Professional'noe dvizhenie*, pp. 140–42; Milonov adds, on p. 21 of his introduction, that it was adopted by the assembly of electors at Countess Panina's *narodnyi dom* on February 17. That is a mistake. Somov writes that the declaration was prepared in case workers' deputies did get into the Shidlovskii Commission (and gives its full text, except for the concluding "Down with . . ." and "Hail to . . .") but does not mention its adoption by an assembly of electors. Nor is this mentioned in the Petersburg Group's summation of the campaign in *Iskra*, No. 92; and the detailed newspaper reports on the assembly of February 17 give no indication that such a declaration was on the agenda for discussion or voting. It was, however, issued on February 18 by the Petersburg Group as a leaflet, with the same heading as the one *Iskra* gives it; and it undoubtedly did reflect the feelings of the majority of the electors. Perhaps they did approve it explicitly—not at a formal assembly, which it was no longer possible to convoke, but during talks in front of Countess Panina's *narodnyi dom* and at the assemblies of the nine groups on the same day. Be that as it may, nothing that was published then or later suggests that the declaration did not in fact express the feelings of the majority of the electors.

[79] For the text of Shidlovskii's answer, see the Kats and Milonov collection, *1905. Professional'noe dvizhenie*, p. 144.

groups, and seven of the groups refused to elect deputies to the Commission. "The electors left the electoral assemblies in a state of excitement, shouting, 'It's a new betrayal,' 'Comrades, stop working,' and dispersed to their sectors to urge the workers to strike. The strike was all but general."[80] On February 20, upon receiving Shidlovskii's report, the tsar "deigned to order that the activity of the commission instituted under the chairmanship of State Council member Senator Shidlovskii be discontinued."[81]

The Mensheviks and the Bolsheviks had at first disagreed sharply on the subject of calling a general strike. The Mensheviks had agitated for it, the Bolsheviks had rejected it. Gusev wrote in his letter (No. 10) to Lenin, from which I have already quoted:

A general strike did not enter into the Committee's plan (personally, I did include it in the plan from the first—as long as two weeks ago). In any case, the Committee considered it impossible to take the initiative in calling for a general strike without the workers' taking some initiative first. *Now*, when it has been decided by the electors, when one third of the factories are already striking, when the strike cannot conceivably be halted—now, today, we are coming out with such an appeal.[82]

The Bolshevik and Menshevik attitudes are seen from a special angle in a report of the chief of the Petersburg Division of the Okhrana, Gerasimov, to the director of the Police Department on the electors' assembly of February 17, written on the same day:

. . . According to information received, closing the Commission's work would result in strong agitation for a general strike, although the "Bolshevik" faction of the Social-Democratic organization considers the present time unsuitable for any upheavals. The "Menshevik" faction is calling for a strike in special proclamations.[83]

V. I. Nevskii, quoting this report, remarks:

The information was indeed close to the truth. The Bolsheviks did not intend to turn the Commission into the kind of political

---

[80] Somov, "Iz istorii sotsialdemokraticheskogo dvizheniia . . . ," *Byloe*, April, 1907, p. 55.

[81] *Novoe Vremia*, February 23, 1905. The government communiqué to this effect is given in full in the Kats and Milonov collection, *1905. Professional'noe dvizhenie*, pp. 144–45.

[82] *Proletarskaia Revoliutsiia*, February, 1925, p. 47.

[83] *Istoriia Proletariata SSSR*, 1935, II, 199.

center that the Mensheviks were dreaming of. In the Bolsheviks' report after February 13, we read: "Now it remains to carry out the rest of the plan, demonstratively to block the second elections, for Shidlovskii will never satisfy the demands put forward at the elections and the electors will not vote unless the demands are satisfied."

This was what the disagreement between Bolsheviks and Mensheviks was all about. The former, without boycotting the elections in the early stages, sought to make them fall through in the later stages; the latter dreamed of creating an all-Russian political center and therefore decided to pressure the government, even by a general strike, into satisfying the demands presented by the electors. An appeal for a general strike was in fact made in a special proclamation of the Petersburg Group of the Central Committee of the Social-Democratic Party.[84]

But once the electors had called for a general strike and, as Gusev says, every third factory was already striking, the Bolshevik Petersburg Committee also issued a brief announcement about the strike and then a lengthy direct appeal to the workers for a general strike.[85]

Thus the three-week "experiment" of the Shidlovskii Commission ended in a general strike and in a new wave of arrests. In conclusion, let us see how the history of the campaign is treated in later Communist publications. Beginning with Gusev's letters to Lenin, full of perfectly fantastic assertions about the campaign, the Bolsheviks have produced a myth of brilliant and successful Bolshevik strategy and complete Menshevik disarray. In his very first letter about the campaign, writing of Bolshevik achievements and Menshevik ineptitude, Gusev had predicted: "We shall show them how one can act and, I am almost sure, settle the hash of the whole miserable Group."[86] Later this became the historical stereotype.[87]

---

[84] Nevskii, "Vybory v komissiiu senatora Shidlovskogo," *Arkhiv Istorii Truda v Rossii*, 1922, Book 3, p. 88.

[85] *1905 god v Peterburge*, I, 121–24. It should be noted that on February 18 the Petersburg Committee issued a leaflet, "Pochemu my otkazalis' vybirat' deputatov v komissiiu Shidlovskogo," in the form of a "Pis'mo k tovarishcham g. Peterburga" from "a group of electors" (*ibid.*, pp. 119–20); but it said nothing about a general strike.

[86] Gusev's letter has been extensively quoted earlier in this book; for example, on p. 110.

[87] Even *Bol'shaia Sovetskaia Èntsiklopediia*, though without Gusev's aggressive

But we have seen how "brilliantly" the Bolsheviks had conducted the campaign. They missed its beginning, which forced them to give up their idea of boycotting the elections of electors; they were late with their leaflets (the first one appeared only on February 12, on the eve of the elections of electors); they were not in evidence at the assembly of seven groups on February 16, when the demand to open the eleven locals, which they had avoided raising, was put at the head of the list of demands. True, they did get their resolution passed at the assembly of the fourth group on February 16, but there was nothing specifically Bolshevik about it except for its silence about the locals; and they did not even try to defend it at the general assembly on the seventeenth, when the fourth group unanimously joined in the resolution adopted by the seven groups on the sixteenth. And having, after some initial wavering, rejected the general strike, they became its champions after it had started. No wonder the *History of the CPSU: Short Course* [*Istoriia VKP(b), Kratkii kurs*] (1938) and the *History of the CPSU* [*Istoriia KPSS*] (1959) do not even mention the campaign around the elections to the Shidlovskii Commission.

To counterbalance the Bolshevik story of their own and the Mensheviks' roles in the campaign, let us quote Somov:

> If we overlook certain divergencies on secondary organizational details, there were at first no major disagreements between Bolsheviks and Mensheviks. . . . It soon became apparent that it was not minor organizational disagreements that divided the two factions but a deeply rooted difference in their understanding of Russian reality, disagreements on the proximal course of the Russian revolution and on the tasks of the Social-Democratic Party.

> The guiding tactical premise of the Bolsheviks of that time was

---

tone, said in its first edition: "On the subject of workers' participation in the Commission, disagreements arose between Bolsheviks and Mensheviks. The Bolsheviks considered it imperative to make use of the electoral campaign to this Commission for the purpose of unmasking the government and for the workers' political education. The Mensheviks displayed in this matter the usual wobbling of opportunists. . . . The Bolsheviks carried out the electoral campaign with great success and gave it a pronounced political character. . . . The elections, which took place February 13 amid mass strikes, produced brilliant results. . . ." (Vol. LXII [1933], col. 382.) The second edition's account (Vol. XLVIII [1957], p. 33) is essentially the same as the first, except that it does not mention the reopening of the eleven locals as among the demands drawn up by the assembly of electors.

that the Russian revolution "hinged on uprising." In their opinion, only a victorious uprising could and must resolve the political crisis in Russia; therefore it must play the decisive role in the tactics of Social-Democracy: only that was important which fostered and speeded an uprising; anything that could retard its coming in any way must be put aside. . . . Hence, when discussing any mass actions by the proletariat, it was necessary, in their opinion, to ask first of all: Is the proletariat capable of, and ready for, the uprising which must inevitably follow its mass actions—and to refrain from the latter if the proletariat seemed insufficiently prepared for an uprising. But the Bolsheviks' estimate of the workers' revolutionary readiness and consciousness was on the whole so high that they saw no obstacles on this score even to an immediate uprising; they viewed readiness for an uprising mainly from the technical point of view. This point of view also determined the Bolsheviks' proposal to boycott the elections to the Shidlovskii Commission and their doctrine of abstention from individual campaigns by the proletariat in general and from a May Day street demonstration in particular. The proletariat should not dissipate its strength in skirmishes but accumulate it against the day of the decisive battle, the nationwide uprising. . . .

The Menshevik Group in Petersburg, while also considering an uprising inevitable, viewed it, however, as the result of a lengthy process, a whole series of actions in which the fighting capacity and the consciousness of the proletariat would keep growing in breadth and depth. Although the Mensheviks, too, had a strong tendency to overestimate the revolutionary spirit of the working masses, they conceived preparation for an uprising chiefly as popularizing the idea, not only by propaganda and agitation, but also through the proletariat's active response to the major events of the day, through constant support and expansion of the strike movement.[88]

The Effect of the Campaign on the Development of the Labor Movement

January 9 had stirred up all the workers in Petersburg, and not only in Petersburg, but it had had no organizational consequences whatsoever. It was the campaign around the elections

---

[88] Somov, "Iz istorii sotsialdemokraticheskogo dvizheniia . . . ," *Byloe,* May, 1907, pp. 161–62.

to the Shidlovskii Commission that brought home to the workers the advantages of organized unity and representation. Oversimplifying a little, one might say that January 9 had an immense *propaganda* value in revolutionizing the masses; and the campaign, though incomparably lower in political resonance, a great *organizational* value.

From the standpoint of organization, the fact that workers had to elect electors at individual factories, and only the electors could elect deputies to the Commission, was a distinctly positive fact. The officials who had planned the Commission naturally did not see it this way; nor did the labor organizations appreciate the value of the two-stage procedure—they had actually demanded direct elections. But the workers felt it instinctively, as witness their spontaneous choice of such elections at certain giant factories, with shops electing representatives and these in turn electing electors.

For the first time in Russian history, there was to be an elected representation of a large body of workers (only in Petersburg, it is true) and not merely of workers in separate factories, as provided for by the misbegotten "factory elders law" of 1903. To be sure, the government expected the workers and electors to retire from the scene as soon as the deputies to the Commission had been chosen. It did not expect the electors to continue as workers' representatives in the factories or the assembly of electors to remain active as a body supporting the deputies to the Commission. But the government was no longer able to control matters of such scope. To the electors themselves as well as to the working masses, the elections meant creating in every factory an authoritative body of representatives. If the elections of deputies had gone through, and the Commission begun to function with workers in it, the assembly of electors would have turned into a kind of permanent house of representatives of the Petersburg workers.

How much the workers felt the need for organized unity is clear from the popularity of the demand to reopen the "eleven locals." No one, of course, thought of reviving the police-tainted statute of the Gapon Assembly. The locals were to be centers uniting the workers on the broadest basis; one of their purposes was to keep the deputies to the Shidlovskii Commission in constant touch with the rest of the workers. But the Shidlovskii Commission never materialized and no deputies were elected. This made it impossible to preserve the assembly of electors as a permanent organ. Nor were the locals reopened. At many factories, however, the electors remained spokesmen for the workers, and the idea of workers' representation never died out again.

About much of this, we have the testimony of P. N. Kolokol'nikov, the foremost Menshevik party organizer [*praktik*], who rose to prominence during the Mensheviks' integration with the mass labor movement. (Later Kolokol'nikov was influential in shaping the theoretical views of the leaders of the trade-union movement, whatever their political bent.) He arrived in Petersburg (from Nizhnii Novgorod) in February, 1905, too late to take part in the campaign but not too late to see its "living legacy." This is what he wrote about the first two weeks following the disbandment of the Commission:

My own party work was in the Neva sector. Here, from the very first, I came into contact with the living legacy of the electoral campaign to the Shidlovskii Commission, in the persons of the electors, who had retained their mandates and become factory committees [*sic*] after the liquidation of the Commission. At the time, almost all the current work of the Menshevik party organization, with the exception of its propaganda circles, was connected with the boards of deputies-electors and based on them. No less important was the factory electors' role as precursors of the metalworkers' trade union: up to 1906 factory representation provided a substitute for a trade union, and later it served as starting point for the organization [of a union]. The first attempts to organize a union, in the spring and summer of 1905, were also based on factory representation. This is why it is worth while to consider in some detail this form of workers' organization, out of which grew, in October, the Petersburg Soviet of Workers' Deputies.

The most enduring and viable factory representation developed in the Neva sector out of the boards of electors of the Semiannikov and the Obukhov works. At the Aleksandrov plant it was weaker. The textile mills—Pal', Maxwell, Thornton—retained only some vestiges of it. Factory management, of course, looked askance at workers' representation. Forced by the workers' pressure to recognize it, it tried, on the basis of the police law about factory elders, at once to legalize workers' representation and to curtail its powers and weaken its ties with the mass. The workers energetically resisted the appetites of management. . . .

A number of remarkable workers came to the fore and joined forces through factory representation. At the Obukhov plant the leader of the representatives was P. A. Zlydnev, whose influence among the workers was enormous; he took part in all the negotiations, rather frequent at the time, with the factory management, which set great store by his opinions. During the Days of Freedom Zlydnev, who had played a conspicuous role in the Petersburg Soviet of Workers' Deputies, was a member of its presidium and . . . of the delegation to Witte. He was also a spokesman for the other accused during the trial of the Soviet. . . .[89]

The role played in the factories by the electors who emerged during the elections to the Shidlovskii Commission—a role that lasted for a long time and was of course not limited to the Neva sector—has often been described in the literature, but since all the other accounts are less reliable and precise than Kolokol'nikov's, we need not consider them here.

Kolokol'nikov notes that the electors laid the groundwork for the organization of the metalworkers' union, even though it proved impossible to establish one immediately. Similar strivings in the textile industry are reported by Perazich on the strength of the interrogation of several former electors more than twenty years later. At the assemblies of electors of February 16 and 17, 1905, many electors from textile mills discussed the creation of a union. This had no immediate practical consequences either, but during these discussions several men emerged who later became leaders of the Petersburg union of textile workers.[90] The situation was no doubt much the same in other branches of industry. The printers alone were more successful. Kolokol'nikov writes:

Soon after my arrival I found a former fellow deportee, the typesetter I. M. Liubimtsev, who had been chosen elector by the printing press where he worked. . . . After the liquidation of the Shidlovskii Commission on February 20, only the printers maintained organized contact among the electors of various enterprises. A group of electors from printing presses took it upon itself

---

[89] P. Kolokol'nikov, "Otryvki iz vospominanii, 1905–1907 gg.," in *Materialy po istorii professional'nogo dvizheniia v Rossii* (Moscow: VTsSPS, 1924), II, 214–15.

[90] Perazich, "Tekstil'shchiki v komissii Shidlovskogo," pp. 55 ff.

to direct the wage-rate struggle, and at the same time began to organize a trade union.[91]

This attempt, in which Liubimtsev had an active part, succeeded.

The campaign around the Shidlovskii Commission also had a strong influence on the political education of the Petersburg working masses, in particular in preparing them for the idea of a Soviet of Workers' Deputies:

> The majority of the electors issued a statement in which they gave an accounting to their constituents. Pointing to the ruinous consequences of the war precipitated by the government, to the loss of thousands of young lives, to the unemployment and hunger, to the military defeats, to the fact that all strata of the population were protesting against the policy that was destroying the country, and to the carnage of January 9, the workers' deputies emphasized their negative attitude toward all bureaucratic commissions, incapable of solving the vital problems. . . . The electors recommended that the workers insist on their demands: an eight-hour working day, factory inspectors from among the working class, state insurance, immediate termination of the war, freedom of assembly, freedom of speech and of the press, freedom of unions and strikes, freedom of conscience and inviolability of person and abode, free universal public education, and broad participation of the people in administration.
>
> The fiasco of the Shidlovskii Commission coincided with the Mukden defeat, which made the broad working masses especially receptive to the words of their deputies. But even apart from this, the Shidlovskii Commission had been of tremendous significance for the labor movement in Petersburg, and not only in Petersburg. It had drawn new strata of the city's workers into the movement. In the persons of the electors it gave the Petersburg workers . . . a new organization, better equipped for the tasks of the moment. True, many electors were arrested and exiled from Petersburg, but the model for an all-Petersburg organization through representatives of individual factories had been given, and the masses liked it. . . .[92]

The Bolshevik literature tends to ignore or minimize the role played by the campaign around the Shidlovskii Commission in popularizing the idea of workers' representation in factories and

---

[91] Kolokol'nikov, "Otryvki iz vospominanii, 1905–1907 gg.," pp. 213–14.
[92] Kol'tsov, "Rabochie v 1905–1907 gg.," pp. 199–200.

in paving the way for trade unions and for the idea of a Soviet of Workers' Deputies. Milonov writes that Kolokol'nikov "exaggerates the role of the Shidlovskii Commission" in these matters: "It is much more accurate to connect the emergence of both these institutions [trade unions and the Soviet of Workers' Deputies] with the strike movement of January and October."[93] But to *counterpose* the strike movement and the elections to the Commission in this way is to distort historical truth. In reality they were intimately related. The electoral campaign stimulated the strike movement, and the strike movement strengthened the idea of making factory representation a permanent institution. Two Bolshevik authors have recently painted a vivid picture of this process, using archival data inaccessible before the Revolution. Their view of the labor movement in Petersburg in 1905 is very biased, but they have put together a great deal of factual data and have done it well:

At the assembly of February 14, 1905, the workers of the L. Nobel plant decided to create a permanent commission of workers "to eliminate misunderstandings between the management of the plant and the workers and also to set pay rates for new articles of production." The workers of the Beyer copper-smelting works, having declared a strike, demanded of the owners "that deputies be elected from among the workers of all the shops, who would have an equal voice with the management and in turn defend the interests of the workers. So that the factory management could not dismiss workers without the consent of the deputies." Factory commissions were formed at the Putilov plant, the Semiannikov plant, the Baltic shipyards, the Okhta mills, and other enterprises.

The factory commissions actively intervened in matters of intra-factory life. They directed the strike struggle of the workers, drew up the demands [presented] in their name to the factory management, took part in clearing up conflicts between workers and owners, gave material help to strikers and their families. Thus, on February 23, 1905, the factory commission of the Baltic shipyards demanded that the management institute personal immunity for deputies and all other workers, that it create a free factory hospital and an elementary school for all workers' children, abolish fines and overtime work, raise wages, especially for unskilled workers and

---

[93] Milonov in the introduction to the Kats and Milonov collection, *1905. Professional'noe dvizhenie*, pp. 22–23.

women, abolish humiliating searches, hire "persons deported for the workers' cause," and so on.[94]

In this way the campaign around the Shidlovskii Commission introduced some elements of organization into the mass labor movement and new organizational concepts into the social consciousness of the masses. The impact of the campaign on the Social-Democrats' organizational ideas was less obvious. In the Bolshevik faction it was hardly felt at all. What elements of progress had begun to emerge during the campaign were short-lived. In May, 1905, the so-called Third Party Congress, as we have seen, returned to the conceptions dominant in Bolshevism before the campaign.

But the campaign had a notable effect on Menshevik thought. It stimulated its quest for organizational forms that would insure closer contact with the masses. This was, however, a laborious and barely beginning process, which entered its next phase at the Menshevik All-Russian Conference of Party Workers in May. Yet the *Iskra* article "What Shall We Do with the Shidlovskii Commission?" had already advanced, if still in embryonic form, the notion which was soon to become a basic principle of Menshevism, namely, that the forces of Social-Democracy should be maximally "utilized" to promote a mass movement far exceeding the Party—in contrast to the Bolshevik principle of maximally "utilizing" every manifestation of the mass movement to strengthen the Party organization.

[94] E. I. Shalaeva and I. P. Leiberov, "Profsoiuzy Peterburga v 1905 g.," *Voprosy Istorii*, October, 1955, pp. 19–20.

CHAPTER 3

The Strike and Trade-Union
Movements and Social-Democracy

THE events of January 9 were set off by a strike at the Putilov plant, which in turn had begun over a relatively minor incident (the dismissal of four workers) but had soon grown into a movement that spread to other Petersburg factories and, after Bloody Sunday, reverberated across the land. These strikes were part of a nationwide unrest that had been growing intermittently since the beginning of the century, had flared up in the summer 1903 in a series of general strikes in southern Russia and the Caucasus, abated, then flared up again in the latter half of 1904. The major event in the new upsurge was the Baku oil workers' strike in December, 1904. It developed into a general strike in Baku, which stimulated the unrest in other industrial centers and soon fused with the movement sparked by the Petersburg events.

Social-Democracy and the Strike Movement

It is a surprising feature of the strike movement that it developed despite the almost total absence of even rudimentary trade unions. The illegal Social-Democratic organizations made up for them to some extent. They existed in virtually every industrial center of any size and wielded a far greater influence in the

129

workers' world than their relatively small membership seemed to warrant. Hence it often fell to these little underground organizations to unify and partly direct the labor movement.

Both branches of Social-Democracy supported the strikes, sometimes initiated them, and tried to bring some organization into the movement. The Bolsheviks, however, tended more and more to "utilize" it for the political struggle. The Mensheviks, while not forgetting the political import of the strikes, stressed satisfaction of the workers' immediate economic needs. The differences were more of emphasis than of principle; they were unformulated and partly unconscious.

During the Baku strike the differences of principle became clear. Before going into them, I must point out that the Baku strike was unusual in several ways. Though it came in the wake of earlier, spontaneous outbreaks of labor unrest, it was the first large-scale strike in Russia that did not begin spontaneously. It was planned, organized, and successfully carried out by the Menshevik RSDRP Organization of Balakhany and Bibi-Eibat Workers, while the Bolshevik Baku Committee, which was against starting it, gave it only scant support after it had started and wanted to end it too soon. The great majority of workers in the oil industry unquestionably sided with the Menshevik Organization.[1] (See Appendix 6, pp. 301–14, for details.) The Baku strike was also the first in which Mensheviks and Bolsheviks tried out their ideas on the role of mass strikes in bringing about a revolution. The tactics dictated by their divergent conceptions remained a subject of controversy throughout 1905.

---

[1] Years later, a Bolshevik historian wrote: "The official history of the Party organization recognizes that in Baku 'at the end of 1904 there were two to three thousand Mensheviks and Shendrikovites and only two to three hundred Bolsheviks.' True, by the end of 1905 the Bolshevik organization counted in its ranks not less than two thousand people; but, again according to history, 'the Shendrikovites in fact led (until early 1906) the Baku workers in their economic struggle.'

"The same is told by Bolsheviks, members of the Bolshevik organization of that time. A. Rokhlin writes: 'To be frank about it, from the end of 1904 until the beginning of 1906 the Shendrikovites in fact led the masses of Baku, while we, with all our *political* influence, were forced (at least in the area of the economic struggle) to fall into line with their front.'" (V. Nevskii, *Rabochee dvizhenie v ianvarskie dni 1905 goda* [Moscow: Vsesoiuznoe Obshchestvo Politkatorzhan i Ssyl'noposelentsev, 1930], pp. 309–10.) "Shendrikovites" was a term applied to the Mensheviks in Baku; it was derived from the name of the brothers Shendrikov, the leaders of the Menshevik organization in that city. Nevskii is quoting from the collection *Dvadtsat' piat' let bakinskoi organizatsii bol'shevikov* (Baku, 1924), pp. 24, 79.

The Mensheviks observed the rising labor movement with hope and were eager to help it to organize, sure that it would lead to increased socialist consciousness and to a desire for vaster labor organizations, which were bound to be socialist in spirit. The Bolsheviks, on the other hand, observed its development with mixed feelings—with hope of course but also with some trepidation—for two reasons: first, fear that the "elemental" spontaneous labor movement, with its emphasis on economic demands, might result in bourgeois rather than socialist consciousness and in bourgeois leadership of the masses (see Appendix 9, pp. 325–30); second, fear of "dispersal of strength," of using up prematurely the revolutionary energies of the working class needed for the "decisive blow" which only a well-organized party could correctly prepare and time. These considerations explain the Bolsheviks' seemingly incomprehensible policy in Baku in late 1904.

The same general attitude toward mass movements—which under the Russian conditions were perforce spontaneous or semi-spontaneous—determined the Bolsheviks' party work in Russia after January 9, 1905, and the decisions of the so-called Third Party Congress in the spring. The Petersburg events had erupted against a strike background and in turn had greatly intensified the strike movement, which everywhere combined political and economic issues. The Petersburg Committee could not actually oppose it. As Zemliachka said somewhat wistfully at the Congress, "After January 9, strikes kept breaking out. It was hard to hold them down."[2] The Petersburg Committee reacted to them with frequent leaflets, all of which concentrated on political and studiedly ignored economic demands.[3] In Moscow a wary attitude was even more pronounced. Lunacharskii approved it in his speech at the Congress, "On the RSDRP's Attitude to Armed Uprising":

> A spontaneous strike over individual economic demands is a weapon in the class struggle of a still backward proletariat, and no theories of stages can make us view such a strike as some sort of

---

[2] *Tretii s"ezd RSDRP. Aprel'-mai 1905 goda. Protokoly* (Moscow: Gospolitizdat, 1959), p. 135.

[3] *Listovki bol'shevistskikh organizatsii v pervoi russkoi revoliutsii 1905–1907 g.g.*, I: *Ianvar'-iiul' 1905* (Moscow, 1956), 217–28.

perfection. The Moscow Committee, which has been attacked by *Iskra* for discouraging disorganized striking at present, is in our opinion acting just right in this respect. A political mass strike [on the other hand] is the weapon of a more or less politically advanced proletariat, and we can conceive of it only in conjunction with an armed uprising.[4]

The attitude to the ongoing strikes with their stress on economic demands was not discussed at the Congress but merely touched upon in the debates on an armed uprising. Both reporters on the question of an uprising, and all the delegates who spoke on the subject, considered only *political* strikes and their role in the uprising.

Lunacharskii's description of the semispontaneous strike

---

[4] *Tretii s"ezd RSDRP . . . 1905 . . .* , p. 105. According to n. 48 to the protocols of the Congress, Lunacharskii was referring to a Moscow correspondent's report in *Iskra*, No. 93, March 17/30, 1905. The workers connected with the legal (Zubatov) organizations had been extremely restive since January 9; a meeting was scheduled for March 12, at which fifty board members of these societies, rabid Zubatovites to a man, were to be present, and four hundred representatives of other societies, mostly of non-Zubatovite orientation. The meeting was to work out the definitive formulation of the political demands discussed at previous meetings of these societies and to decide whether to include the crucial demand for a constituent assembly and to support it by "an almost general political strike" (immediately or potentially is not clear from the report). Some participants in the earlier meetings had asked Menshevik friends if the Party wouldn't help them with leaflets and agitators to get this demand included. The Mensheviks had consulted the Moscow Committee, which was entirely Bolshevik at the time. *Iskra*'s correspondent continued: "We pointed out that a strike with categorical demands [*ul'timativnye trebovaniia*] would (1) draw into the political struggle led by Social-Democracy . . . tens of thousands of workers still lagging behind even the legal societies; [and] (2) greatly enhance the self-awareness of the Moscow proletariat, which would unite in actual fact around one political slogan and realize from experience that there was nothing left for it but an armed uprising. But the Committee resolved to reject the proposal. The reasons: a general or almost general strike could, in its opinion, jeopardize the armed uprising by (1) weakening the organization, since there would be arrests, and (2) deflating the [workers'] mood because of the lack of concessions [on the part of the government] and the losses sustained. [The Committee] thought, moreover, that an ultimatum to the government would lower the revolutionary spirit of the masses by raising hopes that the government might satisfy the demands and that in general it would mean entering into negotiations with the government that were unworthy of Social-Democrats. Therefore, the Committee decided that [the societies' meeting had better] just pass a resolution on the necessity of armed uprising, with no strikes or ultimatum."

Iskra also carried a letter about a strike at the Morozov textile mills in Orekhovo-Zuevo (in the Moscow Committee's area), of which the Committee disapproved. *Iskra*'s correspondent said quite plainly: "In general the Moscow Committee considers that workers should now be kept from striking because strikes supposedly harm the future armed uprising."

movement as "disorganized striking" was topped by A. A. Bogdanov, the other reporter on armed uprising. (Lunacharskii discussed the political, and Bogdanov the technical, problems of it.)
He called the Petersburg strikes following January 9 "anarchic
striking" and gave such a distorted account of them that one
cannot read it without amazement: "All it took was for one
worker to cry, 'Fellows, stop working!' and a strike was on, and
anyone who spoke up against it was dubbed *provocateur*." Bogdanov insisted that Social-Democrats must propagandize "the
importance of discipline for saving and concentrating the revolutionary forces," unabashed by "unreasonable accusations that
they are slowing down the development of the revolutionary
mood of the masses."[5]

The delegate of the Caucasus Union, L. B. Kamenev, also
sharply criticized the strikes:

> The broad masses of the January strikers had labor demands but no
> particular proletarian policy. The workers' January demands did
> not exceed the limits of what is admissible from the bourgeois point
> of view. They lacked the idea characteristic . . . of S-D proletarian
> policy—that no real improvement in the situation of the working
> class is possible under the capitalist system.

And here danger lurked:

> Unless Social-Democracy takes the present movement in hand, we
> are running the risk that the worker will enter the revolutionary
> movement with only bourgeois-democratic demands, without ad-
> vancing a political platform of his class. . . . The spontaneous
> mass movement of the working class will not carry us on its
> shoulders, or, rather, it isn't *us* it will carry.[6]

The resolution "On the RSDRP's Attitude to Armed Uprising,"
proposed by Lunacharskii, had been drafted by Lenin: the Congress was to resolve that

> organizing the forces of the proletariat for a direct struggle against
> autocracy *by means of political mass strikes and armed uprising*
> . . . is one of the important tasks of the Party at the present
> revolutionary moment. Therefore the Congress enjoins the CC
> [Central Committee] and also local committees and unions to

[5] *Tretii s"ezd RSDRP . . . 1905 . . .*, p. 110.
[6] *Ibid.*, pp. 147–48.

begin preparing a political mass strike as well as organizing special groups for acquiring and distributing arms, working out a plan of armed uprising, and directing it.[7]

Here, strike and uprising stand side by side in the scale of political values. Preparing for them is a single task, "one of the important tasks of the Party." Some members of the Congress objected to this formulation as giving too much weight to political strikes at the expense of the armed rising. A compromise resolution was passed, to the effect that it was "one of the most important and urgent tasks of the Party" ("most" and "urgent" were added) to organize the proletariat—and so on, as in Lenin's draft—but that autocracy was to be fought not by "political mass strikes and armed uprising" but simply by armed uprising. Thus it no longer was "one of the important tasks" to prepare political strikes. They were mentioned only in the concluding (new) part of the resolution, in which the Congress enjoined all Party organizations to

> *a*) clarify to the proletariat, by means of propaganda and agitation, not only the political significance but also the practical, organizational side of the coming armed uprising;
> *b*) *clarify in this propaganda and agitation the role of political mass strikes, which may be of great importance at the beginning and in the actual course of the uprising;*
> *c*) take the most energetic measures toward arming the proletariat and also toward working out a plan of armed uprising and closely directing the same, forming special groups of party workers for this purpose, as the need arises.

The changes in the resolution show the downgrading of political strikes in the Bolsheviks' view of the Party's tasks.

This wary attitude to the growing strike movement prevailed among the leading Bolsheviks right up to the general strike in October. It was not, however, a hostile attitude. In the climate of 1905, a hostile attitude was psychologically impossible for a revolutionary party. In many places the Bolsheviks found themselves drawn into the strikes and playing an active part in them despite themselves, as it were—especially where they made up most of the Party organizations, as, for instance, in central Russia.

---

[7] *Ibid.*, p. 104 (original draft of the resolution), p. 162 (compromise draft), and pp. 450–51 (final text); italics added.

A case in point is the economic general strike in Ivanovo-Voznesensk in May/June, 1905, the most important event in the economic strike movement in Russia (excluding Poland) between January and the political general strike of October, 1905. The Social-Democratic organization in Ivanovo-Voznesensk was not large, but it was the only revolutionary organization of any influence in the city, and its leaders were Bolsheviks to a man. At its head stood a "group" (changed into a "committee" only during the strike, when it had become more important) subordinated to the distant and rather sluggish Northern Committee (whose competence extended over Vladimir, Iaroslavl, and Kostroma provinces). The organization was unique among the Social-Democratic organizations of the time in that factory workers were more influential in it than *intelligenty*. M. K. Dianova noted this in her study "The Life and Work of the Ivanovo-Voznesensk Social-Democratic Bolshevik Organization in 1905," included in a collection published by the local Istpart in 1925:

> Until the end of 1904 there was a complete absence of *intelligenty* in the organization, they appeared only at the end of 1904, and until mid-1905 there were so few of them that one could count them on one's fingers. In mid-1905, they appeared and began to help with the organization's work. . . . The newly arrived professionals did provide leadership in the work, but because it was the kind of town where no newcomer remained unnoticed, they did not last long and either had to leave Ivanovo after a short while or were arrested.
>
> The Ivanovo workers, who had been left to their own devices until the general strike, were exceptionally active and tenacious in pursuing their goals; they developed into stalwart cadres of revolutionaries and organizers directing the labor movement.[8]

This made for a greater closeness than usual between the "Group" and the workers, but even so the strike arose in a largely spontaneous fashion, getting organized as it progressed and bringing its own leaders to the fore instead of being led by the Party organization. In fairness to the latter it has to be said, however, that it stepped in at the right time.

On May 11 the Group called a meeting of workers, including

---

[8] *1905 god v Ivanovo-Voznesenskom raione* (Ivanovo-Voznesensk: Istpart, 1925), p. 80.

those who did not belong to the organization. It was decided to strike all the textile mills, and the strike began the next day. This in itself shows how ready the workers were for it—the Group had only to pick up the idea. Yet the Group paid no attention to the elections of workers' delegates [*upolnomochennye*] on the fourteenth, in which Social-Democratic workers took an active part.[9] (These elections were held partly at the suggestion of the senior factory inspector and with the governor's consent.) When two members of the Group were elected, the Group's leader, M. V. Frunze, actually expressed alarm that their duties might interfere with their work in the Group. It was no accident that both the chairman of the *Sobranie Upolnomochennykh* ("Assembly of Delegates") and its secretary (later, its three secretaries) were non-party people. (See Appendix 11, pp. 335–38, for details.)

In the twenties, Communist literature began to depict all this quite differently. Dianova writes, for instance:

> The overall leadership of the strike remained in the hands of the Party organization and was implemented through the Soviet of Workers' Deputies [*sic*]. Every night, after the meeting, the local

---

[9] Dianova says, it is true, that the elections were held under the guidance of cell members, to whom the Group had "given the directive to get mostly non-party sympathizers elected as deputies, saving Party members for other party work" (*ibid.*, p. 75). But this was written in the early twenties, when the groundwork for the myth about the Ivanovo-Voznesensk "Soviet of Workers' Deputies" (see Appendix 11, pp. 335–38) was already being laid. Where Social-Democratic cells existed, their members no doubt took part in the elections and did not refuse to serve if they were elected—that would have been psychologically impossible and would not have been understood by the masses. But there certainly was no "directive" from the Group, least of all to elect non-party and save Party people. Fedor N. Samoilov, who was both a delegate from his mill and a member of the Group (and later a delegate from the workers of Vladimir Province to the Fourth Duma), corroborates this in his reminiscences, *Po sledam minuvshego*, p. 70 (I am quoting from the 1948 edition): "On May 14 the strikers elected one hundred fifty deputies to conduct negotiations with the authorities and direct the strike. This was done with the knowledge and consent of the governor, who had guaranteed the personal immunity of the workers' deputies. The elections of deputies were held at the mills, under the guidance of the local Party cells. There had been no special instructions in this matter from the Group of the Northern Committee, and it had not discussed the composition of the Soviet of Deputies. When I saw M. V. Frunze and told him that I and S. Balashov ("Strannik") had been elected deputies by the workers of our mill, Mikhail Vasil'evich asked in a puzzled way: 'But, Arkhipych—both of you are members of the Group, who is going to work in the Group then?'

"In reply to my remark that the workers trusted us and had elected us unanimously and that we would manage to work both in the Assembly of Deputies and in the Group, Frunze said, after some reflection: 'I guess it is just as well—through you, the Group will be linked more closely to the Assembly of Deputies and, through the Assembly, with the mass of the workers as well.'"

Group held a conference by a fire deep in the woods, at which the results of the struggle for that day were summed up, the further course of the strike was discussed, and proclamations on topical issues were composed; late at night [the Group] dispersed to sleep in various places, avoiding their own homes so as not to be arrested. Early in the morning they were already at the plenum of the Soviet of Workers' Deputies, explaining the directives of the Party organization; and at the meeting later in the day these directives were carried out. . . .[10]

This is something hardly imaginable for 1905. It was the actual strike leaders who met at night in the woods; any comrade able to give useful advice, whether a member of the Group or a visitor (lecturers often came to the town at that time), was probably included in the discussions; but all this was quite informal, not in the least like *Group conferences* making *decisions* and working out *directives*. What is true is that the Group issued the leaflets to help the strike.[11] Quite a few came out, and all were signed by the Group—though most of them, as far as their content went, could just as well have been signed by the *Sobranie Upolnomochennykh*.

In Ivanovo-Voznesensk the Bolsheviks were friendlier to the strike movement than anywhere else at the time. The strike had repercussions in other textile centers, of Vladimir and especially of Kostroma provinces. Yet even this did not change their basic misgivings about mass strikes, whether economic or political—as their behavior in the political general strike in October would show.

The general strike was preceded, in September and early October, by spirited economic strikes in Moscow and Petersburg

---

[10] *1905 god v Ivanovo-Voznesenskom raione*, p. 76. Dianova depicts the 1905 events in the light of the organizational ideas developed later, under the Communist dictatorship, with its sharp demarcation of Party members from non-party people. "The most active elements at the mills were the members of the organization and the sympathizers who had not yet joined the Party but were preparing for it and often attended circles and mass meetings" (*ibid.*, p. 75). For 1905, this sounds fantastic: no one "prepared" to join the Party, and usually there was no formal joining—workers were drawn into the circles, and those who attended regularly were considered members of the organization.

[11] Eight such leaflets are printed in *1905 god v Ivanovo-Voznesenskom raione*, pp. 357–65. Possibly the leaflets were issued in the name of the Group because only the Group had an illegal printing press and the *Sobranie* could not have issued leaflets without the Group's help.

(always with an admixture of political demands, sometimes included merely for the record) and by the general railroad strike announced on October 7 by the central bureau of the railroad workers' union. The decision to call a nationwide general strike came hard to the revolutionary organizations: too much was at stake, and the risk was great since there was no certainty that the masses were ready to respond. The Bolsheviks argued, in addition, that a great strike might eclipse the idea of an armed uprising.

Twenty years later a Bolshevik historian, A. Shestakov, himself a participant in the 1905 events in Moscow, admitted that the Bolshevik Moscow Committee "may have been overcautious in this matter."[12] "Both the Petersburg and the Moscow Bolshevik Committees adhered to wait-and-see tactics and perhaps erred on the side of caution. The PC's call to a general strike did not come out until October 9 or 10."[13] Even this is doctoring history a little. As we shall see, the decision was made on October 10 in Moscow and not until October 12 or 13 in Petersburg.

Shestakov quotes from the reminiscences of a party worker of the Bolshevik Moscow organization, B. A. Breslav ("Zakhar"): "For a long time there was no appeal for a general, concerted strike, from an organ carrying authority in the eyes of all the Moscow workers. Only the Bolshevik MC of the RSDRP was such an organ, and it was undecided on this question." When the nationwide railroad strike had already been announced,

> a meeting of the MC rather heatedly discussed the question: Should the MC at this time, considering the conditions in Moscow, call the Moscow proletariat to a general strike? By a majority of 7 to 2 it was decided to refrain from such an appeal . . . An end was put to this indefinite situation on October 10, at a general conference of the Moscow organization attended by as many as eight hundred to one thousand persons, when it was unanimously decided to announce in the name of the MC a general strike from twelve noon on October 11.[14]

---

[12] A. Shestakov, "Vseobshchaia oktiabr'skaia stachka 1905 goda," in M. N. Pokrovskii (ed.), 1905. Istoriia revoliutsonnogo dvizheniia v otdel'nykh ocherkakh, II: Ot ianvaria k oktiabriu (Moscow-Leningrad: Gosizdat, 1925), p. 280.

[13] Ibid., p. 190.

[14] Ibid., pp. 285–86. Evidently this was not yet the end of the wavering. In the section on October, 1905, in M. N. Pokrovskii (ed.), 1905. Materialy i dokumenty,

The Petersburg Bolsheviks found it even harder to come to a decision. The story is vividly told by Vladimir Voitinskii, later an economist of international repute but at the time a student at Petersburg University and a popular Bolshevik speaker at meetings (under the name of Sergei Petrov). On October 11 he spoke at a meeting at the Military Academy of Medicine. The immense auditorium was packed, mostly by workers of the Vyborg sector (after the Neva sector, the most advanced sector of the local Social-Democratic organization). The railroad strike had already paralyzed most of the main junctions; the Petersburg junction was grinding to a standstill, and the workers' mood was tense. Voitinskii was asked to speak on political strikes:

Feeling that the workers had to be given a straight answer to the question that was worrying them but not daring to take the responsibility in such a serious matter, I asked a comrade to go at once to the secret meeting place [iavka] of the Petersburg Committee and ask for instructions on what to say about the strike. While waiting for the reply, I began a speech on political strikes in general as one of the weapons of the proletariat. When I had finished, the chairman (also a Bolshevik Social-Democrat) proposed that the audience be sounded about the mood at the factories. Speeches from the audience began.

After an hour, the comrade I had sent to the Committee returned; the answer he brought was this: "The Petersburg Committee is concluding the discussion of the question, directives will be sent in half an hour."

A half-hour, then an hour, passed. No news from the Committee. Meanwhile the meeting was going on. The speakers were almost exclusively workers—and all said the same thing: A strike is imperative, a strike must be announced immediately, the Petersburg workers cannot lag behind other cities!

"Now let the *Party people* speak! Let the comrade *orator* tell us!"

I was asked to take the floor. Yielding to the general impulse

---

III: *Bol'shevistskie proklamatsii i listovki po Moskve i Moskovskoi gubernii* (Moscow-Leningrad: Gosizdat, 1926), p. 282, we read: "Only after the all-city conference of October 10, apparently on October 12 or 13 [the Moscow Committee] issued two appeals . . . 'To All Moscow Workers' ['Ko vsem moskovskim rabochim'] and 'A General Strike' ['Vseobshchaia zabastovka'], urging the proletariat to begin a general strike and boldly repulse the government's offensive." The two leaflets are in the same collection, pp. 289–90.

despite myself, I began my speech: "Comrades! What can I add to what has already been said? *Hail to a general strike!*"

Thunderous applause. People rise from their seats.

At that moment a student comes running to the chairman's little table, hands him a folded note, whispers something in his ear. The chairman glances at the note, makes as if to hand it to me, changes his mind, puts the paper aside, and continues listening to my speech.

When I had finished he gave me the note. It said, *literally:* "*Directive to agitators—Clarify pros and cons of striking. PC of the RSDRP.*"[15]

The Petersburg Committee vacillated throughout the next day. Only in the evening of the twelfth or in the small hours of October 13 did it finally decide to call a strike.[16]

---

[15] V. S. Voitinskii, *Gody pobed i porazhenii* (Berlin: Gzhebin, 1923), I, 95–96. Soviet authors generally avoid mentioning the unfortunate "clarify pros and cons of striking." An exception is E. Krivosheina, *Peterburgskii Sovet Rabochikh Deputatov v 1905 godu* (Moscow: Voprosy Truda, 1926), p. 80.

[16] At the time I was a student at Petersburg University and the Bolshevik "chief agitator" of the Peterburgskaia Storona sector, very active in the meetings campaign. About noon on October 12 the meeting agitators gathered as usual to receive the last instructions of the Petersburg Committee and to plan who would speak where (meetings were going on at several institutions of higher learning). We kept in touch with the PC through the "chief agitators" of the PC (themselves members of the Committee). There were two of them at the time: Anton (P. A. Krasikov) and Ruben (B. M. Knuniants). We waited for an hour or so but no one came. Probably a conference of the PC was in progress, and both Anton and Ruben were waiting for its decision. We knew of the "Clarify pros and cons of striking" directive of the day before but felt sure it would be changed. Reluctant to disobey it, however, we discussed the matter among ourselves and decided to use the formula "Hail to *organizing* a strike."

I went to the Technological Institute, where several meetings were already going on. After strolling around a bit to glean information, I went to one of the ze auditoriums. A Menshevik, S. M. Zaretskaia, was making a remarkable speech, appealing to the audience to support a general strike. I remember I listened with a feeling of envy: bound by the PC's directives, I would not be able to speak as she did. When she had finished, I took the floor in the name of the Bolsheviks and spoke rather fervently of the enormous importance of the strike and the need to prepare and conduct it in exemplary order and with complete success. The audience got the impression that I had said much the same as Zaretskaia and loudly applauded me. But when I stepped down, Igor (Boris I. Goldman, the representative of the CC in the Petersburg Committee and a member of the latter, subsequently known as the writer I. Gorev) came up to me and asked very crossly who had given me leave to make such a speech in the name of the organization, when I was in fact going against its directives. His tone was offensive, but I kept my temper and told him that a meeting of agitators a few hours earlier had decided to speak on *organizing* the strike—since none of us felt we could speak on the "pro and con" theme. I also said that if he was so furious about my speech, the speakers' rostrum was open to him as well as to me, and he could present his point of view. (*Note continued on p. 141.*)

The Mensheviks' attitude toward the strike movement evolved quite differently, but in their propaganda, too, there were echoes of the Bolshevik dogma that all attempts to improve the workers' lot would be fruitless until autocracy was overthrown. As early as February 17 (O.S.) Martov had written in *Iskra*, No. 88, in the article "What Shall We Do with the Shidlovskii Commission?" (discussed in the preceding chapter):

> We shall not tire of repeating to the proletariat that participating in the Commission will give it *absolutely nothing* in real improvements [italics here and below added]; we are constantly emphasizing that the workers can expect *no* real reforms to result from their participation in the Commission, that this participation will do something for them *only insofar* as it can be used to organize the workers and propagandize the workers' demands.

The "absolutely nothing" was less categorical than it sounded since it referred not to all improvements but to "*real* improvements," "*real* reforms." But this was merely a verbal evasion of the difficulty.

Mutatis mutandis, the argument was applied to the economic struggle as well, though only theoretically. It was completely forgotten whenever concrete economic demands supported by a strike (or the threat of one) were at stake. The Mensheviks took part very actively in the workers' economic struggle in 1904 and 1905. Surprisingly, however, the notion of supporting economic strikes received very little attention in the Menshevik press. *Iskra* barely mentioned it editorially; only its correspondents' reports

---

From Igor's reaction I concluded that the PC had not yet reached a new decision. But on the thirteenth a hectographed leaflet calling for a general strike was distributed—which meant that the Petersburg Committee had arrived at an affirmative decision either in the late evening of October 12 or during the night.

The leaflet, "Bastuite, tovarishchi!" is printed in the Leningrad Istpart collection *1905 god v Peterburge*, I: *Sotsialdemokraticheskie listovki* ([Leningrad-Moscow, 1925], pp. 308–9), with the comment that it came out "after October 9" [*sic*]. In the Leningrad Istpart collection *Listovki peterburgskikh bol'shevikov, 1902–1917*, I: *1902–1907* ([Leningrad: Gosizdat, 1939], p. 261), the same leaflet is dated "not later than October 9, 1905." In *Revoliutsiia 1905–1907 g.g. Dokumenty i materialy. Vserossiiskaia politicheskaia stachka v oktiabre 1905 goda* ([Moscow-Leningrad: Akademiia Nauk SSSR, 1955], I, 352), it is dated "not before October 8 and not later than October 12"; and in *Peterburgskie bol'sheviki v period pod"ema revoliutsii 1905–1907 g.g.* ([Leningrad-Moscow: Leningradskii filial IMÈLS pri TsK KPSS, 1955], pp. 337–38), "not later than October 12." All these notes attempt to obscure the fact that the leaflet came out *not before the twelfth,* or more precisely, *only on the thirteenth.*

from Russia show how active the Mensheviks were in this matter.

Supporting the strikes became for the Mensheviks one of the prime aspects of the blanket formula of "unleashing the revolution." Martov writes in his *History of Russian Social-Democracy:*

> All over Russia, and especially among the most backward strata of the proletariat, the impetus given by the Petersburg events brought forth a series of strike movements on economic grounds, which under the circumstances naturally turned into political movements. In connection with these movements *Iskra* launched the slogan "unleash the revolution." It meant encouraging the spread of these individual movements, despite their lack of co-ordination, as factors increasing the general disorganization of the reactionary forces and drawing new strata of the popular masses into the decisive struggle begun in the capital. "Seizure" by the agitated masses of the rights that the distracted government did not dare refuse them was pointed to as the most reliable method . . . of organizing the people widely and solidly in the course of the struggle for changing the political system of the country. The tactics *Iskra* recommended were based on the spontaneous tendencies of the movement itself, in the political as well as the economic sphere: by the "seizure method" the workers of large cities had in fact won a certain freedom of meetings, factory representation, and so on. . . .[17]

The Soviet literature represents these policies as hostile in principle to an uprising and contrasts them with the Bolshevik policies, which made an uprising their cornerstone. But whereas the Mensheviks felt that "unleashing the revolution" was the best way to a genuine uprising, the Bolsheviks thought that it was the Party's task to prepare an uprising in a centralized fashion.[18] The Menshevik slogan called for a positive, and the Bolshevik slogan

---

[17] L. Martov, *Istoriia rossiiskoi sotsialdemokratii* (2d ed.; Moscow-Petrograd: Kniga, 1923), p. 112.

[18] The resolution "O vooruzhennom vosstanii" of the Menshevik "All-Russian Conference of Party Workers," recognizing that it was the Party's task to prepare the masses for an uprising, stressed political, rather than organizational and technical, preparation as the foremost task:

"Taking into consideration (1) that timing a simultaneous nationwide uprising for a date set in advance, and doing this by the means available to a secret organization, is impossible—if only because the more advanced proletariat is weakly organized, and because the revolutionary movement of the popular masses, on whose quick involvement in the battle . . . our victory depends, can only be spontaneous in nature; (2) that it is the continual unrest of the masses and the growing disorganization of the forces of reaction that primarily create favorable conditions for a victorious uprising,

"Social-Democracy, in order to prepare the uprising, must first of all (a)

of "saving strength for the decisive blow" for a far warier, attitude toward semispontaneous, "uncontrolled" strikes. This profound difference was especially noticeable at the peak of the strike movement in September/October, 1905, which brought the first major, if indecisive, victory over tsarism—the Manifesto of October 17; while the Mensheviks helped the movement along, the Bolsheviks were passive, almost holding it back. This difference has been illustrated above. It will be shown in greater detail in chapter iv.

Social-Democracy and the Trade-Union Movement: Some Prehistory

In its full scope, the problem of whether to build up trade unions confronted Social-Democracy only during the great strikes of 1904–5, when the masses displayed a sudden urge to organize to defend their economic interests. On a smaller scale, Russian Social-Democracy had chosen to encourage trade unions as early as the nineties, in connection with the Jewish workers' unions in Lithuania and Poland, where conditions were most favorable for illegal labor organizations. Social-Democratic thought tended in that instance toward the idea of an indivisible economic and political labor movement and of a Social-Democratic party based on trade unions. When a Jewish Social-Democratic party was founded in 1897, it even assumed the name "General Jewish Labor Union in Russia and Poland" (later, "in Lithuania, Poland, and Russia"). In Russia proper, the problem hardly existed until 1905. Mutual-aid associations made up to some extent for the absence of trade unions. But their activity was severely limited by statutes which had to be approved by the Ministry of the Interior in every single case, and there was little that Social-Democracy as

---

expand its agitation among the masses on the basis of current political events; (b) link the independently arising social and economic movements of the proletariat to its own political organization and bring them under its influence; (c) reinforce in the masses the consciousness that a revolution is inevitable and that it is imperative to be always ready for armed defense, which can at any moment turn into an uprising. . . .

. . . .

"Only on the basis of such comprehensive work by Social-Democracy can the moment of the uprising be brought nearer, our leadership of it be facilitated, and the [Party's] technical military preparations for it acquire any serious significance." (*Pervaia obshcherusskaia konferentsiia partiinykh rabotnikov*, a separate supplement to *Iskra*, No. 100 [Geneva, 1905], pp. 18–19.)

such could do in them. The broader legal organizations that emerged here and there in the early years of the century were sponsored by the police to counteract the revolutionary movement, so that participating in them was out of the question for Social-Democrats. Only one illegal union came into being, after a successful strike of printers in September, 1903—the Union of Moscow Workers in the Printing Trade for the Struggle To Improve Labor Conditions. (It came out of the underground in 1905 and played a big role in the September/October strikes.) In this union the mutual relations of trade unions and Social-Democracy had to be defined quite early. I shall return to this topic.

In 1902 the Social-Democrats happened to get hold of a long confidential memorandum of the Ministry of Finances on the legalization of strikes and unions, with compulsory membership in the unions for all workers and, needless to say, various measures designed to insure the authorities' tight control over the unions. The Social-Democrats had to define their attitude to this new development. The memorandum was published in Geneva with a long article—a pamphlet, really—by Martov, outlining the possible tactics. In chapter v of this pamphlet, "What Kind of Unions Do We Need?" Martov protested against compulsory membership: workers must have the right to unite in "free, voluntary organizations." In chapter vi, the last, "How Shall We Use the New Law?" he wrote:

> If Witte's project becomes law, we advocate the following tactics:
>
> 1. Energetically demand that the police not interfere in strikes. . . .
>
> 2. Demand immunity from arbitrary police action for participants and leaders of strikes. . . .
>
> 3. Demand that appeals for financial support of strikes may be published in legal newspapers. . . .
>
> 4. Demand that cases of disorder and violence arising in connection with a strike be tried before juries. . . .
>
> . . . .
>
> 7. Demand the right for workers' societies to establish contact with other similar societies in Russia and abroad.
>
> . . . .
>
> Only such tactics will enable the workers to extract from the new laws at least some good for their economic struggle. And in

order to carry out these tactics it is necessary to organize *politically*, that is, rally more closely around the Russian Social-Democratic Labor Party. Behind every "official" workers' society let there be a secret workers' circle conducting agitation in that society and linked with the local committee of our Party. Let every instance of clashes with the government over a strike or a union be exposed on the pages of the "underground" press. . . . Let the government be forced, under the menacing pressure of the expanding political movement, to look the other way when Russian workers in "authorized" societies and by means of "authorized" strikes consolidate their battle positions for fighting capital.[19]

The dominant idea here is the political utilization of the proposed reform. There is an appeal to organize *politically* (underscored in the original) but no appeal to organize economically; an appeal to expose clashes with the government but not clashes with employers. At the end, it is true, fighting capital is mentioned. Probably the task was to be facilitated by the organizational plan: behind every "official" society a secret circle of agitators connected with the Social-Democratic committee. The whole program was evidently to be carried out within the Party framework or with the Party's guidance.

The proposed reform was not enacted, however, and at the Second Party Congress in 1903 the question of trade unions was treated in an even narrower context. Martov's resolution "On the Economic Struggle," from which I have quoted in chapter i, was adopted without debate.[20] True, it called the economic struggle "an inevitable consequence of the proletariat's position in a capitalist society" and "one of the chief means of counteracting the tendency of the capitalist system to lower the workers' living standards"; yet it entirely subordinated this struggle to the "leadership" of Social-Democracy:

Taking into consideration that the workers' economic struggle, if it develops apart from the proletariat's political struggle led by Social-Democracy, tends to break up the proletariat's forces and subordinate the labor movement to the interests of the propertied

[19] L. Martov, "Novaia pobeda russkikh rabochikh," in *Samoderzhavie i stachki. Zapiska ministerstva finansov o razreshenii stachek* (Geneva: Liga Russkoi Revoliutsionnoi Sotsialdemokratii, 1902), pp. xxiv–xxvi.

[20] *Protokoly 2-go s"ezda RSDRP* (Moscow, 1932), p. 547. Before being offered, Martov's resolution was signed by fifteen members of the Congress, some of them Bolsheviks.

classes, the Congress recognizes that, in the area of the economic movement, *it is the task of the RSDRP to direct the day-by-day struggle of the workers for the betterment of labor conditions* and to agitate for the removal of the obstacles that the laws of Russian autocracy are putting in the way of the trade-union movement—in other words [?], *to combine the individual skirmishes of separate groups of workers into a single organized class struggle.*

At the same time, in view of the increasingly obvious intent of the tsarist government to seize control of the economic struggle . . . the Congress recommends that all comrades continue the tireless struggle against Zubatovism . . . [continue] *to urge the workers to unite in a single class movement of struggle for the political and economic emancipation of the proletariat.* . . . Party organizations [should] support *and direct* strikes initiated by legal labor organizations [Zubatovite organizations?—S. S.]. [Italics added.]

Lenin had drafted an even more outspoken resolution, stressing the need to "secure the Social-Democratic character of the movement from the very first" (meaning the trade unions' subordination to the Party).[21] He did not offer his resolution, and the Congress adopted Martov's.

I have already mentioned the illegal Union of Moscow Workers in the Printing Trade, formed in 1903. Before 1905 it played a modest role in the printers' economic struggle,[22] but we cannot go into this. Here I merely want to illustrate how the Social-Democrats of that period approached the relationship between Party and trade-union organizations. In December, 1903, the "center" of the Union declared its solidarity with the RSDRP's program but added: "The Union considers it premature to join the RSDRP." This resolution was printed in *Iskra,* No. 57, January 15/28, 1904, with the editorial comment:

Now it remains for the Union to take one more step, a step it considers "premature" for the time being: join the ranks of the RSDRP. We have no doubt whatever that this step will soon be taken, because it inevitably follows from the correct understanding

---

[21] Lenin's draft of the resolution was first published in Vol. VI of *Leninskii Sbornik* (1927). See also Lenin, *Sochineniia* (4th ed.), VI, 429.

[22] On this union, see V. V. Sher, *Istoriia professional'nogo dvizheniia rabochikh pechatnogo dela v Moskve* (Moscow: Nauka, 1911), pp. 136–82. During and after the First Revolution Sher stood very close to the printer's trade-union movement in Moscow, and his book is valuable as a participant's testimony.

of political action in general and of the Social-Democratic program in particular.

Here the idea of trade unions belonging to the Party is taken as a matter of course by both sides. And if the Bolshevik *Vpered* had already been in existence, it probably would have reacted in the same way as *Iskra*. The Union, in No. 6 of its *Vestnik*, explained its reluctance to join the Party by the Party's lack of unity and the fear of losing its "independence." *Iskra* refuted these arguments in the article "The Moscow Printers and Our Party," in No. 79, December 1/14, 1904, but no longer sounded quite so sure that *unions* should belong to the Party: "We insistently appeal to the *members* of the Union to join the ranks of the Party" (italics added). For the Mensheviks, this was the beginning of the reversal—still tentative perhaps, by no means emphasized, and probably unnoticed by most readers. Basically, the idea of trade unions led by the Party was held in common by both wings of Social-Democracy until the upheavals of early 1905, when it was revised—in different ways—by both.

The First Steps of the Free Trade-Union Movement

Against the background of civic enthusiasm of the winter 1904/5 there appeared the first free labor organizations existing out in the open. They grew from three roots:

1) the weak legal mutual-aid societies, overcoming their limitations and turning into a semblance of trade unions;

2) the remnants of Zubatov-Gapon organizations, shedding their police origins and beginning to reflect the true feelings, and to protect the true interests, of the workers (a process that began before the Gapon organizations were closed as a result of Bloody Sunday);

3) the main root—the attempts to organize unions in the *fait accompli* way, partly in connection with the recently introduced workers' representation in factories and partly in imitation of the professional-political associations of the intelligentsia, which combined in January into the Union of Unions.

These developments seemed to invite Social-Democratic participation, but for a truly positive attitude toward free labor unions to emerge a psychological block had to be overcome—the ingrained fear that the economic struggle might distract the workers from the political struggle and even revive the ideas of the notorious "Credo" (1899), which rejected the very notion of a labor party in Russia.[23] ("All the talk about an independent labor party is nothing but the result of transferring to our soil the tasks and achievements of others." "For the Russian Marxist, there is only one way: participation, that is, assistance, in the proletariat's economic struggle and participation in the activity of the liberal opposition.") No matter that the foremost Economists had rejected the Credo's extreme formulations—the ghost of that conception continued to haunt Social-Democracy. The long struggle against Economism had ended in victory, but a residue of the struggle itself seemed to persist in the minds of the party workers.

---

[23] E. D. Kuskova was the author of the "Credo." She tried later to minimize its importance. In her review of F. Dan's book *Iz istorii rabochego dvizheniia i sotsialdemokratii v Rossii v 1900–1904 godakh* for the October, 1906, issue of *Byloe*, she related the origin of the "Credo": "Once, after a heated discussion, M. M. [Kuskova] was asked to formulate [her] views on the vexed questions, as it would be convenient to have something orderly and well-rounded to fall back on in arguments. M. M. alone, without anyone's participation and not for publication, hastily jotted down a résumé of [her] views. The scrap of paper [!] was taken by someone who had been involved in the discussion. The author of the 'views' set forth on the scrap had quite forgotten about its existence. . . . One day M. M. came across a 'protest' of seventeen Social-Democrats against some heretical 'Credo.' Reading it, M. M. saw to [her] amazement that the 'Credo' was nothing else than [her] own scrap of paper with the hastily jotted-down points for arguments. . . . Who had printed this 'Credo' and who had written this title on the scrap (the original had no title), M. M. does not know to this day. All the above is exact, for I who am writing these lines was the author of the 'Credo' . . ." (pp. 325–26).

Lenin, then in Siberia, had composed the sharp "Protest rossiiskikh sotsialdemokratov protiv 'Kredo'" together with other deportees. The protest, quoting the Credo in full, was published in *Rabochee Delo* (No. 4/5 [September/December, 1899]), the main organ of the Economists, and the editors indorsed it: "We heartily welcome this forceful protest of our comrades in Russia against the views set forth in the 'Credo,' in that attempt to distort the true character of the Social-Democratic movement in the West and in Russia. But we are firmly convinced that this 'profession of faith' represents nothing but the opinion of individuals, reflects merely the confusion of ideas in the heads of its authors. Such views testify only to the lack of scientific understanding and revolutionary political tact in these 'young oldsters' [p. 24]. . . . Such programs or, rather, such personal fantasies of political infants (even if of respectable age) have appeared before and will appear again— until Russian Social-Democracy reaches unified views on the basic tasks of the revolutionary movement in Russia, by working out a definite Party program and tactic" (p. 26).

In émigré circles this uncalled-for rudeness was taken as a symptom of the Economists' fear that the Credo's extremist ideas might be identified in the Party's infighting as their own—as indeed they were.

It made even the Mensheviks pause before plunging in to support the trade-union movement, to say nothing of the Bolsheviks, who had long since evolved a well-rounded anti-trade-union philosophy.

Only these feelings can explain the fact that it was the liberal-democratic *Osvobozhdenie* and not the Social-Democratic press that broached the subject of broad organization—this, in the article by Peter Struve "A Vital Task of the Times" (*Osvobozhdenie*, No. 63, January 7/20, 1905). Struve was still thinking in terms of legalized unions:

> This is how we visualize the matter: The local committees of the "Union of Liberation" enter into an agreement with the local Social-Democratic committees and, having enlisted in the cause some influential members of the intelligentsia and the more advanced workers, press for the authorization of economic labor organizations. . . . This movement, being an economic movement, must be formally non-political, but we have not the slightest doubt that it will be the main source of large and stable cadres for the Labor Party. *Intelligenty*, both Liberationists and Social-Democrats, will have in this movement only the role of initiators and conscientious helpers; very soon the whole movement is sure to pass in the most natural way into the workers' own hands; in fact, even the first steps of such a movement are possible only if there are elements in the working class that are ready for it.
>
> . . . .
>
> In saying that it is necessary for Liberationists to take the initiative in creating a trade-union movement, we are not at all giving them a "party" task or suggesting that they "raid" workers from Social-Democracy. In our opinion the economic organization of workers, no matter who does it or even how it is done, will almost certainly create cadres for *the Social-Democratic Party*.

The Menshevik *Iskra* (No. 84, January 18/31) disagreed with Struve in an ironical article, "A Grade-School Liberal Politician," which, however, did not contribute anything essentially novel to the discussion.[24] The Bolshevik *Vpered* simply ignored Struve's article.

---

[24] A discussion of the Liberationists' role in the trade-union movement would make us digress from our main topic, but since it cannot be ignored it is dealt with in Appendix 7, pp. 315–19.

The Mensheviks and the Organization of Trade Unions

Struve had put his finger on the sensitive spot that had to be dealt with by leaders who wanted to base the labor movement on the organized activity of the masses. Life itself had made trade unions an urgent issue, and the Mensheviks had to do more than just argue with the Liberationists about it. Barely a month after its polemical article, *Iskra* on its own initiative expressed the opinion that the Mensheviks should encourage trade unions (No. 88, February 17 [O.S.]). In the article "What Shall We Do with the Shidlovskii Commission?" Martov wrote:

> During the era of industrial boom, when the political pulse of our country was beating sluggishly, it was easy to get overinvolved in economic agitation among the politically inexperienced Russian proletariat, to follow the "line of least resistance," and lose sight of the Social-Democratic policy while organizing the struggle for individual economic improvements; but now that the proletariat is getting political impulses from all sides, when it is itself brimming with political discontent and is carrying on its struggle in conditions of complete economic bankruptcy among Russia's rulers—now, when this danger is past, we should use a good part of our forces to organize the economic self-defense of the working class, to unify its disjointed economic struggle, rally the broad proletarian masses around it, and link this struggle to the proletariat's basic political tasks of the moment. *At one time, the trade-union movement in Russia may have been historically antipodal to any kind of "politics,"* but now every new stride made by Russian society in the whirlpool of revolution [*sic*] is linking this movement more firmly to the nationwide political struggle; and our task, the task of Social-Democracy, is, precisely, *not to let [this movement] become a support of liberal-democratic politics* (to say nothing of reactionary monarchist politics). And this we can do only to the extent that we *use the political forces of our Party to lighten for the proletarian masses the work of organizing in trade unions* and bettering their condition themselves—[a work] they are doing so skilfully, taking advantage of the hour of autocracy's disintegration. [Italics added.]

This is still an attempt to vindicate retrospectively the wary, not to say inimical, view of "economics" in the labor movement (note the passages I have underlined), but that view is considered a thing of the past. The task of the future is to use the political resources of the Party to help the proletariat organize in trade unions.

The Mensheviks gave a large place in their plans to the *fait accompli* method. Unlike Struve, whose January article spoke of legally organized unions, *Iskra* said on March 3/16:

> One must openly, independently, asking no one's permission, organize mass meetings of workers. . . . Openly, and not secretly as before, organize among the broad masses of workers all kinds of trade unions, mutual-aid societies and funds; only where the money is should perhaps be kept secret, so that it cannot be taken away. One must organize in the open reading circles for workers, of legal and illegal literature alike. In general, one must try during this period to convert a great deal of what is now illegal into something that is, if not legal, at least quite open and broad, functioning thanks to the masses' revolutionary action.[25]

This did not mean renouncing attempts to legalize trade unions. It was merely an appeal not to let formal obstacles interfere; and in the climate of 1905 this was often possible.

The Menshevik All-Russian Conference of Party Workers, held in Geneva in April/May, recommended in its resolution "On Trade Unions" that all Party organizations

> 1) assist the workers in all their attempts to create unions for the defense of their economic interests and urge them to organize such unions despite the laws still extant prohibiting them;
>
> 2) arrange regular meetings of representatives of various trade unions or factories (elders, deputies, and so on) in order to establish continuous contact among them;
>
> 3) maintain continuous contact between Party organizations and trade unions and constant assistance to them by all the forces and technical means at the Party organizations' disposal;
>
> 4) require all Party-member workers to belong to trade unions existing or being formed at their places of employment;
>
> 5) have the trade unions that accept the Party program represented in the Party organization.[26]

---

[25] "Rabota v revoliutsionnoe vremia," an article by Moskal'—a pseudonym that was never decoded.

[26] See the special supplement to *Iskra* about the Conference, No. 100, May 15/28.

The fifth point still contained, in a greatly diluted form, the idea of Party trade unions. Before long, the Mensheviks were to discard it for good (unlike the Bolsheviks, as we shall see). It is true that certain former Economists evolved a variant: not trade unions subordinated to the Party but a Party based on trade unions; not so much "Party trade unions" as a Social-Democratic party in fact transformed into a trade-union party. This conception did not influence Menshevism as a whole, though there were remote echoes of it when the idea of a workers' congress was discussed (see chapter v).[27]

The fact that the Menshevik Conference adopted the resolution meant that the idea of "utilizing" trade unions to aggrandize the Party had been definitely abandoned; the relationship between Party and trade unions was to be built on co-ordination, not subordination; the Party was to assist in the creation of trade unions. This was the Mensheviks' firm policy from then on.

In early 1905, when the Gapon movement suddenly emerged as a true mass movement with an unexpectedly great revolutionary potential, the Mensheviks became more conscious than ever of the need to overcome the Party's remoteness from the masses. The campaign around the Shidlovskii Commission and the Mensheviks' keener interest in all forms of the labor movement helped to bridge the distance, but the process was not as rapid as it seemed to the party workers. The failure of the May Day demonstration proposed by the Menshevik Group made this painfully clear and led to more enterprising efforts at rapprochement. The party work was influenced in this direction by a resolution adopted on May 3/16 by a group of Menshevik agitators (S. I. Somov was its author). It was published in *Iskra,* No. 100, May 15/28, with a supporting editorial, "May Day Successes and Failures." This resolution is outstanding among the documents that shaped Menshevik "public opinion" in regard to the trade-union movement. I shall cite it in full:

> The failure of the May Day celebration this year has shown the lack of contact between the Party organization and the working

---

[27] The main champion of this conception was V. Akimov (Vladimir Petrovich Makhnovets), at one time the most enterprising spokesman for Economism and an editor of *Rabochee Delo,* who never did join the Mensheviks formally. See Appendix 8, pp. 320–24, for his views on the interrelations of the Party and the trade unions.

masses. This sad fact made the meeting of agitators of the City sector examine our methods of work more closely. Having discussed this question, the meeting has come to the following conclusions:

1. Until now the proletariat's struggle for its immediate needs has been carried on with little participation on the part of Social-Democracy, which has been losing contact with the life of the broad masses because of this.

2. Since, at the present time, underground work alone does not afford the masses enough participation in Party life, and in a sense leads to opposing the masses as such to the Party as an illegal organization, it is indispensable that [the Party] take in hand the workers' legal economic struggle, while strictly linking it to Social-Democratic aims.

3. To this end the Party must not only take a most active, direct part in already existing trade unions, funds, and so on, but also take the initiative in creating such organizations, which make it possible to unite broader masses on the basis of class interest.

4. In this connection, the meeting considers it necessary to emphasize the pressing need for further new steps toward democratizing our Party, so as to afford its members greater independence of action.

The strongly expressed wish for internal reform also met with *Iskra*'s approval. The Mensheviks stepped up their activity in the trade-union movement, and Menshevik thought began to search for new ways of organizing the masses and restructuring the Party accordingly. I shall return to this in chapter v.

The Bolsheviks and the Organization of Trade Unions

Far more arduous and tortuous was the road by which the Bolsheviks came to the acceptance—the forced acceptance, one might say—of trade unions as a positive factor in the labor movement. Throughout 1905 their stand was still based on Lenin's theory of spontaneity articulated in 1902 in *What Is To Be Done?*:

The *spontaneous* development of the labor movement leads to its subordination to bourgeois ideology, *it leads straight to the program of the "Credo,"* for the spontaneous labor movement is trade-unionism, is *Nur-Gewerkschäftlerei*, and trade-unionism means the ideological enslavement of the workers by the bourgeoisie. Hence it is our task, the task of Social-Democracy, to *fight spontaneity*, to *divert* the labor movement from this spontaneous tendency [to move] under the wing of the bourgeoisie, and draw it under the wing of revolutionary Social-Democracy.[28]

Lenin himself was not always disposed to pursue his formula to its extreme conclusions: in the section "Organizations of Workers and Organizations of Revolutionaries" he sought a compromise answer to the question of the Party's stand on the economic movement.[29] But the formula had a mystic power over the Bolshevik party workers as they faced the trade-union problem in 1905, as well as over the Bolshevik orientation in general.

The question was not on the agenda of the so-called Third Party Congress but it was touched upon in the resolution "On Overt Political Action by the RSDRP." Dissatisfied with a draft (never published) by P. P. Rumiantsev and with his own amended version of it, Lenin wrote a new draft, which proposed to use the available legal means of creating trade unions—and then, of course, to use the trade unions to strengthen the Party. This draft was not brought before the Congress. Another version, from which the first part of the proposal had disappeared, was unanimously adopted. It had been prepared by Lenin and Rumiantsev jointly. The difference between the two versions is so significant that I am quoting the corresponding sections for comparison:

Lenin's Draft	*Lenin-Rumiantsev Draft*
b) Utilize all legal and semi-legal ways of creating workers' societies, unions, and organizations and endeavor to insure (in one way or another) that Social-Democratic influence predominate in such unions. . . .[30]	b) Utilize all legal and semi-legal workers' societies, unions, and other organizations to insure that Social-Democracy's influence predominate in them. . . .[31]

Who persuaded Lenin to make the change, and on the basis of what arguments, has never been established, but the incident

---

[28] Lenin, *Sochineniia*, IV, 356.

[29] *Ibid.*, pp. 423–25. Since my book is concerned with the events of 1905, I can do no more than touch upon the conception Lenin expressed in *Chto delat'?* But this conception had such a deep influence on Bolshevik trade-union policy—especially, though not only, in the years of the First Revolution—that a brief reference is inadequate. It is therefore discussed somewhat more fully in Appendix 9, pp. 325–30.

[30] *Ibid.*, VIII, 345–46.

[31] *Tretii s"ezd RSDRP . . . 1905 . . . ,* p. 453.

shows that he wavered on one of the basic tenets of Bolshevik trade-union policy. His original draft remained unknown for over twenty years, until it was published in 1926 in Volume V of *Leninskii Sbornik*.

For a long time the Bolshevik press, both *Vpered* and *Proletarii*, which replaced *Vpered* soon after the Third Congress, simply ignored the problem of trade unions. *Vpered* never did discuss the Bolsheviks' attitude toward them, and only its last issue (No. 18, May 5/18) carried three items about trade unions. One was the resolution of a printers' union in Riga, recognizing the leadership of the Party Committee and pledging to "support the Committee by all the means at our disposal, such as: conducting Social-Democratic agitation among the working masses, distributing Committee publications and general Party literature, and being in the first ranks of the fighters for the people's freedom at the moment of the uprising." It also promised to "require every member of the Union to contribute fifty kopeks monthly toward Party needs and purchasing arms." The second item, also from Riga, was a declaration by a Social-Democratic union of railroad employees that it "unreservedly aligns itself with the local Committee of the Russian Party." The third was a report from Moscow, that a "Union of Railroad Employees of the Moscow Junction, attached to the Moscow Committee of the RSDRP," had been founded. The new union's appeal to all the railroad workers of Moscow to join the Party (!) was printed in the same issue of *Vpered*. I have never come across any other references to either a Riga or a Moscow railroad union belonging to the Social-Democratic Party.

Two months passed before *Proletarii* took up the issue. The lead article of No. 8, July 4/17, "The Trade-Union Movement and Social-Democracy," groped for a compromise solution:

> The trade-union struggle carried on entirely within the framework of bourgeois society . . . does not pass without effects on the self-awareness of the working masses. [It] makes bourgeois notions stick to the proletarian's psychology, which obscure his proletarian consciousness or prevent its development. The enthusiasm for the economic struggle is dividing the proletariat into trade groups, alienating it from its class interests, that is, its political interests; not only that, but it frequently turns [the proletariat] against the

political struggle and Social-Democracy. This opposition of the economic to the political movement bespeaks a profound crisis in the life of the proletariat as a class, its political defeat, in fact, even if it is accompanied by flourishing trade unions and the working masses' material prosperity.[32]

The author nevertheless concluded, after some unconvincing leaps, that it was necessary to "combine trade-union organizations with the political Party":

Close communion between the two types of organization, recognition by the first of the political leadership of the second, defense by the second of the economic interests of the proletarian class—in a word, *Social-Democratic* trade unions and a political *labor* party—that is the quickest way for the Russian proletariat to become a "class in itself," that is, a powerful social force capable of overthrowing the dominance of capital.

These verbal tricks proved too complex for the Bolshevik party workers, who drew straight anti-trade-unionist conclusions from the argumentation. A case in point was a resolution of the Conference of the Bolshevik Southern Committees in late July:

Granted that organizing trade unions . . . is one of the tasks of Social-Democracy, we consider, nevertheless, that in the present revolutionary period Social-Democracy must not take the initiative in creating trade unions—on the contrary, it must [emphasize in its agitation] that all the energy of the working class must now be concentrated on the political struggle and that organizing purely economic unions might weaken the revolutionary energy of the working class and divert its attention from the political tasks, which is precisely the reason for the liberals' and the government's protective attitude toward trade unions. As to already existing trade unions, and new ones that come into being without the influence of Social-Democracy, we must try to make use of these organizations to instil a revolutionary Social-Democratic consciousness in the broad masses of the working class.[33]

This anti-trade-unionist conception was very popular with the Bolshevik party workers at the local level but met with some opposition from the leaders, who were fearful that such a stand

---

[32] According to Iu. Kamenev's *Ukazatel'*, the probable author of this article was Orlovskii (V. V. Vorovskii).

[33] *Proletarii*, No. 15, August 23/September 5.

might isolate the Bolsheviks from the mass labor movement. At a meeting of the Bolshevik Odessa Committee in September, the speaker, Gusev ("S" in the protocols), who was close to the Bolshevik center abroad, proposed that the Bolsheviks be guided by the following rules in their stand on the trade-union question:

1. To expose in our propaganda and agitation all the illusions about trade unions, stressing especially their narrowness in comparison with the ultimate aims of the labor movement.

2. To clarify to the proletariat that a broad and stable development of the trade-union movement is unthinkable under an autocratic regime and that such a development requires first of all the overthrow of tsarist autocracy.

3. To strongly emphasize in propaganda and agitation that the most vital, primary task of the struggling proletariat is to prepare immediately for an armed uprising to overthrow tsarist autocracy and win a democratic republic.

4. To carry on an energetic ideological struggle against the so-called Mensheviks, who are reverting, on the issue of trade unions, to the narrow, erroneous viewpoint of the Economists, which demeans the tasks of Social-Democracy and holds back the thrust of the proletarian movement.

But at the same time:

5. To use every means to insure Social-Democratic influence and, if possible, leadership, in all the newly emerging or already existing legal and illegal trade unions.[34]

The last point evoked protests from the Committee. Here is an excerpt from the protocols of the meeting:

A.: "Comrade S. is overlooking the fact that Point 5 of his resolution flatly contradicts all the preceding points. What do they say? That one must expose, one must destroy, illusions, one must, in short, disarm the trade unions, in other words, demolish them. And Point 5 suddenly speaks of leadership. To me, a trade union has a definite content. If I assume its leadership, I am thereby taking on

---

[34] This resolution was believed lost, but in the mid-twenties a copy of it turned up in police archives. It is printed in the notes to Vol. VIII of the third edition of Lenin's *Sochineniia*, pp. 502–3, as well as in the collection *Vserossiiskaia politicheskaia zabastovka v oktiabre 1905 goda* (Moscow, 1955), I, 161–62, with one difference: in Point 4, the Economists' viewpoint is described as "restricting" (*suzhivaiushchaia*) not as "holding back" (*sderzhivaiushchaia*) the thrust of the proletarian movement.

this content, I must organize funds, and so on. This is a Menshevist misconception. . . ."[35]

Gusev managed to overcome the objections, explaining that the first four points referred to "principles" and the last to "practice." The resolution was unanimously passed and sent to Lenin in Geneva, who subjected it to severe criticism, showing more understanding of the role of trade unions than his followers in Russia. He wrote Gusev on September 30/October 13, 1905:

> We must beware of overstressing the struggle with the Mensheviks over this question. Trade unions are likely to start emerging very soon now. We must not stand aside from them and above all give no cause to think that one should stand aside, but try to participate, influence, and so on. . . . It is important for Russian Social-Democracy to strike the right note about trade unions from the very beginning, to create from the first a tradition of Social-Democratic initiative in this matter, of Social-Democratic participation, Social-Democratic leadership.[36]

But these views, like Lenin's draft of a resolution at the Third Congress, remained unknown to most of the party workers; they were insufficiently aired in Lenin's *Proletarii*, and were not published until the mid-twenties. Lenin's practical sense warned him that the negative policy toward trade unions would lead Bolshevism into an impasse; but, a captive of his own theory, he did not openly reverse it.

In 1905 this policy consisted mainly of propaganda in favor of Party trade unions: since it was politically impossible to oppose the formation of trade unions openly, the Bolsheviks settled for trade unions led by the Party. As we have seen, *Vpered* first acknowledged the emergence of unions by printing announcements about three Party trade unions, two of them in Riga.[37]

---

[35] "Perepiska N. Lenina i N. K. Krupskoi s Odesskoi organizatsiei," *Proletarskaia Revoliutsiia*, December, 1925, p. 62.

[36] Lenin, *Sochineniia*, XXXIV, 309.

[37] The idea of setting up trade unions subordinated to the local Committee of the RSDRP was especially hideous in Riga, where there also functioned organizations of Latvian Social-Democracy and of the Bund, at this time not even connected organizationally with the RSDRP and yet exercising more influence among the workers than the Riga Committee of the RSDRP, as the latter itself recognized in a report to the Third Congress first published as a supplement to the 1955 edition of the protocols of the Congress. The report is also in the 1959 edition, pp. 581–601.

Proletarii's editorial "The Trade-Union Movement and Social-Democracy" (see pp. 155–56 above) had evaded a plain answer to the question of Party trade unions. Its hazy formulations could not suffice for long, and the editors returned to the subject in No. 11 (July 27/August 9), in the article "The First Steps of the Trade-Union Movement," quoting a "standard statute" for such unions, proposed by the Bolshevik Saratov Committee:

> A union is a Party organization whose activity is under the control of the local Party committee; it is guided in its activity by the decisions of the committee, with the right of lodging complaints about them with the CC of the Party and with Party congresses. [Art. 8.]

There was to be a board consisting of a deputy of the local Party committee and four members elected by factory representatives (Art. 15). But even the factory representatives who were to elect the four board members were to be "appointed [only] upon agreement between the union members of the given factory and the local committee" (Art. 17). Moreover, the union was to contribute 20 per cent of all receipts to the fund of the local committee (Art. 11).

While "welcoming the initiative of the Saratov comrades," the editors of *Proletarii* had "serious doubts" about the formal rule that "a union is a Party organization":

> The Rules of our Party as well as the general principle on which it is built admit as Party members (consequently, also as members of a Party organization) only persons accepting the Party program and directly working for the Party. Hence identifying a trade union as a Party organization would limit the union's membership to conscious Social-Democrats. This in our opinion would be a mistake which in practice is bound to lead either to anemic trade unions or to diffuse Party organizations. Either [outcome] is undesirable. . . . In our opinion it would be better to consider trade unions not Party organizations but organizations connected with the Party. . . . Our task is to make the unions Social-Democratic in the sense of their recognizing the Party's guidance and the tenets of its program. If, however, a union consciously joins the ranks of the Party in order to fight for its interests, and becomes a Party organization on its own, then we can only rejoice in our victory.

This was the first flicker in the Bolshevik press of the thought that a harmful ideological "diffuseness" in Party organizations might result if trade unions formally joined the Party and had a voice in its policies. Unions merely "connected" with the Party and submitting to its "guidance" were preferable.

The idea was elaborated in *Proletarii*, No. 21 (October 4/17) in the article "The Trade-Union Movement and the Tasks of Social-Democracy," by M. Borisov,[38] which was flatteringly commented upon by the editors (that is, Lenin) and reprinted on November 21 in *Novaia Zhizn* when that first legal Bolshevik publication in Russia made its appearance. The author started from two contradictory premises: that the trade-union movement could easily divert the Party from the socialist to the general democratic path and that the movement was legitimate, necessary, and inevitable:

> The urge to unite in trade unions is now noticeable everywhere; workers are constantly attempting to form them, questions about them are asked at mass meetings, and so on. This phenomenon is far from fortuitous and cannot be ascribed to deficiencies in our Party organization, as some comrades believe. . . .

Hence:

> Taking trade unions into account as an inevitable fact of life, we must work out a definite attitude toward them and devise forms for them that will best serve the expansion of our Party. To begin with, we must renounce the myth of neutrality. We cannot stand on the sidelines, saying neither yea nor nay, and merely observe their emergence and development. If we consider them useful for the Party, we are obliged to help their inception as much as we can. Not friendly neutrality but active assistance—that must be our motto in regard to the trade-union movement.

While rendering "active assistance," one must remember, however, to "safeguard the trade-union movement from the influx of politically opportunistic elements." But, "unless we are able to inculcate into the trade unions our political and socialist program in its entirety"—and the author is sure that this is impossible—"it is better not to inculcate any [program], so as to have

---

[38] I have not discovered the identity of "Borisov"; he is alluded to as "a comrade active in Russia."

at least full freedom of agitation and not to feel we are in the company of official liberals." In addition, "While encouraging the creation of trade unions, we must restrict their activity to purely economic limits." The author then "goes even farther":

As I see it, we should not attach to trade unions the Social-Democratic label, even when a considerable majority of the members of a union subscribe to the Party program. We musn't forget that the stronger a trade-union organization becomes, the more independent significance it acquires in the eyes of its members. . . . The Social-Democratic slogan is "Proletarians of all countries, unite!" The German workers organized in trade unions have translated it into "*Pfennigs, unite!*" Yet most of them are Social-Democrats, read *Vorwärts*, call Bebel and Kautsky "*unsere Genossen*" (our comrades). Now imagine that these trade unions have officially adopted the Party program and belong to the Party. As Party units, they have the right to discuss the principles of Social-Democracy and to determine its tactics. You can see what a gorgeous liberal-bourgeois salad they would cook up if leadership of the Party's life fell into their hands! All the articles of the Erfurt program would be reappraised from a penny-saving standpoint; all the revolutionary dogmas would be sacrificed to a policy of "real interests." . . . Unionism would ruin the Party.

This argumentation had a strong impact on Bolshevik policy. It killed the idea of Party trade unions—though not right away: Borisov's plan called for "unofficial agents" in the unions. He said quite candidly: "Members of a trade union who belong to the Party, and officials of the union, use every means to insure Social-Democratic agitation in their union"; "the Party has unofficial agents in the union but no official representatives." This may have been the germ, too, of the idea of "cells" that later figured so prominently in Bolshevik trade-union policies.

But the Bolshevik leaders were still unable to reconcile the contradictions in their stand on trade unions that had been besetting them since the beginning of the revolution. Only on November 3/16 did the Bolshevik Central Committee publish in *Proletarii*, No. 25 (its next-to-last issue), the draft of a resolution on trade unions it had "submitted to the Party organizations." This was its first document on the subject. The announcement was unusual and denoted hesitancy. What did "submitted to the

Party organizations" mean? For discussion? And then? The resolution itself was inconsistent. It seemed to begin in a new spirit: "We acknowledge the enormous significance of trade unions for the practical education of the working class in its struggle with capital [Really only for "education"?—S.S.] . . . and for the political emancipation of the people"; but it went on to state:

> So long as the old order holds, the Party's boundaries are perforce narrow in comparison with the workers' irresistibly growing need to unite; the unity provided by trade unions may partly make up for this deficiency of the secret organizations, in satisfying the urge to unite of the broader circles of the working class not yet able to join the Party, besides serving them as gateway to eventual union within the Party.

That is, trade unions would serve as party surrogates ("while the old order holds") for those who could not be included in a secret organization. But even this was not all. There followed a *warning* against too much enthusiasm for trade unions:

> Excessive infatuation with the trade-union form of organization would also carry notable dangers for the growth of the proletariat's political movement. On one hand, with the chronic shortage of forces [even] for the most essential party work, diverting them to organize trade unions might seriously weaken the Party organizations themselves. On the other hand, in a revolutionary political atmosphere trade unions easily acquire a political coloring; and this coloring, because of the developmental level of most workers in the unions, might turn out to be not Social-Democratic but more moderate, democratic-liberal; this holds a threat of the workers' political demoralization, their education in a spirit of trite opportunism.

In view of all this, the resolution proposed that the Party organizations

1) systematically utilize, in accord with the directives of the Third Congress, all existing or emerging trade unions to expand Social-Democratic propaganda and agitation and attract new forces into the Party organizations. Overt action by Social-Democrats in the unions and secret organizational work must complement each other; the aim must be to secure in every union the dominant

influence of Social-Democracy—not to change the union into a secret Party organization, at the cost of narrowing the union.

This sounded like a renunciation of the idea of Party trade unions. But Article 2 specified support of unions that had accepted the entire Party program or were "granting Social-Democracy an open forum for propaganda and agitation." And Article 3 said that unions which accepted some other, non-Social-Democratic program must be "systematically influenced to induce them to accept the program of our Party." If this did not work, the resolution continued, the Party should seek to draw out of the union those members who might establish (instead of a non-Social-Democratic union) either a purely economic or a Social-Democratic one, depending on the type of workers in the union and their preferences.

Here, for the first time, the idea of dividing recalcitrant unions was spelled out. At the end, as at the beginning, there was a sugar-coated pill (Art. 4):

> . . . The Party organizations must assume the initiative of organizing trade unions in all cases where the proletarian masses manifest a desire for broad organization on the basis of trade unity, and [they must] draw into organizational work the workers themselves, those [workers] who are most able to do it and who accept the Social-Democratic program and tactics.

Instead of being discussed and amended by the Party organizations and returned to be passed or rejected by the Central Committee or by a Party conference, the draft of the resolution was simply forgotten. The CC's first attempt to formulate a trade-union policy was a complete fiasco.

Bolshevism remained in a state of ideological confusion until the end of the year. In November Lenin returned to Russia. Sensing some inner flaw in the Bolsheviks' attitude to the innumerable organizations springing up all over the country, he tried to outline a new approach in the article "The Socialist Party and Non-Party Revolutionism" in *Novaia Zhizn* (in the issues of November 26/December 9 and December 2/15). It dealt with Party members' participation in "non-party unions and soviets," "non-party revolutionary organizations created now by workers, now by peasants, now by soldiers, and so on." Apparently Lenin did not have trade unions specifically in mind, but the article influenced the Bolshevik stand on participating in them.

Lenin's main points were these: "Strict partisanship [*partiinost'*, literally "party spirit"] is a concomitant and a result of a highly developed class struggle."[39] "Non-partisanship is a bourgeois idea. Partisanship is a socialist idea."[40] Under the circumstances, "Is it admissible for socialists to participate in non-party organizations? If yes, on what conditions is it admissible? What tactics should they pursue in such organizations?" Lenin explained:

> The first question cannot be answered with an absolute no, a no in principle. . . . In an era of democratic revolution, refusal to participate in non-party organizations would amount in certain cases to refusal to participate in a democratic revolution. Of course socialists must delimit these "certain cases" narrowly, they can admit such participation only on firmly defined restrictive conditions. . . . Such participation may prove necessary, for example, in the interests of socialist propaganda before a vaguely democratic audience or in the interests of a joint struggle of socialists and revolutionary democrats against counterrevolution. . . . In either case it is admissible only if the independence of the workers' party is fully protected and if the Party members or groups "delegated" to non-party unions or soviets are controlled and led by the Party as a whole.[41]

Here Lenin came close to Borisov's "unofficial agents." The following year the notion was further developed, and it determined the Bolsheviks' basic policy for years. It led them to abandon the idea of subordinating the trade unions to the Party. At the time, however, *Novaia Zhizn* was still leaning toward a modified form of Party trade unions. In its lead article of November 30/December 13, 1905, "The Trade-Union Movement and Socialism," we read:

> The Party's tasks: saturating the labor movement, and consequently, its most characteristic form, the trade-union movement, with socialism; awakening Social-Democratic consciousness in

[39] Lenin, *Sochineniia*, X, 57.
[40] *Ibid.*, p. 61.
[41] *Ibid.*, pp. 62–63,

"trade-union" workers; drawing them *and whole unions* into the ranks of the Party as conscious Social-Democrats. Clearly the motto "Party trade unions" would restrict both the composition of these unions and the sphere of Social-Democracy's influence over the labor movement. To this motto we must oppose another: broad trade unions, encompassing all workers if possible; ideological propaganda of Social-Democracy with the aim of converting these unions into Social-Democratic unions—*that is, unions that can join the Party!*[42]

A resolution on trade unions drafted by Lenin for the Stockholm ("Unification") Congress, held in April/May, 1906, was still asking the Congress to "recognize"

1) that all Party organizations must assist the formation of non-party trade unions and induce all [the workers] in the given trade who are Party members to join them;

2) that the Party must strive in every way it can to educate the workers who are members of trade unions in the spirit of a broad understanding of the class struggle and of the proletariat's socialist tasks, so as to gain . . . *de facto* leadership in such unions and . . . enable these unions under certain conditions to *join the Party directly*—though by no means excluding from membership their non-party members.[43]

As a natural result of such a policy, the Bolsheviks' role in the labor movement was insignificant. There were only two Bolsheviks (a delegate from the Petersburg Union of Retail Salesmen, Leontiev, who was also a member of the Central Bureau of Trade Unions, and the editor of *Vestnik Prikazchikov*, A. A. Belozerov) among the twenty-two delegates to the so-called Second (actually the first) All-Russian Conference of Trade Unions (still illegal) in February, 1906, which in a sense provided a measure of the

---

[42] Italics added. The article was signed Iu. Adamovich. This was one of V. V. Vorovskii's pseudonyms.

[43] *Chetvertyi (Ob"edinitel'nyi) s"ezd RSDRP. Aprel' (aprel'-mai) 1906 goda. Protokoly* (Moscow: Gospolitizdat, 1959), p. 487 (italics added). This resolution was not brought before the Congress, and the Commission of the Congress (predominantly Menshevik) worked out another draft, which was adopted unanimously (with two abstentions) without debate (p. 455). To the idea of trade unions *organizationally* linked to the Party, that is, Party trade unions, it opposed the Menshevik idea of non-party trade unions linked to the Party *"organically, in struggle and agitation"* (p. 529). This expressed the idea of *co-ordinating* the two aspects of the labor movement instead of *subordinating* the unions to the Party.

development of the Russian trade-union movement during 1905. The other delegates included eleven Mensheviks, five members of the Bund, one non-faction Social-Democrat (D. B. Riazanov), and three non-party people.[44]

[44] *1905–1907 g.g. v professional'nom dvizhenii. I i II vserossiiskie konferentsii professional'nykh soiuzov,* compiled by P. Kolokol'nikov and S. Rapoport (Moscow, 1925), pp. 420–26.

CHAPTER 4

The Soviets of Workers' Deputies

Tʜᴇ official history of the Communist Party says very little about the soviets of workers' deputies of 1905. The *Short Course* gives them barely a page and a half. Their genesis and the attitude toward them of the two wings of Social-Democracy are dealt with in a few lines:

> In the stormy days of the October political strike, in the heat of the struggle with tsarism, the revolutionary creativity of the masses forged a new mighty weapon—the soviets of workers' deputies. . . . They were a manifestation of the independent activity of the people rising to fight tsarism.
>
> The Bolsheviks regarded the soviets as embryos of a revolutionary government. They considered that the power and significance of the soviets depended entirely on the force and success of the uprising.
>
> The Mensheviks regarded the soviets neither as embryonic organs of revolutionary government nor as organs of uprising. They regarded them as organs of local self-government, something like democratized city councils. . . . Lenin was not yet in Russia at the time, he was still abroad. The Mensheviks took advantage of Lenin's absence, wormed their way into the Petersburg Soviet and seized leadership in it. . . .[1]

The last charge is not repeated in the amended version of the book, and the Mensheviks' alleged view of the soviets is rephrased

---

[1] *Istoriia Vsesoiuznoi Kommunisticheskoi Partii (bol'shevikov). Kratkii kurs* (Moscow: Gospolitizdat, 1938), pp. 75–76.

167

as "only strike committees and organs of local self-government."[2]
This remains the official credo, along with the fiction that the
Bolsheviks saw the soviets as organs of the revolutionary struggle.
Realities were quite different.

The Menshevik Idea of Revolutionary Self-Government and Its Critique by the Bolsheviks

At the high tide of the revolutionary movement of 1905, the
sociopolitical life of the country was breaking out of its narrow
legal bounds and developing in the *fait accompli* fashion, by right
of "seizure" (to use the expressions current at the time). Social-
Democracy was looking for ways to promote this movement and
the workers' organized participation in it. By the summer, with
elections to the Duma in the offing, this became an immediate
problem.

The idea of "revolutionary self-government," which was to
play such a marked role in Social-Democratic thinking, was first
put forward in *Iskra*, No. 101, June 1, 1905, in F. Dan's article
"The Present Situation":[3]

> Semilegal, autonomously formed *agitation committees of workers*
> must be formed at once. In close contact with our legal organiza-
> tion, they must mobilize all the available forces of the working class
> to agitate for the convocation of a constituent assembly and to
> make full use of the electoral campaign, no matter what classes and
> groups take part in it. . . . To elections *without the people* accord-
> ing to [the terms of] the zemstvo law of 1864, they must oppose
> the idea of elections *by the people*—by universal, equal, direct, and
> secret suffrage. They must call upon all the strata of the population,
> urban and rural, to begin carrying out this idea immediately, to
> elect their own true representatives concurrently with the elections
> of "legal" deputies. *Uezd* and provincial assemblies of these repre-
> sentatives of the revolutionary people, if they in turn can send their
> representatives to an all-Russian assembly, might create a powerful
> organization for the entire revolutionary movement aimed at win-
> ning an all-Russian constituent assembly. They will form a kind of

---

[2] *Istoriia Kommunisticheskoi Partii Sovetskogo Soiuza* (Moscow: Gospolitizdat,
1959), p. 98.

[3] The article was unsigned. I have taken the author's name from the collection
Iskra za dva goda (1906).

network of elective organs of revolutionary self-government, with the revolutionary all-Russian assembly of representatives at its head.

"The genuine organization of an armed uprising," insisted Dan, lay in the establishment of such "popular" organs of representation.

Other groups proposed different tactics: boycotting the elections and the Duma (the Union of Unions and the SR's) or "actively boycotting" them (the Bolsheviks and especially the Bund), that is, demonstrating in front of electoral meetings, breaking them up, staging a general strike on the Duma's opening day, and so forth. *Iskra*, No. 106, July 18, pointed out (in F. Dan's article "Defense or Attack?") that its own plan by no means excluded demonstrations and a strike. On the contrary,

> that is when a mass action such as a political strike assumes a quite different character from that in the plans of the Union of Unions. . . . Then a *political strike* will not be a mere "demonstration of discontent" but a fighting move—either directly supporting the moves of the organ of revolutionary self-government, if its creation "aborts" the Duma; or supporting the revolutionary moves of both the organ of revolutionary self-government and the Duma against autocratic officialdom, if the Duma does convene and decides on a revolutionary course; or supporting the organ of revolutionary self-government against both autocracy and the Duma, if the latter turns out to be reactionary.
>
> We can see that offensive and organizing tactics, not hobbling us by the modes of action other parties and classes choose to adopt, will best prepare us for war on any front. But then the political strike entirely loses its character of peaceful demonstration. We must definitely regard it as a *possible* prologue to the uprising; and the organization of revolutionary self-government that we shall have called to life should provide enough support for this uprising to turn it into a nationwide uprising.[4]

Lenin dismissed this plan as "good for nothing," in the article "Boycott of the Bulygin Duma and the Uprising" in *Proletarii*, No. 12, August 3/16, completely disregarding the *fait accompli* possibilities of a revolutionary era: "The organization of revolu-

---

[4] This article was also unsigned; the author's name was taken from *Iskra za dva goda*. In this collection, which appeared legally in Russia, certain words are changed, for example, "uprising" to "stormier events."

tionary self-government, the election of representatives by the people, are not the *prologue* but the *epilogue* of the uprising."

> Setting oneself the aim of achieving this organization now, before the uprising, apart from the uprising, means setting oneself a ridiculous aim and confusing the revolutionary proletariat. First we must have a victorious uprising (if only in one city) and establish a revolutionary provisional government, [which], as the organ of the uprising, as the acknowledged leader of the revolutionary people, can start organizing revolutionary self-government. To obscure or even to defer the motto of uprising by the motto of organizing revolutionary self-government is like suggesting [that one] catch a fly and then dust it with fly powder.[5]

In *Iskra's* plan, "revolutionary self-government" did not mean local self-government in the usual sense: its autonomously, *lawlessly* emerging organs were to represent the revolutionary people, to mobilize the social energies for the conquest of a constituent assembly. In the ambience of the swelling mass movement, as Dan wrote much later, "the Mensheviks believed it possible to struggle for the transformation of the Bulygin Duma into something like the French Estates General of 1789, out of which there emerged, as we know, first the Constituent Assembly and then the Convention with full powers."[6] The Mensheviks believed that the victorious revolution would come by way of "revolutionary self-government," with or without an uprising, as the case might be—the two were not mutually exclusive. Lenin viewed their idea as "opportunism" and as a renunciation of the uprising. "In the Wake of the Monarchist Bourgeoisie or at the Head of the Revolutionary Proletariat and Peasantry?" asked his article in *Proletarii*, No. 15, August 23/September 5.[7] The first meant following the motto of revolutionary self-government; the second, the motto of uprising and a provisional government—two opposite conceptions of the probable course of the revolution. For the Mensheviks, the revolution meant a spontaneous popular movement; it was the task of Social-Democracy to help it take shape organizationally and politically and culminate in the formation of

---

[5] Lenin, *Sochineniia* (4th ed.), IX, 161.

[6] F. Dan, *Proiskhozhdenie bol'shevizma* (New York: Novaia Demokratiia, 1946), p. 407.

[7] Lenin, *Sochineniia*, IX, 189–200.

a mass labor party. For the Bolsheviks, the people remained a sphinx whose immanent tendencies were dangerous; it was the main task of Social-Democracy to make sure that the revolution was led by a strictly centralized, ideologically homogeneous party. Thus already in 1905 two attitudes were emerging, one democratic and the other authoritarian. In October the storm broke, and both factions put their ideas to the test.

The Beginnings of the Petersburg Soviet of Workers' Deputies

The railroad strike which began in Moscow on October 8 soon spread to other parts of the country, leading almost everywhere to general strikes. The Petersburg junction was struck on October 12, and all the city's workers were seething. For a general strike to begin, only an organizing center was needed. It was provided by the Soviet of Workers' Deputies.

The myth about the beginnings of the Petersburg Soviet which the Bolsheviks launched twenty years later is still alive in Soviet literature and we must analyze it, but first let us see what the truth was. Let us take the accounts of five eyewitnesses: two members of the Menshevik Group, Evgenii Maevskii (Gutovskii), who was also a member of the Organizational Committee, and S. S. Zborovskii; two members of the Bolshevik Petersburg Committee, B. I. Gorev (Goldman), who was also the representative of the Bolshevik center, and B. Radin (Knuniants); and a gifted young Bolshevik agitator, V. S. Voitinskii.[8]

Maevskii writes of the trends in leading Menshevik circles in early October:

> Even before the Moscow strike, in discussions of revolutionary self-government in the Petersburg Group, the opinion was expressed that, although *Iskra* linked the revolutionary elections and the Duma elections, the idea could be carried out during any revolutionary upswing, whether brought about by elections to the Duma or anything else. . . .

[8] Evgenii [Maevskii], "Peterburgskii Sovet Rabochikh Deputatov," *Otkliki Sovremennosti*, No. 5, 1906, pp. 1–11; A. Kuzovlev [Zborovskii], "Kak voznik Sovet," in *Istoriia Soveta Rabochikh Deputatov g. S.-Peterburga* (Petersburg, 1906), pp. 22–44; B. I. Gorev, *Iz partiinogo proshlogo. Vospominaniia, 1895–1905* (Leningrad, 1924); B. Radin [Knuniants], *Pervyi Sovet Rabochikh Deputatov. 13 okt.–3 dekabria 1905 g.* (Petersburg, 1906); V. S. Voitinskii, *Gody pobed i porazhenii* (Berlin: Gzhebin, 1923), Vol. I.

Several members of the Menshevik Petersburg Group thought so, and hence it was decided . . . to pitch to the Petersburg proletariat the slogan of revolutionary elections.[9]

Zborovskii's account complements Maevskii's:

On October 10 the Petersburg Group of the RSDRP debated the question of what to do, of what outlet to give the revolutionary mood of the proletarian masses.

It was decided to call upon the workers to [elect] a workers' committee and to [start] a general strike.

In deciding this question, all the members of the Group started with the idea of "revolutionary self-government," but they came to different conclusions.

Some feared that agitation for creating a workers' committee, which the workers were bound to regard as a strike committee for directing this particular strike, might cramp the proletariat's political range and hamper the realization of "revolutionary self-government." Wouldn't it be better to call right away for nation-wide elections to organs of "revolutionary self-government"? Then a workers' committee would also be formed—but already under the banner of "revolutionary self-government," in contact with the revolutionary movement of other classes. No concrete proposal was put forward, however.

Other members of the Group also considered a workers' committee an indispensable component of "revolutionary self-government"; they, too, saw the tactical pivot of the revolution in the creation of organs of its self-government; but they believed that this idea was not yet popular with the masses, unfamiliar to them, and sure to founder, while the idea of a workers' committee was more or less understood by the workers and was dictated by the impending struggle. Besides, at a time like this, the formal functions of the workers' committee, even if they were extremely narrow—which they would not be—could not narrow the proletariat's political horizon. Finally, the workers' committee would be a superb organ of education and agitation, an organ that would prepare the nation-wide organization of the revolution, the very "agitation committee" of which *Iskra* had written long ago.

It was decided to call for elections to a workers' committee immediately.[10]

As in the elections to the Shidlovskii Commission, there would be

---

[9] Evgenii, "Peterburgskii Sovet Rabochikh Deputatov," p. 3.
[10] Kuzovlev, "Kak voznik Sovet," pp. 41–42.

one deputy for every five hundred workers; factories employing more than five hundred would send two or more deputies.

Agitation began on October 11. Kuzovlev (Zborovskii) writes that "about fifty agitators carried the Group's appeal everywhere" and, "in an atmosphere of enthusiastic agreement, fervently appealed to the workers to decide at once at their factories the question of striking and to elect deputies to the workers' committee." Here and there elections took place as early as the twelfth. On the thirteenth, the deputies met in conference:

> At the first meeting there were no more than thirty or forty deputies; and many of them had not been elected in a strictly formal way. The question of striking and of setting up a workers' committee was discussed. It was unanimously decided to call the men and women workers of Petersburg to a general strike at once and to elect a committee, on the basis of one deputy per five hundred workers.
>
> The Petersburg Group of the RSDRP was charged with issuing the appeal in the name of the Soviet. The basic content of this appeal was outlined.[11]

Kuzovlev (Zborovskii) omits mention that he was the first chairman of the Soviet. At the next day's meeting there were eighty or ninety deputies. Maevskii writes that Zborovskii was too hoarse to preside[12] and passed the gavel to Khrustalev, "who was well known to the Petersburg workers and had good connections among the workers in the printing trade."[13]

That the Petersburg Group was asked to issue the appeal proves that the Soviet in its early stages was very largely a Menshevik enterprise. The next day the appeal (with the mention, "published by the Petersburg Group of the RSDRP") was distributed among the workers. It was signed "Assembly of Deputies [*Sobranie Deputatov*] of Petersburg Factories and Plants" and

---

[11] *Ibid.*, pp. 42–43.

[12] Evgenii, "Peterburgskii Sovet Rabochikh Deputatov," p. 10.

[13] Khrustalev proved such a good chairman that the original plan to elect a new one at each meeting was abandoned, and he presided over the meetings until his arrest on November 26; see D. F. Sverchkov, *Na zare revoliutsii* (Moscow, 1921), p. 100. Khrustalev's importance gave rise to the myth (discussed in Appendix 10) of the Liberationists' exceptional role in creating the Petersburg Soviet. (In 1905 Khrustalev was a Liberationist; he went over to the Mensheviks only in November.)

printed three days later in No. 1 of *Izvestiia Soveta Rabochikh Deputatov*.

Knuniants, who soon became the representative of the Petersburg Committee in the Executive Committee of the Soviet of Workers' Deputies and was later arrested and sentenced in the trial of the Soviet, writes in his book on the SWD:

> To direct the strike it was necessary to create a broader and more suitable apparatus than the Party organization. The Soviet of Workers' Deputies resulted from that necessity. The initiative in creating it belonged to the "Mensheviks," who had always been in favor of broad mass organizations.[14]

Gorev is interesting mainly in what he says about the Bolsheviks' stand on soviets after the strike, but he, too, notes that the initiative in taking part in the elections to the Soviet came from the Mensheviks.[15] Voitinskii also tells, in greater detail, of the Menshevik Group's decision on October 10 to call for a general strike and a workers' committee.[16] The Mensheviks linked the latter to the idea of "revolutionary self-government," which was what turned the Bolsheviks against it:

> . . . The Bolsheviks extended their mistrust of "organs of revolutionary self-government" to the Soviet of Workers' Deputies, as an institution originally conceived by the Mensheviks in the form of *Iskra*'s "Workers' Committee."
>
> It goes without saying that there would have been no such mistrust if only the Menshevik Group had said outright in its decision of October 10:
>
> "A general strike is beginning. To direct it, let us create a *strike committee* which will include deputies from all the striking factories and trade unions!"[17]

Voitinskii elaborates on the sources of the Bolsheviks' mistrust:

> Born of *Iskra*'s "utopian" plan, the Soviet suddenly rose before the Party like a Medusa head, claiming to direct the struggle of the Petersburg proletariat. Naturally the Bolsheviks regarded this pretension as unheard-of insolence.

---

[14] Radin, *Pervyi Sovet Rabochikh Deputatov* . . . , p. 7.
[15] Gorev, *Iz partiinogo proshlogo* . . . , p. 76.
[16] Voitinskii, *Gody pobed i porazhenii*, p. 134.
[17] *Ibid.*, p. 142.

Our contingent of agitators learned of the birth of the "Workers' Committee" from Krasikov.

"The Mensheviks have started a new intrigue," he told us, "they're electing a non-party Zubatovite committee."

And although "Comrade Anton" was far from the brightest head in the organization, I think that at the time almost all Bolsheviks shared this view of the Menshevik enterprise.[18]

It is quite true that the immense majority of Bolsheviks viewed the Soviet as a "new intrigue" of the Mensheviks but not that "almost all" of them actually shared Krasikov's view of it as a new variant of Zubatovism.[19]

But opposing the Soviet further endangered the Bolsheviks' already tenuous contact with the mass movement, and they revised their stand after the publication of the above-mentioned appeal of the "Assembly of Deputies." A Bolshevik historian of the Petersburg Soviet, E. Krivosheina, writes:

As early as October 14 or 15 the Bolsheviks began to take a most active part in organizing the Soviet. [They] had unwittingly already made a mistake in taking a very hostile attitude to it from October 10 to 13 [on the grounds that creating a soviet meant] creating a non-party organization.

This mistake was inevitable since the Mensheviks, the initiators of the organ, attached to it the label of revolutionary self-government, thus provoking a negative attitude on the part of the Bolsheviks.

The usual Menshevik striving for broad non-party organizations and for legalization of the Party also made the Bolsheviks take a very cautious view of their original creation. Thus the initial tactics of the Bolsheviks toward the Revolutionary Workers' Committee logically stemmed from the earlier movement and from the Mensheviks' precedents in this respect.

---

[18] *Ibid.*, p. 188.

[19] In October, 1905, I too was a Bolshevik agitator, somewhat friendlier to the Soviet than most other Bolsheviks but in the main keeping to the official view. I was not present when Krasikov called the Soviet "Zubatovite," but if that had really been the opinion of "almost all Bolsheviks," I would have heard of his remark and it would have surprised me very much. I first learned of it in 1923 from Voitinskii's book. Krasikov was at the time one of the two members of the Petersburg Committee in charge of directing its agitators (in Party hierarchy, *otvetstvennye agitatory*). Knuniants was the other. About early November, G. A. Aleksinskii ("Petr Alekseev") arrived from Moscow and became a member of the PC and its third "chief agitator." Knuniants alone was popular with the agitators.

Here we only want to note that the strikers' enthusiasm, the revolutionary mood evidenced in the brisk elections to the Revolutionary Workers' Committee, forced the Bolsheviks, too, to approach the problem from a practical standpoint.

The elections going on among the working masses, mainly for the purpose of directing the strike and unifying the movement—for realizing the announced slogans—inspired in the Bolshevik Party the natural apprehension that a continued negative stand on the "organ of revolutionary self-government" would in effect result in shutting Bolshevism out of the movement.

As it was, the latter was outgrowing the [Party] organizations and heading toward workers' representation to lead the struggle . . . [with] a general strike as the first, tentative method of struggle under the Russian movement's conditions.

. . . .

And it was the initial tactic of the Bolsheviks to criticize revolutionary self-government and agitate in favor of elections to the Workers' Committee purely as a strike committee.[20]

As I have shown, the *History of the CPSU* accuses the Mensheviks of trying to keep the Soviet merely a strike committee. This quotation from a Bolshevik source shows that the reasons for the friction over the Soviet were the direct opposite of the ones given in the official history. Maevskii writes that, once the Bolsheviks had joined in the elections, the two factions worked quite harmoniously at workers' meetings, except that

. . . we Mensheviks were sometimes obliged to add to, or broaden, the appeals to hold elections that comrades from the "Majority" made at meetings. I myself addressed several meetings right after speeches by Bolshevik comrades calling for elections to a "strike committee."

Willy-nilly we had to explain that the Revolutionary Workers' Committee would not be a mere "strike committee." Born not so much of the strike as of the general revolutionary enthusiasm, it was not meant to die with the end of the strike. Just as striking was only one of the weapons during a revolutionary tide, so also leading the strike was only one of the functions of the Revolutionary Workers' Committee.

---

[20] E. Krivosheina, *Peterburgskii Sovet Rabochikh Deputatov v 1905 godu* (Moscow: Voprosy Truda, 1926), pp. 92–94. "October 14 or 15" is typical of the vagueness of this and later studies. Krivosheina remarks on page 96 that "the exact date has not been ascertained."

The higher the tide of revolution rose, the more complex and diversified would the Committee's activity become.

Only the ebb of the revolution or complete victory over the old order would make the further existence of such an institution unnecessary and impossible.[21]

Krivosheina actually goes even farther than Maevskii. She explains the Bolsheviks' decision to support the elections by their wish to prevent the Mensheviks from making the Soviet a broad revolutionary organ:

It was imperative to prevent Menshevik tyranny in the future Soviet of Workers' Deputies, [a tyranny] that would be only natural after the initiative they had taken; hence the Bolsheviks decided to take the Soviet in hand by sending their "own" people into it for an organized struggle against Menshevik tendencies in general and against the attempts to turn the Soviet into revolutionary self-government in particular.[22]

Below I shall discuss the evolution of Bolshevik and Menshevik attitudes toward the Soviet, but first it is necessary to touch on another matter. For two decades the Menshevik initiative in creating the Petersburg Soviet remained undisputed. This hampered Bolshevik propaganda. In the twenties there began a search for arguments that would permit the Soviet's emergence to be credited to the Bolsheviks.

One popular argument was advanced by N. I. Podvoiskii in 1922: the Petersburg Soviet had not been the first soviet; the first was the Ivanovo-Voznesensk *Sobranie Upolnomochennykh*, elected in May, 1905, during the textile strike.[23] That strike was indeed a historic event in the labor movement, but even the members of the *Sobranie* did not consider themselves a revolu-

---

[21] Evgenii, "Peterburgskii Sovet Rabochikh Deputatov," pp. 6–7.

[22] Krivosheina, *Peterburgskii Sovet Rabochikh Deputatov*, p. 95.

[23] Podvoiskii expressed this idea in the article "Pervye Sovety Rabochikh Deputatov," in *Raboche-Krest'ianskii Kalendar'* (Petersburg, 1922). The relevant part of his article was published in 1925 as a pamphlet, with the loaded title *Pervyi Sovet Rabochikh Deputatov (Ivanovo-Voznesenskii)* (No. 12 in the "Deshevaia Biblioteka" series of the journal *Katorga i Ssylka*—the edition I am using). Podvoiskii has a rival in F. N. Samoilov, in whose *Vospominaniia ob Ivanovo-Voznesenskom rabochem dvizhenii* (1922), the Ivanovo-Voznesensk *Sobranie Upolnomochennykh* is called *Sovet Rabochikh Deputatov* ("Soviet of Workers' Deputies"). This passed almost unnoticed, however, and the idea is generally attributed to Podvoiskii.

tionary organ, as the Petersburg Soviet did from the beginning; the tasks they set themselves were connected with the strike only, and when the strike ended, the *Sobranie* disbanded. Its origin, too, was different: no revolutionary party brought it forth, nor even the workers themselves—it had been suggested by the factory inspector, who wanted the delegates to negotiate with the employers. The governor had promised personal immunity to the delegates.[24] How untenable it is to trace the soviets back to Ivanovo-Voznesensk is clear from yet another fact: when soviets of workers' deputies began to spring up in many industrial centers in the fall of 1905, Ivanovo-Voznesensk was one of the few that did not produce a soviet.[25]

As the alleged cradle of the soviets, Ivanovo-Voznesensk was a suitable choice since its Social-Democratic organization was entirely in Bolshevik hands in 1905, and there were no other revolutionary organizations in the city.[26] This, however, makes the failure to elect a soviet in late 1905 even more revealing. Other centers where Bolsheviks predominated also lagged behind in this matter. In Moscow a Bolshevik appeal to the workers to form a "Soviet of Deputies from All Moscow"[27] allegedly went out in September, yet the Moscow Soviet of Workers' Deputies was formed late, when everything was nearly over: its first meeting took place on November 21.[28]

The Soviet of Workers' Deputies and the Social-Democratic Party

Once the Bolsheviks had reversed their stand on participating in the Soviet, party squabbles subsided. The Soviet was engrossed

---

[24] See Appendix 11, pp. 335–38.

[25] V. I. Nevskii's monumental work *1905. Sovetskaia pechat' i literatura o Sovetakh*, in *Materialy i dokumenty* (Moscow-Leningrad, 1925) contains in full the "Izvestiia" and "Biulleteni" of soviets of workers' deputies of fourteen cities (including the Sulino plant) and gives information (gleaned from local and central publications) about fourteen more cities (including the Votkinsk and Nadezhdinsk plants), but there is not one word about an Ivanovo-Voznesensk Soviet of Workers' Deputies. Nor does it appear in the list of thirty soviets in Nevskii's later study, "Sovety v 1905 godu," in *1905. Istoriia revoliutsionnogo dvizheniia v otdel'nykh ocherkakh*, ed. M. N. Pokrovskii (Moscow-Leningrad, 1927), III, 52. There is no doubt about it—it did not exist.

[26] According to more recent data, about one-third of the elected representatives were Bolsheviks, and there were no Mensheviks or members of any other party in the *Sobranie Upolnomochennykh*. See *1905 god v Ivanovo-Voznesenskom raione*, ed. O. A. Varentsova et al. (Ivanovo-Voznesensk, 1925), p. 75.

[22] Krivosheina, *Peterburgskii Sovet Rabochikh Deputatov*, p. 95.

[28] See Appendix 12, n. 3.

in managing the strike; whether it was a strike committee or something else had become an academic question. Differences revived, however, when the strike ended on October 21, at the decision of the Soviet.

As yet neither faction was ready to formulate its views distinctly. The basic points of dissent were somewhat blurred and not wholly conscious. We can try to reconstruct them.

The Mensheviks attached immense importance to the Soviet and wanted to strengthen and preserve it as the possible basis for a movement that would in the end transform the Social-Democratic Party into a mass labor party (see chapter v). True, within Menshevism there also were differences of opinion on the role of the working class in the bourgeois-democratic revolution, Axelrod representing one extreme and Trotsky the other. In October these differences, too, receded into the background, and Trotsky became the unchallenged leader of the Mensheviks in the Petersburg Soviet.

The Bolsheviks were leery of the very existence of the Soviet. Radin (Knuniants), one of the more levelheaded of their leaders in 1905, writes in his book on the Petersburg Soviet:

> So long as the entire Petersburg proletariat was engaged in a vast strike struggle, the Soviet was indispensable. With the low level of organization of the workers, no other agency could replace it. All we could do was prevent *possible harmful consequences in the future* and try to use the Soviet and its organization to propagate the Party's ideas.[29]

And, even more distinctly:

> The Party had to ask itself whether the proletariat would emerge from the revolutionary storm conscious enough to realize that an independent political party was the only effective form of organization for it and that the program of international Social-Democracy was its own class program. The existence of the Soviet, an organization politically amorphous (from a programmatic point of view), standing outside the Party, could be a poor asset in the future work of rallying the whole proletariat around Social-Democracy. Under the impact of demagoguery many backward elements among the workers *might see the Soviet as the germ of an "independent labor party"* as opposed to socialism.

No matter how sharply the Soviet's policy differed from the

---

[29] Radin, *Pervyi Sovet Rabochikh Deputatov* . . . , p. 102 (italics added).

"Independents'" [*Nezavisimtsy*] policy or how revolutionary was the mood of the masses, *the mere existence of an informal, non-socialist political organization* of the proletariat could look like something of a menace to the free development of the class movement toward Social-Democracy.[30]

In keeping with his own attitude, Knuniants' description of the Bolsheviks' motives is relatively restrained. Gorev writes more bluntly that "when the Petersburg Soviet expanded its activity, became a united revolutionary force, the Petersburg Committee took fright."[31] He bases this on a remark by "Nina L'vovna" (M. M. Essen, an influential member of the PC) and on some resolutions of sector meetings:

> I remember "Nina L'vovna"'s words: "But where do we come in? So we have to reckon with them! The Soviet issues decrees, and we trail behind it, we cannot put through our own decrees," and so on.
> This was also reflected in the resolutions of sector meetings, especially of the Peterburgskaia Storona, where the leader[s were] Doroshenko . . . and the Bolshevik Mendeleev, now the well-known Menshevik Schwarz-Monoszon. They demanded that the Soviet either turn into a trade-union organization or accept our program and in effect fuse with the Party organization.[32]

The situation was far more acute and the hostility to the Soviet far deeper than one would assume from the Peterburg-skaia Storona resolution mentioned by Gorev. I was the author of that resolution and remember its origin very well. It was passed on October 27 or 28 at a sector meeting of agitators and propa-gandists—really an enlarged meeting of the sector committee. N. V. Doroshenko ("Viktor Semenych"), the chief organizer for the sector, through whom we kept in touch with the Petersburg Committee, informed us that the PC had discussed its attitude to the Soviet but had not yet reached a decision. Some members wanted to have it boycotted as unnecessary since there was the

---

[30] Radin, *Pervyi Sovet Rabochikh Deputatov* . . . , p. 102 (italics added). The "Nezavisimtsy," or "Ushakovtsy," were the members of the police-sponsored Nezavisimaia Sotsial'naia Rabochaia Partiia founded by M. A. Ushakov, a worker at Ekspeditsiia Zagotovleniia Gosudarstvennykh Bumag (the printing office of the Mint). It was the last organization of the Zubatov type.

[31] Gorev, *Iz partiinogo proshlogo* . . . , p. 75.

[32] *Ibid.*, pp. 75–76.

Party organization; others advocated joining the Soviet, getting as many of our own people into it as possible, and "exploding the Soviet from within"—also because it was "unnecessary." I, the chief agitator for the sector, was still inexperienced in this kind of strategy and Doroshenko's report simply bowled me over. To my semirhetorical question—Hasn't anyone in the PC spoken up for supporting the Soviet as a useful organization in the labor movement—Doroshenko replied in a shocked tone that certainly no one had expressed such a notion. The resolution in question was adopted after a heated debate, in which all the members of the sector committee sided with me. The next morning I wrote an article and took it to *Novaia Zhizn*, where it appeared on November 2. (I shall return to this article.) I also got a workers' meeting at the Semenov plant to pass a similar resolution, which was printed in *Novaia Zhizn* on November 1. Gorev notwithstanding, neither of the two poorly formulated resolutions expressed the hostile official attitude of the Petersburg Bolshevik leaders to the Soviet. Both were, on the contrary, meant to combat it.

That the Bolsheviks' official attitude in late October, 1905, was hostile to the Soviet was subsequently confirmed by Gorin: "Denouncing the inconsistency and lack of principles of the Mensheviks, the Bolsheviks intended to boycott the Soviet."[33] And Trotsky wrote in his well-known letter to the Istpart of August 25, 1921:

> The Petersburg contingent, led by Bogdanov, of the Bolshevik Central Committee resolutely opposed the creation of an elective non-party workers' organization. The negative attitude of the Bolshevik summit in Petersburg to the Soviet continued until Comrade Lenin's arrival in Russia. I was present at the meeting of the Bolshevik CC (or Bureau of the CC or Petersburg Bureau of the CC) at which the tactics toward the Soviet were worked out. Bogdanov proposed the following plan: Put before the Soviet, in the name of the Bolshevik faction, the proposal to accept immediately the Social-Democratic program and the general leadership of the Party; [and] if the Soviet decided against it, leave the Soviet. . . . Bogdanov's "ultimatum" ("recall") tactics were expressed with perfect clarity even then. All the objections to facing the Soviet

---

[33] P. Gorin, *Ocherki po istorii Sovetov Rabochikh Deputatov v 1905 godu* (Moscow, 1925), p. 60.

with the ultimatum about the program were judged invalid. . . .
The meeting indorsed Bogdanov's plan.

A few days later Comrade Anton (Krasikov), in the name of the
Bolsheviks, did propose to the Soviet that it accept the Party
program and recognize the Party's leadership. As far as I remember, the debate was very brief. Khrustalev objected. Krasikov's
proposal received hardly any support. But, contrary to Bogdanov's
plan, the Bolsheviks did not leave the Soviet.[34]

This meeting of the Soviet took place on October 29.[35]
Khrustalev describes it in his "History of the Soviet":

> The Social-Democratic "Majority" faction demanded "clarifica-
> tion of the Soviet's political physiognomy". . . . The "Majority"
> faction definitely posed the dilemma: the Soviet must either accept
> the Social-Democratic program or be disbanded. The "Majority"
> faction argued that a vague political amalgam like the Soviet could
> not be the political leader of the working class. The matter was put
> in an "either-or" form. . . .
>
> Such an approach, without increasing the Party's strength,
> threatened to destroy a mighty revolutionary organization of the
> proletariat. The forces of life removed the question from the
> docket.
>
> There is no need for me to show the untenability of such at-
> tempts. Life itself has done that.[36]

All this helps in understanding a resolution which was passed
at about this time by the Social-Democratic Federative Council
formed in mid-October to co-ordinate the activities of the Bolshevik Petersburg Committee and the Menshevik Petersburg Group
and pave the way for a unification congress. Recent Bolshevik
writings maintain that this resolution expressed the Bolshevik

---

[34] In Sverchkov, *Na zare revoliutsii* (Leningrad, 1921), pp. 6–7; Trotsky's letter
serves as foreword. A skeptical reader may ask how Trotsky, at that time a leading
Menshevik, came to attend a meeting of the Bolshevik center. This was not too
strange in late 1905, when Social-Democracy was preparing for unification. Gorev
writes in his reminiscences that Bolsheviks, including Lenin, "visited a Menshevik
conference held in Petersburg in November" and that a representative of the
Mensheviks, Smirnov (Gurevich), attended the Bolshevik conference in Tammer-
fors in December (*Iz partiinogo proshlogo* . . . , p. 78).

[35] For a report on this meeting, see *Novaia Zhizn*, No. 5, November 1, and
Peterburg v 1905 g., II, 21.

[36] G. Khrustalev-Nosar', "Istoriia Soveta Rabochikh Deputatov (do 26-go
noiabria 1905 goda)," in *Istoriia Soveta Rabochikh Deputatov g. S.-Peterburga*
(Petersburg, 1906), pp. 150–51.

viewpoint, but it was in fact a compromise, as could be expected from its source. It toned down the Bolsheviks' views enough to enable them to retreat from their "ultimatum" stand.

This resolution is quoted in *Novaia Zhizn* in a report on a joint conference of meeting-orators of both factions on October 27:

> At the present time, when the old regime is crumbling under the onslaught of the revolution, the workers must closely unite into a single party and tirelessly fight for our interests in its ranks. Otherwise the bourgeois parties will grasp all the fruits of victory we shall have won. The workers need a single party. The workers' party must adopt a program that expresses the interests of the proletariat of the whole world. The program of international Social-Democracy is such a program. . . . Russian Social-Democracy is a part of world Social-Democracy. All organized labor unions must stand under the banner of the RSDRP. We therefore appeal to the workers' soviet formed during the last political strike . . . to continue the struggle for a democratic republic, a people's militia, the eight-hour working day, and socialism, in the ranks of that party.[37]

The Bolshevik Central Committee tried to give this resolution a more extremist interpretation than its text warranted. Citing it—ostensibly to popularize it—in a "Letter to All Party Organizations" on October 27, the Committee pointed out the danger of "politically amorphous and socialistically immature workers' organizations created by the spontaneous revolutionary movement of the proletariat. . . . Every such organization represents a certain stage in the proletariat's political development, but if it stands outside Social-Democracy, it is, objectively, in danger of keeping the proletariat on a primitive political level and thus subjugating it to the bourgeois parties. . . . One such organization is the Petersburg Soviet of Workers' Deputies." The Central Committee asked the Social-Democratic members of the Soviet (1) to invite the Soviet to accept the RSDRP's program and, when this was done, to recognize the leadership of the Party and "ultimately dissolve in it"; (2) if the Soviet refused to accept the program, to leave the Soviet and expose the antiproletarian nature of such organizations; (3) if the Soviet, while refusing to

---

[37] *Novaia Zhizn*, No. 2, October 28. See also Radin, *Pervyi Sovet Rabochikh Deputatov* . . . , p. 103.

accept the program, reserved to itself the right to decide its political stand in every case as it came up, to stay in the Soviet but reserve the right to speak out on "the absurdity of such political leadership."[38]

Voitinskii tells us how the young Bolshevik agitators reacted to this profoundly anti-Soviet conception of their elders:

> The Soviet represented the *spontaneous* side of the labor movement. It was necessary to subordinate it to an organ embodying the revolutionary *consciousness* of the proletariat. Hence the idea of making the Soviet of Workers' Deputies a Party organization, a cell of the RSDRP, subject to the discipline of the Petersburg Committee. The question was heatedly debated in Party circles and the press.
>
> As far as I remember, in the end the majority in our organization were inclined to act step by step: first get the Soviet to decide in principle that it subordinated itself to the RSDRP, then raise the question of which of the Party organizations should give directives to the Soviet. The first blow would thus be directed at the non-Social-Democratic elements in the Soviet, that is, the SR's, and the final maneuver would "dislodge" the Mensheviks from the Soviet.
>
> . . . .
>
> Let me say that among us agitators the question of the Soviet's subordination to the Party caused much dissent. There were some proponents of drastic measures, up to *dispersing* the Soviet if it did not obey the Committee's directives. I remember an ardent speech to this effect by Abram (N. V. Krylenko). Others feared that turning the Soviet into a Party cell might undermine its influence over the non-partisan working masses. Personally I was definitely against the proposed "campaign."
>
> Getting ahead of my story, may I mention here that after the flop of this campaign, strained relations persisted between the Bolshevik organization and the Soviet.[39]

It was of course almost impossible to defend the Bolsheviks' extreme stand at workers' meetings, and their agitators hewed to the Federative Council's resolution. This suited them tactically,

---

[38] Nevskii, "Sovety v 1905 godu," pp. 39–40, 70. Usually a reliable writer, Nevskii here surprisingly identifies the text of the CC's letter with that of the Federative Council's resolution.

[39] Voitinskii, *Gody pobed i porazhenii,* pp. 193–94.

too, since the Mensheviks had been displeased with it.[40] Within the Bolshevik faction the arguments continued, however, and they were aired in *Novaia Zhizn.*

The most important among these expositions of Bolshevik views were two articles "On Organization" by B. Radin (Knuniants), the second with the subtitle "The Soviet of Workers' Deputies or the Party?" in *Novaia Zhizn* of October 29 and November 1 (Nos. 3 and 5). Knuniants was the chief representative of the CC in the Soviet, very popular in the Bolshevik organization and by nature averse to intraparty feuds. He avoided a sharp formulation of the problem and even tried to shake off the traditions of the underground. The main present task of the working class, he wrote, was to create a mass organization.

> To be sure, the working class has organized before, and its conscious elements have expended much effort on attracting comrades into the proletarian Party, but all this was done on a small scale, in the underground. Now both the scale and the organizational form must change sharply. Now there must be open recruiting of members, open discussion of the proletariat's class aims, open action by Party members as such. Now it is time to organize a broad labor party.

This was not the only novel idea. Fearing a "temporary dominance of bourgeois ideology" unless the new organizations *formally* joined the Party, Knuniants said: "The existence of any groups following Social-Democratic policies but not linked to the Party organizationally is not in the interests of the proletariat's struggle for emancipation." What about the Soviet? Knuniants replied:

> It was the composition of the Soviet that made it effective during the political strike, when the entire proletariat was acting as

---

[40] The article "K voprosu o Sovete Deputatov," *Novaia Zhizn*, No. 1, October 27, tells of a joint meeting of Bolshevik and Menshevik sector committees, at which the resolution of the Federative Council was discussed. The Mensheviks were against making the resolution obligatory and "recommended not hurrying to turn the Soviet into a Party organization but . . . quashing the question of the Soviet's nature even if it arose in the Soviet itself."

At the Soviet's meeting of October 29 the Mensheviks, according to Voitinskii, decried the Bolsheviks' attempt to subordinate the Soviet to the Party as "an attempt to dynamite the Soviet" (*Gody pobed i porazhenii*, p. 194).

a class, battling for its interests. A strike commission, if it wants to
conduct a strike successfully, must include representatives of all
strikers. . . . In our country, owing to the police conditions of
work, the Social-Democratic Party, the strongest and most influential among the workers, was unable to set up an organizational
apparatus capable of rallying the masses associated with the Party.
Because of this . . . the emergence of the Workers' Soviet as
leader of the strike was inevitable. It was not only inevitable, it was
useful. . . .

But can an agency formed in this way be the political leader of
the working masses? Not under any circumstances. To be a political
leader, one must have a clear program, precisely defined aims. One
must have an orderly organization of people accepting this program
and willing to fight for these aims. The Soviet can direct only
specific actions of the proletariat, take the lead in clear-cut mass
operations. It can set concrete tasks that will draw the proletariat
together, but directing class policies is not its role.

Therefore,

the proletariat must clearly know under what banner its elected
body is standing, which party's slogans and directives it will be
carrying out in its practical actions. Playing blindfold in politics is
not in the interests of the proletariat. A clear-cut statement by the
Soviet as to which political party it recognizes, which political
program it adheres to, is imperative.

P. N. Gvozdev expressed the prevailing view more sharply in
the article "Social-Democracy and the Soviet of Workers' Deputies" in *Novaia Zhizn*, No. 7, November 3. He began by explaining
why the Soviet's competence should be so limited:

The Petersburg proletariat elected the Workers' Soviet to fulfil a
definite function—conduct the political strike the proletariat had
announced. Thus the genesis of the Workers' Soviet is clear: it was
elected . . . as *the executive organ for a specific proletarian action.
Neither more nor less.* . . . From the Party's viewpoint it would
of course be most desirable if the masses trusted the Party enough
. . . to regard the Party organizations as the already acknowledged
executive organs directing all mass movements. In such cases the
masses do not even think of elections. Unfortunately . . . the
organizational forms of the Party, under the conditions of underground work, were too imperfect to allow the Party to capture the

masses not only ideologically but organizationally as well. [Italics here and below added.]

In other words, it had been necessary to put up with the creation of the Soviet for a "specific proletarian action," and the Soviet had acquitted itself creditably. What of the future?

> The strike is over; yet the Workers' Soviet continues to exist. More than that, it is displaying a strong tendency to become the movement's political leader. Its physiognomy is thus drastically changed.
>
> The RSDRP's attitude toward it must change accordingly. *If Social-Democracy vigorously supported the Workers' Soviet as the executive organ of the proletarian action, it must now no less vigorously combat all attempts on its part to become the political leader of the working class.* . . .
>
> The Workers' Soviet could unwittingly push the labor movement onto the path of opportunism . . . become the loophole the bourgeois parties have been seeking in vain so far, in their desire to lead the workers on the leash of the bourgeoisie. That is why Social-Democracy . . . must resolutely fight all attempts to put the labor movement under the leadership of such a vague political organization as the Workers' Soviet.

Without saying so, the author obviously felt that the Soviet should disband. He spoke of creating a *new* soviet if needed:

> But what if there is a new proletarian action? Will not the need for an executive organ . . . arise again? This can be answered as follows: By intensifying our Social-Democratic agitation, by having our Party come out of the underground and act openly, by organizing the trade-union movement under the leadership of a workers' soviet which has joined our ranks—by all this we hope, by the time of the new proletarian action, to have extended the organizational influence of our Party over the proletarian masses to the point where *these masses, when they rush into battle, will turn to our Party Committee, will say, Here are our leaders, we need no others!* And if we fail in this, if the proletariat wishes to elect its leaders itself, we shall go to the proletariat, just as we did before the October events, and say, Elect a *new workers' soviet,* a new executive organ for the new proletarian action.

Gvozdev added a warning: "But just as we do now, we shall *fight this new workers' soviet* if, instead of [acting as] the *executive organ* of a proletarian action, it tries to become a *political organ* of the proletarian movement." A workers' soviet "could not fail to be . . . a political hodge-podge . . . a vague and unstable organization." Only a firm, class-conscious Party could direct the political movement of the proletariat while keeping its slogans pure.

At about the same time, the article "The Problem of the Soviet of Workers' Deputies," by N. Mendeleev (Schwarz), appeared in *Novaia Zhizn*. The discussion at the sector meeting from which it had resulted had been little more than an argument between Doroshenko and myself. He had defended the official stand, and I the value of the Soviet to the labor movement. All my comrades shared my point of view, but none of us had really thought through the issues involved. When I tried to write them down, I capitulated at once on the point of keeping the Party at the political helm of both the labor movement and the Soviet and concentrated on the Soviet's role as organizer of mass actions and of the workers' economic struggle. The article was so poorly constructed that the rejection of the Soviet as political leader seemed to be the main point, while the arguments in its favor melted into the background.[41] This explains why other writers later referred to it as expressing the official Bolshevik viewpoint, hostile to the Soviet.

The theoretical discussions in *Novaia Zhizn* abruptly ceased in early November when a second general strike broke out, over the threatened court-martial of the Kronstadt insurgents and the introduction of martial law in Poland. When the strike ended (on November 7) the discussion was not resumed, at least not in its old form. The Mensheviks had no need to rehash the unfortunate resolution of the Federative Council, since the Soviet, at its meeting of October 29, had by an overwhelming majority refused to discuss its subordination to the RSDRP. Besides, they momentarily lacked a forum: the appearance of *Nachalo* had been delayed, and the little one-kopek *Russkaia Gazeta*, which had

---

[41] I remember how dissatisfied I was with this article when I saw it in print. I thought the editors had made changes in it, though they probably hadn't. I decided never to use that pen name again. An additional reason was that my signature, N. Mendelev (after my friend Mendel Osipovich Levin), had been printed "Mendeleev," which seemed unpleasantly pretentious.

become Menshevik in late October, did not have space for polemics. Furthermore, a wave of "unification" feelings swept over the Petersburg Mensheviks, as can be seen from short reports on sector meetings of their party workers in *Russkaia Gazeta*. Let us draw on two sources for the Mensheviks' views on the Party-Soviet interrelation after the November strike—an "Open Letter to the Federative Council and to Social-Democratic and Non-Partisan Comrade Deputies," signed "A Proletarian," in *Russkaia Gazeta* of November 11; and A. Martynov's article "The Soviet of Workers' Deputies and Our Party" in *Nachalo*, No. 2, November 15 (the only article in *Nachalo* on the problem of the Party and the Soviet). Both posited the need to preserve the Soviet as a "political institution" until there was "one Social-Democratic Party with a single program and uniform tactics," which would reflect through elections (to its various offices) the workers' own initiative (the "Open Letter")—in other words, both sources expressed the need to "reform our underground Party organization into a broad organization of a labor party existing out in the open, broad enough to absorb and render superfluous such organizations as the Soviet of Workers' Deputies, broad enough to [lead] the working masses unified by the Soviet" (Martynov).

The Bolsheviks, too, had lost their eagerness to reopen the question again and again. At the time their restraint was somewhat puzzling. Now we know that it had to do with Lenin's return to Russia.

Two Lenins

Lenin remained abroad for almost a month after the appearance of the Soviet of Workers' Deputies. He left Geneva in late October, spent about a week in Stockholm, was in Helsingfors on November 5, and in Petersburg only on November 7 or 8. In Stockholm, from November 2 to 4, he wrote an article, "Our Tasks and the Soviet of Workers' Deputies (A Letter to the Editors)," intended for *Novaia Zhizn*.[42] Most likely he did not

[42] On all this, see "Daty zhizni i deiatel'nosti Lenina," in Lenin, *Sochineniia*, X, 503. Lenin's official biography (Moscow, 1960), p. 138, gives November 8 as the date of his arrival in Petersburg. The article in question is in *Sochineniia*, X, 3–11.

mail it but took it with him, since he left Sweden right after finishing the article. It was not printed and remained unknown even to Party historians until it was suddenly "found"—thirty-five years later!—and published in *Pravda* on November 5, 1940. The strange fate of the article to which Lenin attached great importance—for good reason, as we shall see—suggests that it met with violent opposition from the Bolshevik leaders in Petersburg and that Lenin agreed not to publish it. It is inconceivable that *Novaia Zhizn* would have refused to print Lenin's "Letter to the Editors" had he insisted.[43]

But let us look at the article itself. After some introductory remarks, Lenin polemizes against Radin's articles in *Novaia Zhizn* (No. 5 was the last issue Lenin had seen in Stockholm): "It seems to me that it would not be expedient for the Soviet as a whole to join any one party." The Soviet is carrying on both an economic and a political struggle. Of the first, Lenin says:

> Should such a struggle be conducted only by Social-Democrats or only under the Social-Democratic flag? I would say no; I am still of the opinion which I expressed in *What Is To Be Done?*—namely, that it is not expedient to limit the composition of trade unions, and consequently participation in the economic struggle, to members of the Social-Democratic Party alone.

As I have noted (in Appendix 9, p. 329) this opinion remained unassimilated in Bolshevik ideology. Now Lenin went even farther:

> But this half of the question, concerning the economic struggle, is relatively simple and probably does not even cause particular controversy. The other half of the question, about political leadership, the political struggle, is a different matter. At the risk of surprising my readers even more, I must, however, state from the outset that here, too, it seems inexpedient to me to demand that the Soviet of Workers' Deputies adopt the Social-Democratic program and join the Russian Social-Democratic Labor Party. It seems to

---

[43] Lenin's introductory remarks to the article indicate some uncertainty: "I am still forced to write from the accursed far-away, the émigré's distasteful 'abroad.' . . . I am therefore leaving it to the editors' discretion whether or not to publish this letter written by an uninformed man. I am reserving the right to change my opinion when I shall at last have a chance to acquaint myself with the problem not just 'from paper.' " (*Sochineniia*, X, 3.)

me that for leading the political struggle the Soviet (*reformed* in the direction described below) and the Party alike are indispensable at present.

Lenin's proposed "reform" of the Soviet must have surprised his faithful followers still more:

> As I see it, the Soviet of Workers' Deputies, as a center of political revolutionary leadership, is not too broad but on the contrary too narrow an organization. The Soviet must proclaim itself the provisional revolutionary government, or form such a government, and be sure to draw in new deputies to this end—not only from workers but also, first, from sailors and soldiers, who are already reaching out for freedom everywhere; second, from the revolutionary peasantry; third, from the revolutionary bourgeois intelligentsia. . . . We are not afraid of such a broad and variegated membership—we want it, for unless proletariat and peasantry unite, unless Social-Democrats and revolutionary democrats fight as allies, the great Russian revolution cannot be a complete success. This will be a temporary alliance for clear-cut, immediate political objectives; the still more important, fundamental interests of the socialist proletariat, and its ultimate aims, will be steadfastly watched over by the Russian Social-Democratic Labor Party.

This conception came close to Trotsky's variant of the Menshevik viewpoint. It must have had a shattering effect on the Bolshevik leaders in Petersburg. The Party at large was not told about the article,[44] and *Novaia Zhizn* stopped discussing the

---

[44] In the process of improving on history, all this is now presented differently. In *Lenin v Peterburge* (*Mesta prebyvaniia i revoliutsionnoi deiatel'nosti V. I. Lenina v Peterburge-Petrograde, 1890–1900 g.g., 1905–1907 g.g., 1917–1920 g.g.*) (Leningrad: Istpart, 1957), we are informed that on the very day of his arrival in Petersburg, November 8, 1905, Lenin spoke on the attitude toward the Soviet of Workers' Deputies, at a meeting of the Petersburg Committee and Party workers: "In his speech Vladimir Il'ich sharply criticized the 'leftist' orientation of some Party members (Bogdanov, Knuniants, and others) who insisted that the Petersburg Soviet must adopt the program of the RSDRP. [Lenin] enlarged upon the ideas he had already expressed in a letter to the editors of *Novaia Zhizn*, 'Nashi zadachi i Sovet Rabochikh Deputatov,' during a stopover in Stockholm on his way to Russia. Lenin said that the demand of obligatory adoption of the program of the RSDRP by the Soviet of Workers' Deputies was fundamentally wrong—it showed that those who proposed it failed to understand the essence of the Soviet as a fighting political mass organization, failed to understand the relationship between the Party—the vanguard—and the class" (p. 70). This statement is allegedly based on archival materials and on three published sources. Only the latter could be verified, and all three references turned out to be false.

issue of the Party's relation to the Soviet, waiting for Lenin to change his mind or to find a formula less blatantly contradictory of everything the Bolsheviks had been saying before his return.

Lenin wrote in *Novaia Zhizn* almost daily, but at first he avoided the crucial question. He touched on it briefly in a small article, "Learn from Your Enemies!" on November 18 (*Novaia Zhizn*, No. 16)[45]—a reply to the left-democratic *Nasha Zhizn*, which had criticized the Social-Democrats' opposition to non-partisan class organizations. "Learn from your enemies!" Lenin exclaimed. "Down with non-partisanship! Non-partisanship has always been a weapon and a slogan of the bourgeoisie." Much was left unsaid, but in spirit the article was already the direct opposite of what he had written in Stockholm. On November 23, his article "Dying Autocracy and the New Organs of a People's Government" appeared in *Novaia Zhizn*, No. 19.[46] It had been prompted by a suggestion in the liberal-democratic *Rus'* that all freedom-loving parties join in creating a national soviet of deputies, which would become "a mighty instrument for exerting pressure on the government if it is still able to function or else an organ of popular government all ready to take over temporarily the government's duties in the event of the latter's complete incapacitation and collapse." Lenin interpreted this as a bid by the liberal bourgeoisie for a share in the government when the regime fell. It would have been consistent with his Stockholm article to oppose his "reformed" Soviet to the "national soviet of deputies." But that would have focused public attention on the Soviet of Workers' Deputies and its special role. Clearly wishing to avoid this, Lenin spoke vaguely of "organs of popular government,"

> growing on their own, on the soil plowed up by the political strike, fertilized with the blood of the fighters for freedom. These organs are the revolutionary parties and the fighting organizations of workers, peasants, and other popular elements carrying on the actual revolutionary struggle.

It is certainly no accident that in this passage the Soviet of Workers' Deputies was not mentioned by name. Keeping this up was too difficult, however, and later in the article Lenin said:

---

[45] Lenin, *Sochineniia*, X, 42–43.
[46] *Ibid.*, pp. 48–52.

We are forming a temporary fighting alliance with all of revolutionary democracy for the attainment of our common immediate aim. To this end, while strictly preserving our separateness and independence as a party, we are also in the Soviet of Workers' Deputies and in other revolutionary unions.

There is a sense of constraint in all this. "We" are in the Soviet for the sake of a "temporary fighting alliance with all of revolutionary democracy." Was this really the only reason? And, not to feature the Soviet too prominently, "we are *also* in the Soviet and in other revolutionary unions."

The real issues were getting harder and harder to avoid. On November 23 the Executive Committee of the Soviet, with the Bolsheviks' approval, rejected a request by the Anarchists to have their representatives admitted to both the Soviet and its Executive Committee on an equal basis with representatives of the socialist parties. *Novaia Zhizn* could not pass this over in silence. No. 21, of November 25, carried an article by Lenin, "Socialism and Anarchism," explaining the Anarchists' exclusion:[47] "The Soviet of Workers' Deputies is not a workers' parliament and not an organ of proletarian self-government, not an organ of self-government in any sense, but a fighting organization for the attainment of specific aims"—aims that the Anarchists did not share. And once more a somewhat enigmatic but essentially restrictive remark: the Party is represented in the Soviet "on the basis of a temporary, informal fighting agreement."

This was still treading water. Finally Lenin spoke out, in the article "The Socialist Party and Non-Partisan Revolutionism" (already discussed in chapter iii) in *Novaia Zhizn*, Nos. 22 and 27, November 26 and December 2.[48] Of his Stockholm views, nothing remained. "Strict partisanship is a concomitant and a result of a highly developed class struggle." "Non-partisanship means indifference to the parties' struggle," and since there could be no "abstention" from class struggle in a capitalist society, "indifference means tacit support of the strong, of those in power." Yet, "in an era of democratic revolution, refusal to participate in non-party organizations would amount in certain cases to refusal to participate in a democratic revolution. Of course, socialists *must*

---

[47] *Ibid.*, pp. 53–56.
[48] *Ibid.*, pp. 57–64.

delimit these 'certain cases' narrowly, they can admit such participation only on *firmly defined restrictive conditions.*" (Italics added.)

This was a complete return to the Bolsheviks' stand before Lenin's arrival. Lenin even added a safeguard the Petersburg Bolsheviks had not thought of:

> Circumstances may *force* us to participate in non-Party organizations—especially in an era of democratic revolution, particularly a democratic revolution in which the proletariat plays an outstanding role. [But] such participation . . . is admissible only if the independence of the workers' party is fully protected, and *if the Party members or groups "delegated" to non-Party unions or soviets are controlled and directed by the Party as a whole.* [Italics added.]

This was the first mention of the idea, so important later in Bolshevik tactics, of having the Party direct non-Party organizations through a system of "cells."

In substance, the thesis that Lenin from the very beginning favored the soviets as organs of revolutionary government is correct insofar as his Stockholm article is concerned. But the idea of assigning to the Soviet a leading role in the revolution was so foreign to the Petersburg Bolsheviks that they persuaded Lenin to give it up. He returned to it only when the soviets had ceased to exist and the danger of their competition was past. In 1927 Nevskii disputed the story, which was then just gaining acceptance, that Lenin had consistently (including all his articles in *Novaia Zhizn*) defended the Petersburg Soviet as a revolutionary government in embryo. Nevskii maintained that Lenin had expressed this idea for the first time only in March, 1906, in his booklet *The Victory of the Kadets and the Tasks of the Labor Party (Pobeda kadetov i zadachi rabochei partii)*.[49] In Lenin's published works there was indeed no indication of such a view before March, 1906; but Nevskii was unaware of the Stockholm article. After its publication it became easier to defend the thesis of Lenin's early approval of the soviets. Possibly the article was "found" (and published with a facsimile of its first page) for this very purpose. Lenin's Petersburg writings of November, 1905, are all the more interesting as evidence of the hostility of the local

---

[49] Nevskii, "Sovety v 1905 godu," p. 42.

Bolshevik leaders to the Soviet—a hostility so deep that Lenin bowed to it.[50]

---

[50] The Conference of (Bolshevik) Northern Committees in Moscow from November 21 to 23, attended by delegates from the Moscow, Nizhnii Novgorod, Tula, Tver, Ivanovo-Voznesensk, Iaroslavl, Kostroma, and Vladimir District (*okruzhnoi*) Committees of the Party, the Moscow representative of the CC, and one other agent of the CC, adopted the following resolution "Ob otnoshenii k Sovetam rabochikh deputatov i t.p. rabochim organizatsiiam": "Soviets of workers' deputies need to be created only where the organization cannot direct the proletariat's mass action in any other way or where it is necessary to detach masses that have fallen under the sway of bourgeois parties. The Soviet of Workers' Deputies must be the Party's technical apparatus for carrying the RSDRP's political leadership to the masses. Therefore it is imperative to gain control of it and to persuade it to recognize the program and the political leadership of the RSDRP." (*Novaia Zhizn*, November 29, 1905.) Here the inimical attitude to the idea of soviets is formulated perhaps even more forcefully than it was by the Petersburg Bolsheviks before Lenin's arrival.

CHAPTER 5

The Organizational Problems
of Social-Democracy

THE surge of the labor movement in 1904–5 made Social-Democracy very conscious of the inadequate state of its organization. I pointed out in chapter i the contrast between the Party's poor organization and its political influence, between its weakness and the immensity of its tasks. It was vital for the Party to solve the "organizational question," and the arguments about it were exceptionally intense.

Basic differences over Party organization had already arisen at the Second Party Congress in the summer of 1903 (also under the immediate stimulus of a sudden swell of the mass movement, a wave of industrial strikes in southern Russia). These differences had then focused on the definition of Party membership in Article 1 of the Party Rules. Lenin had wanted to define a member of the RSDRP as "one who accepts its program and supports the Party by personally participating in a Party organization";[1] Martov, as "one who accepts its program, supports the Party by material means, and renders it regular personal assistance under the direction of a Party organization."[2] In practice, Lenin's formula would

---

[1] *Vtoroi s"ezd RSDRP. Iiul'-avgust 1903 goda. Protokoly* (Moscow: Gospolitizdat, 1959), p. 262.

[2] *Ibid.*, p. 425.

have restricted the membership to a small circle of "professional revolutionaries"; Martov's extended it to include the large number of people who, although not members of an underground organization, were associated with the Party and were giving it sustained support.

What ingenuity, what inventiveness went into those arguments! "I think we must separate the concepts 'party' and 'organization,'" said Axelrod, supporting Martov.[3] Martov said, "We can only rejoice if every striker, every demonstrator, in answering for his actions, can call himself a Party member."[4] No, replied Lenin: "Better let ten people who work not call themselves Party members than give one windbag the right and the possibility to be a Party member."[5] This would unduly narrow the Party? Not at all: "We need a great variety of organizations of all kinds, ranks, and shadings, from extremely restricted and secret ones to very broad, free, *lose Organisationen*"; one thing, however, should be required for all—"confirmation by the Central Committee."[6] These points were passionately debated during almost two entire sessions. Besides Lenin and Martov, eighteen delegates spoke on the subject, including practically all the Party elite: Plekhanov, Axelrod, Trotsky, the *Rabochedel'tsy* Martynov and Akimov, the Bund leaders Liber and Medem, the leader of the Caucasus Social-Democrats Noah Zhordania, and others. Martov's formula won, 28 to 23.[7]

Many of the delegates were people of keen intellect and long experience in politics. Yet, as the reader can judge from the above samples, their arguments had about them a weird irreality. It was as if the debaters sensed some disease in the Party and were groping in the dark for a cure. For at least a year and a half—until January, 1905, brought forth other, vaster problems—the "organizational question" remained the focus around which eddied the Party's internal struggle, washing Bolsheviks and Mensheviks farther and farther apart.

---

[3] *Ibid.*, p. 262.
[4] *Ibid.*, p. 263.
[5] *Ibid.*, p. 277.
[6] *Ibid.*, p. 265.
[7] *Ibid*, pp. 262–81. See also chap. i, n.1.

The Arguments about Centralism, Discipline,
and Independent Activity

At the Congress, both factions professed to be staunch centralists. Lenin tried to attenuate his centralism by speaking of Party organizations "of all kinds," up to *"lose Organisationen."* Martov wished the Party to break out of the small, almost closed circle of "professional revolutionaries," yet declared that "strict centralism, not broad autonomy, is our organizational principle"[8] —this, it is true, in an argument not with Lenin but with the Bund. Most of the fine points discussed at the Congress were soon forgotten; the post-Congress disputes shifted to other matters, and the underlying attitudes of the two sides gradually became clear—in the first place to themselves.

The basic organizational idea of the Bolsheviks was to develop the Party as a centralized organization consisting mainly of people dedicated to revolutionary work above all else ("professional revolutionaries"), who would submit to strict Party discipline and in turn educate the masses in a spirit of unquestioning obedience to, and trust in, a party they could not join and whose decisions they could not directly influence.

The basic organizational idea of the Mensheviks was to draw as many intelligent workers into the movement as possible, to let them participate in the Party organization and have a voice in its decisions, so as to overcome the hegemony of "professional revolutionaries" which inevitably gave the Party a closed, "conspiratorial" character and prevented it from becoming truly the spearhead of the working class.

The Bolsheviks' conception is most clearly expressed in Lenin's "Letter to a Comrade about Our Organizational Tasks,"[9] written in the fall of 1902 when Petersburg comrades had asked him to criticize the rules they had drawn up for the local organization. The hectographed letter remained an internal Party document until early 1904, when it was printed and widely distributed by the Central Committee, entirely Bolshevik at the time.

---

[8] *Vtoroi s"ezd RSDRP . . . 1903 . . .* , p. 259.

[9] Lenin, *Sochineniia* (4th ed.), VI, 205–24. Page numbers in parentheses on the next few pages are from this reference.

Throughout 1904 the letter played a big role in the discussion of organizational problems.

The plan outlined in the letter rested entirely on the principle of tight control over local and nationwide party work by the local committees and the Central Committee (for the nationwide work, this was difficult to achieve since there were two centers—the Central Organ for ideological, and the Central Committee for practical, leadership). The local committees were to be formed with the "participation" and "consent" of the Central Committee (p. 211). They were to consist of "fully conscious Social-Democrats devoting themselves entirely to Social-Democratic activity" (in other words, professional revolutionaries) (p. 211). "There should not be too many committee members (to insure quality, and greater specialization in their exercise of their revolutionary profession), yet enough of them to manage all aspects of the work and insure full discussion and firm decisions" (pp. 211–12). The committee would organize and control sector groups, factory committees, and "diverse groups serving the movement—groups of university and high-school youth; groups of, let us say, co-operating government employees; transport, printing, passport groups; groups arranging for secret apartments; groups for detecting spies; groups of the military; groups for procuring arms; groups for organizing, for example, a 'paying commercial enterprise'; and so on" (p. 215). All would be subordinated to the committee; some would belong to the Party and some would not, but all would be organized on authoritarian lines. Let us consider the most important of these bodies, the sector groups and the factory committees.

The sector groups (not sector committees!) were to be direct organs of the local committees: "The composition of the sector groups must be determined by the committee, that is, the committee *appoints* one or two of its members (or even non-members) as delegates to a given sector and intrusts them with *the formation of a sector group*, all members of which are in turn 'confirmed' by the committee. The sector group is a subsidiary of the committee, getting its authority from it alone" (pp. 214–15; Lenin's italics here and below). "One of the most important tasks [of the sector groups] is the properly managed distribution of literature. I think that sector groups should be mainly *intermedi-*

aries between the committee and the factories—intermediaries or even mainly *transmitters*. . . . A sector group should be allowed independence only in technical matters of transmission and distribution" (pp. 213–14).

The group should not even engage in propaganda in its own sector—that was the committee's job:

> The committee instructs several of its members to organize a group of propagandists. This group, using the *services* of sector groups in underground matters, must conduct propaganda *in the entire city*, the entire area of the committee's "competence." If necessary, this group may form subgroups—delegate a part of its functions, so to speak—but only with the committee's sanction; the committee must always have the unconditional right to send its delegate into any group, subgroup, or circle at all connected with the movement. [P. 215. Incredible as it seems, this was the plan for Petersburg! —S.S.]

Similar rules, with perhaps even greater stress on the authoritarian principle, were to be applied to factory committees—or factory subcommittees, as Lenin often called them, to distinguish them from the main local committee (I am capitalizing the latter in the following quotation, to prevent confusion):

> A factory group or committee should consist of a small number of *revolutionaries* getting their instructions, and the authorization to conduct all the Social-Democratic work at the factory, *directly from the Committee*. All members of the factory committee must consider themselves agents of the Committee, duty-bound to observe all the "laws and customs" of the "active army" which they have joined and which they have no right to leave in time of war without their superiors' permission. Hence the composition of the factory committee is very important, and it must be one of the Committee's main concerns to set up these subcommittees properly. This is how I see it: the Committee assigns to some of its members (plus perhaps certain persons from among the workers—persons not included in the Committee for various reasons but who could be useful by their experience, intelligence, knowledge of people, or their connections) the organization of factory subcommittees everywhere. This commission consults with representatives of the sector, arranges a number of interviews, thoroughly examines the candidates for membership in factory subcommittees, subjects them to "trial by ordeal," subjects them to tests if necessary, while trying

to look over and personally examine the *greatest possible* number of candidates to the subcommittee of the given factory, and finally asks the Committee to confirm such-and-such composition of every factory circle or to authorize this or that worker to form, designate, pick out the entire subcommittee. In this way it is again the Committee that determines which of these agents is to communicate with it and *how* he is to communicate. . . . Finally, it should perhaps be mentioned that, instead of a factory subcommittee of several members, it may sometimes be necessary, or more *convenient*, to appoint just one agent of the Committee (and one alternate). [Pp. 217–18.]

The relations between the center and the local organizations —not just the local committees but all Party and non-Party groups working under them—were to be regimented in the same utopian bureaucratic-revolutionary way. The Central Committee and the Central Organ (the letter did not foresee the conflict between them) were to be informed of every detail of local work:

A group of students [or] officers [or] employees, engaged in self-education *with the assistance* of one or two Party members, sometimes need not even know that [the latter] are Party members, and so on. In one respect, however, we must *absolutely* require *maximal formality* in running all these subsidiary groups: every Party member participating in them is formally responsible for the conduct of work in these groups, is obliged to take *all* measures to *lay bare to the fullest* before the CC and the CO the composition of each such group, and the whole *mechanism* of its work, and the entire content of that work. . . . This is absolutely essential in all cases. [P. 220.]

Oddly enough, the letter describes this extreme centralism as "a necessary corrective" to centralism (p. 221), as "*maximal decentralization* of responsibility to the center and of [the center's] intelligence about all the big and little wheels of the Party" (p. 222).[10] The center can direct the Party effectively only if it receives information in this "decentralized" way:

To enable the center not only to advise, persuade, and argue (as it has done until now) but truly to conduct the orchestra, it is imperative that it know exactly who is playing what violin and where,

---

[10] It was not specified that the central agencies in turn should inform the lesser "wheels" of what they were doing—which would have been a "corrective" to extreme centralization, a possible germ of decentralization.

where and how he learned or is learning to play what instrument; where and why he dissonates (when the music offends the ear); who should be moved where, and in what way, to correct the discordance, and so on. [Pp. 222–23.]

From that time on, the words "conduct the orchestra" and the more emotionally charged "conductor's baton" kept cropping up in intraparty polemics.

Besides regular reports to the center on the composition of every subsidiary group and the "mechanism of its work," the letter required "*obligatory* transmission to a safe place (the Party bureau at the CO or the CC) of contacts [*sviazei*] with that circle, that is, the names and addresses of several of its members" —in code, naturally. Only when he had done that, could a Party member working in a circle be considered to have discharged his duties. Arrests would not mean a bad setback since "it will be easy for the delegate of our CC to find replacements and have the work resume. The arrest of a committee will not destroy the entire machine but only snip off the leaders, for whom alternates are available" (pp. 220–21).

Lenin expressed the same ultracentralist ideas in *One Step Forward, Two Steps Backward,*[11] an analysis of the debates and votes of the Second Congress, published in the spring of 1904. So cluttered with detail that sometimes the reader can get his bearings only if he also consults the protocols of the Congress, this work did not reach a wide Party audience in Russia, and it was from the letter that most young Bolsheviks learned their ideology of organization.

That these views strongly influenced the Bolshevik party workers at the local level can be seen from the "Answer to the Letter of the CO from Representatives of the Ufa, Middle-Ural, and Perm Committees" printed in a supplement to *Iskra,* No. 63, April 1, 1904, which became widely known in Party circles as "Pis'mo Ural'tsev." I shall refer to it as "the Ural Letter." Responding to "the official invitation of the CO's editors" (in a letter sent to the committees) to comment on the situation in the Party, the Ural Committees criticized "*Iskra*'s new opinions" and expressed their own beliefs:

---

[11] Lenin, *Sochineniia,* VII, 185–392.

Only an all-Russian centralized organization of revolutionaries in *full control* of the local committees can foresee the political struggle of the proletariat, prepare for it, march ahead of the masses. . . . Both the committees and individual Party members can be given very broad powers, but this must depend on the Central Committee. On the other hand, the Central Committee can also—if it finds it necessary or useful—*disband a committee or another organization* or deprive this or that Party member of his rights. Otherwise the proletariat's struggle cannot be successfully organized. [Italics added here and below.]

The Ural Letter rejected as "purely opportunistic" the view expressed in *Iskra* that "in Germany the question of the conductor's baton lost importance in direct proportion to the growth of the proletariat's class consciousness. The proletariat's class consciousness relentlessly, if slowly, does its work." The Ural Committees felt that the Party should be educated in a spirit of *unquestioning obedience.*

Preparing the proletariat for dictatorship is such an important organizational task that all others must be subordinated to it. The preparation consists, among other things, in building up a favorable attitude toward a strong, *masterful* proletarian organization and fully making clear its importance. *One might retort that dictators . . . appear spontaneously. But that is not always the case, and in a proletarian party it must not happen spontaneously or opportunistically.* Here the highest degree of consciousness must be coupled with *unquestioning obedience.*

The authors wanted all "incorrigible revisionists, opportunists, backhangers [*khvostisty*]" to be ruthlessly expelled from the Party; and a spirit of "voluntary, conscious, and necessary *unquestioning obedience*" to be created. "Long enough have we floated in flimsy boats at the mercy of currents; we are building a big ship, the last word in science and skill, and *we need a good captain* for it."

To be sure, these were the views of extreme, "rockhard" centralists, but the underlying attitude was quite common among Bolshevik party workers.[12] Long before the Ural Letter, in *Iskra*

---

[12] Some ten years later I realized with surprise how deep and persistent these feelings were. In the winter of 1913/14 I was in jail in Petersburg and conversed with the inmate of the next cell by knocking on the wall. He was a prominent

of December 15, 1903, P. B. Axelrod had quoted from the rules (!) of a local organization:

> Recognizing that under the present conditions a forcible overturn can be achieved in Russia only with the support of the working masses of large industrial centers *prepared to obey* and [ready for] an open uprising, we are making the organization of the working class the main focus of our work.[13]

The Mensheviks' organizational ideas underwent a more complex evolution. At the Second Congress, as we have seen, they too had favored a centralized organization. The Party did not yet exist as an organized entity, and in the face of the rising mass movement the need to be done with "amateurism" was acutely felt. Axelrod wrote of that time: "The motto 'Away with organizational anarchy, hail to merging all the forces of Social-Democracy into one strictly centralized organization!' soon became the common cry of most members of our Party."[14]

Yet in their understanding of "centralism" and of the role it should play in the development of the unified Party, the future Mensheviks and the future Bolsheviks had clearly begun to differ. At the Congress, over Article 1 of the Rules, the disagreement had flared up with a virulence that must have surprised all concerned. Axelrod, as we have seen, proposed to differentiate between the concepts "party" and "organization"— a broadly understood "party" and a necessarily narrow, closed "organization." This was a throwback to the terminology of the seventies and eighties, when the term "revolutionary party" embraced all who held revolutionary views and the entire gamut of revolution-

---

Bolshevik party worker and a good journalist, whom I had met in the course of our work. In jail we became quite friendly. Once he told me that we Mensheviks were unfortunate in having neither a final, absolute authority nor a "homeland," while the Bolsheviks had both: Lenin and Cracow! I was flabbergasted and replied that he didn't seem to understand what a terrible thing he had said. My neighbor died a martyr's death in 1938, and I would rather not give his name.

[13] Axelrod did not name the organization whose rules he was quoting, but in the second edition of his pamphlet *Narodnaia duma i rabochii s"ezd* (Petersburg: Novyi mir, 1907), p. 16, he mentions that it was the Viatka Committee.

[14] P. Axelrod, "Ob"edinenie rossiiskoi sotsialdemokratii i ee zadachi"—two articles in *Iskra*, subtitled, respectively, "Itogi likvidatsii kustarnichestva" (No. 55, December 15, 1903), and "Obshcherevoliutsionnye i proletarskie tendentsii v nashem dvizhenii" (No. 57, January 15, 1904). The quotation is from *Iskra*, No. 55.

ary organizations. But the Congress had been concerned with the "organization" and its rules: a "party" in this broad sense could not have rules. Axelrod had seen that Lenin's brand of centralism would lead the Party into an impasse. *In substance, he was right* in rebelling against it. His argumentation, however, rather missed the mark, even if Martov, Trotsky, and others supported it. *Formally, Lenin was right* when he wrote in *One Step Forward*, in reply to Martov's remark at the Congress that a conspiratorial organization made sense only if it was "encased in a broad Social-Democratic workers' party": "It would have been more exact to say . . . 'encased in a broad Social-Democratic workers' *movement.*'"[15]

The Menshevik leaders' outcry against Lenin's centralism was a natural reaction against the ugly idea of a closed organization. But an underground party hounded by the police could hardly be anything else, as both Mensheviks and Bolsheviks knew. The difference was that the Bolsheviks elevated centralism into a principle, whereas the Mensheviks accepted it as a temporary evil, trying wherever possible to encourage the workers' *independent* activity and to give them a share in Party life. Criticizing *One Step Forward*, Martov wrote:

> By European standards, the organization that has worked out its Rules at the Second Congress . . . is only an organization of *leaders* of the proletarian struggle, not an organization of struggling proletarians.
>
> . . . .
>
> This kind of political leadership of the proletariat cannot be considered truly Social-Democratic leadership. To make it such, our work must be substantially reformed in such a way that along with the spreading and increasingly revolutionary mass movement there may be a corresponding development and growth of an independent *class party of the proletariat*, with the "committees" as its recognized *political representatives*. . . . The policy of the Russian Social-Democratic Labor Party must not only "ideally," not only from the point of view of the purity of its "leaders'" principles, but in fact, in reality, become the active policy of the conscious stratum of the Russian proletariat, whose representatives those "leaders" would be; it follows that this conscious stratum . . . must actively

---

[15] Lenin, *Sochineniia*, VII, 242.

participate in all manifestations of Party life, in the process of working out the Party's program, the principles of its tactics, and its organizational methods. When this is so, we shall really have the right to call ourselves the *vanguard* of the Russian proletariat.[16]

Only in this way could the Party change from an "organization of leaders" into "the skeleton of an *independent proletarian class party.*"

Axelrod expressed similar views, more decisively, in a letter to Kautsky on June 6, 1904:

> Through self-criticism (of the Party's past and present, its one-sidedness, and so on), we are calling the comrades' attention to the question vital to our Party: *What should we do so that Russian Social-Democracy (before the decisive moment in the struggle with absolutism) may be transformed, at least partly, from a politically intermediate creature into a true proletarian class party?* Unless we solve this problem, we are running the risk that at the decisive moment events will sweep [Social-Democracy] off the stage of history.[17]

Stress is laid on solving the problem "before the decisive moment in the struggle with absolutism." When Axelrod published his letter in *Iskra,* he added a "note to Russian readers, especially to perceptive ones," in which he once more expressed strong disagreement with the view that it was "utopian" to strive for a systematic self-transformation of Social-Democracy "while still in the shackles of absolutism," from a party of the revolutionary intelligentsia *leaning* on the proletariat into a party of the proletarian class itself. To understand these remarks, one must remember the atmosphere of the time, when the approaching storm could already be felt and the old order had clearly begun to crack.

Several leaders of German Social-Democracy were drawn into the dispute. Until the First World War, Russian Social-Democracy looked up to its German counterpart, and after the Second Congress both wings of the RSDRP sought the backing of German theoreticians, especially of the "orthodox," "anti-Bernstein"

---

[16] L. M., "Vpered ili nazad?" Part 2: "Proletarii i intelligenty v russkoi sotsialdemokratii," supplement to *Iskra,* No. 69, July 10, 1904.

[17] Axelrod, "K voprosu ob istochnike i znachenii nashikh organizatsionnykh raznoglasii (Iz perepiski s Kautskim)," *Iskra,* No. 68, June 25, 1904.

ones. They turned first to Karl Kautsky, the internationally recognized authority on revolutionary Social-Democratic theory, and to Rosa Luxemburg and Parvus, who knew Russian and were popular with the international left. All three expressed their solidarity with the Mensheviks' view. Rosa Luxemburg's article "The Organizational Questions of Social-Democracy," printed in Kautsky's weekly *Die Neue Zeit* (1903–4, Nos. 42 and 43) as well as in *Iskra* (No. 69, July 10, 1904) especially influenced the Social-Democrats in Russia.

Rejecting Lenin's "ultracentralism," she stressed the profound difference between Social-Democratic and Jacobin-Blanquist centralism:

> The Social-Democratic movement is the first in the history of class societies to be geared in all its aspects and its overall course to the organization and the direct independent activity of the masses.
>
> In this regard, Social-Democracy is creating quite another type of organization than did earlier Social-Democratic movements, for example, those of the Jacobin-Blanquist kind.
>
> Lenin does not seem to appreciate this sufficiently when he says in his book that a revolutionary Social-Democrat is nothing else than "a Jacobin inseparably bound up with the *organization* of a proletariat which has *become conscious* of its class interests." For Lenin the whole difference between Social-Democracy and Blanquism boils down to the organization and the class consciousness of the proletariat as against a conspiracy of a small minority. He forgets that this entails . . . filling the concept of centralism with an entirely new content, an entirely new understanding of the correlation between organization and struggle.
>
> Blanquism was not based on the direct class activity of the working masses and hence did not require their organization. On the contrary, since the broad popular masses were to appear on the battlefield only at the moment of the revolution, and the preliminary work of preparing the revolutionary thrust was done by a small minority, a sharp demarcation between the individuals designated for this specific work and the popular mass was downright indispensable for the success of their task. . . .
>
> The conditions of Social-Democratic work are fundamentally different. It takes its historical growth from elementary class struggle. . . . Organization, the development of consciousness, and the struggle are not distinct, temporally separated aspects . . . but

merely different facets of one and the same process. . . . Just from this, it follows that Social-Democratic centralization cannot be based on blind obedience, or on mechanical subordination of the Party's fighters to the rule of its center.[18]

Lenin's plan looked to Rosa Luxemburg like "a mechanical transfer of the organizational principles of the Blanquist movement of conspiratorial circles to the Social-Democratic movement of the working masses":

> And perhaps Lenin characterizes his own standpoint more shrewdly than any of his opponents could when he defines his "revolutionary Social-Democrat" as "a Jacobin bound up with the organization of a proletariat which has become conscious of its class interests." Actually, Social-Democracy is *not bound up* with the organization of the working class; it is itself the *genuine movement* of the working class. Consequently Social-Democratic centralism must essentially differ from Blanquist centralism.

Russia, it is true, did not yet offer all the necessary conditions for Social-Democratic centralism, but *the elements for it were being created in the process of the labor movement's development.*

> . . . It would be a mistake to think that "for the time being" the autocratic rule of the Party center can be substituted, "by proxy," for the still unattainable supremacy of a majority of conscious workers in their Party organization or that control by the CC over the activity of the revolutionary proletariat can make up for the lack of open control by the working masses over what the Party organs do or do not do.[19]

---

[18] The quotation from Lenin used by Luxemburg may be found in *Sochineniia*, VII, 353.

[19] In late September Lenin sent to *Die Neue Zeit* a reply to Rosa Luxemburg's article, but instead of explaining the controversy in Russian Social-Democracy, he filled his article with remarks about her wrong interpretation of what had happened at the Second Congress and after. Kautsky refused to print it. Surprisingly, Lenin did not publish his article, either as a pamphlet through his publishing house or in *Vpered*, which began publication three months later. Perhaps he himself was dissatisfied with it. The article remained unknown until 1930, when it was printed in Vol. XV of *Leninskii Sbornik*. Later it was included in *Sochineniia*, VII, 439–50. Lenin must have been stung by Luxemburg's criticism. Repeatedly in 1905 he referred in passing to "the notorious theory of 'organization as process' (see especially Rosa Luxemburg's articles)," "the theory of Rosa Luxemburg, who discovered 'organization as process,'" "Axelrod's (or Luxemburg's?) recondite theory of organization as process." (Lenin, *Sochineniia*, VIII, 45, 131, 260.)

The Arguments about Intelligenty and Workers in the Party

The post-Congress disputes between Mensheviks and Bolsheviks often led in the end to the question of the respective roles of *intelligenty* and workers in the Party. It was not the intelligentsia in the broad sense that was meant but the Party intelligentsia of bourgeois or petty-bourgeois origin as opposed to the workers, including the workers' intelligentsia brought forth by the labor movement.

In his already quoted article "The Unification of Social-Democracy and Its Tasks" (see n. 14), Axelrod placed the question in a broad historical context: the RSDRP "is only trying to become the political organization of the working masses; in reality, in the composition of its leadership, *it is as yet, in the main, only an organization of partisans of the proletariat among the revolutionary intelligentsia*" (italics added). Nor is this accidental: "Objectively, historically, the very leaning of the radical intelligentsia toward socialism and the proletariat is called forth and determined, in the last analysis, not by the proletariat's class struggle but by the general democratic urge of the nation and the classes to be rid of the remnants of the era of serfdom." On the other hand, "some elemental forces of history itself are pushing our movement toward bourgeois revolutionism—against our wishes and our reason."[20] Hence there is danger that "our labor movement may be reduced to the role of mere tool in the process of our bourgeois revolution."

In the West, Social-Democracy had emerged when the goals of the bourgeois revolution had already been attained, whether through revolution or evolution. In Russia the very foundations on which to build the bourgeois order still had to be gained. This

[20] Dan notes in *Proiskhozhdenie bol'shevizma* (New York: Novaia Demokratiia, 1946), p. 288, that this remark seems to bring Axelrod close to Lenin's theory about the labor movement's tendency to become "bourgeois" but points out that Lenin set his hopes on the intelligentsia to supply "from without" the socialist consciousness lacking in the proletariat, whereas Axelrod saw "the greatest danger" in the fact that the proletariat had to be awakened and activated by an element extraneous to it.

made an enormous difference for the development of Social-Democracy:

> In the West, Social-Democracy is, and has been from the first, nothing else than a part of the *proletariat itself*, flesh of its flesh, bone of its bone. [The proletariat] is at once the agent and the object of its own class education and unification. The systematic influence exercised by Social-Democracy on the working masses is the influence exercised by their own most advanced, ideologically conscious, and organized layers upon the comparatively still backward layers of the same working masses. In the West, the development of the proletariat's class consciousness and independent activity is therefore a process of *self*-development, *self*-education. . . . With us, the systematic influence exercised by Social-Democracy upon these masses has meant influence *from without*, by a social element alien to them; and educating them has been tantamount to subordinating them to the leadership of the radical intelligentsia.

This state of affairs was likely to have deep historical and political consequences:

> Let us imagine for a moment that our movement has achieved ideal results in all these respects [that is, in attracting the sympathies of the revolutionary intelligentsia and in drawing the workers into the latter's sphere of influence.—S.S.]. All the radical elements of the intelligentsia are arrayed under the banner of Social-Democracy, grouped around its central organization, support the latter in every way, and supply it with constantly growing contingents of professional revolutionaries, who alone can belong to these organizations. This on one hand. On the other—the working masses, to a still greater extent than now, follow [Social-Democracy's] directives and are ready to obey it. . . . What would that mean? . . . A revolutionary political organization of the democratic bourgeoisie would be leading the working masses of Russia in its wake as its fighting army. To top off the malicious irony, history might even give us as leader of this bourgeois-revolutionary organization not just a Social-Democrat but an ultra-"orthodox" (by his origin) Marxist.

In the climate of 1904 the problem of the Social-Democratic leaders' social origins loomed very large, especially at the local level. The Bolsheviks denied its existence, maintaining that under Russian conditions the Party machine *had* to be directed at all levels by tested "professional revolutionaries"—who, with rare exceptions, came from the bourgeoisie or the petty bourgeoisie. The Mensheviks' standpoint—expressed in the articles by Axelrod in *Iskra*, Nos. 55 and 57 (from which I have been quoting), and soon espoused by all Mensheviks as the basis of their organizational, and largely their theoretical, views—called for active participation by workers in the organization, for rapprochement between the local Party organs and the masses. Because of police persecution (and provocation) this met with almost insuperable obstacles, and in practice the *social composition* of the organizations led by the Bolsheviks and by the Mensheviks was about the same. The difference lay in their attitudes toward the respective roles of workers and *intelligenty* in Party organizations. In Bolshevik eyes, it was "opportunism" even to raise this question. The quintessence of this attitude is perfectly if crudely expressed in the Ural Letter quoted above, which blithely equates "revolutionary Social-Democracy" with "intelligentsia" (assuming that this is as it should be). The Mensheviks tolerated the immense preponderance of *intelligenty* among local party workers as an inevitable temporary evil but tried to palliate it by seizing every opportunity to stimulate the workers' activity in all Party organizations. In many cities where the Bolsheviks dominated the local Party committee, conflicts arose over this issue between the committees and their Menshevik-leaning "peripheries." In the second half of 1904 these conflicts led to the formation, side by side with the Bolshevik "committees," of Menshevik "groups," far more influential among the workers.[21]

---

[21] The conflict sharpened over the question of the Third Congress. Martov wrote in the article "Partiinyi s"ezd ili s"ezd kruzhkov?," *Iskra*, No. 94, March 25, 1905: "It is no secret that for a whole year many committees have been doing little else than 'dismissing' organized proletarians, for the specific purpose of keeping the mandate to the Congress in a certain group. This work has been so brilliantly successful that in almost all the main centers various 'groups' of all kinds of 'outcasts' have now been formed side by side with the 'rockhard' committees; and these groups *always* are much stronger, have more members and more influence, than the committees and shoulder the whole burden of real leadership of the mass movement. To substantiate this, it will suffice to remind [the reader] that during the memorable January days, when the Petersburg proletarian masses surged up spontaneously, all the efforts of Social-Democratic agitation resulted from the energetic work of the 'Group' and that recently this Group managed to crown the campaign around the Shidlovskii Commission with a shining achievement, the acceptance of the 'manifesto' by the majority of the electors, which means that the majority of these freely elected representatives of a hundred thousand workers

But even the Mensheviks could not fully satisfy the workers' wish to make the Social-Democratic Party their own party in fact as well as in theory. The problem of *intelligenty* versus workers was hotly discussed in Menshevik and pro-Menshevik circles. During these debates it became clear that the active workers had begun to realize that they were not considered full-fledged Party members. Bitterness toward the Party intelligentsia, whether Bolshevik or Menshevik, was vented in the pamphlet *Workers and Intelligenty in our Organizations*,[22] signed "A Worker" and published in late 1904 with a long critical preface by Axelrod. It may

---

have in principle joined our Party. No wonder that the organization of the Petersburg Group unites twice as many workers (about five hundred) as the official Committee; the [numerical] superiority of its organizers, propagandists, and agitators is still greater. What we see in Petersburg can be observed in other cities as well. In Riga the group that was forced away from the Committee organized three hundred workers in a short time (the Committee has much fewer); right after it was formed it was heading the strike of Russian workers, with whom the Committee had established no strong ties during the whole year of its existence. In Baku the 'Balakhany and Bibi-Eibat Organization,' made up of comrades 'dismissed' by the Committee, not only prepared the December general strike but saw it through despite the active opposition of the Committee, which was so 'carried away' that it made an agreement with the capitalist industrialists, behind the Organization's back, to end the strike on the most pitiable terms, which it 'enjoined' the strikers to accept. . . . In Ekaterinoslav, as everyone knows, the 'rockhard' Committee simply faded out when the news about January 9 came: it had nothing to do with the masses, having severed all ties with them by its fatal method of 'dismissals.' The Committee's 'press' passed into the hands of the Mensheviks, who did work with the masses and made use of the strike period as Social-Democrats should. In Nikolaev, that old 'stronghold' of *Vpered* people, the Committee likewise fell into the Mensheviks' hands when the mass strike began. In Odessa the Mensheviks and 'conciliationists' who had been ousted from the Committee organization formed a Group in January, and two months later they were many times stronger than the Committee and had distributed during that period several times the number of proclamations [distributed] by the Committee. In Moscow the 'Menshevists' and 'conciliationists,' who had sparked all the work in January, are now being subjected to Turkish—excuse me, Odessa-Baku—'atrocities' by the firm Committee, which feels obliged to expend its valuable energy on obstructing the development of the masses' strike and political movement because —strikes and demonstrations interfere with 'preparing the uprising.' One could cite a couple of places where the 'rockhard' comrades have none of this criminal attitude to the interests of the movement and work very well (Tver, Batum, Kutais). But the exceptions only prove the rule. . . ."

[22] *Rabochie i intelligenty v nashikh organizatsiiakh*, signed "Rabochii" ("A Worker") and published by the Menshevik party press in Geneva. Before the pamphlet came out, Axelrod's "Vmesto predisloviia" appeared as an article in *Iskra*, No. 80, December 15, 1904, with the title "Pis'ma k tovarishcham-rabochim." The letter "Intelligenty i rabochie v nashei partii" was somewhat expanded in the pamphlet. My quotations are from the pamphlet; they are identical with the text of the *Iskra* article.

have been, in part, a reverberation of the earlier struggle between "Economism" and "politicism" (*Iskra* had been the main champion of the latter), during which the economic problems of the workers had been somewhat neglected in favor of political problems. This had naturally reduced the workers' influence, small to begin with, over local party work. After the Second Congress the Mensheviks had tried to correct these undesirable consequences, but it was a difficult task, complicated by the split in the Party, which even the rank-and-file Party members found it hard to understand. (The workers tended to regard it as mere "intelligentsia wrangles.")

For the author of the pamphlet, the basic question ("perhaps the most important in our Party life"), which had to be solved "to insure the healthy and successful development of our Party," was that of "the mutual relations of workers and *intelligenty* in our organizations" (p. 18). He accused "our *praktiki*" (i.e. the *intelligenty* engaged in "practical" as against "theoretical" party work) of actually wanting to prevent workers from influencing local party work, however slightly. (This criticism was applied only to party workers at the lower level; of the central, especially the "theoretical," leadership the author spoke quite differently, as we shall see.) The pamphlet's indignation with local *praktiki* was boundless:

> Our *intelligenty* leaders have never, or hardly ever, made it their primary task to develop the consciousness and independent activity even of those workers with whom they came into fairly close contact. Worse, lately things have gotten so that our *praktiki* not only haven't tried to draw conscious workers into the Party leadership but have consciously or unconsciously systematically persecuted all such strivings on their part for independent activity from the bottom up. On this ungrateful soil an unhappy *antagonism* between workers and the intelligentsia has arisen which at present especially needs to be liquidated (p. 18).

During the period of Economism, the pamphlet continued, the workers' trade-union organizations had enjoyed a certain autonomy, which had given a mighty impulse to the workers' striving for independent activity. In the following period, the era of "politicism," such autonomy had been denied them. In their "harsh struggle" against the workers' organizations, the advocates of the political struggle "made no effort to secure for the conscious workers, of which there were already a few, a further and more correct development of their independent activity." Indeed, "such aspirations began to look so suspicious to our *praktiki* that it was almost with pride that some of them observed that there were no workers in the Party's leading agencies. . . . The enemy had been vanquished!" (pp. 19–20). Having "vanquished the workers" and secured for itself a position "permitting it to be independent of the workers in the matter of leadership and to take the road of 'generalship' with a light heart" (p. 36), the Party intelligentsia had in fact become "a carrier of antiproletarian tendencies" (p. 37).

For this state of affairs the author had a sociological explanation. He told the *intelligenty* party workers: "This attitude of yours toward workers and consequently toward the proletarian movement is not a product of your will but a product of your psychology, which in turn is . . . a product of your class, or group, instinct" (p. 50). Rather naïvely, he advised them to break free of their hostile class "instinct" by frankly admitting their mistake, "if these actions of yours are directed against the proletariat's strivings for independent activity" (p. 50).

These strictures were by no means confined to the Bolshevik, "Leninist" intelligentsia: "It is better not to harbor undue illusions about the so-called Martovite intelligentsia either" (p. 42). Still, the highest "theoreticians" were exempt; all the blame lay with local party workers: "Getting no response to its legitimate aspirations" from them, the conscious proletariat "naturally expects a response from our theoreticians" (p. 33). "Fortunately, despite long years of strife, our Party has not lost these genuine leaders of the proletariat, such as the 'Minority' theoreticians, without whom it could not exist as a *proletarian* party" (p. 29).

Just adding workers to committees was not the solution: "I am of course not talking about introducing one or two dozen workers into the committees but about transferring the conscious work of leadership from the top of the Party to the stratum of conscious workers" (p. 34). By "top of the Party" the author evidently meant the leaders of the local organizations. How the transfer was to be accomplished he did not say.

Axelrod in his foreword agreed up to a point.

> This pamphlet shows your growing proletarian self-awareness and the intense desire in your ranks for broader and more energetic independent activity in your own Party. Needless to say, any Social-Democrat . . . devoted to the cause of elevating the proletariat politically cannot but rejoice in this drive, of paramount importance just now, when the immediate fate of our Party and the role of the proletarian masses in the coming decisive battles of democracy with absolutism so largely depend on the broad initiative and activity of our Social-Democratic workers. [P. 3.]

But what would happen if the Social-Democrats followed the pamphlet's suggestion and changed the makeup of Party committees so as to give workers numerical superiority over the intelligentsia?

> In the first place, this would revive the defunct "democratism" which is incompatible with the conditions under which revolutionary organizations have to exist under absolutism and which therefore always . . . degenerates into its opposite and serves as shield for ambitious plotters, even gives clever *provocateurs* access to the organization. In the second place, a struggle would develop between the proponents and the opponents of this alleged "democratism" in the Party organization. Far more than the motto of the era of Economism, "Purely a Workers' Movement!" would the motto "Hail to Genuine Proletarians, Down with *Intelligenty*," serve all kinds of demagogues to corrupt the workers and disorganize the Party. Readers who remember the exploits of police demagogues of the Zubatov school can easily imagine in what way the representatives of reaction could exploit intraparty conflicts on those grounds. [Pp. 6–7.]

Resolving the crisis in Social-Democracy was a more complex process than the author of the pamphlet realized. The "antagonism between workers and *intelligenty*" was not the whole problem, or the main problem, but a part of it, which could not be solved separately (p. 5). It could be radically solved

> only in the process of our Party's conscious collective work consistently aimed at organizing ever broader masses of the proletariat and drawing them into a *conscious* and organized struggle for their class interests. . . . Only on the basis and in the atmosphere of that struggle can class consciousness develop and the proletarian masses

unite into an independent political party. . . . And it is precisely in the process of developing the independent class activity of the working masses, by acting as prime movers, leaders, and organizers in the struggle for the economic, political, and cultural interests of the proletariat, that our "workers' intelligentsia"—engulfing the *intelligenty* and thus merging with them—can win in Russian Social-Democracy a position in accord with its program, its principles, its designation as the party of the proletariat. [P. 9.]

Axelrod appeared to be feeling his way toward the "Party reform" that was to preoccupy the Mensheviks in 1905 and which the Bolsheviks considered a heretical and "opportunistic" idea. Of course even the Bolsheviks could not help seeing that the workers were dissatisfied with a Party organization that gave all "power" at the local level to "committees" of "professional revolutionaries" directed and controlled from above. Hence they, too, discussed including workers in committees—but not in order to change the nature of the organization but only as a means of strengthening the committees' ties with the workers. Often their basic aim was "social-decorative" rather than Social-Democratic.[23]

Conservatism or Party Reform?

This "decorative" intent was very noticeable at the so-called Third Party Congress in the spring of 1905. By then, with the swelling mass movement and its natural gravitation toward Social-Democracy, the relationship between *intelligenty* and workers in

---

[23] This is very clear from a March, 1905, letter of Gusev, the secretary of the Petersburg Committee and of the Bureau of the Committees of the Majority. V. Nevskii writes in *Rabochee dvizhenie v ianvarskie dni 1905 goda* (Moscow, 1930), p. 159: "Only in March [1905] did the Bolshevik organization, under the blows of reality, take account of the tremendous drive of the working masses for independence and independent activity and attempt to vitalize its intelligentsia organization by an influx of live forces from among the workers:

"'A circular on organizational questions is needed,' wrote Comrade Gusev to [the center] abroad, 'particularly on the issue of drawing workers into the committees. It is necessary to stress the importance of the condition on which this can be done. The criterion for bringing in workers should not be how well read they are, but how revolutionary, how devoted, energetic, and influential. Nowadays there are many such [people], and *mainly among unorganized workers*, most of them very young and lacking the political qualities of political leaders, although they are well read in Social-Democratic literature. Further, I have already written you about moving the base of the organization, the secret work, to workers' homes. Concretely, this means that *a part of our best illegal forces must become outwardly proletarianized*'" [italics added].

the Party organizations had become a crucial issue, especially in the cities where the Bolsheviks predominated in the committee. It was one of the points on the agenda of the Congress.[24]

Maksimov (A. A. Bogdanov) read the draft of a resolution (later it was said that it had been written by Lenin and Maksimov[25]) which began by explaining that the matter had been put on the docket because "the right wing of our Party continues its systematic attempts to sow enmity and mistrust between *intelligenty* and worker Party members, its attempts to depict our organizations as purely intelligentsia ones . . . to accuse the Social-Democratic organizations of trying to shackle the independent activity of the working class by Party discipline . . . to flaunt the slogan of the elective principle, usually without taking any earnest steps toward its realization."[26]

The debates were somewhat disorderly and at times quite sharp. The next speaker, Gradov (Kamenev), felt that the question should not be discussed at all since the only reason it had been put on the docket was the struggle with Mensheviks:

> I must express my strong opposition to . . . this resolution. As an issue of the relationship of workers and the intelligentsia in Party organizations, this question does not exist. (LENIN: It does.) No, it does not: it exists as a demagogic question, that is all.[27]

Zharkov (Leshchinskii) agreed: "The question of intelligentsia and workers exists only insofar as it has been raised by Mensheviks."[28] But several delegates sharply objected. Liadov: "I do not agree with Comrade Gradov that the question of *intelligenty* and workers does not exist. . . . I think the fact that [it] has arisen cannot be explained merely by the Mensheviks' demagogic activity; it has arisen because there really are two strata in our Party— the proletarian and the petty bourgeois."[29] Leskov (Romanov):

---

[24] This point did not appear in Lenin's first draft of the agenda, written in December 1904 (*Leninskii Sbornik*, V (1926), 191), or in his draft of February, 1905 (*ibid.*, p. 193), but it was included in the brief (eight-point) agenda Lenin worked out either on the eve of the opening of the Congress or at its very beginning (*ibid.*, p. 224).

[25] *Tretii s"ezd RSDRP. Aprel'-mai 1905 goda. Protokoly* (Moscow: Gospolitizdat, 1959), p. 326.

[26] *Ibid.*, pp. 253–54.

[27] *Ibid.*, p. 255.

[28] *Ibid.*, p. 256.

[29] *Ibid.*, p. 257.

"We must introduce workers [into the committees] because the movement is growing, not because the Mensheviks are 'sowing discord.' "[30] Mikhailov (Postolovskii): "The workers are interested in the question of the relationship between workers and *intelligenty* (*Shouts:* There are the Rules) and impatiently wait for the Congress to answer it."[31]

The inclusion of workers in local committees was debated with particular heat. Filippov (Rumiantsev) said that there was only one worker in the Petersburg Committee although work in Petersburg had been going on for fifteen years. (LENIN: Outrageous!)[32] Leskov (Romanov) said that in the Northern Committee things were even worse:

> At one time three of the seven members of our Northern Committee were workers; now not one of the eight Committee members is a worker. Very soon this question will become even more complex. The labor movement is growing irresistibly, quite apart from Party influence, and the newly emerging masses must be organized. This weakens the ideological influence of Social-Democracy.[33]

Osipov (Zemliachka), one of the Bolshevik center's agents-at-large, who had traveled extensively in preparation for the Congress, reported:

> Not so long ago I toured the Caucasus committees. . . . At the time, there was one worker in the Baku Committee, one in the Batum Committee, and none in the Kutais Committee. Only the Tiflis Committee had several. . . . Could it be that our Caucasus comrades prefer *intelligenty* committeemen to worker committeemen?[34]

Orlovskii (Vorovskii) commented that "a workers' party in which leadership is the hereditary property of the intelligentsia is doomed to be anemic."[35] A. Bel'skii (Krasikov) declared: "In our committees, and I have seen plenty of them in my work, there is

---

[30] *Ibid.*, pp. 332–33.
[31] *Ibid.*, p. 333.
[32] *Ibid.*, p. 267.
[33] *Ibid.*, p. 265.
[34] *Ibid.*, p. 334. Osipov's data for Baku were, however, challenged by Golubin (Dzhaparidze) and for Batum by Barsov (Tskhakaia) (*ibid.*, pp. 334–35).
[35] *Ibid.*, p. 275.

some kind of phobia toward workers."[36] Lenin stepped in, and the session became even noisier:

It will be the task of the future center to reorganize a consider-able number of our committees. The committee members' inertia must be overcome. (*Clapping and hissing.*)

I hear Comrade Sergeev hissing, while non-committeemen are applauding. I think one should look at the matter more broadly. Bringing workers into the committees is not only a pedagogical but also a political task. Workers possess the class instinct, and with a little political experience they quite soon become tempered Social-Democrats. I should be very pleased if there were eight workers to every two *intelligenty* in our committees.[37]

Mikhailov (Postolovskii), speaking immediately after Lenin, added coals to the fire:

We must see to it that our committees are immediately expanded to fifteen–twenty members, with an elective board. The main contin-gent of a committee must consist of workers. It is said that we do not have workers capable of sitting on a committee. That is not true. The criterion for admitting workers . . . ought to be different from the one applied to *intelligenty*. There is talk of tempered S-D's, but . . . first- and second-year students, familiar with Social-Democratic ideas from the Erfurt Program and a few issues of *Iskra*, are already considered tempered S-D's. Thus in practice the requirements for *intelligenty* are very low, and for workers they are extremely high. (LENIN: Very true! THE MAJORITY OF THE DELE-GATES: Not true!) The only valid criterion for admitting workers into a committee must be the degree of their influence among the masses. (*Hissing, shouting.*) All workers who are leaders and have been in our circles must be members of our committees. (Right!) I think this is the only way to settle the vexed question between workers and *intelligenty* and to cut the ground from under dema-goguery.[38]

Later Lenin returned to the subject:

I could not sit quietly when it was said that there were no workers fit to be committee members. The question is being put off;

---

[36] *Ibid.*, p. 335.
[37] *Ibid.*, p. 262.
[38] *Ibid.*, p. 263.

evidently there is some sickness in the Party. Workers must be brought into the committees. It's funny—there are only three publicists [*literary*] at the Congress, the rest are committee people, and it is the *literary* who approve of bringing in workers, while the committeemen are all worked up for some reason.[39]

The issue was shelved until the Congress had worked out new Party Rules,[40] but the subsequent debates confused it even more. In the end the Congress passed a resolution—on the undesirability of passing a resolution on the principle of the problem.[41]

No doubt the reason it proved impossible to reach a decision lay in the delegates' reluctance to revise their basic authoritarian conception of the Party. This reluctance had been quite obvious in the debate over the revision of the Party Rules. Maksimov (Bogdanov) had noted "the need for political leadership of huge masses of the proletariat entering the political arena with unprecedented energy." This, he had said, required two things of the Party: (1) maximal order and cohesion, which "entailed" stricter enforcement of centralism; (2) maximal closeness to the masses, which "entailed" a "tendency toward organizational democratism." Because of "tremendous obstacles," both these problems could be solved only in part; and *"since conditions have not changed very considerably in this respect since the Second Congress, the reforms in Party organization in both of the indicated*

---

[39] *Ibid.*, p. 333.

[40] *Ibid.*, p. 269.

[41] This "resolution" said, literally: "The Congress considers it superfluous to adopt a separate resolution on the relationship of workers and *intelligenty* in Party organizations, and passes on to the next point on the agenda" (*ibid.*, pp. 333, 465). Twelve delegates (with 24 votes) voted for this resolution and ten (with 19 votes) against it, with one abstaining—Rybkin, the only worker at the Congress (1 vote) (*ibid.*, p. 336).

Among the minority (!) were Lenin, Bogdanov, Rumiantsev, Krasin, Orlovskii, Tskhakaia, Postolovskii, and the "advisory" delegates Lunacharskii, Liadov, Krasikov, Avilov (*ibid.*, p. 725, n. 146)—in other words, the overwhelming majority of the most influential Bolsheviks, including *all* the reporters on *all* the points of the agenda, with the sole exception of the reporter for the credentials committee.

The disparate majority had rallied against them for different and sometimes opposite reasons. Rykov, Kamenev, Litvinov, and Zemliachka were some of the better-known members who voted for the resolution. As Lenin observed, basically it was an insurrection of committee people against the ideologues and publicists, the *literary*. This was the only time in the history of Bolshevism that Lenin found himself in the minority at a Bolshevik congress after putting up a fight and that a speech of his was booed.

directions cannot be especially radical."[42] From this labored, vague formulation one idea stood out clearly: No basic changes!

Partial changes were made, however, and in both directions at once—toward greater centralism and toward some democratization; the first in a clear-cut, the second in a muddled and tentative, way.

The Party Rules adopted at the Second Congress had provided for two central agencies, the Central Committee and the Central Organ. The CC and the editor of the CO were elected by the Congress. To co-ordinate their activities, a third agency had been created—the Party Council (*Sovet Partii*), to which the CC and the CO elected two members each; a fifth member, who was also the chairman, was elected by the Congress. This complex system had been intended to mitigate the possible bad effects of extreme centralization. It did not work well, however, and the Third Congress abolished the Party Council. But instead of trying to straighten out the difficulties by democratizing the central leadership—whether by strengthening the collective principle in it or by giving the local organizations some degree of influence over the center—the Third Congress reinforced centralism and authoritarian leadership even more.

The new Rules vested all power in one organ, the Central Committee, which appointed from among its members the chief editor of the Central Organ—a single *otvetstvennyi redaktor*, not an editorial board as before. This chief editor was given a remarkable prerogative: Article 3 of the Rules provided that at the next congress the Central Committee would be represented by two delegates and that the chief editor must be one of them. That Lenin would be the chief editor no one at the Congress doubted.

The Rules contained still tighter guaranties of "firm" leadership: until the next congress, new members could be co-opted into the Central Committee only by the CC's unanimous decision. In principle, the old Rules also required unanimity, but they left some room for non-unanimous decisions. The nominations of the CC became final only if dissenters did not file a complaint with the Party Council. If such complaints were filed, the Council was empowered to annul the CC's nominations. But the CC in turn had the right to raise the issue once more and, if it did so, to settle

---

[42] *Ibid.*, p. 269.

it by majority vote. Now, with the Party Council abolished, unanimity in co-opting members into the CC became an absolute requirement. Many delegates objected to this. Petrov-Kvitkin moved that the clause be stricken from the Rules ("unanimous co-optation would strengthen the influence of [the group residing] abroad"). This was defeated, 13 to 6;[43] but the next day eleven delegates, some of whom had voted for unanimity in co-opting members into the CC, presented a formal request to have the decision revised. With an even vote for and against revision, the request was refused—but only because the top leaders applied pressure (protesting against the "irresponsible attitude" to debates, and so on).[44]

In the other direction, the new Rules granted the local organizations some "rights" which they had not formally had before. No longer could a local committee be "dismissed" by the Central Committee. The old Rules had not formally given the CC this right either—they had said nothing on the subject—but "dismissing" local committees or adding new members to them against their wishes had become standard practice. Without explicitly forbidding it, the new Rules eliminated this practice by providing, in Article 12, that co-optation into local committees of persons nominated by the Central Committee was to take place by simple majority vote. In the *Communication about the Third Congress of the RSDRP*, the clause was amplified: "The committee's membership has been declared inviolable, that is, the CC has been deprived of the right to expel members from local committees or to add new ones without the committee's consent."[45]

Local committees were also given the formal right (Article 7) to publish Party literature—that is, to put "RSDRP" on the leaflets and pamphlets they issued at their own expense and in their own name. The final version of the Rules added that the CC was obliged to transport the publications of any organization—on condition, however, that five fully qualified committees demand it.[46]

---

43 *Ibid.*, p. 302.
44 *Ibid.*, pp. 323–25.
45 *Ibid.*, p. 2.
46 *Ibid.*, pp. 270, 461.

How hard it was to win even these modest "rights" for local organizations is clear from the fate of the next article in the draft, which read: "All peripheral organizations (that is, all Party organizations besides the general and local centers) have the right to extensive and prompt information about general and local Party affairs, insofar as underground conditions present no obstacles to this." Many delegates realized the awkwardness of including such a provision in the Rules. After debates that sound almost fantastic,[47] the Congress decided to exclude the article from the Rules and to pass instead a resolution, in which the idea was reformulated:[48] "It is part of the duties of the CC as well as of local centers to inform the Party organizations as fully as possible about all general and local Party affairs, insofar as underground conditions present no obstacles to this."[49]

The draft of the original Article 8 had granted the peripheral organizations two more "rights": that of voting "in an advisory

---

[47] To understand the following, it is necessary to know that *krome* may mean either "except" or "besides." Orlovskii, with some justification, ridiculed the wording *krome obshchikh i mestnykh tsentrov* (in the passage quoted a few lines above in text, where *krome* is perforce translated "besides"): "Almost every word here is a joke. It says, 'all except the general and local centers have the right to be informed.' That would mean that the general and local centers do not have that right. Furthermore, it isn't a matter of rights but of obligations. The leading centers are obliged to inform the organizations without waiting for the periphery to try and enforce its right by asking questions." Sosnovskii (Desnitskii) concurred: "Everything that has been put into Article 8 is taken for granted in any Social-Democratic party and doesn't need to be put in the Rules. All the Congress must do, since this elementary rule has been violated, is to refer to it in a special resolution." Kamskii (Obukhov) put it more strongly still: "Such truisms are not written into rules. This Article must be stricken from the Rules lest it become a laughingstock. But since the leading centers have not always remembered the axiom contained in Article 8, there should be a reminder in a special resolution." Postolovskii disagreed: "I think it is imperative to put this article into the Rules. It is being said here that this is elementary, but in abnormal times even the ABC's are occasionally forgotten. Lately every higher organization has been keeping secrets from the one below it. In my work I have gone through all the stages, from member of the periphery to agent of the CC, and I have met with this phenomenon everywhere. Thus, in Odessa the Committee refused to communicate to me, a member of the Odessa periphery, its plan of organization and work. The CC concealed from me, an agent of the CC, one of the points of its agreement with the BCM [Bureau of the Committees of the Majority]. Since the axiom of information is being forgotten, it has to be written into the Rules." (*Ibid.*, pp. 293–95.)

[48] *Ibid.*, p. 295.

[49] There was a mixup in this matter too. The Congress agreed to use Orlovskii's draft (*ibid.*, pp. 325–26) "as a basis," and it was given to the commission together with other drafts (*ibid.*, p. 328), but the Congress never returned to this question, and Orlovskii's draft was printed in the protocols among the "resolutions of the Congress" (*ibid.*, pp. 458–59).

capacity" in the local committees' discussions of general and local Party affairs (naturally, insofar as "underground conditions" did not interfere) and that of "proposing official candidates" for co-optation into the local committee. These candidates, like the candidates proposed by the Central Committee, were to be co-opted by simple majority vote (Article 12). As in the case of the "right to information," the "advisory right" was replaced, in a resolution, by "the local committees' duty" to include representatives of peripheral organizations "in an advisory capacity" in their discussions of "all general and local Party affairs."[50]

The practical effect of these resolutions was almost nil. Neither in the press of the time nor in reminiscences have I come across a single instance of representatives of peripheral organizations' being asked to attend committee sessions (or of representatives of local committees' being enlisted in the CC's work), nor a single instance of peripheral organizations' formally proposing candidates for co-optation into a local committee. The CC's practice of dismissing members of local committees and foisting new ones on them did cease, it is true, or at least was sharply curtailed. On the whole, however, the structure of the Bolshevik wing of the Party did not change after the Third Congress. It even "solidified" in a sense, which may explain why the faint attempts to adapt the Party's organization to the changing demands of life brought no results. Conservatism had triumphed.

The Bolsheviks' conservatism in matters of organization was also evident in their wariness of "informal organizations" and the *fait accompli* method of creating them. The Third Congress did not touch upon these questions in any of its numerous resolutions. As we have seen in chapter iii, it even removed from the resolution "On Overt Political Action by the RSDRP" the recommendation contained in the original draft to utilize "semilegal ways" of creating workers' unions.

The Mensheviks' organizational ideas ran ahead of the concrete possibilities of the times. The discrepancy between what

---

[50] When Article 8 was replaced by a resolution, there remained no explicit mention of the peripheral organizations' right to propose candidates for co-optation into local committees, but since Article 12 stated that candidates proposed by primary organizations could be co-opted into a local committee by simple majority vote, the right of peripheral organizations to propose such candidates was recognized by implication.

was possible and what the Mensheviks wanted made for a certain vagueness in their attempts to remodel the Party organization. They held that new possibilities for reform were apt to arise in the course of events, especially in a developing labor movement. This was what Lenin had derisively called "organization as process." His formula, coined for polemical purposes, was essentially correct.[51]

In Somov's reminiscences there is a story about the Mensheviks' search for new organizational forms in late 1904. At this time the Petersburg Group discussed a new "organizational plan" (Somov does not mention that it was his):

> According to this plan, the basic nucleus of the organization would be the factory group consisting of the more advanced and influential workers of the given factory. It would be the main task of this group to react with leaflets to the major events of factory life, [such as] clashes with the management, the latter's abuses, both in matters concerning the material conditions of the workers' life and the worker as citizen. . . . Representatives of all the factory groups of a sector would form a sector assembly in charge of the affairs of the whole sector, including studies in propaganda circles. The author of this plan thought that the factory groups might serve as germs of the trade unions of free Russia; and the sector assemblies, as initiators of political clubs and political unions. This was, however, an extreme view, in opposition to which there arose in the Group itself another extreme view, that no kind of organization was possible under the police conditions of autocratic Russia and that the role of the Social-Democratic committees was confined to political agitation through leaflets, pamphlets, and to their distribution among the workers. . . . The majority of the central Group vacillated between these two extreme viewpoints. [The Group] did not have time to arrive at a definite decision . . . for events intervened that put organizational experiments out of mind.[52]

This was little more than the embryo of a plan. It did not attend to the difficult problems of creating an all-city center and defining its relations with the sectors; it hardly touched upon the vast political tasks of Social-Democracy. Somov's own past may have accounted for this, as also for the good points of his plan,

---

[51] See n. 19 for some of Lenin's remarks in 1905.
[52] *Byloe*, April, 1907, pp. 28–29.

such as its boldness in calling for independent organizational activity on the workers' part: former *Rabochedel'tsy* often proved to be the most progressive people in the Menshevik camp.

The upswing in the labor movement after Bloody Sunday stimulated the Mensheviks' search for more democratic forms of Party organization and, more broadly, for new forms of organizing the whole labor movement by the *fait accompli* method of creating "informal" mass organizations. The two sets of problems were closely interlocked.

All these questions were discussed at the Menshevik "All-Russian Conference of Party Workers" in Geneva in April/May, 1905. Regrettably, no detailed account of the Conference exists, and I cannot analyze the debates as I have done for the simultaneous Bolshevik "Third Congress." Only a small pamphlet, containing little more than the resolutions adopted, was ever published—as a supplement to *Iskra,* No. 100. However, the resolutions suffice to show the development of Menshevik organizational thought in 1905.

The resolution "On Organizational Rules" is the most interesting, though inexplicably it attracted hardly any attention in the literature of the time or later. Its introductory part stressed flexibility:

> Wishing to guarantee participation in working out and orienting Party policies to a wider circle of party workers, the Conference proposes some organizational norms for reforming local work in this direction. The Conference deems it necessary to point out, however, that the proposed norms for local organizations are merely intended to bring into the Party's organizational life the degree of democratism for which the time is ripe and which can already now be applied in all advanced organizations. At the same time the Conference recommends that wherever conditions are favorable the local organizations go farther toward democratization—increasing, on one hand, the degree of influence of lower-level organizational cells on the Party's practical work and, on the other, gradually introducing the elective principle into the local organizational system.

This bears the stamp of that era of transition when the police state had been shaken but no stable democratic order had yet emerged. It is a schema to be followed wherever possible, not a set of rules clearly defining the interrelation of the Party organizations and the rights and duties of their members.

Even so, the organizational rules are of great interest. They made the city Committees little more than co-ordinators of local party work. Political leadership was to be provided, not by the Committee alone, but *collectively* by the city Committee and the sector committees. The latter were to consist of people "actively participating in the work of the sector's organizations" plus a representative of the city Committee, whom the Committee was to recall and replace by another "if the majority of the sector committee's members demanded it." Only in very special cases, when there was no time to consult the sector committees, could the Committee act on its own and report on its actions to the sector committees afterward. And if the majority of the latter's members then expressed "lack of confidence," the Committee was to be reorganized by mutual agreement of the regional [*oblast-noi*] Committee and the sector committees. New Committees, in localities where there had been none before, were to be formed "by mutual agreement of the regional Committee and a conference of responsible [party] workers."

The "collective leadership," that is, the local Committee and the sector committees, would also work out the election rules to regional congresses, each of which would elect a regional Committee of three to five members. This would be a permanent organ co-ordinating the work of the local organizations and linking them together; all its members were to "participate in local work as much as possible." Finally, as the organ unifying all party work, there would be a "regular conference" [*reguliarnaia konferentsiia*] of representatives of all the regional Committees, with an executive commission it would elect.

It was characteristic of the period that the mass labor movement, though close to Social-Democracy in its essence, and inspired by dimly perceived notions of struggling for democracy and socialism, *could not be fitted into any party-organizational mold*. Realizing this, the Menshevik leaders looked for ways to convert the Social-Democratic Party into a broad labor party. A separate resolution of the All-Russian Conference of Party Workers explained "the motivation of the organizational resolutions":

Recent events attest that the RSDRP is an enormous political force strongly influencing broader and broader strata of the working class. But the same events also show that the growing political influence of Social-Democracy is not adequately reflected in a commensurate development of the Party as a self-governing organization of the proletarian vanguard. . . .

In the Party, the number of people capable of directing the proletarian mass movement on their own is growing too slowly. Among the proletariat ideologically influenced by Social-Democracy, there is at the same time a growing number of politically mature elements capable of participating in party work, and sometimes acting on their own as leaders of the masses, but remaining outside our Party organizations.

The awakening activity of the masses was instinctively seeking some simple organizational forms. A multitude of embryonic organizations were springing up almost spontaneously. The political parlance of the time grouped them under the term "informal organizations." In keeping with the general Menshevik orientation, the Conference was entirely in their favor. The resolution "On Informal Organizations" stated that "in the prevailing atmosphere of revolutionary ferment there arise among the broad masses various kinds of informal unions of workers," which, "because of the historical circumstances, become starting points for the political unification of the proletariat" and thus create a basis for the "quick expansion and strengthening of an independent party of the working class under the banner of Social-Democracy." The Conference recommended that party workers "(1) help such unions to emerge and multiply and (2) endeavor to turn them into permanent revolutionary organizations of the proletariat (workers' clubs) directed by Social-Democracy and making it their business to intervene constantly in the life of the state and of society in the interests of the working class." The idea of "revolutionary workers' clubs" was no doubt inspired by the clubs which had played a similar role in the French Revolution.

The informal organizations usually emerged in a *fait accompli* manner (see chapter iii), in total disregard of laws and official administrative practice. A favorable attitude toward them came so naturally to the Mensheviks that nobody seems to have thought of expressing it in the resolution "On Informal Organizations." The resolution "On Trade Unions," however (quoted in chapter iii) did recommend that trade unions be organized "despite the laws still extant prohibiting them."

Whereas the Mensheviks discerned exceptional opportunities in the rising labor movement, the latter disconcerted the Bolsheviks, prejudiced as they were by their dogma of "spontaneity and consciousness" (see Appendix 9, pp. 325–30). *Iskra*, No. 101, June 1/14, 1905, contrasted the responses of the two factions in a long article, "On the Work of the 'Firm' Congress," summarizing the organizational decisions of the Third Congress:

> The "firm" comrades still haven't grasped the truth that a Social-Democratic party directing the *masses* cannot be anything but a union of *Social-Democratic workers' organizations*. An aggregate of committees is not yet a party; at best, it is only an aggregate of its executive and directing organs. An aggregate of professional agitators, propagandists, and organizers is not yet a workers' party but only its "spinal column." A party must be the aggregate of all the advanced, conscious elements of the proletariat willing to wage a co-ordinated struggle for the interests of their class, willing to submit to the discipline of the organized whole. . . . And if we are still in the process of transition from an "organization of professional revolutionaries" to a Social-Democratic labor party—if, for historical reasons, this transition cannot take place "from one day to the next"—it is the duty of all forward-looking Social-Democrats to move consciously toward that goal when they build or rebuild the Party organization.

"Transition from an 'organization of professional revolutionaries' to a Social-Democratic labor party"—the words express in a nutshell the task that faced Russian Social-Democracy in the summer of 1905. This was the "reform" that challenged the Menshevik leaders. But during the months between the All-Russian Conference of Party Workers and the events of October even the Mensheviks barely began to rebuild their organizations in the democratic spirit suggested in their resolution "On Organizational Rules." *Iskra* carried many reports about these efforts from provincial centers but none from Petersburg, where the Menshevik leaders had been arrested in May and June. (They had been denounced by Dobroskok, nicknamed *Nikolai-Zolotye ochki* ["Nicholas–Gold Spectacles"], the main *agent provocateur* among the Mensheviks during the years of the First Revolution.)

The Menshevik propaganda for a more democratic Party organization often influenced Bolshevik workers as well. It also influenced the negotiations, launched soon after the Third Congress, between the two Party centers (the Central Committee elected by the Third Congress and the Organizational Commission elected by the All-Russian Conference), which resulted in October in the federation of the two factions.

In late summer, almost on the eve of the October events, another new idea arose in Menshevik circles which markedly affected the Mensheviks' views on organization—that of an all-Russian congress of workers.

The Problem of a Workers' Congress

P. B. Axelrod elaborated the idea of a congress of Russian workers and became its ardent promoter. To be sure, the idea was in the air. Many labor leaders were painfully aware of the discrepancy between the great revolutionary tasks of the working class and the absence of mass organizations truly representing them. The idea of remedying this by calling a congress of workers first occurred in the summer of 1905 to the organizers of the trade-union movement just arising all over Russia. They began to talk of a national congress of trade unions—not so much to unite the weak new unions as to speed the nationwide organization of the movement. When the soviets of workers' deputies emerged in October, the idea shifted to a congress of representatives of the soviets to unite the country's laboring masses. Trotsky, its strong advocate, wrote down the schema of the plan later, in July, 1906, in prison, in the pamphlet *Our Tactic in the Struggle for a Constituent Assembly (Nasha taktika v bor'be za Uchreditel'noe Sobranie)*:

1. Local soviets of workers' deputies.
2. An all-Russian workers' congress.
3. An all-Russian workers' soviet as a permanent organ created by the workers' congress.[53]

---

[53] L. Trotsky, *Sochineniia* (Moscow-Leningrad: Gosizdat, 1925), Vol. II, P. 1, p. 435.

From his argumentation it is clear, however, that Trotsky meant the all-Russian Soviet to be "permanent" only for the duration of the revolution. Axelrod's version of a workers' congress was broader, more complex, and closely related to the idea of either creating a vast new labor party or transforming the Social-Democratic Party into such a party.

Axelrod first raised the question of a workers' congress in letters to members of the Organizational Commission elected at the April/May Menshevik Conference. These letters were not written for publication, but the response to them among Menshevik leaders was so enthusiastic that *Iskra* published them in Geneva as a pamphlet, under the title *The People's Duma and the Workers' Congress (Narodnaia duma i rabochii s"ezd)*— practically on the eve of the October events.[54] The title, and the fact that Axelrod discussed the issue in connection with *Iskra's* plan to hold illegal elections concurrently with the elections to the Bulygin Duma,[55] created the impression in rank-and-file Party circles that the idea of a workers' congress was bound up with the idea of a people's duma. Actually the letters posed the issue more broadly. The first of the three letters[56] does not discuss the people's duma at all. It deals with reinforcing the "position" of the working class, which is identified with the "position" of Social-Democracy:

> It seems to me that the advanced and enterprising units of the Party should focus their attention on one practical matter—organiz-

---

[54] In the foreword to the second edition of this pamphlet (Petersburg, 1907), Axelrod wrote that his pamphlet had been printed "abroad in the fall of 1905; but so few copies got into Russia that very few comrades could acquaint themselves with it" (p. 3). *Iskra* listed all the Menshevik writings published abroad or in the Russian underground, but its last issue, No. 112, October 8/21, 1905, does not mention Axelrod's pamphlet. This seems to indicate that it came out in the last days of September at the earliest.

[55] On February 18, 1905, the tsar ordered the minister of the interior, Bulygin, to draw up a plan for convoking a duma. On August 6 a law about the duma and the method of elections was published. It was a badly reactionary law, which was never put into effect—the events of October swept it away. This was the "Bulygin Duma."

[56] The first letter was written about the middle of July (O.S.), the third and last partly before the Manifesto about the Duma and partly after. Besides the three letters, the second edition of Axelrod's *Narodnaia duma i rabochii s"ezd* (Petersburg, 1907) contains a long foreword (pp. 3–17) written in the spring of 1907; a chapter from a pamphlet Axelrod had begun after the disbandment of the First Duma (pp. 37–48); and his article "Po povodu agitatsii protiv 'idei' rabochego s"ezda" (pp. 48–55), which had appeared in No. 1 of *Sotsialdemokrat* for 1907.

ing and convoking a general workers' congress to discuss, and definitely decide on, the program of the next demands and methods of action of the working class. Side by side, simultaneously, and in connection with this general congress, a congress of Social-Democrats must also be convoked and hold sessions; most of its delegates should also be workers.

This is how I see the order and the course of agitation: the "Organizational Commission" convokes a conference of ten or so party workers known to it; having discussed [at this conference] the plan of agitation among workers in favor of a congress and the draft of its agenda, [the Organizational Commission] addresses an appeal to the workers; [this appeal] must, first, briefly give the facts about the moves of the official organs of the liberal and democratic bourgeoisie and describe the social composition and the program of action of these organs (the "Union of Unions," the "Bureau of the Zemstvo Congress," and so on) and, second, describe what is in store for the workers if they do not immediately organize into a separate union with an independent program and tactic instead of tailing along in the rear of bourgeois unions and joining them, individually or even in groups.

Third, it is necessary to point to the workers' congress as the first step toward the formation of such a union.

It should be the congress's main task to discuss current civic questions—the convocation of a constituent assembly, the attitude toward the government's travesty of popular representation and toward the tactics of the organizations and meetings of the bourgeois opposition . . . the economic and political reforms that the constituent assembly will have to carry out and for which it will be necessary to agitate before and during the elections to that assembly.[57]

Here the organization of a workers' congress is left to the Organizational Commission, that is, to the Menshevik center. Bolshevik participation is not mentioned (it seemed hopeless at the time; I shall return to this), nor is the idea of making the organization of a congress a non-partisan undertaking of all workers. At the end of the letter Axelrod says once more that the ideal, in his opinion, would be to "convoke a general workers' congress exclusively on the initiative and in the name of the Party"—of its Menshevik part, that is.

---

[57] Axelrod, *Narodnaia duma i rabochii s"ezd*, pp. 19–20.

Less than a month later, however, in answer to questions about his first letter from a member of the Organizational Commission, Axelrod expressed a much broader view: the Organizational Commission must issue the appeal—there is no one else to do it—but it must not try to turn the workers' congress into a Party affair. The objective is political representation of the working class:

> The advanced strata of the working class must create their own political organization, having its own center and uniting the working masses—in a *variety* of ways—around its own banner, tirelessly sustaining their live interest in events and mobilizing them . . . for determined revolutionary action whenever there are issues at hand that concern the vital interests of the working class and the popular masses generally. . . . But the political organization of workers I am envisaging can of course be brought into being only with the energetic influence and direct participation of Social-Democrats (workers and *intelligenty*) acting as a *united* nucleus, following a definite plan, and inspiring the proletariat caught up in the social movement with the idea of independent action by their class in the social-political arena.[58]

In the process, Social-Democracy itself must reform and become truly the party of the masses. Its role as the nucleus of such a party is "historically determined." It must instil higher aspirations and principles into the masses' struggle for partial improvements, while acting as their conscious revolutionary vanguard.[59]

A year later, Axelrod would carry this thought to its logical conclusion:

> We used to regard our intelligentsia Social-Democratic Party as a transitional organization, as an instrument in the historical process of politically organizing the working masses. And from the point of view of its . . . historical mission our Party must now . . . take the first preliminary steps toward radically rebuilding its own organizational edifice (not only in the formal and technical sense) on wholly proletarian foundations. These preliminary steps I consider to be the convocation of a workers' congress and the Party's agitational and organizational work in preparing for it. This preparation and the congress itself can and must serve as the first stages

---

[58] *Ibid.*, p. 27.
[59] *Ibid.*, p. 30.

of converting Russian Social-Democracy from a party of the revolutionary intelligentsia influencing the advanced elements of the proletariat ideologically and politically into a party of the proletarian class itself.[60]

And still more pointedly:

I personally consider it entirely likely that the congress will adopt our program for its own (even if with substantial modifications) and work out a tactical line for the immediate future that will fully conform to this program. In that case our Party organization will have to merge with the new, the workers', Social-Democratic organization into one Social-Democratic party. Thus it will fulfil its last duty to the proletariat, for it will itself help its advanced elements to make a revolution to eliminate . . . the intelligentsia's organized tutelage over the working masses awakened to conscious political life and substitute for it . . . their organized *self-government*. In this ideally favorable case the workers' congress will play the role of a proletarian constituent assembly, which will liquidate our old party order and initiate a new party regime in Social-Democracy and . . . the proletariat. Such a congress would be the greatest triumph for our Party.[61]

After October, Axelrod's plan lost its topicality, and the workers' congress virtually ceased to be discussed in broad Party circles. However, according to a member of the Organizational Commission, M. Panin, the Commission and the editors of *Nachalo* held joint conferences on the subject and sought ways of combining the trade-union and soviet movements to create a stable proletarian organization that would be both a political and a mass organization.[62] Yet even *Nachalo* paid no attention to this "search."[63] In the provinces the average party worker did not

---

[60] *Ibid.*, pp. 45–46.

[61] *Ibid.*, pp. 47–48.

[62] M. Panin, "Rabochii s"ezd na partiinom s"ezde," *Otkliki* (Petersburg), April, 1907, p. 8.

[63] In all of its short existence (November 13 to December 3) *Nachalo* did not carry a single article that even incidentally discussed the problem of a workers' congress. In its large current events section I found only two references to it: the question had been on the agenda of a Menshevik meeting in the Neva sector on November 23, but the meeting didn't get around to it and it was postponed until the next meeting (*Nachalo*, No. 10, November 25); and in Kiev a conference of Menshevik party workers had noted "the importance of immediately convoking a workers' congress with representatives of all the organizations of the proletariat" (*Nachalo*, No. 14, November 30).

know anything about these problems.[64] In mid-1906 the idea of a workers' congress would be revived in the Menshevik press; but this part of the story is beyond the bounds of my book.

The Bolshevik leaders opposed the idea of a workers' congress from the start. In 1905 they showed their disapproval mainly by their total silence on the problem. In 1926 the draft of a pamphlet Lenin had prepared in 1905 was published in Volume V of *Leninskii Sbornik*, under the title "On P. B. Axelrod's Pamphlet *The People's Duma and the Workers' Congress*."[65] It was a caustic review, calling Axelrod's plan "the archetype of all *Iskra* stupidities," "a mass of oddities," "nonsense," "chaotic ideas," and so on. Lenin's pamphlet did not appear in print[66]—perhaps because the events of October shifted all organizational problems to a new plane: the question of a workers' congress seemed to have lost its urgency or at least to call for a different kind of analysis.

The Party Organizations during the Days of Freedom

Between October 17 and early December, 1905—the short stretch of time known as the Days of Freedom—Social-Democ-

---

[64] P. A. Garvi in *Vospominaniia sotsialdemokrata* (New York, 1946) says, it is true, that the problem was discussed at the Conference of Menshevik Organizations of Southern Russia in Kiev in the late summer of 1905. Just released from jail in Rostov-on-the-Don, Garvi arrived in Kiev the day after the Conference closed, but he took part in the final editing of its resolutions. He writes that the latter envisaged, among other things, the realization of the plan "developed in P. B. Axelrod's well-known pamphlet *Narodnaia duma i rabochii s"ezd*" and that in one "lengthy resolution" the Conference "gave concrete form to this plan" (p. 509). Here Garvi is certainly in error. He was an honest chronicler, but he wrote a quarter-century after these events and did not always check his memories against documentary evidence. A report on the Conference in *Iskra*, No. 111, September 24/October 7, quotes its major resolutions, and the text of the resolution "Po povodu Gosudarstvennoi Dumy" does not even contain the words *narodnaia duma* and *rabochii s"ezd*. There is, however, the embryonic idea of a workers' congress in the resolution "O predstoiashchem s"ezde predstavitelei professional'nykh soiuzov." In it the Conference resolves to "propose to the bureau organizing the trade-union congress to give properly organized assemblies of workers the right to be represented at the congress; [these representatives], in the presence of representatives of the corresponding trade unions, will lay the foundations of new trade unions." At best, this still left the question of a workers' congress where it had been before Axelrod's letters.

[65] Lenin, *Sochineniia*, IX, 385–88.

[66] There is a strange editorial note to this "draft" in Lenin's *Sochineniia*, IX, 419: "Lenin's pamphlet on this subject did not appear in print." Every word has of course been weighed. Does the note mean that the pamphlet had been written but not published? In the fifth edition of *Sochineniia* (XI, 488), the mystery deepens: "Lenin's pamphlet or article on this subject did not appear in print."

racy came out of the underground and existed openly in the *fait accompli* manner; a democratization of the Party's structure began almost everywhere, and the desire for Party unity surged with renewed force. The drive for democratization and unity was all the stronger because pressure from the Party's lower strata had been building up since the spring. Incidentally, in the minds of the factory workers associated with the Party, the two issues of democratization and of healing the rift in the Party were closely intertwined. This pressure influenced the leadership, which soon found itself going farther in both directions than either the Bolshevik Congress or the Menshevik Conference had contemplated.

Right after the Congress and the Conference, the Bolsheviks' Central Committee and the Mensheviks' Organizational Commission discussed, in Geneva, the chances of reconciliation. The discussions came to naught because the representatives of the CC insisted that their Congress must be recognized as the Third Party Congress, and their Central Committee as the CC of the whole Party. They offered to co-opt some Mensheviks into the CC and the editorial board of the Central Organ and proposed to unify the local organizations, also "on the organizational principles laid down by the Third Congress."[67] These conditions deadlocked all further negotiations, even though during the next few months rapprochement seemed at times possible.[68] Only

---

[67] Reported by a participant in these talks, a member of the Organizational Commission, in the section "Iz partii" of *Iskra*, No. 108, July 13/26, 1905.

[68] The unification of the Party as an agreement between two sides of equal status was formally considered for the first time at a meeting of representatives of the CC and of the OC on July 12. The Mensheviks proposed the following reforms as the basis for an agreement:

a) To strengthen the influence of the periphery in Party affairs, sector committees must be given votes in all local organizations on questions concerning the general policies of these local organizations.

b) To the same end, all organized workers must be given the right to vote on all cases of mass action. In these cases the decisions of the majority of organized workers must be binding on the committees.

c) For the collective will of the Party to be more fully expressed during the intervals between congresses, there must be organized "central conferences" of representatives of regional committees, or, as long as this is not feasible, of representatives of the major local committees and groups of committees. The Central Committee must be guided by the directives of these central conferences in the general planning of major political campaigns.

d) The Central Committee will include representatives of both parts of the Party.

the Days of Freedom finally brought a change, with the formation, right after the Manifesto of October 17, of the Petersburg Federative United Council (*Federativnyi Ob"edinennyi Sovet*) of the Bolshevik and Menshevik organizations. As early as October 18 there appeared an announcement of the Federative Council, in No. 2 of *Izvestiia Soveta Rabochikh Deputatov*[69] (it probably came out in the evening):

> The Petersburg Committee and the Petersburg Group of the RSDRP, despite existing differences of opinion on tactics and organization, have decided to form a Federative United Council to direct jointly the political actions of the Petersburg proletariat in the coming events.
>
> The tasks of the Federative Council will include the unification and systematic planning of oral and written agitation and of all public actions of the proletariat, as well as liaison with all the other

---

e) If the two parts of the Party unite, both *Iskra* and *Proletarii* must function as official organs of the Party, free to defend this or that tactical position. The heading "CO" is either to be left to both or else to be removed from both.

The representatives of the CC suggested, and the representatives of the OC agreed, that discussion of point e be postponed until the editors of both papers had been consulted. The CC's representatives found all the other proposed measures "highly desirable" but difficult to carry out "at the present time." "Moreover, the CC definitely feels that it has no right to force these reforms on local organizations which may not find it convenient to introduce them, as this would run counter to the autonomy the Congresses have guaranteed the local organizations in their internal arrangements." (Protocols of the meeting of July 12, in *Iskra*, No. 107, July 29/August 11.)

Very soon it became clear, however, that the Bolsheviks still understood unification with the Mensheviks *as a return to the Party of a splintered-off part*. Right after this conference the CC published an "Otkrytoe pis'mo" to the OC (*Proletarii*, No. 11, July 27/August 9), expressing readiness to do all it could toward "unification according to the organizational principles worked out by the Third Congress." And in *Proletarii*, No. 12, August 3/16, returning to the "Otkrytoe pis'mo," the editors "reminded" their readers that "for unification, a common organizational basis is necessary. So far we know of only one such basis, the Rules of the RSDRP adopted at the Third Party Congress."

The protocols of the third conference of the CC and the OC, in September (the second conference had not been reported in the press), were published in *Proletarii*, No. 20, September 27/October 10, with the CC's comments and a note by Lenin. From these it is clearer than ever that the Mensheviks insisted on immediate local mergers and that the Bolsheviks were extremely wary of the idea, demanding "unification of the two parts of Russian Social-Democracy on the basis of the decisions of the Third Congress." This, Lenin explained, meant the Mensheviks' "joining the Party" on that basis. As the *sole* possible alternative, the CC and Lenin proposed that a unification congress be convoked upon the mutual agreement of the two sides (real mutual agreement in this case).

[69] It was also printed in *Proletarii*, No. 25, November 3/16. *Iskra* was no longer in existence.

revolutionary organizations of Petersburg on technical fighting problems.

The admission that there were "differences of opinion on tactics and organization" was a concession to the anti-unification feelings still harbored by some of the Party leaders.

The announcement stated that "besides representatives of the Petersburg Committee and the Petersburg Group, the Federative Council includes representatives of the Central Committee and of the Organizational Commission." No Federative Council combining the CC and the OC had been formed, and the Petersburg Federative Council acted as a unifying center for the Party as a whole. Similar councils (but without representatives of the CC and the OC) were soon founded in Moscow[70] and here and there in the provinces.[71] Almost everywhere, however, the basic trend was toward plain merging of the organizations; and even where federative organs were formed, they immediately or very soon set out to effect complete fusion.

The Petersburg Federative Council was a breakthrough that the average Party members greeted with almost unanimous joy. This in turn impelled the leadership to approach the question of unification in a new way. The Bolsheviks found it hard to give up their idea that the Third Congress had been a Party congress and that the Mensheviks were a splinter group which could return to the fold but not "federate" with what was properly "the Party."[72] Still less acceptable to the Bolsheviks was the idea that federation was only a stage, soon to be followed by fusion. Hence their moves after the creation of the Federative Council tended mainly

---

[70] *Novaia Zhizn,* No. 5, November 1.

[71] In Baku (*Novaia Zhizn,* November 16), in Kharkov (*Nachalo,* November 29), and so on.

[72] A good example is a resolution of the Ivanovo-Voznesensk Committee printed in *Novaia Zhizn,* No. 5, November 1: "Having discussed the state of affairs in the Party and taken cognizance of the progress of the negotiations between the CC of the RSDRP and *the OC of its splintered-off part,* the Ivanovo-Voznesensk Committee considers . . . that unification is highly desirable . . . but declares that unification is possible only on the basis of the decisions of the Third Congress or can be achieved by convoking an extraordinary unification congress" (italics added). Even this resolution passed by a majority of only 8 to 4. "Four comrades accept this resolution, save the words 'or can be achieved by convoking an extraordinary unification congress.' They consider that unification must come about *only* on the basis of the decisions of the Third Congress." *Novaia Zhizn* added: "The same resolution was put before a conference of sector committees and was passed after prolonged discussion, by 26 votes against 4, with 7 abstentions."

to slow down the change from federation to unity. Bolsheviks and Mensheviks both realized that after the two separate conventions and the creation of two Party centers the rift had gone too far to be patched up without a new congress. The Bolsheviks attempted to apply the "federative" principle even to the organization of the unification congress, while the Mensheviks tried to settle the quarrels beforehand and to make the new congress the constituent assembly of an already united Party.

Riadovoi (A. Bogdanov), an influential member of the Central Committee, wrote in an article, "Concerning Unification," in *Novaia Zhizn*, No. 5, November 1 (O.S.):

> For the congress to attain its goals more surely and easily, there are two prerequisites—equality of the sides at the congress itself and elimination of competition in electing delegates. For this in turn it is necessary that both sides have an equal number of votes at the congress and that they hold elections separately.
>
> In a word, the "Majority" and the "Minority" must convoke simultaneous separate congresses in one locality; then, having agreed on a common agenda, combine into one congress, at which a definite equal number of delegates on both sides will be given the right to vote; who exactly, each side will decide separately.

To make everything quite clear, Bogdanov expressed strong disapproval of "direct common elections to a joint 'constituent' congress."

On November 10 the Central Committee published in *Novaia Zhizn*, No. 9 an appeal "To Convoke the Fourth Congress of the RSDRP." It was being convoked, the appeal said, "on the basis of the Rules of the Third Congress," and not by any "federative" organ but by the Bolshevik CC elected at the Third Congress; only the Bolshevik part of the Party would be represented. (That it was only a "part" of the Party was now conceded.) All this was supposed to "preserve continuity with all the prior ideological and organizational work of the Party." There followed a detailed plan for organizing the two simultaneous congresses, similar to the plan in Bogdanov's article, but the "fourth consecutive [*ocherednoi*] Party congress" which the CC would convoke had somehow turned into "a part of the unification congress."

True, the appeal said that the other part of the Party had not yet agreed to the plan: the Organizational Commission had proposed that the congresses or conferences of the two sides merely agree on the method of elections to the "constituent" congress and set up a common electoral apparatus, which in due time would also convoke the congress. The CC hoped that "the other half of the Party will not refuse to call a new conference or congress simultaneously with our congress," to avoid needless delay in settling "the sore subject of unification."

The plan aroused no enthusiasm even in the Bolshevik faction. The process of mending the rift by direct local mergers was well underway; it was in fact going on with such headlong force that the very idea of two congresses seemed downright silly. The many local organizations that had already united would have had to stay away from the separate congresses or else to send delegates to both. It is significant that *Novaia Zhizn*, in its comprehensive coverage of current events, reported hardly any cases of positive response from local organizations to the Central Committee's appeal. Nor were the Mensheviks disposed to accept this dualistic approach. In the article "The Tasks of Unification" in *Nachalo*, No. 8, November 23, Martov "insisted" on cutting short, or even entirely bypassing, the "federation phase": the Party was ripe for unification; there was no need to dawdle in that transitional stage. If the coming conventions of the factions could agree on a plan of union, "it [would] be possible soon after to hold a congress of a *united Party*, to which the organizations [already] united locally [would] send Party, not factional, delegates."

Events fully vindicated this optimistic view of the organizations' psychological readiness for union. Barely three weeks after the CC's "federalist" appeal, the Petersburg Committee, that bastion of the "firm" attitude, suddenly surrendered on the issue of unification.[73] *Novaia Zhizn*, No. 19, November 23 (O.S.),

---

[73] The Petersburg Committee's decision of November 22 must have been very sudden indeed. Only a week earlier, at a meeting of the Petersburg Federative Council on November 15, the Bolsheviks had hotly argued with the Mensheviks and got the "federative" principle adopted for all the Petersburg sectors except Vyborg, for which they had made some concessions (for a detailed account, see *Novaia Zhizn*, No. 19). But the supporters of the federative principle were so clearly losing ground that the Petersburg Committee passed its resolution of November 22 (also printed in *Novaia Zhizn*, No. 19, and quoted below in my text) *on the same day* that the Federative Council finally passed its resolution about carrying out mergers everywhere. (The passage on November 22 of the Federative Council's resolution was announced at a meeting of the Menshevik committee of the Neva sector on November 23; see *Nachalo*, No. 10, November 25.)

carried an announcement, "On the Unification of the Party," stating that the Petersburg Committee, at the suggestion of the Federative Council, had adopted the following "resolutions":

1. For the speediest possible merger of the Party all along the line, the PC insists on an immediate merger of the Party centers.

2. The PC has resolved to start on the complete unification of its organization with the organization of the Petersburg Group immediately, without waiting for a congress, or a conference, or the unification of the centers.

3. To effect the merger, the PC will elect its representatives to an organizational committee consisting of members of the PC and the PG in equal numbers. The organizational committee must work out mutually agreeable Rules based on the application of the electoral principle from the bottom up. The Rules must be ratified at a general meeting of the Committee, the Group, and all sector committees. The decisions of this meeting are to be binding on both organizations.

On the same day, the Mensheviks published in *Nachalo,* No. 8, a plan worked out by their Organizational Commission: For immediate unification from the bottom up—

1. The Organizational Commission enters upon negotiations with the Central Committee about the forms of reorganizing the Party and immediately merging the two factions. . . .

2. The Organizational Commission considers it an indispensable condition for unification that both sides recognize the democratic principle of organization . . . and strictly apply the elective principle at all levels of the Party organization.

3. The Organizational Commission and the Central Committee form a committee to unify the Party. . . . The unification results in a single elected center. The unification of the Party culminates in the convocation of a Party congress, on the principle of democratic representation in proportion to the number of organized workers.

At the same time, about November 22 or 23, a temporary organizational committee was formed, "with an equal number of representatives of the Petersburg Committee and the Petersburg Group," to carry out the unification and provide political leadership until the election of a new, joint Petersburg Committee. The organizational committee began work at once and as early as November 27 published (in *Nachalo,* No. 12, and *Novaia Zhizn,*

No. 23) the draft of Rules for a Petersburg Organization of the RSDRP. The draft was built on democratic principles, with one significant exception, clearly a concession to the Bolsheviks:[74] Not all Party members could vote in the factory and sector "assemblies" that were to be the basis of the Party and elect its leaders—but only those Party members who actually "conducted Social-Democratic work" at the given factory or in the given sector. When all these lower-level organizations had united, the Organizational Committee would disband, and a new Petersburg Committee take its place.

During its short existence in the open, Social-Democracy introduced some new organizational forms to fit the needs of a broad, overt labor movement. These forms, not carefully devised beforehand, were created more or less empirically. In November Social-Democratic "political unions" and Social-Democratic or plain "workers' clubs" began to appear in Petersburg and soon afterward in the provinces. The political unions were meant to become the basic form of the new Party organization. The term "unions" (soiuzy) was adopted to underline the new democratic spirit. The old organs of leadership ("committees") continued to exist, many already as united organs of Bolsheviks and Mensheviks, but were supposed to be replaced in the near future by elected committees which the system of "unions" would bring forth. The workers' and Social-Democratic workers' clubs were mostly non-partisan organizations, often not even aspiring to formal Party membership but concentrating on political and general education.

The club and union movement really began only in the middle of November. It was initiated mainly by Menshevik and pro-Menshevik workers. Not surprisingly, the Menshevik Nachalo and even the little Russkaia Gazeta carried more information about the unions and clubs than Novaia Zhizn. Although the Bolsheviks had immediately taken up the idea of this new type of organization, they wanted to preserve for an indefinite period of

---

[74] These points of the Rules were particularly criticized at a Menshevik meeting of the Petersburg (Peterburgskaia Storona) sector; see Nachalo, No. 15, December 1, and the article by Evgenii [Maevskii] in Nachalo, No. 14, December 2.

time the old, secret organizations as well. It would have made sense to keep a skeleton underground apparatus to fall back upon if the new freedom did not last, but this was not the Bolsheviks' main consideration. The old setup often remained the basis of the Party, with the role of the new organizations reduced to that of auxiliaries to the secret apparatus.

The first article Lenin published after his return to Russia, "On Reorganizing the Party" (*Novaia Zhizn*, Nos. 9, 13, and 14, November 10, 15, and 16) contained the following:

> The secret apparatus of the Party must be preserved. At the same time it is absolutely necessary to take the fullest advantage of the present relatively greater latitude. It is absolutely necessary to create alongside of the secret apparatus more and more new overt and semi-overt Party organizations (and organizations associated with the Party). Without this work it is impossible to adapt our activity to the new conditions and to be able to solve the new problems.[75]

Creating new organizations was an urgent task, but they should remain under the tutelage of the existing "Party institutions":

> The question of creating Party unions, organizations, groups, is to be raised immediately at all meetings. Every union, organization, group, will immediately elect its bureau or board or administrative commission—in a word, a permanent central agency to conduct the organization's business, to maintain contact with the local Party institutions, to receive and distribute Party literature, collect dues for party work, organize meetings, lectures, talks, [and], finally, to prepare the elections of delegates to the Party congress. The Party committees will of course help every such organization, supply it with material [about] the RSDRP, its history, and its great present tasks.[76]

The elections to the Fourth Congress must conform to the Rules (that is, the Rules established by the Third Congress); delegates with a vote must be elected by the local committees, but the CC, making use of its right to invite persons in an advisory capacity to the Congress, will ask the new organizations to elect them (in proportion to the size of their membership); and at its very first

---

[75] *Lenin, Sochineniia*, X, 12.
[76] *Ibid.*, pp. 17–18.

meeting the Congress must pass a resolution giving them the vote.

Lenin remarked that it would be necessary to "combat" the conservatives in his own camp to whom his plan might look like "a threat to Social-Democracy," but he advised his readers not to "exaggerate the threat." The arguments he used are somewhat surprising, coming as they did from the father of the doctrine of "spontaneity and consciousness":

> The working class is instinctively, spontaneously Social-Democratic, and more than ten years of Social-Democratic work have done a great deal toward turning this spontaneity into consciousness. Do not imagine non-existing terrors, comrades![77]

This was one of the "zigzags" characteristic of Lenin in those years—a "bending of the pole the other way," deliberately a little too far the other way, to straighten it out.[78] In this article Lenin did not raise the question of the relations between the old Party organs and the new ones that the Congress would create. Perhaps he had not yet decided it for himself, especially the question of preserving the secret Bolshevik apparatus after unification. But the general trend of his thoughts is quite clear from the subsequent history of the Party, not only after the Stockholm Congress in the spring of 1906, at which the Mensheviks had the majority, but after the London Congress in the spring of 1907, where he and his followers triumphed. Despite his victory, Lenin created within the Party a secret Bolshevik center—secret even from the Bolshevik rank and file.

The transformation of Social-Democracy into a broad, freely organized movement in the open that began during the Days of Freedom was cut short in the first week of December. The Petersburg Soviet of Workers' Deputies was arrested. The Moscow and the provincial soviets disbanded. The Social-Democratic papers were closed, and the Social-Democratic and other workers' organizations swept away by the tidal wave of victorious reaction. Social-Democracy found itself back where it had been

---

[77] *Ibid.*, p. 15. For a discussion of Lenin's theory of "spontaneity and consciousness," see Appendix 9, pp. 325–30.

[78] *Ibid.*, p. 21.

before the Days of Freedom. And although the Stockholm Congress did take place—in the main, in accord with the Mensheviks' plan—the internal strife between Bolsheviks and Mensheviks continued with increasing acerbity.

But the experiences of 1905 left their mark on both factions. The Mensheviks' work from this time on was influenced ever increasingly by the conviction that the "conspiratorial" tradition, which pre-Revolution circumstances had forced upon the Party, must be discarded; that Social-Democracy must come out into the open, if not formally as a Party, then as a movement openly active in the social and political arena and thus paving the way for the really broad Social-Democratic Party of the future. The Bolsheviks, on the other hand, moved more and more in the opposite direction, toward a more centralized Party, a more authoritarian leadership, toward the conversion of Social-Democracy into a "party of the new type." During 1911/12 the two factions formally and finally divided into two separate parties, the RSDRP of the Bolsheviks and the RSDRP of the Mensheviks. The Bolsheviks kept this name until their Seventh Congress in March, 1918, when they changed it to Communist Party of the Bolsheviks, and later to plain Communist Party. But already by 1917 the Menshevik RSDRP was in fact a Social-Democratic, and the Bolshevik RSDRP a Communist, party in the modern sense of these terms. Accordingly, the Menshevik RSDRP played a major role in the first, democratic phase of the Revolution, from February to October, 1917; and the Bolsheviks, who came to power after organizing the overturn of October, put an end to the democratic development of the Revolution.

The Theory of Permanent Revolution: Parvus and Trotsky

It took Marxist thought many years of development to arrive at a clear demarcation between bourgeois-democratic and socialist revolution. The French socialist circles of the second quarter of the nineteenth century entertained in a vague form the idea of continuous (permanent) revolution until socialism was fully established. The idea was faintly echoed in one of Marx's early articles (1843), but there is no trace of it in the *Communist Manifesto* (February, 1848). Immediately thereafter the revolutionary-socialist ("communist") leaders treated "permanent revolution" essentially as a problem of tactics: depending on circumstances, the same people now advocated, now rejected, it. In Cologne during several months of 1848/49, Marx vigorously promoted the theory that communists should merge with the democratic movement until the victory of a democratic republic—warring with Dr. Andreas Gottschalk, the leader of the left wing of the Communist Union, who championed permanent revolution.[1] In London in early 1850, after the bitter experience of 1849, the same Marx, having made his peace with the left wing of the Communist Union (whose most radical spokesman was August von Willich) and expecting a revolutionary resurgence because of the continuing economic slump, composed together with Engels the "Address of the Central Committee to the Communist Union," in which we read:

---

[1] B. I. Nicolaevsky and O. Mänchen-Helfen, *Karl Marx, Man and Fighter* (Philadelphia: J. B. Lippincott, 1936), chaps. xiii and xiv.

Whereas the democratic petty bourgeois want . . . to end the revolution as soon as possible, our interests and our task consist in keeping up a permanent revolution until all the more or less propertied classes have been forced out of power, until the proletariat has conquered state power, and the union of proletarians has progressed, not only in one country but in all the major countries of the world, to the point where competition between proletarians has ceased . . . and at least the decisive productive forces are concentrated in the proletariat's hands.[2]

The address actually ends with an appeal to the German workers to make continuous revolution their battle cry.[3]

At about the same time, referring to "revolutionary socialism," or "Communism," Marx wrote in *The Class Struggle in France from 1848 to 1850: "*This socialism is a declaration of permanent revolution [*Permanenzerklärung der Revolution*]; [it is] the class dictatorship of the proletariat as a necessary stage in the abolition of all class distinctions."[4] Neither he nor Engels ever again returned to the subject of permanent revolution.[5]

During the second half of the nineteenth century, there gradually emerged in Marxist literature and in the social-democratic parties of continental Europe a well-defined conception of a socialist program-minimum (achievable in a bourgeois society) and a socialist program-maximum. In this connection, the idea of permanent revolution revived in a new guise. After the outbreak of the Revolution of 1905 in Russia, the most responsible socialist publications began to discuss permanent revolution, but the term no longer referred to the direct transition from a bourgeois-democratic to a socialist revolution. "Permanent revolution" now had two basic connotations: first, the pursuit of democratic reform in Russia to its completion, to prevent the revolution from ending in a compromise with the old order; and second, a revolutionary development in the West, under the influence of the Russian events, with a clear-cut tendency toward socialism.

Immediately after January 9, Rosa Luxemburg wrote of the need "*den revolutionären Zustand in Permanenz zu erhalten*";[6] and Karl

---

[2] Karl Marx and Friedrich Engels, "Ansprache der Zentralbehörde an den Bund der Kommunisten vom März 1850," in *Werke* (Berlin: Dietz-Verlag, 1960), VII, 247–48.

[3] *Ibid.*, p. 254.

[4] *Ibid.*, p. 89.

[5] B. I. Nicolaevsky, "Who Is Distorting History?" *Proceedings of the American Philosophical Society* (Philadelphia: The Society, 1961), Vol. CV, No. 2, p. 219.

[6] Rosa Luxemburg, "Nach dem ersten Akt," *Die Neue Zeit*, February 4, 1905, p. 613.

Kautsky, of *"die Revolution in Permanenz in Russland."*[7] Franz Mehring's argument in *Die Neue Zeit* in early November, 1905, about the limitations of continuous revolution in Russia was widely accepted in Social-Democratic circles:

> Of course, the saying that miracles do not happen from one day to the next also applies to the Russian workers. It is not in their power to skip the stages of historical development and instantly to create a socialist community out of the coercive tsarist state. But they can shorten and smooth the road of their struggle for emancipation if they do not sacrifice their hard-won revolutionary might to the deceptive mirages of the bourgeoisie but keep asserting it, so as to accelerate the historical, that is to say, the revolutionary, development. In months or weeks they can now obtain what would take them decades of laborious effort if, after victory, they left the field to the bourgeoisie. They cannot write the dictatorship of the proletariat into the new Russian constitution; but they can [obtain] universal suffrage, the right to unite, the legally regulated working day, unrestricted freedom of press and speech, and [they can] extract from the bourgeoisie guaranties for all these demands as firm as those the bourgeoisie will extract from the tsar for its own needs. But [the workers] can do all this only if they do not for an instant lay down arms and do not permit the bourgeoisie to advance by as much as one step without also advancing another step.
>
> That is what constitutes the "permanent revolution" with which the Russian working class will reply—and, judging by the news to date, has already replied—to the frightened bourgeois clamor for "peace at any price."[8]

After this, the term underwent reversion. It came to denote the direct "growing-over" of a bourgeois-democratic into a socialist revolution. And this is how it is usually understood when Parvus and Trotsky are named as the fathers of the theory of permanent revolution in Russia. The literature has long since cast them both in the role of its energetic promoters during the First Russian Revolution. This is correct as far as Trotsky is concerned but only partially true of Parvus. As I am going to show, the latter never advocated the idea in its definitive form. And yet it may be only fair to attach both their names to it, and even to give Parvus pride of place, since Trotsky came to the idea partly through Parvus.

---

[7] Karl Kautsky, "Die Folgen des japanischen Sieges und die Sozialdemokratie," *Die Neue Zeit*, July 2, 1905, p. 465.

[8] Franz Mehring, "Die Revolution in Permanenz," *Die Neue Zeit*, November 4, 1905, pp. 169–72. A Russian translation is given in *Nachalo*, No. 10, November 25, 1905.

Trotsky had been a very active member of the Menshevik literary "nucleus" since the Second Party Congress in 1903, but during the "political thaw" of the summer and fall of 1904, he found himself at odds with Axelrod, Martov, and others over their attitude toward the liberals and left Geneva for Munich, without, however, breaking with *Iskra*. During the several months of his stay in Munich, he often saw Parvus, who was considerably his senior and a recognized authority in leftist European Social-Democracy. A quarter-century later Trotsky himself wrote that Parvus had influenced the development of his political thought.[9] After January 9—he was back in Geneva by then—Trotsky decided to go to Russia. As soon as he obtained the necessary papers, he and his wife set out for Munich, probably to see Parvus once more. Trotsky writes:

> Parvus put us up at his home. There he read my manuscript about the events of January 9, and it put him in an elated mood. "Events have fully borne out this prognosis. Now no one can deny that a general strike is the basic method of struggle. . . . It is only necessary to add that the revolution in Russia may carry a democratic government to power." Parvus wrote a foreword to my pamphlet to this effect.[10]

For Trotsky this was the beginning of the theory of permanent revolution. It was not mentioned in the pamphlet itself (*Before January 9*, published by *Iskra* in February), but Parvus' foreword lays down some of its basic elements, such as the peasants' incapacity for independent revolutionary action and the outstanding role of workers' representatives in the future revolutionary government:

> Greater and greater masses of peasants will be drawn into the movement. But they can only increase the political anarchy in the country and thus weaken the government; they cannot form a compact revolutionary army. As the revolution develops, more and more of the political work will fall to the proletariat. This will also broaden its political self-awareness and increase its political energy.
> The Russian proletariat has already built up a revolutionary force

---

[9] In *Moia zhizn'. Opyt avtobiografii* ([Berlin: Granit, 1930], I, 193), Trotsky wrote: "Parvus was unquestionably an outstanding Marxist figure of the end of the last century and the beginning of this one. His expert use of the Marxian method, his broad outlook, the fact that he kept abreast of all important world events—all this, plus an uncommon audacity of thought and a virile, sinewy style made him a truly remarkable writer. *His earlier writings had brought me close to the problems of social revolution, having definitely changed for me the proletariat's conquest of power from an astronomical 'ultimate' aim into a practical task for our times*" (italics added).

[10] *Ibid.*, pp. 192–93.

that surpasses anything other peoples have achieved during revolutionary uprisings. . . . When the Russian proletariat finally overthrows autocracy, it will be an army tempered in the revolutionary struggle, firm and determined, always ready to use force to back up its demands.

As early as 1848 the French proletariat forced the inclusion of its people in the provisional government. . . . The Russian workers, having already written their proletarian demands into the political program of the revolution, will be much stronger at the moment of the uprising, and will certainly show no less class consciousness, than the French workers in 1848. They will undoubtedly appoint their own people to the revolutionary government. Social-Democracy will be faced with the dilemma of assuming responsibility for the provisional government or standing aside from the labor movement. The workers will regard this government as their own, whatever attitude Social-Democracy takes. . . .

A revolutionary overturn in Russia can be accomplished only by the workers. The revolutionary provisional government in Russia will be a government of the workers' democracy. If Social-Democracy heads the revolutionary movement of the Russian proletariat, that government will be Social-Democratic. If Social-Democracy lags behind the proletariat in revolutionary initiative, it will become an insignificant sect.[11]

Should a Social-Democratic government introduce socialist measures? No, replied Parvus, without even mentioning that things might change if there were a social revolution in the West:

A Social-Democratic provisional government cannot effect a socialist overturn in Russia, but the very process of liquidating autocracy and establishing a democratic republic will provide a favorable soil for its political work. . . . It will be a . . . government with a Social-Democratic majority, formed at a revolutionary moment, when a government's power is very great. . . . And this government will be faced at first with the political tasks for which the whole Russian people united in the revolutionary struggle. A Social-Democratic provisional government will of course do this work more thoroughly than any other.[12]

The words "at first" do suggest that the "political tasks" (that is, the bourgeois-democratic revolutionary tasks) might change, but Parvus did not say so outright, either then or later. Soon after Trotsky's departure he wrote a leaflet, "No Tsar, and a Workers' Government,"[13] in which he defined the tasks of the workers' government:

[11] Parvus' foreword to Trotsky's pamphlet *Do 9-go ianvaria* (Geneva, 1905), pp. x–xi. The foreword was reprinted in Parvus' book *Rossiia i revoliutsiia* (Petersburg: N. Glagolev, 1906), with the title "Chto nam daet 9-oe ianvaria."

[12] *Ibid.*, pp. xi–xii.

[13] This leaflet, signed by Parvus, was printed by the *Iskra* press but without the Party imprint.

It is the task of the working people not only to abolish the tsarist government but to take power themselves.

The whole people must have political rights, and the working class must stand guard over these rights.

There must be political rights and a *workers' government.* There must be a government appointed by the revolutionary army of workers which has accomplished the political overturn.

The government of representatives of the working class will have the task of consolidating the people's rule, democracy. It will ruthlessly abolish all remnants of autocracy and pave the way for the convocation and the legislative activity of a Russian parliament.

Trotsky was therefore right when he attacked K. Radek's peculiar notions about Parvus' stand in 1905:

Radek in fact refutes himself elsewhere in his article when he points out, in passing but quite correctly, the difference between my views of the revolution and Parvus'. Parvus did not think that a workers' government in Russia . . . could grow over into a socialist dictatorship in the process of fulfilling the tasks of democracy. . . . Parvus limited the tasks of the workers' government to *democratic* tasks. . . . Parvus, already at that time, had in view the establishment of a workers' regime of the "Australian" type after the revolutionary overturn. . . . Parvus in 1905 saw the conquest of power as a way to democracy, not to socialism.[14]

Yet it was from Parvus that Trotsky originally drew the idea of Social-Democracy's leading influence in the provisional government. He wrote on this theme for the first time in *Iskra* in March, 1905:

If Russia's renewal were following the road of compromise and bargaining, our working class could not dream of the role it has today. The revolution is moving the proletariat into the forefront and giving it hegemony. . . . Only the proletariat can insure the victory of the uprising and the triumph of the revolution as a whole. Other groups of the urban population, as well as the peasantry, will play their role in the revolution to the extent that they follow the proletariat, support it, facilitate its work. Neither the peasantry, nor the petty bourgeoisie, nor the intelligentsia will play an *independent* role in the revolution at all comparable with that of the proletariat.

Consequently, the makeup of the provisional government will depend mainly on the proletariat. This means . . . that the development of the revolution is leading the proletariat, and with it our Party, toward temporary political supremacy.[15]

---

[14] L. Trotsky, *Permanentnaia revoliutsiia* (Berlin: Granit, 1930), p. 66.
[15] "Politicheskie pis'ma. II," *Iskra*, No. 93, March 17, 1905 (O.S.).

Here the role of Social-Democracy in the government is defined, essentially, "according to Parvus." Nothing is said as yet about socialist tasks, and the supremacy is viewed as "temporary."

In April Trotsky wrote down his theses on participation in the provisional government. At the insistence of L. B. Krasin, the *de facto* head of the illegal Central Committee of the Party in Russia, he refrained from predicting a Social-Democratic majority in the government. And by and large, the theses were still within the framework of the ideas Trotsky had developed in the *Iskra* article.[16]

But his views were rapidly evolving. In July he wrote in the foreword to a Russian translation of Lassalle's *Speech to the Jury:*

> *Now* the bourgeoisie is likely to show even less initiative and firmness than it did in 1848. For one thing, the obstacles are far more colossal; for

---

[16] Trotsky relates in *Moia Zhizn'*, I, 199–200, that "my theses were printed in Petersburg, and Krasin undertook to defend them at the expected general Party congress abroad in May. However, no general congress took place. Krasin participated in the debate on the question of the provisional government at the Bolsheviks' Congress and presented my theses as correctives of Lenin's resolution. This incident is so interesting politically that I am compelled to quote from the protocols of the Third Congress: 'As to Comrade Lenin's resolution,' said Krasin, 'its defect, in my opinion, is precisely that it does not point out vividly enough the connection between the provisional government and the armed uprising. The provisional government is really put forward by the popular uprising as its organ. . . . Further, I disagree . . . that the provisional government appears only *after* the final victory of the armed uprising and the fall of autocracy. No, it emerges in the process of the uprising and takes a most active part in its direction, assuring its victory by its organizing influence. It is naïve to think that Social-Democracy can participate in the provisional government from the moment that autocracy has definitely fallen. Once the chestnuts have been pulled out of the fire, no one will think of sharing them with us.'—This is formulated almost verbatim as in my theses. Lenin, who had treated the question purely theoretically in his main speech, took a very favorable view of Krasin's approach. . . . The resolution was revised accordingly."

Since Trotsky stresses his far-reaching solidarity with Krasin on the question of the provisional government, it may be worthwhile to quote another excerpt from Krasin's speech (*Tretii s"ezd RSDRP. Aprel'-mai 1905 goda. Protokoly* [Moscow: Gospolitizdat, 1959], pp. 199–200): "We are all in agreement that the impending overturn will be only political and not socialist. It will result only in strengthening the influence of the bourgeoisie, and there will finally come a moment in the life of the provisional government when the revolution begins to ebb, when the strength of the bourgeoisie impels it to try and deprive the proletariat of its conquests. The proletariat has already won many improvements, whose preservation requires further efforts on its part. And when the proletariat is exhausted from its terrible sacrifices, the bourgeoisie will seize the opportunity to take away from it the rights it has conquered. At that time our representatives will of course have to leave the provisional government, so as not to stain their hands with the proletariat's blood." These words, clashing as they did with the idea of permanent revolution and even with Parvus' conception of a democratic workers' government, were out of harmony with Trotsky's views. But the disagreement was not yet substantial enough to prevent Trotsky from feeling a basic solidarity with Krasin on the question of the provisional government.

another, the social and political parceling of the nation has gone immeasurably farther. The tacit conspiracy of the national and world bourgeoisie presents terrible obstacles to the process of emancipation; it strives to prevent it from going beyond an agreement between the propertied classes and the representatives of the old order for putting down the popular masses. Under such conditions a genuinely democratic tactic can be developed only in conflict with the liberal bourgeoisie. . . . [The working class] will have to assume the role of hegemon—if the country is to have a radical democratic rebirth at all. Under such conditions we have the supremacy of the "fourth estate." Of course the proletariat, like the bourgeoisie in its time, fulfils its mission with the backing of the peasantry and the petty bourgeoisie. It directs the peasantry, draws it into the movement, interests it in the success of its plans. But it remains inescapably the leader. This is no "dictatorship of the proletariat and peasantry"; this is a dictatorship of the proletariat leaning on the peasantry. [The proletariat's] work is of course not confined to state limits. The logic of its position will immediately propel it into the international arena.[17]

Here we already have two basic elements of the theory of permanent revolution—the dictatorship of the proletariat leaning (in Russia) on the peasantry and the emergence of the proletarian revolution in the "international arena."[18] There is as yet no direct admission that the dictatorship of the proletariat is socialist and that the objectives are no longer limited to the program-minimum. Soon Trotsky was to add these elements, too. In November he wrote in the article "Social-Democracy and the Revolution":

The position of the working class as the vanguard in the revolutionary struggle, the direct ties forming between it and the peasantry, the fascination it exerts over the army—all this inescapably pushes it toward power. The complete victory of the revolution means the victory of the proletariat.

This in turn means further continuous revolution. The proletariat carries out the basic tasks of democracy—and at a certain point the logic of its direct struggle to consolidate its political supremacy confronts it with purely socialist problems. A revolutionary continuity is established

---

[17] Lassalle's speech with Trotsky's foreword was published as a pamphlet in 1906 by the Molot press. I did not have it when I was writing this book, and the quotation in my text is taken from Trotsky's book *1905* (Moscow: Gosizdat, 1922), pp. 280–81.

[18] Winfried Scharlau believes that Trotsky arrived at the "internationalism" of his conception of permanent revolution largely under the influence of Parvus' theory of the political effects of an increasingly international economy. See Scharlau, "Parvus und Trockij: 1904–1914. Ein Beitrag zur Theorie der permanenten Revolution," in *Jahrbücher für Geschichte Osteuropas* (München: Osteuropa-Institut; Neue Folge), Vol. 10, Pt. 3, October, 1962, pp. 373–75.

between the minimal and the maximal programs. This is not one "coup," not a day or a month; it is a whole historical epoch. It would be senseless to assess its duration in advance.[19]

In December, 1905, and early 1906, while in prison, Trotsky wrote the long article "Summation and Prospects," a detailed explanation of his conception.[20] And he often returned to this conception in his later writings. In periodic arguments with the Bolsheviks he counterposed the *socialist* dictatorship of the proletariat "leaning on the peasantry" to Lenin's *democratic* dictatorship of the proletariat and peasantry. When the Bolsheviks accepted the so-called April theses in April, 1917, the argument lost its point, as Lenin had virtually endorsed Trotsky's view. A. A. Ioffe wrote Trotsky before he shot himself in 1927 that he had "with my own ears heard Lenin admit that in 1905 you, and not he, were right."[21]

---

[19] "Sotsialdemokratiia i revoliutsiia," published in the Menshevik *Nachalo*, November 25, 1905.

[20] The article "Itogi i perspektivy" was included in Trotsky's book *Nasha revoliutsiia* (Petersburg: Glagolev, 1906). Under the Soviets, it was published separately.

[21] L. Trotsky, *Moia zhizn'*, II, 284. That Lenin in late 1905 came quite close to Trotsky's conception "theoretically," even if he did leave a great deal unsaid in his public utterances, is also evident from his theses about "stages" from which I have quoted. See pp. 26–27 in this book.

The Demonstration of
November 28, 1904, in Petersburg

Communist literature has built up the following myth around the demonstration that led to the formal split between Bolsheviks and Mensheviks in Petersburg. It had been decided on by the Petersburg Committee but was cancelled on Thursday November 25, three days before it was due, at the wish of the Mensheviks, who happened to be in the majority at the Committee's meeting on that date ("Thanks to the absence of three comrades favoring the demonstration, this proposal [that is, the Mensheviks' proposal to cancel.—S. S.] was accepted"); the next day the Committee re-examined the issue, with the three missing Bolsheviks present this time, and decided to go through with the demonstration, but the whole thing was already doomed.

The original source of this story was a letter from "a workman Committee member" in *Vpered,* No. 1, December 22, 1904/January 4, 1905,[1] from which the quotation in the above paragraph is taken. The truth of the matter was different, as can be seen from the protocols of the November 25 and 26 meetings of the Petersburg Committee.[2]

From the letter in *Vpered* we learn that the question of staging a demonstration had been considered by the Petersburg Committee several times during the fall of 1904. In early November

> there appeared some leaflet in the name of a "Social-Democratic students' group" calling for a demonstration on November 14. Having learned of this, the Committee suggested to this organization that they

---

[1] Most of this letter is quoted in Lenin's article "Pora konchat'," in *Sochineniia* (4th ed.), VIII, 19–21.

[2] "K istorii raskola," *Proletarskaia Revoliutsiia,* November, 1925, pp. 47–59.

postpone the demonstration until the end of November, so as to be able to act together with the Petersburg proletariat. The students agreed.

On November 18 the Petersburg Committee decided to hold a demonstration on Sunday November 28. At the November 25 meeting—we are now following the protocols—the Committee called it off. This happened, however, in a paradoxical fashion.

The organizers of the Neva and the Vasil'ev-Ostrov sectors, both Mensheviks, wanted to cancel the demonstration on the ground that since the Committee had failed to prepare the bulk of the workers by issuing leaflets only the organized workers would come. This proposal received only the two Mensheviks' votes and was rejected. But immediately afterward the Committee passed (by three votes against the Mensheviks' two, with one abstention) a resolution proposed by the Bolshevik leader P. P. (Rumiantsev) *cancelling* the demonstration—on the ground that the Committee could not be sure that its outvoted members (the two organizers) "considered themselves bound by the Committee's resolution to organize a demonstration."[3] A worse case of internal crisis is hard to imagine, but that was not all. During the night a large number of leaflets calling for a demonstration was destroyed. ("It was decided not to distribute the leaflets and to destroy those with the appeal," wrote the "workman Committee member" of the meeting of November 25.) The next day, eight—not six—members of the Committee met again, including the three Bolsheviks absent on the twenty-fifth but not the Vasil'ev-Ostrov organizer, who did not appear. It was resolved, seven to one, to participate in the demonstration after all.[4] *Vpered's* correspondent, while stressing his solidarity with this decision, noted that the Committee knew that most of the "appeal" leaflets had been destroyed and that the remaining ones could not be widely distributed because there was not enough time to get them to the factories by Saturday morning, and work ended on Saturdays at 2:00 or 3:00 o'clock. "Thus the leaflets could be distributed to only a small circle of workers—among acquaintances—by no means to the broad masses. Under such conditions the demonstration was in advance doomed to failure, and fail it did."

A good many students and a small number of workers took part in the demonstration. It was quashed with unusual ferocity. *Iskra,* No. 80, December 15, carried three letters from participants, describing what happened. (See also a protest by Petersburg writers against the bloody suppression, in *Iskra,* No. 81, December 22.)

[3] *Ibid.,* p. 55.
[4] *Ibid.,* p. 59.

The Genesis of the Bureau of the Committees of the Majority (BCM)

Official history says that after the Conference of Twenty-two Bolsheviks

> three conferences—of the South, the Caucasus, and the North—took place between September and December, 1904, at which thirteen committees of the RSDRP were represented. The Bureau of the Committees of the Majority was formed at these conferences, under the leadership of V. I. Lenin.[1]

This does not correspond to the truth, and it is no accident that for a quarter-century the Bolshevik literature was almost totally silent about these conferences (except, in part, the belated Northern Conference).

Only the scantiest information has been published about the Conference of the Twenty-two itself. M. Liadov, one of the participants, names fifteen well-known Bolsheviks in his article "The Third Congress of the RSDRP," adding, "and seven more people, whose names I do not remember."[2] R. Khabas, author of the article "The Creation of the Bolshevik Center (BCM) and of the paper *Vpered*," reports that Zemliachka told him in 1924 that

> she and someone else were in July or August, 1904, called from Russia to Geneva. There, at the Lepeshinskiis' restaurant [*stolovka*], a conference

---

[1] *Istoriia Kommunisticheskoi Partii Sovetskogo Soiuza* (Moscow: Gospolitizdat, 1959), p. 71.

[2] *Proletarskaia Revoliutsiia*, 1921, No. 3, p. 62; see also n. 7 to this appendix.

was arranged, which included Maria Il'inishna [M. I. Ul'ianova, Lenin's sister], Gusev, Pavlovich-Krasikov, Lepeshinskii, Ol'minskii, and other comrades. From there, with the "resolution of Twenty-two Bolsheviks" hidden in a mirror frame, Comrade Zemliachka set out on a tour of the Party committees.[3]

There is a strange vagueness about this conference; even its date was never revealed, and no one seems to have remembered it. In *Leninskii Sbornik,* among the documents pertaining to the summer of 1904, a letter from N. K. Krupskaia to M. I. Ul'ianova in Russia cites a "manifesto" adopted by a "conference of partisans of the Majority." An editor's note says: "The date of this letter, 'August 14' (corrected in the original to 'August 12') can safely be assumed to mark the end of the Conference, which probably lasted two to three days."[4] This notion, however, was not taken up. I have never seen it referred to in subsequent publications.

Where did the "conference of partisans of the Majority" meet? Not

---

[3] R. Khabas, "Sozdanie bol'shevistskogo tsentra (BKB) i gazety 'Vpered,'" *Proletarskaia Revoliutsiia,* 1924, No. 11, pp. 25–26.

[4] *Leninskii Sbornik,* XV (1930), 179, 212. Krupskaia's letter surrounds the "conference of partisans of the Majority" with an aura of mystery that can hardly be explained by the need to hide it from the police. More likely, the need was to hide it from public opinion inside the Party. Krupskaia writes: "The following is strictly secret and must not be known to anyone under any circumstances, not a soul except Medvezhonok [M. I. Ul'ianova] and Diaden'ka [L. M. Knipovich]. Diaden'ka must be told as soon as possible. The conference of partisans of the Majority has worked out a manifesto, which I am giving below.

"For many reasons, mainly for secrecy, absolutely no one must know the place of its provenance, but all the committees must as soon as possible learn of its content and express their solidarity with it. For this I propose the following: print it by hectograph and send it privately to all the committees, or better, take it to them. We are asking Diaden'ka to arrange this matter, as secretly as possible."

This letter is in the collection of documents and materials *Tretii s"ezd RSDRP* (Moscow: Gospolitizdat, 1955), pp. 262–63, which also contains other letters (published for the first time) Krupskaia wrote on August 14–to M. M. Litvinov in Riga and V. V. Vorovskii in Odessa. She wrote Litvinov that "Zemliachka has left for your parts and will tell you of our tactic" (p. 263) without mentioning the Conference, but the letter to Vorovskii has a few lines about it: "The rest no one but you must know: we have had a conference; its place is top secret; I am sending the declaration: it must be reproduced and distributed privately, in strict secrecy. Agitate for having the committees indorse it" (p. 265).

A small recent work on the BCM (K. V. Shakhnazarova, "Na puti k III s"ezdu RSDRP. Obzor dokumentov iz fonda Biuro komitetov bol'shinstva Tsentral'nogo partiinogo arkhiva," *Voprosy Istorii KPSS,* August, 1963, pp. 112–16) quotes from a still unpublished letter of Krupskaia to Mysh (P. I. Kuliabko) of August 19 (N.S.): "We have worked out a manifesto here, the place . . . must be kept strictly secret. It must be mimeographed in Russia (privately) and distributed, also privately, to the committees, so that they can rally around one slogan. The manifesto has been sent to Medvezhonok; get it from him through Diaden'ka and do what is necessary" (p. 114).

in Geneva, as Zemliachka later maintained. From early July to mid-September Lenin was not in Geneva,[5] and without him such a conference was unthinkable. According to the editors of *Leninskii Sbornik*, it took place "in some village in the Swiss mountains (its name has not been ascertained)."[6] The same vagueness envelops the names of the participants.[7] Even the announcement about the Conference appeared in a curiously camouflaged form—not abroad but in Russia, in a leaflet, "To the Party," issued by the Riga Committee. It was the address to the Party, written by Lenin, which is known as the "Declaration of the Twenty-two," but it contained no hint that it stemmed from abroad. It began, "Recently there has been a private conference of twenty-two members of the RSDRP who share the viewpoint of the Majority of the Second Party Congress" and have composed an address. The Riga Committee added that it concurred in the initiative of these com-

---

[5] N. K. Krupskaia writes in *Vospominaniia o Lenine* (Moscow, 1957 [pp. 85–86]) that in early summer, 1904, she and Lenin, worn out by their Geneva environment, "took our knapsacks and went off into the mountains for a month. . . . After a month of this kind of life, Vladimir Il'ich's nerves returned to normal. It was as if he had washed in a mountain spring and washed off the cobwebs of petty squabbles. August we spent together with Bogdanov, Ol'minskii, and Pervukhin in a quiet village on the Lac de Bret" (near Lausanne).

[6] *Leninskii Sbornik*, XV, 109.

[7] M. Liadov's enumeration (*Proletarskaia Revoliutsiia*, 1921, No. 3, p. 62) differs from Zemliachka's, quoted earlier. He lists the following as members of the Conference of the Twenty-two: Lenin, Krupskaia, Bogdanov, Lunacharskii, Ol'minskii, Lepeshinskii, Liadov, Desnitskii, Zemliachka, Zver', Vorovskii, Bonch-Bruevich, Velichkina, Gusev, Krasikov. He could not remember the other seven. But not all of the prominent Bolsheviks named by Liadov and Zemliachka were abroad at the time. M. I. Ul'ianova (on Zemliachka's list) was in Russia, where Krupskaia wrote her about the Conference, and on August 14 Krupskaia wrote to Vorovskii in Odessa (see n. 4). There is a relevant comment about Vorovskii in *Leninskii Sbornik*, XV, 177: "It has not been definitely ascertained whether he personally took part in working out the 'Declaration of the Twenty-two' or arrived later; but since he was a prominent organizer and leader of the Majority movement in Russia and unquestionably in agreement with the 'Declaration of the Twenty-two,' his name certainly figured among the signatures of the initiators and participants of the Conference."

"Not definitely ascertained" is good. There also is another indication that Vorovskii was not abroad at the time of the Conference: in D. Kardashev's article "K istorii zarozhdeniia Biuro komitetov bol'shinstva," *Proletarskaia Revoliutsiia*, 1929, No. 10 (93), p. 84, we read that "in the dossier of the former Odessa division of the Okhrana there is an interesting note about V. V. Vorovskii from which one can see that on August 12, 1904 (O.S.) Comrade Vorovskii left for Germany."

Several others on Liadov's list could not have attended the Conference either. Zver' (Zvereva [M. M. Èssen]), for instance, had left Geneva for Russia about June 21 and had been arrested on the Russian border (*Leninskii Sbornik*, XV, 88, 98). A. V. Lunacharskii had recently returned from exile and was working in Kiev; he went abroad at the decision of the BCM toward the end of the year to work on *Vpered* (N. Bychkova and A. Lebedev, *Pervyi narkom prosveshcheniia A. V. Lunacharskii* [Moscow, 1960], p. 6).

rades.[8] For several weeks the document was referred to as "the Riga declaration" or "the Riga resolution."[9]

Apparently there simply had not been any Conference of the Twenty-two, and the Declaration of the Twenty-two had been written in early August by Lenin alone, in a village near Lausanne (perhaps after consulting Bogdanov and Ol'minskii, who were also vacationing there), and then read "at the Lepeshinskiis'" to Lenin's closest followers, who, naturally, approved. All this was kept very dark so that the declaration could be presented as a product of party workers in Russia—a point to which Lenin attached great importance.[10]

The first of the regional conferences which supposedly laid the foundations of the Bureau of the Committees of the Majority was the Southern Conference in late September. It included representatives of the Odessa, Nikolaev, and Ekaterinoslav Committees and of the Southern Bureau of the CC (which had disobeyed the CC's order to disband). The resolutions of this conference were not published until 1930 in *Leninskii Sbornik*.[11] The Conference fully subscribed to the decisions of the twenty-two and resolved that it was necessary

> to form an Organizational Committee [referred to later as OC] which would organize agitation for a congress, allocate the forces of the Majority, and do any other work needed to achieve the convocation of a congress and the . . . unity of Russian revolutionary Social-Democracy. The meeting intrusts the appointment of the Organizational Committee to the Conference of the Twenty-two.[12]

---

[8] These documents were later published in N. Shakhov, *Bor'ba za s"ezd* (Geneva: V. Bonch-Bruevich and N. Lenin, 1904). See *Kak rozhdalas' partiia bol'shevikov. Literaturnaia polemika 1903–1904 g.g.* (Leningrad: Istpart; Priboi, 1925), pp. 326–33.

[9] In the first half of September, Vorovskii wrote the Odessa Committee from Geneva: "The Riga Declaration of the Twenty-two has come out; it expresses the views and the policy of the Majority and must be indorsed" (*Leninskii Sbornik*, XV, 176). On September 16 Krupskaia wrote to Bobrovskii at the Baku Committee, "The Riga Committee has issued an excellent declaration," and on September 20 to Leibovich, a member of the Nikolaev Committee, "The Petersburg and the Moscow Committees have already joined in the Riga resolution" (*ibid.*, pp. 179, 212).

[10] Liadov wrote from Geneva to Litvinov in Riga in the latter half of July: "The old man thinks it would be a good idea for all the stalwarts to issue a manifesto to the Party, expressing their views on our situation. It is especially important that Russia take the initiative in this matter." The commentators on the documents published in *Leninskii Sbornik* remark: "The statement indicates that this was the time Lenin reached the decision that it was necessary for the Party Majority to formulate their views and their stand publicly, which was done by the Conference of the Twenty-two in its declaration 'K partii'" (*ibid.*, p. 99).

[11] *Ibid.*, pp. 217–20.

[12] *Ibid.*, p. 218.

This was not exactly what Lenin wanted.[13] He wrote the participants of the Southern Conference:

> In reply to your resolution about the desirability of forming an OC of the Majority, we hasten to inform you that we are in full agreement with your idea. We should only prefer to call the group not OC but Bureau of the Committees of the Majority. We do not feel we can take it upon ourselves to appoint the BCM; we confine ourselves to recommending Comrades Martyn, Demon and K., the Baron, Sergei Petrovich, Felix, and Lebedev,[14] who (as you know) have in fact begun the work of uniting the committees of the Majority. We think that, provided they have the direct support of several committees, these comrades could act as a private group unifying the activity of the partisans of the Majority.[15]

This letter, published only in 1930, clearly shows Lenin's wish to make it appear that the initiative in the matter of the BCM came entirely from Party workers in Russia. At the time certain details were evidently not yet clear in Lenin's mind: the sentence suggesting that "these comrades" act as a private group originally had "as an OC"; in the manuscript "OC" was first changed to "BCM," then to "private group."[16]

If the Southern Conference had been eager to act in harmony with the Conference of the Twenty-two, even going too far in its zeal, the Caucasus Conference in November—of representatives of the Baku, Batum, Tiflis, and Imeretia-Mingrelia Committees—was something else again. Its resolutions, published a quarter-century later,[17] are appraised by the editors of *Leninskii Sbornik* as follows:

> The mood and the position of the Caucasus committees, as expressed in the resolutions of the Caucasus Conference, differed somewhat from

---

[13] In his letter to Bogdanov of November 2, 1904 (N.S.), Lenin complained that the legal problems which had forced him and Bonch-Bruevich to start a publishing house in their own names were not properly understood in Russia. He wrote about the members of the Southern Conference: "Many take no account of the situation and forget that Bonch-Bruevich and Lenin acted as private persons, not in the name of any group; but in Russia this was not understood and a resolution was passed to support the group headed by Bonch-Bruevich and Lenin. Pretty absurd." (*Leninskii Sbornik*, XV, 233.) The same complaint—ignorance of the legal position within the Party that forced Lenin to resort to various maneuvers—applied to the Southern Conference's resolution about forming a Bolshevik center.

There is a reference to this letter in Lenin, *Sochineniia*, VII, 522, n. 110, but for some reason the letter itself is not in the fourth edition, though it was published in 1930 in *Leninskii Sbornik*, XV, 232–35.

[14] They were Liadov, Zemliachka, È. È. Èssen, Gusev, Litvinov, and Krasikov.

[15] Lenin, *Sochineniia*, XXXIV, 220.

[16] *Leninskii Sbornik*, XV, 221.

[17] *Ibid.*, pp. 249–53.

those of the Southern committees. The Southern Conference was absolutely unanimous in adopting its forthright resolutions about convoking a congress, about creating an OC for convoking a congress, and about supporting the literary group of the Majority; it expressed obvious mistrust of the CC in the matter of convoking a congress; it unreservedly intrusted the formation of the OC to the Conference of the Twenty-two, in other words, to the *de facto* Bolshevik center headed by Lenin. The Caucasus Conference, on the other hand, made its decisions merely by majority vote, admitted into the text of its resolutions the dissenting opinion of one of its members against convoking a congress, counted on the positive participation of the CC in the matter of convoking a congress, took a rather cautious attitude toward the Conference of the Twenty-two and the Majority center abroad, and found it necessary to elect its own special bureau to agitate for a congress without intrusting this work to an all-Russian Bureau of the Committees of the Majority.[18]

This was a far cry from direct participation in forming the BCM, as official history would have it—yet the Caucasus Bolsheviks, led at that time by Stalin, had intensively prepared for the Conference. We read in the Great Soviet Encyclopedia:

Upon his return in February, 1904, after escaping from exile, I. V. Stalin organized the struggle for the convocation of a third Party congress, firmly leading toward a break with the Mensheviks. The Committee of the Caucasus Union of the RSDRP, directed by I. V. Stalin, severed its ties with the Menshevik CC of the RSDRP at that time; in June, 1904, it dissolved the Baku Committee, which had objected to . . . a third Party congress, and organized a Bolshevik Baku Committee. In January-February, 1905, the Committee of the Caucasus Union dissolved the Menshevik Tiflis Committee and organized a Bolshevik Tiflis Party Committee.[19]

---

[18] *Ibid.*, pp. 248–49. Here is an excerpt from the resolution "O biuro": "In order to expedite the convocation of a third, extraordinary congress, this Conference is electing a special bureau from among its members or other persons well known to it, but in any case including a representative of . . . [omission: evidently 'the CC,' to which the following 'itself' then also refers.—S. S.] appointed by itself; the Conference is instructing the special bureau to take any measures it considers necessary for preparing a congress. In particular, the bureau is authorized to conduct appropriate agitation for a congress, on the largest scale, and to enter into agreements with organizations that may prove useful in this matter, such as the well-known group of the twenty-two.

"It is especially desirable to secure the assistance of the CC, without whose participation the bureau is to do its work only if the CC cannot or will not . . . [omission: evidently 'assist.'—S. S.] the bureau in carrying out its assignments. (*Ibid.*, p. 252.)

[19] "Biuro Komitetov Bol'shinstva," in *Bol'shaia Sovetskaia Éntsiklopediia* (2d ed.), VI (1951), 472.

Without having been founded by either the Southern or Caucasus conferences, the BCM was nonetheless very active during the fall of 1904, or, as Lenin had said, "had in fact begun the work." Lenin was anxious to make the *de facto* situation official. Even before the Caucasus Conference, on November 2 (N.S.), he had written Bogdanov:

> The plan is to have a few of our committees elect candidates, then to publish an announcement about the formation of the Bureau of the Committees of the Majority, then to make the rounds of the remaining committees, inviting them to join and to add to the list of candidates one or two of their own.[20]

Lenin's draft of the announcement was inclosed.[21] It appealed to the organizations of the Majority to unite

> in order to struggle for a congress, to struggle against the so-called central organs of the Party which are in fact making a mockery of the Party. We are inaugurating this unity in forming the Bureau of the Committees of the Majority, on the initiative and with the consent of the Odessa, Ekaterinoslav, Nikolaev, Riga, Petersburg, and Moscow Committees.[22]

The announcement, however, was not issued, perhaps because open rebellion against the "so-called central organs" required considerably more preparation. The BCM continued to exist unofficially. In December the BCM itself convoked the Northern Conference, the last of the three regional conferences that allegedly brought it forth.[23] Only after the third conference were any of them mentioned openly and then

---

[20] *Leninskii Sbornik*, XV, 234.

[21] "Izveshchenie ob obrazovanii Biuro Komitetov Bol'shinstva," first printed in *Proletarskaia Revoliutsiia* in 1940 and included in Lenin, *Sochineniia*, VII, 456–60.

[22] *Ibid.*, p. 459.

[23] R. Khabas, drawing on his 1924 talks with Litvinov, who had been one of the organizers of the Northern Conference, writes quite plainly: "The BCM called a conference of the Northern Committees and directed its work" ("Sozdanie bol'shevistskogo tsentra . . . ," p. 26). Litvinov himself wrote later: "The Conference was convoked by the so-called Bureau of the Committees of the Majority, the Bolshevik center in Russia at the time." See Litvinov's comments on his correspondence with Lenin and Krupskaia, *Proletarskaia Revoliutsiia*, 1925, No. 2 (37), p. 86. In all, six people participated in the Conference, which took place in Kolpino, near Petersburg (*Proletarskaia Revoliutsiia*, 1929, No. 1 [36], p. 105). Litvinov names them: Zemliachka, Litvinov, Rumiantsev, Rykov, Vladimirskii, and Liadov (*Proletarskaia Revoliutsiia*, 1925, No. 2 [37], p. 86). About Liadov he is certainly in error: there is a letter from Zemliachka to Lenin and Krupskaia dated December 19, that is, a little over a week after the Northern Conference, in which she insists that Liadov and Gusev should come to work in Russia; see "Perepiska N. Lenina i N. K. Krupskoi s Peterburgskoi organizatsiei," *Proletarskaia Revoliutsiia*, 1925, No. 3 (38), p. 21.

rarely and guardedly. *Vpered*, No. 1, January 4 (N.S.), carried a short item about "Committee Conferences"—of four Caucasus, three Southern, and six Northern committees—and expressed the "hope" to give details before long. "For the present, we shall merely say that all three conferences have declared themselves in favor of immediately calling a third congress and of supporting the literary group of the Majority."[24] Amazingly, even here nothing was said about the BCM. No "details" about any of the conferences ever appeared. The two earlier ones were simply not mentioned again; and nothing but the resolutions of the Northern Conference were published (in the next issue of *Vpered*).[25]

The Northern Conference expressed distrust of the central agencies of the Party; recognized "the literary group led by Comrade Lenin" as "the organ elucidating the principles of the position of the Majority . . . not only in questions of organization but also of program and tactics"; suggested to this literary group that it address a manifesto and an explanatory letter to the Party about the Party's present tasks, "taking its start from the resolutions passed by the Conference on this subject" (there is no resolution about the Party's tasks among the five resolutions printed); and sent an ultimatum to the Central Committee "to make it its business at last to convoke a special congress immediately." It also elected a "special bureau," which was to "declare itself the Organizational Committee" for a congress if the CC failed to comply with the ultimatum within two weeks. The bureau was also intrusted with unifying the Party around the principles of the Majority, "ideologically and in practice"; it was to concern itself with "publication and dissemination of literature, allocation of party workers, and unification of local work." Even now the Conference did not venture to announce the formation of its bureau publicly: "Official action is contemplated only in case of emergency, of which the bureau itself is to be the judge."

The Northern Conference distinguished itself in yet another way: it rejected the CC's proposal to send a representative (only as an adviser, of course) on the ground that "this Conference is a private conference of the committees of the Northern region" and on the further ground that it already knew the CC's stand on the problems to be discussed.

At this conference, even though it called itself a "private conference," the BCM was at last formally established. Neither the members of the BCM nor most of the average Bolsheviks seem to have attached much importance to this event or expected it to change the existing

24 Lenin, *Sochineniia*, VIII, 24.
25 *Vpered*, No. 2, January 14, 1905 (N.S.).

state of affairs. Even Zemliachka, who had played a prominent part at the Northern Conference,[26] could not remember anything about it when she talked with Khabas in the spring of 1924. Khabas writes that she said the BCM "was most likely elected in Geneva. . . . That it had 'to all intents and purposes been appointed in Geneva' is mentioned also by Comrade Litvinov, to whom Zemliachka, upon her return from Geneva, brought the news that he had been elected to the Bureau."[27]

As we have seen, the Northern Conference was in no hurry to announce the formation of an OC or BCM. On this subject, dissent arose between Lenin and the BCM and within the BCM. Little information about it is available. Litvinov shared Lenin's enterprising mood, judging by his letter of December 12 to Lenin. But he met with resistance from the more cautious Zemliachka, the BCM member most active in organizational work (until Gusev arrived from abroad in late December), and from Bogdanov, the leading Bolshevik in Russia, though possibly not formally a member of the BCM at the time (and not a member of the Northern Conference) since he was supposed to leave at any moment for Geneva to become one of the editors of *Vpered*—a move on which Lenin insisted but which Bogdanov kept postponing. As soon as Lenin received the news about the Northern Conference he drafted an "Announcement of the Formation of an OC and of the Convocation of the Third Regular Congress of the RSDRP"

---

[26] Litvinov wrote Lenin about his arguments with Zemliachka at the Conference, just after returning from it to Riga; see *Proletarskaia Revoliutsiia*, 1925, No. 2 (37), pp. 76–78.

[27] Khabas, "Sozdanie bol'shevistskogo tsentra . . .," p. 26. Somewhat simplifying the matter, Litvinov later wrote in his notes to his correspondence with Lenin: "To organize the campaign for convoking a congress, and for the technical preparation of the congress in the event that the CC should definitely decline to take on this task, several persons were designated in Geneva to form an unofficial center under the name of Bureau of the Committees of the Majority. To unify the Party committees in which Bolsheviks were in the majority, it was decided to call a series of regional conferences which, among other things, were to confirm the composition of the Bureau proposed in Geneva. . . . The Conference of the Southern Committees approved the list of BCM members nominated in Geneva. The same list was to be presented for approval to the Northern Conference." (*Proletarskaia Revoliutsiia*, 1925, No. 2 [37], pp. 86–87.)

D. Kardashev describes the birth of the BCM in similar terms. Citing Lenin's letter to Bogdanov and Gusev in which the Bureau is mentioned, he says: "The 'Bureau' that V. I. Lenin refers to in this letter is the all-Russian Bolshevik center, the 'Bureau of the Committees of the Majority,' formed at the famous Conference 'of the Twenty-two' or soon after it" ("K istorii zarozhdeniia Biuro . . .," p. 81). Again the characteristic vagueness: at the Conference or soon after it.

and sent it to the BCM members in Russia.[28] The BCM still procrastinated,[29] and on January 10, 1905 (N.S.), Lenin wrote Bogdanov:

> Now for a complete rift, since we have exhausted all the means. A *Third Congress* against the wishes of the CC and the Council and *without them*. A complete break with the Central Committee. A straightforward statement that we have our own Bureau. Complete elimination of Mensheviks and *Iskra* people from everywhere. . . . For God's sake hurry with an open and incisive statement about the Bureau. . . . Quick, quick, a break with the CC all along the line, and immediately tell in print about the Bureau, that it is the OC and will convoke the Third Congress.[30]

Nonetheless, more than three weeks went by before the BCM issued a formal address to the Party on the tasks of the Third Congress[31] and more than six weeks before an "Announcement of the Convocation of the Third Party Congress," signed by the BCM, appeared in *Vpered*, No. 8 (February 15/28).

Formally neither Lenin nor the other editors of *Vpered* (M. S. Ol'minskii [Aleksandrov], Orlovskii [V. V. Vorovskii], A. V. Lunacharskii) were members of the BCM, and the Bureau functioned as the center for the "practical work" of the Majority in Russia. Basically, however, it is quite true that the BCM worked "under Lenin's direction."

---

[28] Lenin, *Sochineniia*, VII, 503–5, 524.

[29] In the notes to Lenin's and Krupskaia's correspondence with the Petersburg organization, we read: "On the subject of the declaration there were great differences of opinion in the BCM, which are reflected in Comrade Litvinov's letter. Apart from the question of a single center, on which the majority turned out to be with Bogdanov, quite a few arguments arose during the discussion of the rules for the congress proposed by Comrade Lenin. . . . 'Now for a *complete rift*,' Comrade Lenin had written. 'A Third Congress against the wishes of the CC and the Council and *without them*.' This stand did not get enough support in the BCM for two reasons: (1) A considerable number of committees had agreed to participate in the congress only on condition that the CC and the Council would be invited. (2) The soft line taken by Bogdanov, who insisted on not calling the congress the next regular (third) Party congress, which would have greatly irritated the Mensheviks, and on stopping short of a complete break. The first reason had to be taken into account as an immutable fact, and this also determined the position of Liadov and Gusev later (the negotiations and the agreement with the CC), although they supported Lenin's stand on the remaining points. Later, in the agreement with the CC, it proved necessary as well to accept Bogdanov's proposal, which had received the most votes. (*Proletarskaia Revoliutsiia*, 1925, No. 4 [39], p. 38.)

[30] Lenin, *Sochineniia*, VIII, 29–30.

[31] The appeal of the BCM of January 21/February 3 is in "Proklamatsii i listovki Peterburgskogo Komiteta v ianvarskie dni 1905 goda," *Proletarskaia Revoliutsiia*, 1925, No. 3 (38), pp. 78–82.

Zubatovism and Gaponism

Both the Zubatov and the Gapon movements bore the strong personal imprint of the men who had fathered them. In the early 1880's, Zubatov had been a member of revolutionary students' circles in Moscow. Caught by the Okhrana, he betrayed his comrades and became an undercover agent. A few years later he openly joined the Okhrana, in which he rose quickly. In time he formed a coherent new philosophy, apparently under the influence of the chief theoretician of the reactionary *Moskovskie Vedomosti*, Lev Tikhomirov, a reformed revolutionary and ex-member of the Executive Committee of the *Narodnaia Volia* group.

D. Zaslavskii draws an illuminating sketch of Zubatov in his booklet *Zubatov and Mania Vil'bushevich,* valuable for understanding Zubatov's part in the Jewish labor movement:

> Zubatov was the most vivid and colorful figure among the members of the Police Department. He began his career as an *agent provocateur* and came to the Okhrana from the ranks of the intelligentsia. In early youth he had not been free of socialist tendencies. Later he became fascinated with detective work and with setting up a system of "inside agents," a complex system of provocation, and he put no little ingenuity into this work. He was an eloquent, captivating speaker, possessed to perfection the art of sincerity, and strongly impressed even old revolutionaries. It is not surprising that he came to occupy such a high position in the secret police. He was much superior to the old routineers of the gendarmerie world, the old, inept functionaries grown grey in sleuthing.
>
> Zubatov was ambitious. His success went to his head, he wanted to be a statesman, not just a gendarme. And when he conceived a political idea of his own, he believed in it with a passion worthy of any utopian.

267

Perhaps his intelligentsia nature came out in him. He evolved the program and the ideology of a singular tsarist labor party and preached it with ardor and élan to state and privy councilors, Russian workers, and Jewish *intelligenty*. His ultimate aim was victory over the revolution; but for the sake of that victory, he was willing to form alliances with anyone at all.[1]

This unexpected appraisal, not devoid of sympathy, is far from unique. B. P. Koz'min, after thoroughly studying Zubatov's archives, wrote that he was a sincere partisan of autocracy, "and this explains the fact that at the first news of Nicholas Romanov's abdication and the fall of the autocracy he put a bullet through his head."[2]

Having begun as a petty traitor, Zubatov developed over the years into a dedicated believer in the Okhrana as an idea. Although he remained to the end an unrepentant *Okhrannik* and kept up friendly relations with such repulsive Okhrana types as Mednikov[3] and Gurovich,[4] he retained a semblance of humanity. Oddly enough, he may have been influenced by his own proselytes among the Minsk "Independents" and their fervent devotion to the new faith. One of them, Mania Vil'bushevich, wrote him on October 14, 1900, of "the marvelous, dynamic theory of tsarism you have created."[5] She was referring to his peculiar concept of a social monarchy.

Gapon's development was very different. He was the oldest child of a law-abiding peasant family (for several years his father served now as village elder, now as *volost'* clerk) with strong religious traditions, embodied mainly in the mother, who had a marked influence over the boy. It was a harmonious family (Gapon says in his reminiscences that his father never beat him) intent on giving the children some education. In grade school and later at the Poltava seminary, Gapon came under the influence of Tolstoyans—I. M. Tregubov and I. B. Feierman, respectively.[6] This, however, seems to have affected his development

---

[1] D. Zaslavskii, *Zubatov i Mania Vil'bushevich* (Moscow: Krasnaia Nov', 1923), pp. 6–7. The booklet consists of an article published in *Byloe*, 1918, No. 3(9), and a ten-page introduction, from which the quotation is taken. Zaslavskii had never met Zubatov, but having been a member of the Bund in the early 1900's, he knew many people who had shared in the Zubatov "experiment" as opponents or proselytes.

[2] B. P. Koz'min, S. V. *Zubatov i ego korrespondenty* (Moscow-Leningrad, 1928), p. 6.

[3] *Ibid.*, pp. 109–38.

[4] *Ibid.*, pp. 34–35.

[5] Zaslavskii, *Zubatov i Mania Vil'bushevich*, p. 49.

[6] S. Ainzaft, "Gapon," in *Bol'shaia Sovetskaia Éntsiklopediia* (1st ed.), XIV, 546.

only in the humanitarian sense, leaving intact his religious and politically reactionary orientation. Later, at Divinity School (*Dukhovnaia Akademiia*)—which Gapon entered at the age of twenty-eight as a widowed priest—both the humanistic and reactionary traits came out clearly. In Gapon's biography in the Great Soviet Encyclopedia we read:

> In his second year at Divinity School, Gapon was given a priesthood in one of the working-class quarters (at the Second Children's Asylum of the Blue Cross) and began to preach at the Olga Home for the Poor and other places. Here Gapon's ability to galvanize crowds with his sermons manifested itself. Here he also came into close contact with the destitute of Petersburg and was taken with the idea of charitable assistance to the poorest among the population. He composed and forwarded to government circles a lengthy memorandum outlining a plan for establishing a whole network of work houses and colonies for the poor.[7]

This could have been a move to attract attention to himself, but there are other testimonials to Gapon's kindness. The priest M. S. Popov, a fellow student at Divinity School, whose reminiscences breathe envy and animosity, nevertheless says that "at times Gapon astounded everyone with his kindness"; once he gave his new boots to a barefoot beggar and for a long time wore funny-looking ladies' shoes, "provoking astonishment and jokes among his comrades."[8] A member of Gapon's cadres, Nikolai Varnashev, originally a Zubatovite, relates that when Gapon attended meetings of the Zubatov "society" (before the Gapon Assembly was founded) he behaved rather guardedly but "became very animated when a particularly simple-minded and backward worker rose and tried to put something into words. He nodded encouragement, agreed, supplied the words the man couldn't find . . . and no matter what was said he could be heard expressing approval."[9]

At the same time there is no doubt that at the start of his movement Gapon was strictly conservative and looked at the revolutionary and

---

[7] *Ibid.* Zubatov wrote in 1912 that soon after his transfer to Petersburg he learned that the priest Gapon had sent the city governor a "memorandum on the desirability of organizing paupers. . . . The strangeness of the subject did not predispose me to read the memorandum (which remained unread by me) or to meet its author." S. Zubatov, "Zubatovshchina," *Byloe*, 1917, No. 4 (October), p. 169.

[8] N. A. Bukhbinder, "Iz zhizni Gapona" (Po neizdannym materialam), *Krasnaia Letopis'*, 1922, No. 1, p. 103.

[9] N. Varnashev, "Ot nachala i do kontsa s gaponovskoi organizatsiei," in *Istoriko-revoliutsionnyi sbornik*, ed. V. I. Nevskii (Leningrad: Gosizdat, 1924), p. 185.

labor movements from the standpoint of a dyed-in-the-wool reactionary. Below I shall give documentary proof of this.

Zubatovism was an organic outgrowth of the police methods of combating revolutionary tendencies—an attempt to seize control of the labor movement through secret agents and to confine its aims to the economic sphere, in contrast and in opposition to the revolutionary movement and the revolutionary intelligentsia. It emerged in 1901 in two unconnected variants. The Moscow movement—Zubatovism in the narrow sense—was organized by workers or former workers who were paid agents of the Okhrana. Simultaneously there arose in the western provinces, chiefly in Minsk, which was then an important center of the Jewish labor movement, a very different kind of Zubatovism, organized by Bund members converted by Zubatov.

Its emphasis on economic demands made the Zubatov movement unwelcome to factory owners and their ally the Ministry of Finances, but in spite of their opposition[10] the movement lasted in Moscow until 1905, longer than Zubatov himself, who lost his position because of the "independent" labor movement, as we shall see.

The Minsk, or "independent," variant of Zubatovism grew into a broad economic movement not so much guided by the police as making use of police protection to expand its activity. From Minsk it

---

[10] Zubatov skilfully parried the attacks on his policy by Moscow industrialists. In reply to their complaint of March 27, 1902, to the minister of finances about the activity of the Zubatovite Workers' Council (*Sovet Rabochikh*) during the strike at the Goujon plant, Zubatov wrote a memorandum, which he presented on April 2 to the chief of the Special Division of the Police Department, L. A. Rataev:

"It would be impossible in any case to conceal the fact that it was the manufacturers' complaint that led to stopping the activity of the Workers' Council and closing the workers' meetings connected with it. Besides, the belligerent attitude taken by some of them toward the workers' aspirations is perfectly obvious to the latter. But if this fact is publicized it will serve as tangible evidence that the revolutionary and other oppositional elements were right in their views and behavior when they maintained that no monarchist government can be truly absolute, that it is always the servant of the class which holds supremacy at the moment, and that a legal labor movement is therefore by definition an impossibility and its counterfeit in Moscow represents a subtle, camouflaged political inquisition.

"Clearly, reprisals by the government against the Workers' Council will cause joy in antigovernment ranks; the idea of revolution, having received a boost, will find new wide application.

"Furthermore, the workers' quite benign, sincere, and devoted feelings toward the government that have been created in Moscow with great effort will be undercut at their very foundation, for the government will appear in the workers' eyes as having succumbed to the lures of capital and thus deceived the hopes that had been put in it. The workers' mood will change from peaceable to aggressive, and the government from concerned ally into an enemy who can be warded off only in alliance with revolutionaries." (*Krasnyi Arkhiv*, 1922, I, 310.) Zubatov made his point and the Workers' Council was not disbanded.

spread to other cities of the western provinces, then to the South, where it attracted non-Jewish workers and eventually dissolved in the general strike of July, 1903. That was the end of the "independent" Zubatovites. Zubatov was relieved of his duties on August 19, 1903, and never returned to active work.

Gapon's movement began later and was at first connected with Zubatov's. In November, 1902, Zubatov was transferred to Petersburg to head the Special Division of the Department of Police, that is, the entire Okhrana. He took along several of his Moscow agents to set up a similar organization in Petersburg. Gapon attended some of the meetings they organized, but merely as a wary observer. The Zubatovites' demagogy must have gone against his conservative grain. At the same time he was no doubt repelled by their too obvious dependence on the police. Although he was loyal to the authorities and trusted them fully, and although the organization he had begun to think about was a cultural and mutual-aid association on a religious basis, he valued initiative on the part of the workers and did not want too much official interference in the daily life of his movement. The type of organization Gapon envisioned largely met the wishes of important officials. A repetition of the Moscow experiment in Petersburg was firmly opposed by factory owners, whose influence in Petersburg was great.

Gapon began to organize his movement before Zubatov's activity was stopped. The first petition from "representatives of the Workers' Assembly" to "authorize the priest Father Gapon to open workers' meetings with holy prayer and say a short sermon after it" was sent to church authorities as early as March 13, 1903.[11] The meetings remained sporadic, however, and only on August 30, 1903, was the first Gapon tearoom-reading room opened, on Vyborgskaia Storona—the forerunner of all the later "locals." Perhaps it is no accident that its opening immediately followed Zubatov's dramatic dismissal and banishment from Petersburg, though this happened, most likely, not at Gapon's wish—he kept up friendly relations with Zubatov—[12] but at the decision of the Okhrana, which provided "about four hundred rubles"[13] for equipment.

The differences of opinion that came to divide the Gapon from the Zubatov movement actually began inside the latter. Of great interest

---

[11] N. A. Bukhbinder, "K istorii 'Sobraniia russkikh fabrichno-zavodskikh rabochikh g. S.Peterburga.' Arkhivnye dokumenty," *Krasnaia Letopis'*, 1922, No. 1, p. 239, gives the full text of the petition.

[12] Zubatov himself noted in his 1912 article "Zubatovshchina" that when he was forced to leave Petersburg Gapon was one of the few who dared come to the station to see him off (*Byloe*, 1917, No. 4, p. 170).

[13] *Krasnaia Letopis'*, 1922, No. 1, p. 298.

for clarifying this process is a report of the senior factory inspector of Petersburg Province to the chief of the Division of Industry of the Ministry of Finances, dated January 11, 1903, when the Zubatov movement was just gathering steam in Petersburg. After describing the Zubatovites' attempts to intervene in workers' relations with factory owners, he notes

> persistent rumors in the city that there has been a meeting of representatives of the Moscow and Petersburg unions, at which serious disagreements arose between them: the former insisted on the necessity to submit completely to the guidance of the Police Department's agents, whereas the latter thought it more expedient to try and improve their condition entirely through their own efforts.[14]

Since this apparently preceded Gapon's active intervention in the labor movement, it lends support to the theory that in his early days as labor leader Gapon was largely a tool in the hands of others.

Zubatov became acquainted with Gapon in the first half of 1903. He writes:

> After our talks he usually asked for "some fresh illegal literature to read," a request that was never refused. Our talks convinced me that he was rather callow politically, a complete novice in labor matters; he had never heard that there was a literature of the trade-union movement. I passed him on to a helper of mine from Moscow (a workman), from whom he became inseparable, never leaving him night and day, sleeping in his room and leading an ascetic existence, with bread and olives for nourishment.[15]

After Zubatov's dismissal and return to Moscow, Gapon wrote to the "deeply esteemed and unforgettable Sergei Vasil'evich" as a friend and disciple:

> We are not forgetting you, our teacher—we remember. Recently, at a circle meeting, when someone raised a question about you, people spoke up boldly, remarkably boldly and fervently, for you and for your idea. The impression was very good. To sum up, we are not concealing the fact that the idea of a special kind of labor movement is your idea, but we emphasize that our connection with the police is now broken (which is true), that our cause is just and aboveboard, and that the police can only check on us but not keep us on a leash.[16]

---

14 *Ibid.*, p. 295.

15 Zubatov, "Zubatovshchina," p. 169.

16 *Ibid.*, p. 170. The date of Gapon's letter, quoted in full, is not given, but the content indicates the first half of September, 1903.

While remaining personally loyal to Zubatov, Gapon strayed farther and farther from Zubatov's "Economism." In the fall of 1903 he took steps to get his movement legalized. On November 9 he submitted to the authorities the statute of the new organization, but before that, on October 14, he had sent a memorandum to the director of the Department of Police asking him to support the formal legalization of his tearoom-clubs. The memorandum appears in full in *Byloe* for 1925. It is written in such unbelievably contorted Russian that the original is barely intelligible. Some of the excerpts translated below have been cut considerably. Both the style, markedly different from Gapon's easier and more literate style, and the content of the memorandum suggest that at least the parts dealing with ideology were written by someone else. It probably renders quite correctly the ideas that officialdom wanted the Gapon movement to embody:

> The immediate aim of the tearoom-club is to be truly a place where factory workers themselves can make an earnest and, moreover, practical effort at refinement, at self-education, at rational, sober, and honest independent activity in their free time.
> The circle of responsible persons sees a further task in the noble endeavor to foster, under the guidance of truly Russian educated people and clergy, a sober, Christian view of the worker's life and condition and persistently, by their own example, to carry the idea of mutual aid into working-class circles and the lives of workers, helping thereby to improve their working and living conditions without disrupting the orderliness and legality of their relations with proprietors and with the government.[17]

Special stress is laid on "the basic guiding idea which must inspire and set the tone of the entire activity of the circle of responsible persons"; namely,

> to build up among factory workers a sensible and loyal element with a Russian self-awareness, which, while trying in a peaceable, lawful manner to gain real improvements in the spiritual and material life of workers, will not give up that precious heritage of our fatherland, the Russian ethos—will not sell it for a mess of pottage to Russia's enemies. On the contrary, [knowing] that the alleged well-wishers of our country and of the workers, most of them not even of Russian origin, merely impede by their propaganda . . . the beneficial measures . . . planned by His Majesty . . . [this sensible element] will act . . . as a brake . . . as a kind of counterpropaganda. . . . In short, the basic idea . . . is to build nests among Russian factory folk, where the true

---

[17] R. Kobiakov, "Gapon i okhrannoe otdelenie do 1905 goda," *Byloe,* 1925, No. 1 (29), p. 36.

spirit of Russia will breathe and from which healthy, devoted fledglings will fly forth to defend . . . their tsar and their country and really help their brother workers.[18]

This reasoning, typical of the blackest reaction, probably did not quite correspond to the feelings of Gapon and his "responsible circle," of which I shall speak later. But it certainly left its mark on the "cultural and educational" activities of the Workers' Assembly, especially in its early period.

For all its reactionary spirit, the memorandum acknowledged the inescapable advance of the labor movement, combining this insight with an attack on Zubatovism:

> It should not be overlooked that a striving for organization and independent activity is natural in people who have reached a certain level of development. . . . The more highly developed workers are becoming [imbued] with an awakening general self-awareness, which is gaining invincible power. *Therefore it is better to give it a legal outlet.* Let the workers satisfy their *natural* desire to organize for self-help and mutual aid and engage in reasonable independent activity for the good of our country *frankly and openly* rather than (as they otherwise surely will) organize for unreasonable independent activity *secretly and clandestinely, to their own harm and perhaps to that of the entire people.* We especially emphasize this: *otherwise this will be utilized by others, by Russia's enemies.*
>
> Of course, if things are done as they were in Odessa (to say nothing of Minsk), where a Jew turned out to be the leader of Russian workers, or as in Moscow, where the police was the leader, and not a very skilful one . . . then, of course, only a thoughtless person . . . could fail to wonder . . . at the singular labor movement begun and led by . . . the authorities. And there could have been some misgivings at first about similar activities in Petersburg, where the police . . . also began putting into practice the idea we know about, using workers who had stopped working and [proceeding] with some clang and clatter, inconsistently, purely theoretically (a lot of talk) . . . and above all without having formed a nucleus of mature people devoted to the idea and understanding it.[19]

However—and this reveals another characteristic Gapon trait—the police were to keep the new labor organizations under control, without interfering in their internal affairs:

> When the police carries out . . . its ideas, which may be excellent, and [acts as] a vigilant and stern observer, it must yet, for the good of the

---

[18] *Ibid.*, pp. 40–41.
[19] *Ibid.*, pp. 43–44.

cause itself, stand aside as it were, yield the way to independent civic activity . . . cope with the practical implementation of ideas while encouraging . . . reasonable and loyal independent activity. . . . It was in this respect that the police made a mistake in Moscow and, in the beginning, in Petersburg.[20]

In short, Gapon was steering a firm anti-Zubatov course. In his autobiography he says that "in early November [1903] all of Zubatov's agents were unanimously expelled from the society and even forbidden to enter our premises."[21] Gapon also tells of a trip in June, 1904, to Moscow, where he attended a meeting of a Zubatovite union and "hotly protested" against police intervention in labor organizations.[22] This may be exaggerated, but that he did show disapproval is confirmed by a top secret communication of July 6, 1904, from the office of the Moscow governor-general to the minister of the interior. It says that Gapon, "without obtaining the proper authorization," began to attend workers' meetings as soon as he arrived in Moscow and, "not in the least inhibited by the presence of workers, permitted himself to criticize" the Moscow organizations, arguing that their success was negligible because they were governed by the narrow statutes of mutual-aid associations. Worse, in conversation with leaders of the movement, he disparaged the Moscow workers' independent activity, pointed out "the allegedly brilliant results obtained through workers' organizations in St. Petersburg, and ascribed this to the fact that the Petersburg organizations have no direct connection with the authorities and are independent of them."[23]

The independence of the Gapon organizations was of course only relative. But the argument gave Gapon a convenient excuse to refrain from intervening in the relations between labor and capital as the Zubatov organizations did.

Both the Zubatov and the Gapon organizations began to function without formal statutes. In 1901 the Moscow chief of police, Dmitrii F. Trepov—Zubatov's superior but also in a sense his disciple—issued an

---

[20] *Ibid*, p. 45.

[21] G. Gapon, *Istoriia moei zhizni* (Moscow, 1925), p. 60. This is confirmed by Pavlov's account of his talk with Karelin, who told him "around November-December, 1903" that "there are no longer any known Zubatovites in our founders' group; Gapon has managed to expel them" (I. Pavlov, "Iz vospominanii o 'Rabochem Soiuze' i sviashchennike Gapone," *Minuvshie Gody*, 1908, No. 3, p. 28). It is possible that the firm anti-Zubatov line, and Gapon's memorandum of October 14, 1903, reflected the Police Department's changed opinion of Zubatov.

[22] Gapon, *Istoriia moei zhizni*, p. 69.

[23] *Krasnaia Letopis'*, 1922, No. 1, p. 300. The communication to the minister of the interior is given in full.

"instruction" to the newly emerging Zubatov organizations. "Instruction" was merely a convenient temporary label: a "statute" required more red tape. When the statute of the mutual-aid society of machine-shop workers [*mekhanicheskie rabochie*] was finally ratified on February 14, 1902, and that of the weavers' association soon afterward, they reproduced Trepov's (actually, Zubatov's) instruction in all essentials.[24] The Gapon organization in Petersburg did not even have such a surrogate. Its statute, sent to the authorities in December, 1903, was not approved until February 15, 1904, with the proposed name, "Workers' Union," changed to "Assembly of Russian Factory Workers of St. Petersburg."[25]

The Moscow statute set forth the aims of the organization laconically: "To render assistance to its active members and their families." The Petersburg statute was much more explicit: The "Assembly" was established

> *a*) [to enable] members of the Assembly to pass their free time in a sober and sensible manner truly beneficial to them spiritually and morally as well as materially;
>
> *b*) to awaken and strengthen Russian national consciousness in the worker members;
>
> *c*) to form and develop in them responsible views on the obligations and rights of workers; and finally,
>
> *d*) to [encourage] independent activity by the members of the "Assembly," conducive to improving the working and living conditions of workers in lawful ways.

(Note the "finally": improving the workers' lot was the last of the aims.) Both statutes provided for assistance to the unemployed. The Moscow statute specified:

> In the event of unemployment, active members and their families can receive pecuniary assistance only when the worker has lost the possibility to work through circumstances entirely independent of himself and not when he leaves his work to look for more profitable occupations or when he does not wish to work. Likewise, no worker receives assistance if he

---

[24] For the contents of the "instruction," see A. Morskoi, *Zubatovshchina. Stranitsa iz istorii rabochego voprosa v Rossii* (Moscow, 1913), pp. 50–51. For the description of the Moscow statute, I used the statute of the Moscow Mutual-Aid Society of Textile Workers, reprinted in the A. Kats and Iu. Milonov collection *1905. Professional'noe dvizhenie (Materialy i dokumenty,* pod obshchei redaktsiei M. N. Pokrovskogo) (Moscow, 1926), pp. 87–89. The statute of the Assembly of Russian Factory Workers is in the same book, pp. 90–95.

[25] D. Kol'tsov, "Rabochie v 1905–1907 godakh," in *Obshchestvennoe dvizhenie v nachale XX-go veka,* ed. L. Martov, P. Maslov, and A. Potresov, Vol. II, Part 1, (Petersburg, 1910), p. 186.

has lost his income in consequence of some administrative measures taken in his regard.

These rules seemed to preclude aid to strikers, but in practice workers were usually aided during strikes initiated by Zubatovite organizations, both in Moscow and especially in the territories of the "Independents."[26] The Petersburg statute ruled that "in the event of strikes no subsidies may be made out of the Assembly's mutual-aid funds."

The Petersburg statute was more reactionary in its membership rules as well. Both statutes admitted as active members men and women workers but not employees and foremen (the Moscow statute barred even assistant foremen), but the Petersburg statute added that active members must be "of Russian descent and the Christian faith," admitting only as special exceptions "Christian workers of non-Russian descent but Russian subjects."

The rules concerning the leading organs of the two societies reveal the government's profound mistrust. In Moscow, twelve candidates for membership on the board and twelve alternates were to be nominated

---

[26] Altogether different in pattern were the statutes of the "independent" Zubatovite unions and the program of the Independent Jewish Labor Party; there was no trace of the police spirit. (At least in the statutes! In practice, the police sponsored the movement.) They wanted to be bona fide labor organizations, eschewing revolutionary struggle, improving only the economic condition of workers, in the hope that society and the government would finally understand the need for legal trade-union organizations. In a typical appeal of the Independent Labor Group of Odessa, "Ko vsem odesskim rabochim i rabotnitsam!" (August 10, 1902), we read:

"To devote themselves wholly to our interests, to unite the working masses broadly, strongly, is possible only for *economic labor unions* which make this their sole aim, penetrate deeply into the workers' life, study their needs and woes, and tirelessly search for means to satisfy these needs. . . .

"Many will say, Workers' unions are forbidden in Russia, we may well be arrested if we join unions.

"That is true. Workers' unions are forbidden in Russia. But they are forbidden, first, because the need for them has appeared only recently—only recently have the workers themselves, and then only the best and most advanced among them, understood the need for unions and begun to desire them and organize them. But this was too novel, too unaccustomed, for everyone. And the government was alarmed by this novelty and began to repress it. [They are forbidden,] second, because the labor movement, from its very first steps, had been led by revolutionary parties, and thus it happened that neither the workers, nor the parties that led them, nor society, and consequently the government, could see the difference between the revolutionary movement and the workers' urge to unite in order to defend their interests. . . .

"If we organize purely economic unions, 'independent' of any and all parties, the government will have to authorize them, for surely it could not prohibit something without which millions of workers cannot live! Finally, everybody— society, the government, even factory owners—will surely see that what we are asking is just, that meeting our demands will benefit industry as well and the whole country." (*Krasnaia Letopis'*, 1922, No. 4, pp. 307–8.)

at a general meeting of members, and the list sent to the chief of police, who would approve eight board members and eight alternates. The board then chose its president, vice-president, treasurer, and other officials, who also had to be approved by the chief of police.

But this was nothing compared with the Petersburg statute. To begin with, the members of the Assembly were divided into two groups, the regular active membership and a "circle of responsible persons." Over them towered the representative of the Assembly, chosen for a three-year term by the responsible circle "from among educated laymen or clergy" and confirmed in his post by the city governor. Naturally, Gapon was elected. The representative was to all practical purposes the head of the organization. He was "considered to be empowered" by the Assembly to conduct all its affairs; he drew up the agendas of board meetings, "authorized" the addition of new members to the responsible circle (originally composed of charter members), and at his own discretion could expel anyone from the circle. Board members were elected at general meetings but only from among the "responsibles." The board "complied with the opinion of the representative" in electing its president and other officials, and the city governor decided whether they were acceptable.

In money matters the Petersburg statute was a distinct improvement, considering the prevailing practices. For a year after the ratification of the statute, board members and other officials were to discharge their duties "selflessly," without compensation; and it was every Assembly member's obligation "not to refuse without good and sufficient cause" any tasks or offices the Assembly might wish to impose on him. This was made easier by the fact that officials were elected for only three months at a time (as stated in Gapon's memorandum of October 14, 1903) and thus could perform their duties without leaving their wage-earning work. The system was intended to prevent corruption, and it was quite strictly followed. Later the Assembly granted its president a remuneration of forty-five rubles a month.[27]

---

[27] See the interrogation of a "responsible," Vladimir Ianov, by the gendarmerie on January 18, 1905, in *Krasnaia Letopis'*, 1922, No. 1, p. 313. Gapon was apparently an exception, at least in the early period. Zubatov wrote of him in his 1912 article: "One day workers asked me to help 'the Father' with money, because they had observed that he seemed to be in want. I tactfully broached the subject with Gapon, and he did not refuse a monthly subsidy of one hundred rubles. . . . When I was surrendering my office to the person who had forced the acquaintanceship with Gapon on me, the following happened: looking through the record of expenditures, he saw the entry 'Gapon, 100 rubles' and became upset, since he had been paying him as much. Later this man confessed to me that, obliged to inform the city governor in detail about my doings in St. Petersburg in regard to the labor problem and fearful of pestering me with questions, he had attached

All this contrasted favorably with the Zubatovite Moscow organizations. Whether they paid their leaders anything is not quite clear, but that the Okhrana paid them was a fairly open secret.[28] The "independent" Zubatovites, unlike their Moscow counterparts, received no pay from the Okhrana and often lived in extreme penury.[29]

Gapon to me as an informer and had paid him one hundred rubles a month for the information." (*Byloe*, 1917, No. 4, pp. 169–70.) This may be exaggerated. Gapon freely admits in his autobiography—written long before Zubatov's article—that Zubatov once helped him with a sum of money; and Zubatov mentions only one disbursement to Gapon. Yet the story is plausible. Considering his feelings toward the authorities at the time, Gapon would have had no qualms about accepting money.

All this apparently ended when Zubatov fell, that is, just as the Gapon movement began to mutate. During that period Gapon was often in need. A. E. Karelin wrote in 1922: "I suspected, and heard from others, that Gapon was getting money from the Okhrana. But if it had been so, I should have noticed something. Actually, Gapon was very poor. More than once, committing a crime, I subsidized Gapon out of the funds of our organization." (Karelin, "Deviatoe ianvaria i Gapon. Vospominaniia," *Krasnaia Letopis'*, 1922, No. 1, p. 116.)

[28] In 1905, when their cause was clearly lost, Krasivskii, Afanas'ev, Sokolov, and six less well-known Moscow Zubatovites were still drawing pay from the Okhrana. On July 6 they sent a petition to Trepov (no longer chief of the Moscow police but deputy minister of the interior), complaining that they had been "notified almost officially of the cessation of government subsidies from September of this year and of a reduction of the monthly salaries the following month" and begging Trepov to intervene. He ordered the chief of the Moscow Okhrana "not to stop or reduce the salaries of the persons enumerated in the petition and not to sever contact with them." (*Krasnyi Arkhiv*, 1922, I, 291.)

[29] Sent by the Minsk Independents to check on the work of the Vilna Independents, Goldberg wrote to Minsk about the chief Vilna party workers, A. Chemeriskii and two others, a stonemason and a clerk: "The whole bunch work very hard but unfortunately too seldom eat dinner, since none of them except Aleksandr Chemeriskii has any income." (*Krasnaia Letopis'*, 1922, No. 4, p. 298.) Chemeriskii's income apparently consisted of a modest salary from the organization, and of course all three lived on it. In 1921 or 1922 Chemeriskii described his life in Odessa: "I and the joiner Hillel lived in a flat on Razumovskaia. We had neither mattresses nor linen. I starved worse than in Vilna, sometimes didn't eat for two days. When my suit and boots were stolen one night (there was a flophouse in the yard), I stayed in my room until clothes were procured. At 4:00 or 5:00 in the morning we used to visit the taverns that served as meeting places for various trades. (A. Chemeriskii, "Vospominaniia o 'evreiskoi nezavisimoi rabochei partii,'" *Krasnyi Arkhiv*, 1922, I, 320–21.)

Even among the Independents there was an exception—Shaevich, their chief organizer in Odessa. He was, it is true, a man from another world, without the schooling of the underground labor movement. Reporting on the circumstances of his dismissal to the director of the Police Department, Zubatov wrote that Plehve once asked him, "Tell me, did you pay your Shaevich out of department funds?" and that he replied, "Yes, out of department funds, with the consent of the director, and also out of my own." (*Byloe*, 1919, No. 1, p. 96.)

Still more compromising are Shaevich's own letters after his arrest. From the transit prison in Moscow he wrote to M. I. Gurovich at the Police Department that he had received "what you sent me" just before his arrest, and gave an address "to use from now on." On the point of leaving in a convoy for his place of exile, he

As in much else, Zubatovism and Gaponism also differed in their development. Zubatov wanted to create surrogate trade unions to channel the rising energies of the masses away from revolutionary activities and blunt the impact of subversive propaganda. Gapon, on the other hand, feared the workers' involvement in economic battles and sought to focus their drive for organized unity on cultural pursuits and, to some extent, on improving their lot through mutual aid.

The Zubatov organizations of the Moscow type made a more or less flying start but soon lost what vigor they had, paralyzed as they were by their leaders' obvious aim to make them instruments of the Okhrana. They existed, however, until the Revolution of 1905. The organizations led by enthusiasts of the "independent" economic labor movement[30]—idealistic Zubatovites, so to speak—soon outgrew the stifling bounds of a movement sponsored by and useful to the police. In the south especially, they were swept into the spontaneous revolutionary labor movement, and this was their doom. During the general strike in Odessa in July, 1903, Plehve "suggested" to the Odessa city governor, in a telegram, that he "take the most energetic measures against fomenters of strikes, including the Independents, and restore order in the streets, by armed force if necessary."[31] Storm clouds had begun to gather over the Independents a little before that. Informed of the coming repression, the Minsk organization forestalled it. The Congress of the Independent Jewish Labor Party (*Nezavisimaia Evreiskaia Rabochaia Partiia,* or NERP) of June 3–6, 1903, declared the Party dissolved.[32]

---

wrote Zubatov: "Let M. I. [Gurovich] mail to Irkutsk (if he will be mailing anything), to me, and not to Odessa as I wrote M. V. at first. Ask him to send always by the first [of the month]. The one thing that makes the event a little less awful is that the family will not suffer too much from it (materially)." (*Krasnaia Letopis'*, 1922, No. 2/3, p. 235.) The "M. V." surprises one. According to N. A. Bukhbinder, it stands for "Mania Vil'bushevich." Did she know, then, that Shaevich was in the pay of the Police Department?

[30] The chief of the Minsk gendarmerie, Colonel Vasil'ev, actually calls the Independent Party "the Jewish Economic or Independent Labor Party" in his report to the Police Department of November 1, 1902. (*Krasnaia Letopis'*, 1922, No. 4, p. 326.)

[31] *Krasnaia Letopis'*, 1922, No. 2/3, p. 233.

[32] *Ibid.*, pp. 265–66. The NERP Committee's appeal "Ko vsem evreiskim rabochim" is given in full in this reference. It is a confused, unconvincing explanation of the decision to dissolve the Party. The events that led up to it are described in a report of the director of the Police Department, A. A. Lopukhin, dated August 10, 1903: "In April of this year, when the Jew Shaevich, the leader of the Odessa 'Independents,' had persuaded the workers of an Odessa plant to strike, I at once summoned him and the leaders of the Minsk 'Independents' to Petersburg and warned them that any attempt of theirs to disrupt law and order would entail prosecution on equal terms with any illegal circle. The Minsk organizations then

The Gapon movement began as a most "loyal" undertaking, innocent of the smallest attempts to join in the struggle between labor and capital. Its modest aim was to give workers a chance to gather and soberly spend their free time in edifying pursuits. In the early period, as Gapon wrote subsequently, every meeting at the first tearoom-reading room "began and closed with prayer."[33] At the official opening of the Assembly on April 11, 1904, after it had received its statute, a religious service was held, "God Save the Tsar" was sung three times, and the Assembly sent a telegram to the minister of the interior, "with the respectful request to lay at the feet of His Imperial Majesty the adored Monarch the most submissive feelings of the workers inspired by zealous love for the throne and the fatherland."[34]

The Gapon Assembly was geared to the backward mass, but the need for some kind of cultural intercourse was so great among the more advanced workers that after a while they too began to take notice of the Gapon meetings. Some of them had belonged to the revolutionary "circles" of the early nineties, had known imprisonment and police surveillance, had eventually withdrawn from revolutionary activities, but retained some intellectual interests and read a great deal. One such group joined the Gapon movement long before the opening of the first tearoom and soon became the most active contingent of the "circle of responsible persons." This group and its leader, A. E. Karelin, are described by Varnashev, the almost permanent president of the board of the Assembly, an early member of the Zubatov organization, which he left to join Gapon. He wrote in 1921 or 1922, somewhat idealizing the distant past:

> Most of them had had some experience in politics, had gone through various tribulations, and had been branded politically unreliable. Their self-taught general knowledge deserved respect . . . and this, added to immaculate civic integrity, gave them unshakable authority among the workers of the factory. Certain reservations about the programs of the parties, dissatisfaction with their tactics, made them [maintain] a non-party status. . . .
> They were people whose actions were completely conscious, and they had originally joined the organization because they wanted to criticize it . . . and create an opposition to Gapon. This did not take

---

chose to go out of existence, and Shaevich said the same. He, however, did not take any steps in that direction." (*Krasnaia Letopis'*, 1922, No. 4, p. 389.)

[33] Whether this practice was kept up is impossible to ascertain now.

[34] A report on this meeting in *Peterburgskaia Gazeta* is quoted in Kol'tsov, "Rabochie v 1905–1907 godakh," pp. 186–87, and in V. Sviatlovskii, *Professional'noe dvizhenie v Rossii* (Petersburg, 1907).

long to become apparent, especially at the meetings of the responsible circle. . . . Their joining the organization must be considered an event of decisive consequence for the "Assembly" as well as for Gapon.[35]

Karelin, also writing in 1921 or 1922, actually describes himself as a Bolshevik at the time he met Gapon (however, "when I came to believe in him, I had to break with the intelligentsia and the Party, for they labelled me 'Zubatovite' "). He describes the president of the Kolomna local, Kharitonov, as a Socialist Revolutionary, and Gapon's personal secretary, Kuzin, as a Menshevik.[36] Yet the same people, with Varnashev at their head, tried to resuscitate the Gapon Assembly in November, 1905—after October 17—with the financial assistance of Witte's government.[37] Having elected a board with Varnashev as president, Kuzin as secretary, and Karelin as treasurer, they sought its approval by the city governor.[38] In Soviet times Karelin was still defending Gapon's innocence during the last months of his life, in the winter of 1905–6, when Gapon had sunk to complete degradation.[39]

Varnashev's description of the responsible circle as a whole is probably more realistic:

> By that time (spring, 1904) the responsible circle had grown to about a hundred people, each of them a staunch agitator for the ideas of the Assembly; yet I shall not be far wrong in saying that they all somewhat *disliked politics* and preferred a peaceful economic movement. This could be explained by the level of their political and class development, which allowed for the belief that one could struggle for economic interests without first conquering political rights. They did not even think of these, relying instead on the authorities' benevolent attitude to labor. *The conservatism of the responsible circle* was also partly due to a certain sedateness of its members, family men and *relatively well off.* Earnings of one hundred rubles a month were no rarity in the machine industry. I myself, as a turner in a fairly small shop, made from one to two hundred rubles a month.[40]

Former Gaponites subsequently tried, with some success, to spread the myth that the organization had developed progressive tendencies very early. The fact is, however, that for a long time it did not give the

[35] Varnashev, "Ot nachala i do kontsa s gaponovskoi organizatsiei," p. 195.

[36] *Krasnaia Letopis'*, 1922, No. 1, p. 107.

[37] N. Petrov, "Zapiski o Gapone," *Vsemirnyi Vestnik,* 1907, No. 3, pp. 59–60; see also Sviatlovskii, *Professional'noe dvizhenie v Rossii,* p. 93.

[38] *Krasnaia Letopis'*, 1922, No. 1, p. 306.

[39] *Ibid.,* pp. 115–16.

[40] Varnashev, "Ot nachala i do kontsa s gaponovskoi organizatsiei," pp. 193–94.

police any cause to question its loyalty. An Okhrana "inquiry" of early summer, 1904, states:

> On May 30 of the current year the inauguration of the Assembly's first local in the Narva sector took place in excellent quarters leased for three years. The equipment . . . came to 360 rubles, of which 150 were given by the Special Division of the Police Department, and 210 by the Petersburg Division of the Okhrana. . . .
>
> Observing the activity of the Assembly, one is led to believe in its vitality and its potentially very beneficial influence on the working masses; the experience of the Assembly itself, although brief, is a warranty of this. By now the Assembly of Russian Workers is clearly emerging as a friendly social element. Moreover, it is increasingly attracting sympathy among reasonable and honest Russian workers. This is proven by the earnest requests of active members of the Assembly from various parts of Petersburg to open Assembly locals in their neighborhoods, for only the long distances prevent some of the workers from becoming active members of the Assembly. Unfortunately, the Assembly does not yet dispose of sufficient funds to spend about 400 rubles at a time on the initial equipment of premises and tearoom in various working-class districts of St. Petersburg. Yet the Assembly's tearooms represent the first step, the place to build up a friendly Russian labor element seeking to improve its condition in legal ways.[41]

With Sviatopolk-Mirskii's "thaw," the Gapon movement blossomed out. At its city-wide meeting in September, it was decided to open locals all over Petersburg and in nearby Kolpino and Sestroretsk. By the end of 1904, there were ten in Petersburg and one more in Kolpino.[42] In the atmosphere of civic enthusiasm that marked the last months of that year, the Petersburg workers crowded into them. The Gapon movement was rapidly changing from a tame protégé of the police into a tumultuous, spontaneous drive, full of inherent contradictions and unconsciously revolutionary in nature. The last phase, which climaxed in Bloody Sunday, is so well known that we can omit its analysis.

Let us, however, take another look at Gapon himself, through the eyes of S. Ainzaft:

> A priest in a working-class neighborhood, close to the popular masses, sensitive to their needs, possessing the gift of hypnotizing them with intimate, soul-stirring words, and himself hypnotized by the mighty wave of the mass movement rising around him and lifting him to its

---

[41] *Krasnaia Letopis'*, 1922, No. 1, p. 299.
[42] Sviatlovskii, *Professional'noe dvizhenie v Rossii*, p. 79.

crest; a man who came to the masses from the Okhrana in order to subjugate the labor movement to it and yet carried in his soul some plan of a singular labor movement; [a man] imbued with vestiges of religious views and feelings, yet sowing among the workers a rebellious spirit of discontent, awakening in them the consciousness of their human worth, of the proletariat's might and power, but fitting this revolutionary work into old, patriarchal, conservative forms; a man who rose to the stature of national hero in the stormy days of January, 1905, and sank to vile, base provocation and treachery by the end of the same year—Gapon and the role he played can be understood only in their context, against the backdrop of that contradictory labor movement which combined within itself the concentrated, instinctively hoarded revolutionary energy of the working class, its intuitive awareness of its own roiling, boiling forces destined to perform great deeds and accomplish high purposes, and, side by side with this, still unresolved ancient prejudices and illusions, a still active residue of centuries of slavish subjection, submissiveness to fate, and belief in the possibility of obtaining help from some upper reaches.[43]

[43] S. Ainzaft, *Zubatovshchina i gaponovshchina* (Moscow, 1922), pp. 80–81.

Social-Democracy and the Zubatov Movement

The Zubatov movement began in Minsk, but we shall consider the complex Minsk variant later. In pure form, so to speak, it emerged in Moscow in the spring of 1901, with some experience behind it.

Zubatov started his Moscow program with great circumspection, keeping himself out of sight. In late winter 1900–1901 a group of workers, his paid agents, approached Leo Tolstoy and Professor I. I. Ianzhul with the request to help them organize a mutual-aid society of machine-shop workers. Ianzhul had won popularity as senior factory inspector of Moscow Province, right after factory inspection had been introduced in 1882. He advised the workers to see Professor I. Kh. Ozerov; Tolstoy sent them to Adjunct Professor E. E. Den. Both Ozerov and Den were skeptical about the idea, but the workers persuaded them to try and also to give a series of lectures for workers about mutual funds, consumers' unions, the organization of employment bureaus, workers' clubs, and so on, assuring the professors that they had sounded out some government officials and that the mutual-aid society and the lectures had a chance to be authorized. Ozerov and Den agreed and enlisted in the lecture project several other liberal academics. The lectures were indeed soon authorized. They dealt with diverse aspects of the labor problem, in particular with the statute of the proposed mutual-aid society. Usually there was a discussion period, in which the audience took a lively part. In August, 1901, the lecturers introduced questionnaires, distributed after each lecture, on which the workers could write down facts from their own experience for the discussion following the next lecture. The questionnaires were a great success. Workers began to assemble ahead of time in their sectors to discuss the topics. These meetings, of three hundred people and more, had their permanent chairmen, who in turn began to meet and soon formed a central agency for all these sector meetings—the Council of Machine-Shop Workers. Before long, the Council began to intervene in labor-management relations, with the open backing of the police.[1] Zubatovism was showing its hand.

Rumors spread that workers who spoke up frankly at the preliminary meetings or after lectures were being arrested and sent out of Moscow. By the end of 1901 the liberal professors withdrew from the project. Soon lectures were being given by friends of the reactionary *Moskovskie Vedomosti*.

The Moscow Social-Democrats had to decide on their stand vis-à-vis a labor movement sponsored by the police. The professors may not have realized that the workers who had drawn them into it were Okhrana agents, but the Social-Democrats saw the situation for what it was. Yet they resisted the temptation to denounce these meetings and

---

[1] Much detail on all this may be found in I. Kh. Ozerov, *Politika po rabochemu voprosu za poslednie gody (Po neizdannym dokumentam)* (Moscow: Sytin, 1906), with three questionnaires in full (pp. 202–4). I am quoting the one for Professor A. A. Manuilov's lecture "O prodolzhitel'nosti rabochego dnia":

"1. On what days of the week are you entirely free, not counting overtime work? If you work at the plant the year round, count up how many free days you have during the year. If you go to the country during the year, tell when and for how long.

"2. Do you work only days or only nights; or sometimes days, sometimes nights; or partly in the daytime, partly at night? (Night is defined as 9:00 P.M. to 5:00 A.M.)

"3. Describe your weekly work schedule, without overtime. If you work the same length of time every day of the week, describe one day. If different, describe every day. If you work two shifts, tell how they rotate.

"4. Count up how many hours a week you work, apart from overtime.

"5. Do you do overtime work? How frequent is obligatory overtime work?

"6. If you do non-obligatory overtime work, do you do it regularly or only occasionally?

"7. If you do non-obligatory overtime work, did you ask to be given such work or was it offered you?

"8. If you asked for it, what impelled you to do so?

"9. If you were offered overtime work, why didn't you refuse?

"10. If you were offered overtime work and refused it, why did you refuse?

"11. If you used to work overtime and later refused, tell why.

"12. If you work overtime only occasionally, tell how often and how many hours per day. On weekdays or holidays?

"13. If you work overtime regularly, tell how many times a week and how many hours at a time. Do you also work holidays?

"14. Count up how many hours a week you work in all—including ordinary work and overtime.

"15. Where do you live and how long does it take you to walk to and from the plant?

"16. Do you have time for reading and recreation?"

have the workers boycott them. The maturer workers were duly
warned of the real nature of the meetings but were encouraged to
attend them and use them, with caution, to intensify the genuine labor
movement and broaden its open, legal existence.[2]

This was the policy unanimously adopted from the first by the
editors of *Iskra*. It is most fully explained in Lenin's book *What Is To
Be Done?*, begun in the fall of 1901 and published in March, 1902:

> The legalization of non-socialist and non-political labor unions in
> Russia has already begun, and there can be no doubt that every step
> forward of our rapidly growing Social-Democratic labor movement will
> multiply and encourage the attempts at its legalization—the attempts
> that come mainly from supporters of the present order but also, in part,
> from the workers themselves and the liberal intelligentsia. . . . From
> now on we have to take this trend into account. How to take it into
> account—on this there can hardly be two opinions among Social-Demo-
> crats. It is our duty relentlessly to expose the participation in this
> movement of Zubatovs and Vasil'evs, gendarmes and priests, and to
> explain to the workers the true intentions of these participants. It is also
> our duty to expose any conciliatory, "harmonious" notes that may appear
> in the speeches of liberals at legal workers' meetings—regardless of
> whether they strike these notes because they sincerely believe that
> peaceful co-operation of the classes is desirable, or because they want
> to ingratiate themselves with the authorities, or simply out of ineptitude.
> Finally, it is our duty to warn the workers of the snares often set for them
> by the police, who are looking for men "with a spark" at the public meet-
> ings and in authorized societies and who try to introduce *provocateurs*,
> by way of legal organizations, into illegal ones.
>
> But doing all this does not mean forgetting that *in the long run* the
> legalization of the labor movement will benefit *us* and not the Zubatovs.
> . . . We can tell the Zubatovs and the Ozerovs: Do your best, gentle-
> men, do your best! Inasmuch as you are setting a snare for workers (in
> the sense of straight provocation or in the sense of "sincerely" corrupting
> them with "Struvism")—we shall take care of unmasking you. Inasmuch
> as you are taking a real step forward—even if in the form of a "timid
> zigzag," but a step forward—we shall say: Much obliged, pray go on!
> Only a real, even if tiny, increase of scope for the workers is a real step
> forward. And any such increase will be useful to us and speed the

---

[2] Among the documents pertaining to the stand of the Moscow Social-Democratic organization on the Zubatov movement that have been collected by S.
Piontkovskii ("Zubatovshchina i sotsialdemokratiia. Arkhivnye materialy," *Katorga i
Ssylka*, VIII, 1924, 66–100), there is only one, titled "Predosterezhenie" (pp.
99–100), that urges workers to stay away from a Zubatovite meeting. But that was
in late 1903, when the Zubatovites were already widely discredited among the
workers; and the meeting in question was one of workers in the printing trade,
who were then laying the groundwork for an illegal trade-union organization.

emergence of the kind of legal societies in which *provocateurs* will not be catching socialists but socialists will be catching converts.[3]

Soon the emphasis shifted to the first, the "exposure" part of this double-barrelled program, for by early 1902 the police nature of the Moscow Zubatov movement had become all too evident. Martov's resolution "On the Economic Struggle," unanimously adopted at the Second Congress of the RSDRP (in the summer of 1903), defined the Party's tasks in the Zubatov movement as follows:

> In view of the increasingly obvious intent of the tsarist government to seize control of the economic struggle of the working class under cover of "legalizing the labor movement" and, [once] having corrupted it politically, to make it a plaything of its own policy—in view of the fact that this so-called Zubatov policy, apart from its reactionary political underlay and its police-provocation methods, is a policy of systematic betrayal of the interests of the working class in favor of capitalists—the Congress recommends that all comrades continue the tireless struggle against Zubatovism in all its forms, [continue] to disclose to the workers the egoistic and perfidious nature of the tactics of Zubatovite demagogues, and urge the workers to unite in a single class movement of struggle for the political and economic emancipation of the proletariat. In the interests of this task the Congress deems it advisable that the Party organizations support and direct strikes initiated by legal labor organizations [and] at the same time make use of these conflicts to expose the reactionary nature of the alliance of workers with autocracy.[4]

All this was directed mainly at the Moscow brand of Zubatovism. The relations between Social-Democracy and the Minsk movement (very different, as I have shown in Appendix 3) were largely an internal Party problem at first, and their development was more complex and dramatic.

When Zubatovism appeared in Minsk in 1900 it already had a prehistory. Minsk was a major center of the Jewish labor movement. The title of this appendix, "Social-Democracy and the Zubatov Movement," refers in this context to the Jewish Social-Democratic organization (the Bund) and Zubatovism among Jewish workers. The Bund ("General Jewish Labor Union in Russia and Poland"; after 1901, "in Lithuania, Russia, and Poland"), formed in 1897, was the most cohesive Social-Democratic organization in Russia and the one closest to the masses. It soon attracted the attention of the political police and

---

[3] Lenin, *Sochineniia* (4th ed.), V, 424–25.

[4] *Vtoroi s"ezd RSDRP. Iiul'-avgust 1903 goda. Protokoly* (Moscow: Gospolitizdat, 1959), pp. 432–33.

became the target of a centralized strategy directed by the chief of the Moscow Division of the Okhrana, Zubatov. On July 26, 1898, after months of sleuthing, the homes of several hundred Bund members in various cities were searched simultaneously. Two printing presses and much illegal literature were confiscated, and fifty-five leaders (the figure usually given in the literature is seventy) were arrested and taken to Moscow, where Zubatov talked politics with each of them, trying to convince them that the economic labor movement should be separated from the revolutionary movement and legalized. He had little success with this group of experienced revolutionaries. Subsequent mass arrests netted less sophisticated people, and Zubatov managed to raise real havoc among them.

He saw fabulous possibilities opening up before him. B. M. Frumkin, one of the Bund leaders in the first group (the group that had resisted Zubatov), wrote of these plans, ten years later:

> For some unfathomable reason he was convinced that, as he said, "With the Bund, one can reach an understanding." Whether Zubatov formed this opinion because of the Bund's reputation of being practical or because the Bund's organization, which was still based on professional, economic units, seemed to him closer to the type of organization he considered it possible to legalize, there is no doubt that he hoped to start negotiations with the Bund as a whole, as an established organization.

> Zubatov took a step in this direction when he telegraphed one of the founders and leaders of the Bund to come and see him.[5] The text of the telegram suggested that the object was to discuss the sentences in the 1898 affair and that the invitation was prompted by the idea that his coming might influence the fate of his comrades; it is very doubtful, however, that the talks, had they taken place, would have been limited to the 1898 case. . . . Later Zubatov frankly expressed his annoyance and his puzzlement that the man he had invited did not appear.

> . . . .

> It should be noted that Zubatov almost did quash the 1898 case, perhaps for the same reasons. We need only say that almost all the people arrested at the printing press were sentenced to simple police surveillance not exceeding four years. Only four or five people were sentenced to administrative exile in Siberia.[6]

---

[5] The founder and leader in question was A. Kremer ("Arkadii," "Aleksandr"). He was one of the accused in 1898 but was released on bail in April, 1900, before the case was closed. He fled abroad after Zubatov's telegram. See *Di geschikhte fun Bund* (New York: Unzer Tsait, 1960), I, 131.

[6] B. M. Frumkin, "Zubatovshchina i evreiskoe rabochee dvizhenie," in *Perezhitoe*, A Collection on the Social and Cultural History of Jews in Russia (Petersburg, 1911), III, 207.

N. A. Bukhbinder, in "Razgrom evreiskogo rabochego dvizheniia v 1898 godu" (*Krasnaia Letopis'*, 1922, No. 4, pp. 147–97), gives the following information,

The uncommon leniency was meant to facilitate Zubatov's plans and the success of his proselytes when the people arrested in and after 1898 returned (in some cases released on bail or on recognizance) in the spring of 1900. "Zubatov's hopes were not deceived," writes a historian of the Jewish labor movement. "As soon as they [the young Bund members he had converted] returned to Minsk, they began an intensive propaganda. They rejoined the old organization and thus corrupted it from within."[7]

The surprising thing is that these men were not expelled, or did not start their own organization, but remained members of the Bund. Though a real tempest broke out in the Bund, and in August, 1900, its Central Committee, in a sharply worded leaflet, called for adamant opposition to Zubatovites and their sympathizers, there were no outward changes in the organization. For a long time, the stand on Zubatovism remained a problem for the Bund. The Central Committee's leaflet had said:

> Every revolutionary entering into any relations with Zubatov and other spies of his ilk is harming the interests of the workers and loses the right to be called a revolutionary. We must not talk with Zubatov, give him any information, take money from him, write him letters, ask for assistance, or anything else. . . . No member of the Bund has the right to have any relations with Zubatov or his spies without the knowledge of the organization to which he belongs. . . . Who fails to comply with this will be considered a traitor, and his name published in the Party organs.[8]

---

based on archival material: during the night of July 25–26, 1898, fifty-five people were arrested; later arrests brought the total to sixty-seven (p. 149). But according to a report of the minister of the interior to the tsar on August 6, 1898, printed in the same article, "ninety people in all were arrested in connection with this case" (p. 159). An imperial order of April 11, 1901, set the following administrative penalties (with deduction for preliminary detention): five of the accused were exiled to Eastern Siberia for three to four years; twenty-two were subjected to open police surveillance for from one to four years in localities of their choice (with certain restrictions of choice); proceedings were abandoned against thirty-five; proceedings were "temporarily suspended" against two, "in view of their having left for abroad."

All are named in the article (pp. 153–54), and the total is sixty-four, not sixty-seven. Three future leaders of the Independents are not on these lists—Maria (Mania) Vil'bushevich, Aleksandr Chemeriskii, and Iulii Volin. (The fourth leader, Iosif Goldberg, did not come from the Bund but from the Poalei Tsion.) Apparently they were arrested somewhat later and did not figure in the 1898 case.

[7] N. A. Bukhbinder, "Nezavisimaia Evreiskaia Rabochaia Partiia," *Krasnaia Letopis'*, 1922, No. 2/3, p. 209; see also Bukhbinder, *Istoriia evreiskogo rabochego dvizheniia v Rossii. Po neizdannym arkhivnym materialam* (Leningrad: Akademicheskoe izdatel'stvo, 1925), p. 181.

[8] Frumkin, "Zubatovshchina i evreiskoe rabochee dvizhenie," pp. 210–11.

This had little direct effect on the relations of the Minsk Bund and the future "Independents." Almost a year later, on July 10, 1901, one of Zubatov's correspondents wrote him from Minsk:

The four principal trades—joiners, locksmiths, bookbinders, and workers in bristle—rebelled against the (revolutionary) organization and wanted to leave it, and I kept them from doing so only by force. Chemeriskii is definitely converted to our faith . . . he has become the most fervent protagonist of the ideas I am defending. Being a member of the Minsk Committee, he upset the latter so much that its members completely stopped working and kept running to one another like people possessed, wondering how to save themselves. It came to the point that they forgot all precautions of secrecy and all gathered at my place to come to some agreement with me. I must admit that the struggle was tough. We stayed up all night, and I had to talk twelve hours in a row. Victory was the outcome. The organization has decided that legal institutions are necessary and that it is necessary to legalize the movement, legalize it gradually and systematically, not quickly and haphazardly, so as not to confuse the masses even more. It was also decided to work out a program of legal work, which has been intrusted to me and Chemeriskii, with the obligation to present the result to the Committee. It was also resolved to send someone to the Central Committee to inform it of all these happenings and to hear its opinion.[9]

In the glow of victory, Zubatov's correspondent may have over-stated matters, but we also know from an impeccably reliable source that the situation in Minsk in 1901 was indeed shaping up favorably for Zubatovites and that the future leaders of the Independent Party played an important role in the Bund at the time. M. Rafes, a prominent Bund member and later, after the schism of 1920, the leader of its Communist wing, writes that in the fifteen-volume dossier on the secret Jewish organizations of the western provinces in the State Archives of the RSFSR,

in the volume on Minsk (case No. 355 of the Moscow Division of the Okhrana for 1900), we find a correspondence of 1901 about *a group of Bund intelligenty, among them Chemeriskii and Volin, the future organizers of the "Independent Jewish Labor Party" and very active Bund*

Frumkin notes that Zubatov occasionally "lent" money to released prisoners for their trip home and kept up a personal correspondence with some of them. Frumkin had read one such letter (probably to Shakhnovich) and quotes it from memory: "What is the news about our project [legalizing the union of workers in bristle]? Do your best. You will have served a useful and blessed cause." (*Ibid.*, p. 211.)

[9] *Krasnaia Letopis'*, 1922, No. 2/3, pp. 218–19; see also Bukhbinder, *Istoriia evreiskogo rabochego dvizheniia* . . . , pp. 196–97.

members at the time. Looking through *their program of studies in workers' circles, approved by the Committee of the Bund,* one finds in it all the essentials of the policy which Comrade Lenin called trade-unionist policy in his well-known pamphlet of the time, *What Is To Be Done?*[10]

Zubatov's correspondent was also quite right in saying in the early summer of 1901 that four of the Bund "trades" (*tsekhi*) were strongly Zubatovite. They left the Bund and joined the Independent Jewish Labor Party (*Nezavisimaia Evreiskaia Rabochaia Partia,* or NERP) when it was founded in late July; and in August two others followed them (stonemasons and tinsmiths).[11] What made the Minsk Zubatovites form a separate party is not clear from the documents published so far, but there is no doubt that they left the Bund of their own free will.[12]

The Independent Jewish Labor Party formally came into being on July 27, 1901. It issued a declaration, "The Views of the Party," and a "program."[13] The former calmly but firmly rejected the Bund's claim to the leadership of the Jewish labor movement:

> The present situation, in which economic organizations are led by the Bund, whose aims are primarily political, is in our opinion abnormal because
>
> *a*) economic action is for the Bund chiefly a means of revolutionizing the working masses, and the Bund therefore deliberately ignores in its economic activity many measures that are unquestionably advantageous to the working masses;
>
> *b*) when it admits a worker who is looking only for bread and knowledge into its organizations, which the average worker believes to be purely economic, the Bund foists upon him its own political views and aims, taking no account of the worker's psychology, loyalties, and desires. . . .
>
> . . . The Bund has fulfilled a great historical mission in developing in the working class a spirit of discontent with its economic condition, but now that this has been done and the entire working mass is eager to organize, it becomes impossible to leave economic and cultural activities in the political vise of the Bund.

---

[10] Comments by Rafes on documents published by S. Piontkovskii, "Novoe o Zubatovshchine," *Krasnyi Arkhiv,* 1922, I, 324 (italics added).

[11] Bukhbinder, "Nezavisimaia Evreiskaia Rabochaia Partiia," p. 211.

[12] Bukhbinder says outright: "Feeling they were strong enough, the Zubatovites decided to leave the Bund and create a new political party" ("Nezavisimaia Evreiskaia Rabochaia Partiia," p. 211); see also Bukhbinder, *Istoriia evreiskogo rabochego dvizheniia . . . ,* p. 184.

[13] Bukhbinder, "Nezavisimaia Evreiskaia Rabochaia Partiia," pp. 242–43; Bukhbinder, *Istoriia evreiskogo rabochego dvizheniia . . . ,* pp. 184–86.

The program—very brief, only four points—limited the aims of the NERP to "raising the material and cultural level of the Jewish proletariat through cultural-economic organizations, both illegal and, when possible, legal ones." Politically, the NERP adopted a curious brand of neutrality:

. . . The Party as a whole has no political aims and deals with political issues only insofar as they bear on the day-to-day interests of the workers.

. . . The Party brings together, for economic and cultural activities, workers of all political persuasions as well as [those] without any.[14]

Now that the Independents had their own party, the half-truce between them and the Bund in Minsk might have been expected to turn into open warfare, but this did not yet happen. In August a leaflet of the Minsk Committee of the Bund, "To All Men and Women Workers of Minsk," countered the declaration and the program with some practical arguments. Their burden is beside the point. What is significant is *how* the Committee spoke of the new Party and its leaders: an organization "consisting of a few hotheads" prey to illusion; "how *childish* it is to believe that the government will voluntarily give . . ."; "here in Minsk *some of our brothers* have been caught in the mesh of Zubatov's honeyed words and have begun to dream of 'legalization.'"[15] The Bund leaders of Minsk regarded the converts to Zubatovism as misguided brothers, not traitors, and tried to reason with them in comradely fashion. It would be monstrous to blame them, especially sixty years later.

The influence of the NERP continued to grow. As I have said, by

---

[14] M. Rafes, *Ocherki po istorii Bunda* (Moscow, 1923), cites the declaration and the program of the NERP, adding: "In another document of the 'Independents,' we read. . . ." There follow four points of the July 27, 1901, program in a different version. The third point is formulated much more sharply: "Workers of any political persuasion may join the Party; they must only agree that the labor movement has nothing in common with the revolutionary movement and is in fact its opposite" (p. 76).

But the four points cited by Rafes are apparently not in "another document of the 'Independents'" but are taken from Zubatov's report "O professional'nom rabochem dvizhenii v gor. Minske" of January 22, 1902, to the Police Department. Zubatov does not quote the NERP's program but lists its points (without quotation marks). This report is in *Krasnaia Letopis'*, 1922, No. 2/3, pp. 255–59. The document to which Rafes refers is not among the many published in N. A. Bukhbinder's works "Nezavisimaia Evreiskaia Rabochaia Partiia. Po neizdannym arkhivnym materialam," *Krasnaia Letopis'*, 1922, No. 2/3, pp. 208–84, and "O Zubatovshchine. Po neizdannym arkhivnym materialam," *Krasnaia Letopis'*, 1922, No. 4, pp. 289–328; or in S. Piontovskii's "Novoe o zubatovshchine," *Krasnyi Arkhiv*, 1922, I, 288–314.

[15] *Krasnaia Letopis'*, 1922, No. 2/3, p. 211 (italics added).

August, 1901, six trades had gone over to it. Rafes wrote later: "For a year and a half there existed in Minsk, alongside of the Bund, the far-flung organization of the NERP. At certain periods it *grouped in its ranks a much greater number of Jewish workers* than there were in the Bund in the same city."[16]

Minsk, it is true, was an exception. In other centers of the Bund, the success of the Independents was not nearly as spectacular. Their organization in Vilna, for example, was doing so poorly that in the spring of 1902 the Minsk Committee of the NERP (the Independents' main party center) sent Chemeriskii to build it up. His letters from Vilna paint a picture of grim hostility between the Independents and the Bund, which conducted intensive propaganda for a boycott of the Independents. Yet both sides attended each other's meetings. Matters worsened for the Independents when May Day demonstrators were flogged on the orders of Governor von Wahl, after which a Bund member, Hirsch Lekkert, shot at von Wahl and was hanged on May 28. Even then, however, the boycott was far from total. Chemeriskii wrote his Minsk friends of a common meeting of Bund members and Independents on June 10, 1902. The meeting was stormy. After it, in the street, he spoke to a Bund member who had had a great deal to say during the meeting:

> Since it was late and walking was dangerous, especially as the yardman had gone off to fetch a policeman, I accepted his [the Bund member's] invitation to come to his place. . . . Our talk was extremely sharp. Among other things, he told me that I could expect to be killed. I said that I did. . . . Toward the end the conversation became more peaceable and we parted at dawn amicably enough, agreeing to meet again.

---

[16] Rafes, *Ocherki po istorii Bunda*, p. 76. Elsewhere Rafes explains the success of the Independents in 1901–2 as follows: "Their success can be understood only in connection with the preceding period of the movement. Economism, with its trade-unionist policy, was especially strong in the Jewish labor movement, which in eight or ten years had created cohesive underground economic funds with membership dues, regular meetings, rendezvous places in the streets, and elective councils. The mass had been drawn into the movement in its entirety and was already organized, but neither the mass nor even all of the vanguard proved equal to the demands of the moment or mature enough to grasp the revolutionary class policy of the proletariat. In its *mass*, the Bund of that time (1900) was more a union of workers combating employers and colliding with the government than a revolutionary Social-Democratic Party. Its agitation had many political aspects, of course, and these were increasing, but the mass had not yet had time to grasp even this, and opposition to the leaders' 'politics' was building up.

"Meanwhile the economic struggle had reached an impasse. The Jewish artisans had obtained all that was possible under the circumstances. The Fourth Congress of the Bund (April, 1901) recognized this and urged that [the struggle] be reduced to defensive economic strikes." (*Krasnyi Arkhiv*, 1922, I, 324.)

He asked me to stay overnight but I refused. The impression he made was this: A man of the highest caliber. A self-possessed fellow. I felt sure the whole time that this character wanted to kill me and might do it any minute. He had a gun in his pocket.[17]

Even more striking perhaps is a letter written in late July or early August, 1902, by another Zubatovite, Shmuel the stonemason, who had been sent to help Chemeriskii:

The day after my arrival from Minsk we gathered some thirty-five people in our flat, to tell them how we had celebrated our Party's anniversary. Among them were about fifteen Bund members. I opened the meeting and began my report. . . . My story made a strong impression, although the Bund people interfered. Then they began to ask questions, and the discussion lasted till midnight. As we were breaking up, one Bund member, formerly a member of the Minsk board of trades [razborka], started to argue that all these talks and reports were nothing but provocation. Chemeriskii blanched but did not say anything. The Bund man went on in the same vein and suddenly said he could prove that Vil'bushevich and Chemeriskii were *provocateurs*. I cannot describe what happened then, but here we saw for the first time that we do have people selflessly, utterly devoted to the cause; at that moment they showed it. Fists clenched, voices trembling with rage, they demanded that these words be taken back. A member of the Vilna board of trades announced in an official tone of voice that the Minsk member's words were a lie. This infuriated the other even more. He declared he had facts to prove what he had said. Here Chemeriskii couldn't stand it any longer. Drawing his dagger, he ran to him, shouting: "Prove it, or this knife will be in your breast!" The man from Minsk lost his nerve and said he would furnish proof in a week. All this was somehow fantastic and frightening.[18]

Commenting on Chemeriskii's and Shmuel's letters, Rafes wrote twenty years later:

I remember very well how the workers worried over the question of whether they were dealing with mere *provocateurs* or with honestly misguided people. The Bund member from Minsk meant to strike down the leaders of the "Independents" with his arguments (see the last letter). Chemeriskii's violent reaction, his sincere outrage as he leaped at the Bund member with a dagger, evoked *the workers' sympathy* at this meeting. The representative of the Vilna Committee of the Bund had to dissociate himself firmly from the tactlessness of his too excited Minsk

---

[17] *Krasnaia Letopis'*, 1922, No. 4, p. 291.
[18] *Krasnyi Arkhiv*, 1922, I, 307.

comrade and return the question to the plane of *ideological discussion,* so necessary for the workers trying to avoid the hard struggle with tsarism and still under the illusion of the "independence" of the economic movement.[19]

Rafes' general comments on the Independents, after quoting passages from Chemeriskii's and Shmuel's letters about the great moral significance of the Independent Party for them, are even more interesting:

> And this was written by men reared in the labor movement, written about a party which *they knew* (that is certain!) to be openly protected by the gendarmerie they hated. And they wrote it from Vilna, where the very stones were crying to heaven about the crimes of Governor von Wahl and where quite recently, in May, 1902, a Jewish worker had died on the gallows—the hero cobbler Hirsch Lekkert, who had shot at von Wahl for the flogging of twenty-eight workmen demonstrators. Evidently the NERP's connection with the gendarmerie was not a major issue in the minds of the movement's leaders, or some of its leaders; they, these "leaders," and the masses that followed them were fighting for the "independence" of the labor movement from the revolutionary struggle, the revolutionary Party. What we were facing here was corrupted syndicalism, and the struggle between the Bund and the NERP was a *struggle of two trends* in the labor movement at a critical time for it. This fact complicated the struggle and the liquidation of the "Independents."[20]

For several more months the Independents tried to swim against the current in Vilna, but on February 5, 1903, the Committee of the NERP admitted, in an appeal "To Our Party Comrades," that it could not cope with the Bund's opposition. The explanation it gave is almost unbelievable: "The masses are more backward, unaware, and conservative than in any other city that has the slightest conception of the labor movement. Obtuse, incapable of a critical approach, they had been trembling at the thought of the 'Independents' even before they came to Vilna." Therefore the Committee was temporarily "suspending" work in Vilna and would instead "use its forces in a locality where they can be of real practical help to the working masses."[21]

Chemeriskii wrote later: "The accusation that the 'Independent Party' depended on the police incensed everybody and was taken as a personal affront. All Party members were convinced that it wasn't the authorities that were making use of them but that they were making use of the authorities."[22] But Bund members also quite often regarded

---

[19] *Ibid.,* pp. 323–24.
[20] *Ibid.,* p. 323.
[21] *Ibid.,* p. 302.
[22] *Ibid.,* p. 318.

them as deluded victims, not *provocateurs*.[23] To some extent, both camps felt that their struggle was an intolerable fratricidal war and longed for reconciliation.

Zubatov wrote on August 12, 1902, in a top secret report to the Police Department:

> About three weeks ago a congress of the Bund began in Minsk. Their Central Committee sent one of its members to negotiate with the Independents. At first the delegate was suspicious and caustic, later he became mild and friendly. The conversation with him was unusually long. In the name of the Central Committee he offered peace to the Independents on the following terms: the Independent Party must change into an economic union, cease all polemics with the Bund, observe the strictest neutrality vis-à-vis the revolutionary movement, and sever all relations with the gendarmerie. If they observe these conditions, the Bund will call off the boycott of the Independents, its members will join the Independents' union on a basis of equality, and all the economic work will be in the hands of the Independents. No agreement could be reached because of the point about gendarmes and because Goldberg said that the Independents could not be a party of revolutionary protest in economic matters but wished only to get the economic movement legalized.[24]

This story is disputed by the former Bund members M. Rafes and M. Frumkina (Esther) in their comments "on the documents published above" in the same volume of *Krasnyi Arkhiv*.[25] But their denials miss the point. There must have been some truth in Zubatov's report, though he probably embroidered on it to suit his purpose, as seems to have been his habit (see footnote 14).

The point is not that there was no Bund congress in Minsk at the time (incidentally, Zubatov's wording, *nachalsia s"ezd bundovtsev*, does not necessarily mean a congress of the organization; it could mean that many individual Bund members came to Minsk) or that the Central Committee of the Bund did not negotiate with the Independents. *Formally*, the denials are correct, but some influential Bund members may well have explored the possibility of creating an economic labor organization side by side with the political Bund and may have given some thought to the Independents in this role—on condition that they break with the police. Zubatov points out that the "negotiations" came to nought because of this requirement.

The idea of two organizations, one political and the other eco-

---

[23] *Ibid.*, p. 323.
[24] *Ibid.*, pp. 305–6.
[25] *Ibid.*, pp. 325, 327.

nomic, was rife in Bund circles. In a report of July 6, 1902, to the Police Department, Zubatov had quoted a letter from Chemeriskii in Vilna (apparently to the Minsk Independents):

> I have found out a Bund secret: there is a plan to declare their economic organizations independent of their own political ones; the economic organizations will be directed by special councils [*skhodki*] and will admit people of different opinions and trends. Politically advanced people will be organized separately in an independent political organization. By this move the Bund expects to achieve the final defeat of the Independents. By calling its organizations independent, it will confuse the masses, who will be saying: We are independent, only those others are *provocateurs* but not we.[26]

From this it was only a short step to the idea of using the already existing organizations of the Independents. (Let me remind the reader that the Independents were much more influential among the workers of Minsk than was the Bund.)

To understand how such plans (and rumors of plans) could arise as Zubatov's correspondents reported, one must take into account that the Bund was in the throes of an internal crisis. In his *Essays on the History of the Bund* (*Ocherki po istorii Bunda*) Rafes calls the years 1901–3 "the period of the first crisis of the Bund." Its symptoms had appeared at the beginning of the century. Boris Frumkin wrote later:

> The material for economic agitation had been exhausted. The economic struggle, having produced certain results, could no longer be carried on with the same success; to many trades it no longer applied at all because what improvement was possible had already been attained; the funds [*kassy*] had lost their trade-union [*professional'nyi*] character, and in the absence of the constant stimulation of strikes their existence was largely nominal—the masses had ebbed away from them, only their "political members" remained. . . .
>
> At the Fourth Congress of the Bund (April, 1901) trade-union funds were scarcely mentioned; as for strikes, only a resolution restricting them was adopted. The burden of the debates shifted to the forms of political action; several resolutions recommended organizing demonstrations, celebrating May Day, "giving the local organs a more political character."[27]

Rafes is even more explicit:

> In the artisan industries the economic struggle had reached an impasse, and as early as 1901, when the Fourth Congress of the Bund discussed

---

[26] *Ibid.*, pp. 298–99.
[27] Frumkin, "Zubatovshchina i evreiskoe rabochee dvizhenie," pp. 212–13.

the forms of economic struggle, the need to refrain from economic offensives was formulated. This decision was not popular with the broad masses of Jewish workers, and it helped the Zubatovites in their demagogic agitation against revolutionaries who "subordinate the economic movement to the interests of the revolutionary party."[28]

In this climate, Lenin's *What Is To Be Done?* (March, 1902) had a fatal effect on the Bund. Its leaders interpreted Lenin's ideas too simply and too extremely at the same time. (See Appendix 9, pp. 325–30.) The Fifth Congress of the Bund in August, 1902, proclaimed *"independence from the economic movement"* in its resolution "On the Organizational Principle": "Gearing a revolutionary Social-Democratic organization to the economic struggle could restrict the scope of its activity, and it *diverts the forces from the socialist struggle to leadership of the economic struggle.*" Therefore, it is imperative that the committees and other revolutionary organizations directing the movement at the local level be "quite autonomous and *independent of the trade-union organizations in the manner in which they are constituted* and, although by no means abdicating leadership in the economic struggle," regard themselves "not as representatives of trade-union organizations but as revolutionary organizations putting into effect the principles of international revolutionary Social-Democracy."[29] The fear of "diverting the forces" in order to lead the workers' economic struggle and their economic organizations is especially significant.

The Bund had developed from trade-union funds, and the new, antitrade-union orientation broke with the solidly established organizational tradition. It completely disrupted the Bund's activities. Rafes, who worked in Vilna in 1902, vividly describes that year:

> The whole summer passed in restructuring the organization. We started from the idea that separate trades—cobblers, let us say—if left to themselves and organized within trade limits, did not have a chance to come in contact with Social-Democratic politics and were doomed to follow the line of trade-unionism. We began with an outright repudiation of the preceding era of Economism, which had built the whole organization around the trade-union funds. The Vilna Committee now went to the opposite extreme: *the economic organization was simply broken up.*
>
> The politically more mature vanguard was torn from the economically organized mass and artificially regrouped. The six to seven hundred Jewish workers who comprised the tightly knit political organization of the Bund proper were broken up into groups *regardless* of their trades or, rather, *against* them: every group had to include different trades—

---

[28] Rafes, *Ocherki po istorii Bunda*, pp. 66–67.
[29] See full text in *ibid.*, pp. 80–81 (italics added).

cobblers, joiners, tailors. . . . The "economic" funds were left not to the Independents but simply to their own devices.

When the first consequences of this divorce of the vanguard from the masses began to be felt . . . the Committee had some second thoughts and hurriedly carried out a reorganization on more theoretical lines. The "economic fund" remained the base, with an elective council, to which were elected the selfsame Bund members, the experienced leaders of the economic struggle. And in every trade a *political* group was formed as well. This political council had the double task of conducting political agitation and propaganda and providing *de facto* leadership of the elective economic council.[30]

The arrangement could not last and was soon amended in various ways, but we need not go into this. The facts cited above make it clear enough that the Bund was in turmoil in 1902, and that Zubatov's report about an attempt at negotiation most likely contained some truth.[31]

But the leaders of the Bund did not accept the "conciliationist" policy toward the Independents; and soon the NERP itself disappeared from the scene. After its more or less enforced self-liquidation in June, 1903, the Bund's attitude toward the NERP ceased to matter in any case. The last phase of the Independent Party and the circumstances of its collapse—even in Minsk, where it had been so successful—still await elucidation and analysis.

The Odessa Independents gave the Social-Democrats little trouble. They were quickly absorbed in the spontaneous mass movement and lost their specific traits. The Social-Democrats' propaganda against them accelerated this process, and police repression brought it to a close.

---

[30] *Krasnyi Arkhiv*, 1922, I, 325.

[31] For a criticism of this conclusion and of the analysis on which it is based by an official representative of the Bund, see Ia. Sh. Hertz, "Neskol'ko zamechanii po povodu utverzhdenii S. M. Schvartsa," in Ia. Sh. Hertz and S. M. Schwarz, *Zubatovshchina v Minske* (New York: Inter-University Project on History of the Menshevik Movement, July-August, 1962).

APPENDIX **6**

The Baku Strike of December, 1904: Myth and Reality

Under "Baku Strikes of 1903 and 1904," we read in the second edition of the Great Soviet Encyclopedia (1950; IV, 62–63):

> The Baku strike of 1904, which was directed by I. V. Stalin and P. A. Dzhaparidze, has entered into the history of the labor movement as the beginning of the revolutionary upsurge in Transcaucasia and many regions of Russia. . . . I. V. Stalin's personal direction insured the mighty sweep and the good organization of the 1904 strike.
>
> The Baku strike of 1904 began on December 13 at the Rothschild, Nobel, and Mirzoev oil fields. The strike committee, following I. V. Stalin's directions, led the workers' struggle in an organized way. . . . Between December 14 and 18 the strike spread to most of Baku's industries. Both its preparation and the strike itself went on amid the Bolsheviks' fierce struggle against Mensheviks, SR's, Dashnaks [Armenian Socialists], and the Menshevik-Zubatovite organization of the Shendrikov brothers, who tried to divert the workers from the political struggle and wreck their joint organized action. . . . The workers led by the Bolsheviks steadfastly stood by their demands. The scope of the movement forced the industrialists to make concessions. On December 30, 1904, the two sides signed the first collective agreement in Russia. . . .
>
> The Baku workers' heroic struggle, deployed under the leadership of I. V. Stalin, and the successes they achieved became an inspiring example and a model to the proletariat of the whole country.

This epitomizes the standard Soviet interpretation, except that, of late, "the Bolshevik Baku Committee of the RSDRP" has replaced Stalin's name. The real events were quite different.

301

In the early days of the century the working and living conditions of the Baku workers, especially in the oil industry, were exceedingly harsh even by Russian standards. A great deal of social electricity had accumulated in the Baku proletariat. It had flared up in June, 1903, in a huge general strike that ended in the almost total defeat of the workers. For a time they were relatively quiet, but by the summer of 1904 the unrest was mounting again.

Baku with its mixed population had nationalist revolutionary and socialist organizations besides the Bolshevik Baku Committee and the Menshevik Organization of Balakhany and Bibi-Eibat Workers, but only the last two were influential.[1] In the political climate of the second half of 1904, both naturally faced the question of a new general strike.

The Mensheviks welcomed the idea. This is how a participant in the December strike describes the events that preceded it:

----

[1] To understand the Baku events it is necessary to know how there came to be two RSDRP organizations in that city. Let me quote V. Nevskii, *Rabochee dvizhenie v ianvarskie dni 1905 goda* (Moscow: Vsesoiuznoe Obshchestvo Politka-torzhan i Ssyl'noposelentsev, 1930), pp. 338–39: "In the spring of 1904 the Baku organization was Menshevik, despite the fact that Bolshevik representatives of the CC (L. B. Krasin and I. O. Kunovskii) were living in Baku. That spring A. M. Stopani also arrived there and was charged with disbanding the Baku Committee and building up a new, Bolshevik organization. This task was completed and a new Committee formed. . . . Of course the Mensheviks could not give up their place without a fight. They organized a separate group, pretending that 'the periphery' had rebelled against the Committee."

The term "group" for Party organizations parallel to Party committees came into general use somewhat later (after the Petersburg Group had been formed), and the Menshevik organization in Baku called itself "Organization of Balakhany and Bibi-Eibat Workers," or "Union of Balakhany and Bibi-Eibat Workers," or "Balakhany and Bibi-Eibat Workers" (all with RSDRP), or simply "The Organization"; the members were commonly referred to as "Shendrikovites." Their leader, the student Il'ia Shendrikov, was a gifted man of boundless energy, with an adventurous streak. Nevskii writes: "The 'Union of Balakhany and Bibi-Eibat Workers' had been founded by the Shendrikov brothers. There were three Shendri-kovs—Lev, Gleb, and Il'ia. Il'ia Shendrikov's wife, Klavdia, also was an outstanding worker. The most impressive of them was Il'ia, a remarkable orator and demagogue, as all participants in the movement describe him. Likewise, they all consider that Il'ia Shendrikov was the leader of the 1904 strike. (*Ibid.*, p. 309.)

"Everyone agrees that Shendrikov . . . was the workers' idol. This was so because when he was with workers he 'expressed their interests, inflamed their hearts, called to the struggle with capitalists for the betterment of their condition' [Nevskii is quoting Ivan Golubev.—S. S.]. And since Shendrikov—as Comrade Bobrovskaia, another participant in the movement, notes—preferred to attend workers' meetings rather than Party meetings and discussions, and was an outstanding orator besides, it is not surprising that some backward strata of workers considered him the leader and did not follow our Bolshevik Committee consisting of first-rate professional [party] workers." (*Ibid.*, p. 312.)

The Bolshevik historian is somewhat biased, but in substance he renders the Baku situation correctly. Stopani himself, writing in January to Lenin about the strike, ironically called Shendrikov "our Christ." ("Perepiska N. Lenina i N. K. Krupskoi s Kavkazskoi organizatsiei," *Proletarskaia Revoliutsiia*, 1925, No. 5[40], p. 35.)

In early October, the Organization [that is, the RSDRP Organization of Balakhany and Bibi-Eibat Workers] began to agitate for a general strike. Mass meetings were held, at which the need for a general strike was explained, not merely as a device in the struggle with capitalists but also as a means of making a large-scale political protest. For the same purpose, two proclamations were issued: "To All Workers," on October 20, and "A General Strike." In both, the workers' desperate economic condition was closely tied in with their lack of political rights. . . .

The Organization began working out the demands at one of the large intersector meetings. The demands were . . . issued in six thousand copies the size of a newspaper sheet. The political demands came first: the convocation of a constituent assembly on the basis of universal, equal, direct, and secret suffrage; termination of the war; freedom of speech, assembly, press, strikes, and unions. Then came the local demands and a short appeal to struggle steadfastly, with a final "and we shall conquer." These demands stirred up all the laboring masses.[2]

The Bolsheviks took a different stand. P. A. Dzhaparidze, the *de facto* head of the Baku Committee at the time, wrote in the spring of 1905, in "A Short Outline for a Report at the Third Congress of the RSDRP," that in order to insure "simultaneous action by all the Caucasus committees and to co-ordinate their actions with [those of] the major centers in Russia" the Baku Committee thought it advisable to desist from a local general strike. Dzhaparidze also wrote that when the Group (that is, the Organization of Balakhany and Bibi-Eibat Workers) began to agitate for it,

the Committee made every effort, on one hand, to restrain the workers from spontaneous, unorganized, and isolated action and, on the other, to explain the peculiarities of the given political situation and the need for broad political action and protest. Despite everything . . . the Group started the strike.[3]

This formulation was still somewhat vague. Rybkin, the second Baku delegate to the Congress, put it more sharply in his speech: "As we know, the Baku Committee was against the strike for which the Balakhany–Bibi-Eibat Group was agitating."[4]

---

[2] *Bakinskaia stachka v dekabre 1904 goda* (Geneva: Iskra, 1905), pp. 2–3.

[3] *Tretii s'ezd RSDRP. Aprel'-mai 1905 goda. Protokoly* (Moscow: Gospolitiz-dat, 1959), p. 611. That Dzhaparidze (one of the two delegates from Baku at the Congress) was the author of the "Kratkii konspekt" is noted in *Kratkaia istoriia rabochego dvizheniia v Rossii (1861–1917 gody)* (Moscow: Gospolitizdat, 1962), p. 304.

[4] *Tretii s"ezd RSDRP . . . 1905 . . .* , p. 140. Rybkin's real name, Anashkin, is given in A. Raevskii, *Bol'shevizm i Men'shevizm v Baku v 1904/5 godakh* (Baku, 1930), p. 161.

The Bolsheviks expressed their negative stand in the leaflet "A Necessary Clarification," the Baku Committee's reply to the Menshevik leaflet "To All Workers," mentioned above. It began by saying that the Menshevik Organization of Balakhany and Bibi-Eibat Workers had no right to exist: the Second Party Congress had ruled that there could not be two Party organizations in one and the same city. The main point, however, was this:

> The orientation of the Group's leaflet "To All Workers," inasmuch as it promotes the principle of general strikes and unconditionally condemns strike struggle with individual capitalists, sharply diverges from the program of the RSDRP as well as from the resolution of the last Sixth International Socialist Congress.[5]

The arbitrary interpretation of the resolution of the Amsterdam Congress, of the RSDRP's program, and of the Baku Group's leaflet need not detain us here, but it is important to note that the Baku Committee invoked the authority of the Congress to prevent a general strike.

Almost a quarter-century later, a former member of the Bolshevik Baku organization, Ivan Golubev, wrote in his reminiscences:

> During that period the revolutionary mood was mounting incredibly fast, the idea of a strike was ripening in the working masses, and it has to be admitted that the Baku Committee failed to reckon with the mood of the working masses, was caught unawares, and proved unready to draw the proper conclusions from all the preceding events. . . . This happened because we continued to do our work academically, without descending into the thick of the working masses.[6]

"Academically" is of course a euphemism, but the leaders of the Bolshevik organization in Baku were indeed remote from the masses and the practical issues that preoccupied them, such as better housing, hospital care, compensation for injuries, improved schools, libraries, adult education:

> "It goes without saying that we attended to these matters unwillingly as it were," another active participant in the movement reminisced, "almost

---

[5] The leaflet "Neobkhodimoe raz"iasnenie" is usually omitted from published collections. It appears neither in *Listovki Kavkazskogo Soiuza RSDRP. 1903–1905 g.g.* (Moscow, 1955; 463 pp.), nor in the special collection of documents *Bakinskaia stachka 1904 goda* (Moscow: Glavnoe Arkhivnoe Upravlenie, 1940; 126 pp.). But it is treated in detail in Nevskii, *Rabochee dvizhenie v ianvarskie dni . . .*, pp. 340–42, from which I took the passage quoted, and in Raevskii, *Bol'shevizm i Men'shevizm v Baku . . .*, pp. 107–8.

[6] Quoted by Nevskii, *Rabochee dvizhenie v ianvarskie dni . . .*, p. 311, from the collection *Dvadtsat' piat' let bakinskoi organizatsii bol'shevikov* (Baku, 1924).

under compulsion and I daresay badly, much worse than the Mensheviks-Shendrikovites, who did this work in an inspired, masterly way, and who in their timeserving zeal even shunned the name of 'Social-Democratic organization,' calling themselves first 'Union of Balakhany and Bibi-Eibat Workers' and later 'Union of Baku Workers.' "[7]

"Shunned" is a gross exaggeration, as one glance at the Menshevik leaflets will show. At the top there always figured the inscription "Russian Social-Democratic Labor Party" in large print and below it, in italics, "Proletarians of All Countries, Unite." In content, too, far from eschewing socialism and "politics," these leaflets often stressed political demands, even though it is true that the economic demands also received a great deal of attention—both in the Group's leaflets and in the speeches of its members. This may have been what made the workers like them.

Anxious as they are to prove that the Bolsheviks prepared the December strike, Soviet historians must have diligently searched for leaflets, but they found only one that could possibly be interpreted as supporting their thesis—the Baku Committee's leaflet of November 30. A. M. Pankratova seems to have been the first to have used it in this connection. In her introductory chapter on the Baku strike to the volume of documents on the 1905 strikes, she quotes three leaflets of the Union of Balakhany and Bibi-Eibat Workers, many excerpts from official reports, two documents emanating from the employers' camp, and only one (undated) leaflet of the Baku Committee, "To All Workers."[8] It called for political action, in a relatively calm tone ("Russia is troubled. . . . There are thunderclaps here and there. . . . The government is in a hopelessly disgraceful situation in the Far East. . . .")—and said not a word about the general strike, although its preparation was virtually completed. The leaflet also appears in the collection *Leaflets of the Caucasus Union of the RSDRP* (from which we learn its date, November 30), where its theme is defined as "the rise of the revolutionary movement in connection with the defeat of the tsarist army in the Russo-Japanese war."[9] Its inclusion in materials on the Baku strike can only mean the total absence of leaflets really showing that the Baku Committee took part in the preparation of the strike.

The Bolshevik A. Raevskii writes in his study of Bolshevik and

---

[7] Quoted by Nevskii, *Rabochee dvizhenie v ianvarskie dni* . . . , p. 310, from the collection cited in n. 6.

[8] *1905. Stachechnoe dvizhenie*, compiled by A. M. Pankratova (Moscow-Leningrad, 1925), pp. 1–32.

[9] *Listovki Kavkazskogo Soiuza RSDRP, 1903–1905 g.g.*, pp. 200–204.

Menshevik activities in Baku in 1904/5: "Agitation for the strike began long before it. It began as early as September." The Baku Committee was "opposed to a strike at that time," that is, in the winter (with the opening of navigation, the chances for victory would increase—an argument refuted by the successful December strike). But this, "for all its importance," was not the main point. Though the Bolshevik organization felt that an uprising would be premature, neither did it want to limit the strike to pure "economics." It wanted to

> take advantage of the high tension among the Baku workers . . . also to implant in their minds the necessity of *putting the struggle against autocracy in the forefront;* otherwise the struggle for tangible improvements in the economic area would be difficult. A longer, more thorough and sustained ideological preparation, aimed at giving the struggle a sharper political character, would create the conditions for transforming the Baku workers in the course of the struggle into a fully conscious battalion of the Russian proletariat.[10]

There were more ominous facts as well. A "Shendrikovite" party worker, Studnev, who later went over to the Bolsheviks, wrote of a meeting called by the Organization of Balakhany and Bibi-Eibat Workers on the eve of the strike:

> Having learned that the Bolsheviks had decided to resist the strike (for example, at the machine shop of the Caspian-Caucasus Company, Comrade Sviatoi had declared he would "chase out with clubs anyone who came to stop the plant"), we gathered all the workers who sympathized with us on the shore of Salt Lake, in the evening of December 12.

Among the speakers were Il'ia, Lev, and Klavdia Shendrikov and Studnev himself.

> The gathering was told that in view of possible resistance to the strike at some plants it would be desirable if all those present (about three hundred) stayed overnight on the lake shore and went to stop the plants at dawn. Vania Emel'ianov, also present at the meeting, declared: "I have heard Comrade Sviatoi promise to wreck the strike with clubs, but I have prepared the ground at my plant of the Caspian-Caucasus Company, and the strike will not be wrecked." All remained for the night on the shore of Salt Lake.[11]

---

[10] Raevskii, *Bol'shevizm i Men'shevizm v Baku* . . . , pp. 104, 107–8.

[11] "Vospominaniia t. Studneva," in the collection *Iz proshlogo. Stat'i i vospominaniia iz istorii Bakinskoi organizatsii i rabochego dvizheniia v Baku* (Baku: Bakinskii Rabochii, 1923), pp. 142–43. This volume appeared as a publication of the Bakinskii Komitet Azerbaidzhanskoi Kompartii.

The story about the Bolshevik fanatic threatening to club workers who wanted to strike is so monstrous that one would doubt it if it were not for the fact that it was published by the Communist Party.

Instead of a general strike, the Bolsheviks proposed a demonstration—an armed demonstration, at that[12]—and not in the industrial outskirts but right in the city. The two organizations passionately argued the point. Raevskii tells of joint meetings on November 7 and 14 and December 5 and 11, which merely exacerbated the conflict.[13] Among the Bolshevik documents published since 1917 there is a Baku Committee leaflet of December 7, "To All Workers,"[14] popularizing the demand for a constituent assembly, blaming the liberals for demanding "a parliament without a single worker or peasant," and appealing to the Baku proletariat to be ready at the Party's first call to go out into the streets "under our glorious banners—the red banners of the proletariat" to demand a constituent assembly and a democratic republic. The strike is barely mentioned in passing, and then not to encourage it but to *warn against it:*

> Remember, comrades—so long as the government rules in our country, so long as it helps the capitalists to exploit us, we shall not improve our condition, no matter what grandiose strikes we may stage. Last year's strikes thoroughly proved this to us. Once we have overthrown the tsarist government we shall have a chance to conquer everything, the whole world, but now we shall not obtain even the petty, minor demands that the groups splintered off from the Party have put forward.

This almost unbelievable appeal seems to have been the only Bolshevik leaflet prior to the strike that was at all concerned with the strike.

The leaflet of the RSDRP Organization of Balakhany and Bibi-Eibat Workers of December 6, "To All Conscious Workers" (published in full in Pankratova's collection), throws some light on the dissensions between Bolsheviks and Mensheviks: "False friends are saying that this is a bad time for a strike, one should wait for summer" and hold a demonstration in the streets of Baku instead.[15] The leaflet points out

---

[12] *Ibid.,* p. 142. Studnev says outright that the Bolsheviks called for an armed demonstration.

[13] Raevskii, *Bol'shevizm i Men'shevizm v Baku* . . . , p. 109.

[14] The December 7 leaflet is missing from the collection of documents on the 1904 Baku strike published by Glavnoe Arkhivnoe Upravlenie, but it is given in full in *Listovki Kavkazskogo Soiuza RSDRP, 1903–1905 g.g.,* pp. 209–11, whose editors correctly describe it as "exposing the treacherous policy of the liberals and urging the overthrow of tsarist autocracy."

[15] The leaflet does not mention that the Baku Committee had called for a demonstration in the city, but a Geneva pamphlet does (*Bakinskaia stachka v dekabre 1904 goda,* p. 5). Raevskii quotes from this pamphlet: "The Baku Com-

that this would mean the immolation of the most advanced Baku workers:

> Organize a demonstration? Of whom? What for? Of conscious workers, obviously, and only to have them beaten up and detained. Imagine for a moment that one part of the workers, the best part, is bleeding from the Cossacks' beatings, while the other part remains passive, sweating under the burden of exploitation. . . . Our task is to draw in and stir up the entire working masses. The tsarist government and the capitalists fear these aroused masses, not a handful of conscious [workers] without the masses; it is these masses we must call out to the decisive battle with the sworn enemy—the tsarist government and the capitalists. And a general strike will make them tremble. All the freed workers will come to our meetings and assemblies. And that is where we shall explain over and over who the fell enemy of the workers is and why the capitalists will take away tomorrow what has been gained today with the workers' blood. It is then that a big demonstration, a mass uprising, will become possible.[16]

The Baku Committee's efforts to stop the strike and hold a demonstration instead proved utterly futile. A concerted strike began in the Balakhany and Bibi-Eibat oil industry on December 13 and soon developed into an almost general strike in the Baku region.

In the morning, plant managers were handed a "notification" about the strike, in the name of the RSDRP Organization of Balakhany and Bibi-Eibat Workers. The next day, December 14, the Baku Committee announced its solidarity with the strikers, but in its leaflet "To All Workers" some annoyance can be detected:[17] "The strike has begun. . . . The cup of suffering and oppression has overflowed. . . . Whatever we may think of declaring war on capitalists *at this time,* we must endeavor to make victory ours, the workers'." Significantly, the leaflet contains not one word about the strikers' economic demands ("local demands," in the Baku parlance of the time), concentrating entirely on "our main enemy, the tsarist government." "We shall swear to one another to carry the struggle with tsarist autocracy to the end." The leaflet closes on a recital of "our aims": (1) termination of the war, (2)

---

mittee continued to insist on staging a demonstration, and precisely in the streets of Baku, as the only revolutionary form of protest." Though he engages in polemics against the author of the pamphlet, he does not deny the fact that the Bolsheviks had called for a demonstration "in the streets of Baku" (*Bol'shevizm i Men'shevizm v Baku* . . . , p. 108).

[16] Pankratova, *1905. Stachechnoe dvizhenie*, pp. 5–7.

[17] *Listovki Kavkazskogo Soiuza RSDRP. 1903–1905 g.g.,* pp. 212–13.

a constituent assembly on the basis of universal, etc., suffrage, and (3) a democratic republic.

Subsequently—in the outline of a report to the Third Party Congress—the leaders of the Baku Committee tried to make it appear that

> since before the strike, the Committee together with organized workers had decided to join actively in the strike if it did begin after all, and this was done from the very first day (December 13). On the very first day the Committee issued an appropriate leaflet appealing to all to unite, stand together, come out in the streets, come to meetings.[18]

It was a strange kind of active joining, as we can see from the leaflet just mentioned—of December 14, not 13. The Committee's speakers sounded much like its leaflet. A pamphlet published in Geneva describes a huge meeting of Balakhany workers on December 14 near Sten'ka Razin mountain:

> A Committee orator made a speech which antagonized the strikers from the very first words since he began by saying that the economic struggle was untimely and called for a demonstration in town. He spoke in a lukewarm, listless way, as if carrying out official instructions. "We must make a demonstration, it is our duty," kept coming up in his speech.[19]

The idea of demonstrating continued to dominate in the Baku Committee's propaganda during the strike, but that was not the worst part. Throughout, the Committee behaved not at all like an organization having actively joined in the strike—that is, one would assume, supporting it—but like a weak organization trying to horn in on the strike to bolster its own authority, even if its separatist moves reduced the chances of a successful outcome. We have seen that the Organization of Balakhany and Bibi-Eibat Workers had drawn up a list of demands and widely propagated them by means of a leaflet ("The Demands of the Baku Workers,"[20] on December 1). On December 15 the Baku Bolsheviks bestirred themselves and also issued a leaflet (together with the Armenian Genchakist Party), "The Common Demands of All the Organized Workers of Baku."[21] The demands differed

---

[18] *Tretii s"ezd RSDRP . . . 1905 . . .* , p. 612.

[19] *Bakinskaia stachka v dekabre 1904 goda,* p. 5.

[20] Pankratova, *1905. Stachechnoe dvizhenie,* pp. 7–12.

[21] This leaflet, "Obshchie trebovaniia vsekh organizovannykh rabochikh goroda Baku," is missing not only from Pankratova's collection (the explanation of this may be that it had not yet been discovered in 1925) but also from *Listovki Kavkazskogo Soiuza RSDRP. 1903–1905 g.g.,* published in 1955, although it appears in the 1940 collection of Glavnoe Arkhivnoe Upravlenie (pp. 38–40), cited in n. 5.

little from those of the December 1 leaflet, but the fact of having issued a leaflet of its own permitted the Baku Committee to figure as an independent organ supposedly leading the strike.

In reality it clearly did not intend to give its full support to the strike: already by the next day it had returned to the idea of a demonstration. Its leaflet of December 16, "To All Citizens," calling for a demonstration in the streets of Baku, stated the usual political demands without linking them to the strike or even mentioning it, just as if there were no strike.[22] It is probably no accident that the collection *The Baku Strike of 1904* cites only the leaflet of December 15, omitting the one of December 16, and the collection *Leaflets of the Caucasus Union* cites the one of the sixteenth and not the one of the fifteenth. Side by side, they could suggest to the reader that the Baku Committee's policy was rather inconsistent.

According to Menshevik sources, the strikers elected deputies to negotiate with employers, and representatives of the Organization of Balakhany and Bibi-Eibat Workers took part in these negotiations. According to Bolshevik sources, a strike committee was formed of representatives of several parties, with Bolshevik influence predominating. No data on the strike committee or on its issuing a single leaflet have been published anywhere. The negotiations were conducted in a somewhat chaotic manner, with the people who spoke for the workers constantly changing. On December 27 the Bolshevik Baku Committee jointly with the Armenian Genchakist Party announced the end of the strike—without consulting the workers, without a vote at a strikers' meeting, and without clearing the matter with the Organization of Balakhany and Bibi-Eibat Workers, which had carried most of the burden of preparing and directing it. This is hard to believe, but here is the key part of the leaflet:

> . . . It is not possible, comrades, to continue the strike any longer! No matter how selfless and energetic we are, it is beyond our power to instil the same consciousness, the same energy, in the backward, hungry mass of workers. It is beyond our power to hold them any longer to the dimensions of struggle that we Social-Democrats can accept and that we consider effective at this time. Finally, under the present conditions, unfavorable to striking, we consider that we have no right to continue drawing the working masses into this strike.

---

[22] *Listovki Kavkazskogo Soiuza RSDRP. 1903–1905 g.g.*, pp. 216–17. No one responded to this appeal. Nevskii notes with some bitterness, "The Bolshevik Baku Committee had scheduled a demonstration for a Sunday during the December strike, but Shendrikov to all practical purposes cancelled it, by calling a meeting to which all the workers went" (*Rabochee dvizhenie v ianvarskie dni . . .*, p. 312).

Our final, minimal demands presented to the oil companies in the name of the Baku committees of various parties were satisfied; it was hopeless to count on a greater number of demands being satisfied; let us postpone the complete satisfaction of our demands until another, more convenient time. At present, *declaring the strike ended,* we invite all comrades . . . to resume work on December 28.[23]

The workers did not heed the appeal and the strike continued. On December 28 a large meeting clamored for the remaining concessions. Two days later the bargaining ended in an almost complete victory for the strikers. On December 31 the Organization of Balakhany and Bibi-Eibat Workers issued a leaflet, "Comrade Workers, Let Us Rejoice in Victory!"[24] which also contained a barb: "Various committees avowed their helplessness, only the Workers' Organization stood firm till the end." The leaflet ended with "Long live our Workers' Organization! Down with the government!"

What was the Baku Committee doing during those days? When its appeal of December 27 had been ignored, it addressed another leaflet to the strikers, pointed chiefly at their leaders.[25] In the collection *Leaflets of the Caucasus Union,* it is described as "exposing the treachery of the Shendrikovites' counterrevolutionary activity." But its date is December 31—and the agreement had been signed on December 30 and approved at a strikers' meeting. Nevertheless the Baku Committee castigated those who were trying to "prolong the strike":

Our party foes who wish to drag out the strike are not pursuing the interests of the working class but their own advantage, the advantage of their own small circle: they crave glory at any price. We repeat that the strike begun at a time unfavorable for the workers and favorable for the capitalists must be ended at once; the interests of the entire Baku proletariat demand it. In prolonging the strike for the problematic increase of a few kopeks (5–10 per cent of the increase [already obtained]) we are risking a great deal, risking even what we have already won.

Do not forget, comrades, that we shall be powerless to keep the less conscious, hungry mass from working. . . .

This leaflet is conclusive evidence of the Committee's alienation from the masses—to the point of not knowing what was going on—and, for

---

[23] This leaflet is reprinted in full in the collection of Glavnoe Arkhivnoe Upravlenie, *Bakinskaia stachka 1904 goda,* pp. 45–46, but it is missing from both Pankratova's collection, *1905. Stachechnoe dvizhenie,* and *Listovki Kavkazskogo Soiuza RSDRP. 1903–1905 g.g.*

[24] The text of this leaflet is given in Pankratova's collection, *1905. Stachechnoe dvizhenie,* p. 31.

[25] *Listovki Kavkazskogo Soiuza RSDRP. 1903–1905 g.g.,* pp. 225–27.

that matter, of the total falsity of the claim that it had played a leading role in the strike.

The myth of Bolshevik leadership in the 1904 Baku strike was launched quite early. Already in the twenties it was fully accepted and included in textbooks. Serious historians realized its "legendary" nature. Pankratova obviously did, judging by her choice of materials for *1905. The Strike Movement.* No one, however, dared to say so. The myth had become an article of faith.

A second myth began to grow in the thirties: that Stalin personally had masterminded the Baku strike. Lavrentii Beria originated the new version. A two-day lecture he gave at the Tbilisi *partaktiv* on July 21 and 22, 1935, which ran in *Pravda* from July 29 to August 5 and then appeared separately in one huge printing after another, became the basic "source" for Stalin's biographies. The first version of this lecture, however, did not yet connect him with the strike:

> At the end of 1904 Comrade Stalin went to Baku to invigorate the campaign for the Third Party Congress and advance the struggle against the Mensheviks, in particular the representative of the Menshevik CC, Glebov (Noskov), who was then in Baku.[26]

A colossal, historic strike was being prepared and carried out—and all Stalin could think of was the Third Congress and fighting Mensheviks? In the third, "enlarged" edition of the book (100,000 copies, 1937) the picture is shifted: Stalin arrived in Baku not "at the end of 1904" but "in November," though still for the same purpose. Farther on, however, there is the pregnant addition:

> Under Comrade Stalin's leadership a grandiose strike of Baku workers was carried out in December, 1904, which lasted from December 13 to 31 and ended in a collective agreement with the oil companies, the first in the history of the labor movement in Russia.
>
> The Baku strike marked the beginning of the revolutionary upsurge in Transcaucasia.
>
> The Baku strike served as "a signal for the glorious January/February action all over Russia" (Stalin).[27]

This was startling news to Party historians. The authors of the *Short Course*, which came out a year later, balked at it. They wrote of the Baku strike very nearly in Beria's words, but not quite:

---

[26] L. Beria, *K voprosu ob istorii bol'shevistskikh organizatsii v Zakavkaz'e* (Moscow, 1936), p. 47; see also *Pravda* of August 1, 1935.

[27] Third, enlarged edition of Beria's lecture (Moscow, 1937), p. 38.

In December, 1904, under the leadership of the Bolshevik Baku Committee, a huge, well-organized strike of Baku workers was carried out. It ended in the workers' victory, the first collective agreement in the history of the labor movement in Russia between the workers and the oil companies.

The Baku strike marked the beginning of the revolutionary upsurge in Transcaucasia and in several regions of Russia.

"The Baku strike served as a signal for the glorious January/February action all over Russia" (Stalin).[28]

Obviously the authors had Beria's text before them and wanted to follow it as closely as they could. All the more revealing is their choice of the old formula "leadership of the Baku Committee," not "Stalin's leadership." It means that they rejected the new myth—for the time being, at any rate.

By the late thirties, the personality cult was rampant. In 1940, O. N. Chaadaeva wrote in an introductory article to the collection of documents on the Baku strike (*Bakinskaia stachka 1904 goda*) published by the State Archives Administration:

The Baku Committee, *directed by Comrade Stalin, who arrived in Baku December 14*, conducted the ongoing strike under political mottos. . . . The workers' demands were worked out on the initiative of the Baku Committee *under the direct guidance of Comrade Stalin, who stayed in Baku ten days* [p. 17; italics added].

No matter that several Bolshevik party workers had already written their reminiscences about the strike in the twenties, naming a multitude of people connected with it but never Stalin.[29] A cult has its own developmental laws. Soon the strike was being depicted as an event of which Stalin was the heart and soul. M. D. Bagirov, first secretary of the Azerbaidzhan Communist Party, may have outdone everyone else:

The Bolsheviks *headed by Comrade Stalin* succeeded in arousing the Baku proletariat to a general strike in December, 1904.

The grandiose general strike *organized by Comrade Stalin* began on December 13, 1904. From the first days of the strike, *a strike committee directed by Comrade Stalin* was formed.

At *Comrade Stalin's directions*, the main demands included. . . .

Mensheviks, SR's, Dashnaks, and the camouflaged police agents, the

---

[28] *Istoriia Vsesoiuznoi Kommunisticheskoi Partii (bol'shevikov). Kratkii kurs* (Moscow, 1938), p. 54.

[29] See the two collections issued by the Baku Committee in 1923 and 1924 (cited in nn. 6 and 11 to this appendix) and Zelikson-Bobrovskaia, *Zapiski riadovogo podpol'shchika* (Moscow, 1922).

brothers Shendrikov, did all they could to deprive the strike of its political character, then to wreck it altogether. But the December strike of the Baku proletariat, *directed by Comrade Stalin,* was becoming more and more political in character.

[The Baku Committee] issued *proclamations written by Comrade Stalin personally.* . . .

Comrade Stalin called a joint conference of the Baku Committee and representatives of workers . . . which defined the basic points of the collective agreement between the workers and the oil companies. . . .

This brilliant victory . . . won under the personal direction of Comrade Stalin, was to Russia's working class an added inspiration for future battles. . . .[30]

All this was repeated on every possible occasion until the personality cult was denounced at the Twentieth Party Congress, after which the Stalin version of the myth was scrapped and his name disappeared from the history of the 1904 strike. But the original variant, about the Baku Committee's brilliant preparation and successful conclusion of the strike, lives on in Communist history to this day.[31]

---

[30] M. D. Bagirov, *Iz istorii bol'shevistskoi organizatsii Baku i Azerbaidzhana* (Moscow: Gospolitizdat, 1946), pp. 46–47 (italics added). In view of the fact that Bagirov's book and other Communist sources constantly repeat—with *disapproval* —that the Mensheviks tried to deprive the strike of its political character (which is not true, as the reader has seen), it is interesting to note that a leaflet of the Baku Committee written by Stalin for the fifth anniversary of the 1904 Baku strike described the strike—with *approval*—as "an economic general strike" and appealed to the Baku workers to "raise the banner of an economic general strike for our vital demands. . . . All our past and present, our struggle and our victories indicate that we shall choose . . . the road of a general strike for an increase in the wage rate and an eight-hour working day, for housing developments [*poselki*] and rent allowance [*kvartirnye*], for *narodnye doma* and schools, for medical aid and compensation for injuries, for the right to have factory commissions and unions." The leaflet did not contain a single political demand. (Stalin, *Sochineniia,* II (Moscow, 1946), 169–73.)

[31] A striking example of this falsification of history, by then undoubtedly deliberate, is *Kratkaia istoriia rabochego dvizheniia v Rossii (1861–1917 g.g.)* (Moscow: Gospolitizdat, 1962), pp. 303–6.

The Liberationists and the
Trade-Union Movement

The article in which Peter Struve, even before January 9, called the organization of trade unions "a vital task of the times") *Osvobozhdenie*, No. 63, 1905 has already been discussed in chapter iii (p. 149). It may be useful to quote another excerpt from it:

> . . . The point is that no real mass movement and no true working-class organizations can be achieved without gradually preparing the minds by ceaseless propaganda and organizational work.
>
> Realizing this, all workers for liberation must now include in their program of practical work the creation of workers' trade-union organizations, the organization of workers' meetings, libraries, and so on. . . .
>
> While we insist on the need for "Liberationists" to undertake this work, we do not at all visualize it as some sort of contest with the Social-Democrats. On the contrary, we should like the "Liberationists" to persuade the Social-Democrats that major social achievements are not brought about by verbal incantations and to begin systematic organizational work among the working class together with the Social-Democrats. But whether or not an agreement with the Social-Democrats is reached, the "Liberationists" must undertake this work. In their ranks there are people of energy, knowledge, a certain standing. They must not evade this kind of activity, or the working class will for a long time yet be unable to play its proper role in Russian civic and political life.

The article outlined a plan of collaboration, but the Social-Democrats mistrusted the idea. Twenty years later a thoughtful writer like Kolokol'nikov still saw it as an attempt of "liberal and bourgeois democracy to use the growing labor movement for its own political ends."[1]

Osvobozhdenie's concern was, however, largely theoretical. It reported hardly anything on the fast growth of the trade-union movement in early 1905—not even on the vigorous activity in it of a group of Liberationists headed by Sergei N. Prokopovich (more about this later).

Struve returned to the subject of helping the trade-union movement on May 18/31 in *Osvobozhdenie*, No. 71, with the article "How To Find Oneself," a reply to a letter, "How Can One Not Lose Oneself?" In contrast to his January article, he spoke of creating unions in the *fait accompli* way and did not propose that liberals and Social-Democrats collaborate in this:

> Founding and supporting all kinds of workers' self-help organizations (in the broadest sense)—that must be the task of democracy among the urban population. This is a task of a far broader nature than any party interests or even political interests in the narrow sense. From the "party" viewpoint, the fruits of this work are likely to fall mainly to the Social-Democrats, but that does not trouble or frighten us in the least. The education and self-education of the popular masses is the task of the times; whose party interests will profit from its execution must be a point of less than secondary importance to us. True, a flowering of Social-Democracy in its present form seems highly problematic to me; though the Russian workers will almost certainly organize into a separate and, what is more, a "class" party, the question of whether today's Social-Democracy will be that party has by no means been settled in the affirmative by history as yet. Perhaps our country will evolve a new type of labor party, midway between the British workers' liberalism and doctrinaire German Social-Democracy.

The last may have been an echo of the ideas that were floating around on the outskirts of Menshevism at the time (see chapter v).

It would seem that the Liberationists' activity in the trade-union movement began independently of Struve's theoretical plans. Already in the fall of 1904, Prokopovich and a few others had established contact with Gapon and his workers;[2] after January 9, they began a concentrated drive for the creation of trade unions—or, to be exact, of

---

[1] *1905–1907 g.g. v professional'nom dvizhenii. I i II vserossiiskie konferentsii professional'nykh soiuzov*, compiled by P. Kolokol'nikov and S. Rapoport (Moscow, 1925), p. 23.

[2] The Gaponite Karelin remembered a meeting at Gapon's home in early November, 1904, attended, besides himself and Gapon, by the Gaponites Kuzin, Varnashev, and Vasil'ev, and the *intelligenty* V. Ia. Bogucharskii, S. N. Prokopovich, and E. D. Kuskova, "and two other women." ("Deviatoe ianvaria i Gapon. Vospominaniia. [Zapisano so slov A. E. Karelina]," *Krasnaia Letopis'*, 1922, No. 1, p. 110.)

organizations that would substitute for trade unions, assume the functions usually performed by them. The Gapon pattern clearly influenced
their first plan for such an organization in Petersburg: a "general labor
union," grouping workers not by trade or by type of industry but
geographically, so to speak, like the Gapon locals. Kolokol'nikov
writes:

> Simultaneously with the Social-Democrats, a group of leftist Libera-
> tionists went to the workers with propaganda for unions. They promoted
> the idea of a general labor union. A statute they had drafted was widely
> distributed in the factories. It made factory organizations the basis.
> Factory unions, through their representatives, were to form sector
> unions, then a city union. The crowning achievement . . . was to be
> the unification of city unions into an all-Russian union. The type of
> organization: free federation. Every factory union [would be] auton-
> omous; the decisions of the organization as a whole not binding on its
> component parts. It was meant to be a non-party organization, but the
> draft of a program close to the Liberationists' program was appended to
> the statute.[3]

The plan seems to have intended the "general" or "single" labor
union, like the Peasants' Union and the General Union of Railroad
Employees and Workers, to join the Union of Unions[4] (that was also
Kolokol'nikov's opinion). However, the general labor union did not
materialize, and the Liberationists soon abandoned the idea. Prokopovich wrote in a pamphlet in the fall of 1905 that the attempt had
shown

> the impracticability of such an organization: there was no place in it for
> the defense of economic interests, so different in the various trades and
> so dear to the average worker. Therefore the single labor union was
> replaced by a union of labor unions as the most practical form of prole-
> tarian mass organization at the given moment in history and under the
> given political conditions.[5]

To some extent, it was to take the place of a labor party as well—at
least for a while, "under the given political conditions." Prokopovich
wrote in the same pamphlet:

---

[3] P. Kolokol'nikov, "Kak voznik v Peterburge soiuz rabochikh po metallu," in
*Materialy ob èkonomicheskom polozhenii i professional'noi organizatsii sankt-
peterburgskikh rabochikh po metallu* (Petersburg, 1909), p. 26.

[4] The Union of Unions combined professional-political unions, mostly formed
by various groups of the intelligentsia in the fall and winter 1904/5. It played a
considerable part in the political life of the country until October, 1905. Its
chairman, from May, 1905, was P. N. Miliukov.

[5] S. N. Prokopovich, *Soiuzy rabochikh i ikh zadachi* (Petersburg: E. D.
Kuskova, 1905), p. 26.

The experience of 1905 has shown the workers that to defend their class and political interests it is necessary to have a mass organization, an organization of the working class; that the present trends in the working class, which segregate individual circles of conscious workers from the mass and pull these circles in different directions, cannot [provide] an organized defense of class interests; that detailed programs do not unify the masses but disunite them. Experience has shown that programs cannot precede organizations, that a mass organization is impossible if everyone who joins it must first adhere to some program, that a mass organization must be based only on the principles of class struggle and political freedom and [on the] ideal of . . . social equality. Having united all the workers sharing these principles, such a mass organization will itself work out a program of its demands and develop it as the labor movement develops.[6]

The pamphlet strikes an effective final chord:

The workers have at their disposal such a powerful means as a political general strike. . . . But in order to organize it the working masses must be organized. Organizing the working masses is the next task of the labor movement. This organization can be achieved only by trade unions and by their unification into a single all-Russian union of trade unions.[7]

In Kolokol'nikov's opinion the program was "pointed first and foremost at the Social-Democratic Party."[8] This is probably exaggerated, but it is true that the Party as it was then had no place in such an organization.

This plan was not carried out either. The quickly expanding labor movement passed it by. Prokopovich's group itself was swept into the general movement and lost its specific traits. During all of 1905, however, the Liberationists of the left played a certain role in the Petersburg trade-union movement. Shortly before the "October days" they were very much in evidence at a conference of representatives from Moscow, Petersburg, and some provincial labor unions to discuss an all-Russian congress. The meeting (later it came to be called the First All-Russian Conference of Trade Unions) took place in Moscow, at the Museum of Assistance to Labor.[9] The Petersburg unions were

---

[6] *Ibid.*, pp. 24–25.

[7] *Ibid.*, p. 26.

[8] *1905–1907 g.g. v professional'nom dvizhenii* . . . , p. 26.

[9] Muzei Sodeistviia Trudu, attached to the Moscow branch of the Russian Technological Society, was founded in 1901 as a special bureau to "promote improvement of the working and living conditions of the laboring masses, put to use the inventions most beneficial to them, disseminate scientific knowledge, furnish information and advice on organizing . . . institutions for workers." The museum later expanded its aims; in 1905 it became a center which housed the offices of

represented by the Liberationists S. N. Prokopovich, as delegate from the printing trade,[10] and G. S. Khrustalev-Nosar', from a commission to organize a union of textile workers;[11] and the printer I. Z. Zheludkov, a man close to the Liberationists, from the Petersburg District Bureau for Convoking a Congress of Workers' Mutual-Aid Societies and Trade Unions.[12] Another friend of the Liberationists, Attorney N. K. Murav'ev, the chairman of the board of the museum, presided over the meeting.[13]

This was, however, the last display of Liberationist influence in the trade-union movement. Outside Petersburg it had always been negligible, and even in Petersburg it was dwindling. In the fall of 1905 the Union of Liberation was absorbed by the Constitutional-Democratic Party, and Prokopovich and his group left it. On the other hand, the trade-union movement was rapidly emancipating itself from the intelligentsia. As a result of all this, the role played by the Liberationists in 1905 in the Petersburg trade-union movement was simply forgotten after a while.

---

many trade unions. On the museum, see *1905–1907 g.g. v professional'nom dvizhenii* . . ., pp. 155–60.

[10] *Ibid.*, p. 169.
[11] *Ibid.*, p. 170.
[12] *Ibid.*, p. 168.
[13] *Ibid.*, p. 157.

V. P. Akimov on the Interrelations of Trade Unions and the Party

The Liberationists' "union of trade unions" was to substitute for a labor party and perhaps replace Social-Democracy. V. P. Akimov, also starting from the idea of trade unions as the basis of organizing the working class but wanting to preserve the Party, developed a theory of a Social-Democratic party built mainly (but not exclusively) on trade unions—perhaps after the model of the British Labour Party, though the likeness may not have struck him. It was an ingenious idea, worth examining in some detail.

Akimov was the most gifted publicist in the Economist camp. Finding himself at loose ends after the Second Party Congress in 1903, he settled in Geneva to do some "summing-up" and published two books, *The Work of the Second Congress of the RSDRP* (*K voprosu o rabotakh 2-go S"ezda RSDRP*) in the summer of 1904 and *Materials on the Development of the RSDRP* (*Materialy dlia kharakteristiki razvitiia RSDRP*) in February, 1905. The day the second book appeared, Akimov left for Russia (with false papers, of course), "wishing to try out my ideas in practice, to see how they could be carried out."[1]

In the conclusion of *Materials*, Akimov had spoken of rebuilding the Party from the bottom up, by way of elections, with the Social-

---

[1] Vl. Akimov-Makhnovets, "Stroiteli budushchego," *Obrazovanie*, April, 1907, p. 94. This work, published in the April, May, and June issues of *Obrazovanie*, also appeared as a separate (now very rare) book. Akimov relates his observations and activities in various cities of Russia and draws generalized conclusions from his experiences. For all its subjectivity, this work is one of the best among the semimemoir literature on 1905.

Democratic groups at the factories as the basis.[2] He did not yet mention trade unions as the basis. But in mid-April, talking with leaders of the Moscow union of workers in the printing trade (the strongest trade-union organization in Russia at the time), he tried to persuade the union to declare itself a Party organization and, as the first step toward reforming the Party, to press for the admission of its delegate to the Moscow Committee (with a vote).[3] "If you did that, many other labor organizations would follow suit, and we could build our Party in a way that would make it truly the party of the working class," Akimov wrote in a memorandum the leaders had asked for.[4] But although the latter considered themselves Social-Democrats, they did not agree with him.

In May, in Petersburg, S. I. Somov's criticism made Akimov revise his views:

> Upon reading my last book, Comrade S. I. agreed with my interpretation of the struggle between the trends in our Party but remarked that he could not share my hopes of democratizing the Party organization. At first this surprised me very much, but he explained that it was too late for democratization: "For too long the Party has been processing its members like dried fish, and by no means the best elements of the working class are now grouped in our circles"; before the Party's "demos" could be given self-government, it would be necessary that those who had left the Party rejoin it. Of course, if any worker wishing to serve the liberation of his class could join our Party, broad democratism in the Party would be a must. . . . If a party broadly encompassing the working class were formed outside our Party, I should have no problem deciding in whose ranks to stand.[5]

Later, in *Builders of the Future* (*Stroiteli budushchego*), Akimov wrote:

> Strange to say, I did not at the time pay enough attention to [Somov's] words. I valued Comrade S. I.'s opinion very highly, and he had already been working illegally in Petersburg for over six months, coming in contact with the broadest strata of the working class; but since I had no idea how his thought could be put into practice I merely remembered his words without pondering them; later I often had occasion to recall them.[6]

---

[2] V. Akimov, *Materialy dlia kharakteristiki razvitiia Rossiiskoi Sotsialdemokraticheskoi Rabochei Partii* (Geneva, 1905), pp. 135–36.

[3] *Obrazovanie*, April, 1907, p. 99.

[4] *Ibid.*, p. 102.

[5] *Ibid.*, p. 112.

[6] *Ibid.*

In late July, at a large meeting at a Kharkov locomotive construction plant (during a general strike in Kharkov), Akimov proposed a new idea—no longer a reform of the Social-Democratic Party but a new "single labor party" which would absorb all the existing socialist parties:

> The workers themselves must take this matter in hand, but for this they must act in concert, like one man, and for this they must all unite into a single labor party. Let all conscious workers get together at their plants, factories, workshops, and choose . . . committees, which will speak with the owners as representatives of the workers' interests, defend individual comrades as well as present the workers' general demands, meet in council, take care of the money collected against strikes. Let these committees in turn elect representatives who, gathered together, will form a Kharkov Committee of the united workers of all factories and trades. The Kharkov Committee will send its representatives to a congress of deputies from other cities, and thus an all-Russian labor party will come into being. It will probably set itself the same goals as the workers of other countries, that is to say, it will be a Social-Democratic party; it will send its representatives to international congresses of workers' representatives of all countries. . . .
>
> . . . .
>
> This will not be one more party besides the two that already exist. On the contrary, it will unite all those who wish to pay more than lip service to the cause of the working class; hence it will not aggravate the division of strength but put an end to it. . . . We must put an end to this division, and it seems to me we can do this in the way I have said.[7]

The meeting passed a resolution which "met my [Akimov's] wishes to a considerable degree," though it specified a "workers' union," not a labor party.[8]

In October Akimov settled in Petersburg, took an active part in the trade-union movement, and was elected to the Soviet of Workers' Deputies. He also contributed regularly to the small periodical *Rabochii Golos*, founded by a group of Social-Democratic workmen estranged from the Party organization. Its No. 1, of November 26, 1905, carried a declaration, "From the Editors," doubtless written for the most part by Akimov,[9] in which the idea of a Social-Democratic Party based on trade unions received its definitive formulation.

---

[7] *Obrazovanie*, June, 1907, pp. 59–60.

[8] *Ibid.*, pp. 60–61.

[9] This issue lists the contributors to the periodical, and Akimov is about the only one among them who could have written the declaration. That he was very close to *Rabochii Golos* is confirmed by the fact that the small issue contains two articles signed by him.

The editors stressed that they did not belong to any of the "Majority" and "Minority" factions but believed "in the basic principles of international Social-Democracy." The present Party, however, did not satisfy them:

> We do not have an overall party organization. . . . The present organization of the RSDRP does not at all correspond to the contemporary development of the proletarian movement in Russia; none but the *organized struggling proletariat itself* has the right to be called the party of the proletariat.

What should a true proletarian party be like?

> The proletariat *itself* must organize, and organize for struggle: what is needed is a real *proletarian party.* . . . Such organization is already going on, at a feverish rate, advancing not daily but hourly: the proletariat is organizing in unions according to trade. The mighty rise and growth of trade-union organizations will provide the basis for a genuine class party in Russia. The proletariat's trade-union organizations with all their ramifications and subsidiaries in the form of co-operatives and so forth—that is, the organizations directly linked to its role in industry, to its class basis—constitute [the proletariat's] . . . power and might; they are the pledge of its successful development in every sense and of its complete emancipation from capital.

How should the working-class party be organized?

> We are convinced that an all-Russian labor party, as a single organization of the struggling proletariat, built on a class basis . . . will from the beginning be *Social-Democratic,* that is, will accept all the main tenets of international Social-Democracy. . . . As a group devoted to an idea, we for our part will try to hasten the masses' [assimilation] of Social-Democratic principles. But if reality deceived our expectations, if we proved to have been too optimistic, then we should without a moment's hesitation recognize the labor party and any program it may adopt. Having joined the party, and submitting to its decisions, we should, however, remain Social-Democrats in principle and carry on an energetic struggle within the party to make it become Social-Democratic as soon as possible.

Rabochii Golos had a short life. Some of its contributors, who were associated with the Liberationists of the left, supported the Kadets in the elections to the Duma.[10] Others turned toward syndicalism. The

---

[10] *1905–1907 g.g. v professional'nom dvizhenii. I i II vserossiiskie konferentsii professional'nykh soiuzov,* compiled by P. Kolokol'nikov and S. Rapoport (Moscow, 1925), pp. 137–38.

majority rejoined the RSDRP and became identified with the Mensheviks. Akimov, without formally breaking with the Party, remained alone. In 1907 he attended, as a guest, the Party Congress in London, then retired into obscurity. His idea of a Social-Democratic party based on trade unions was soon forgotten.

Lenin's Theory of Trade Unions, "Spontaneity," and "Consciousness"

In a nutshell, the thesis of *What Is To Be Done?* (1902) is this: Trade unions tend to gravitate toward the bourgeois camp and bourgeois ideology; only the outside influence of the socialist intelligentsia can neutralize this immanent tendency.

This conception began to form in Lenin's mind long before he wrote *What Is To Be Done?* In his "Protest of Russian Social-Democrats against the 'Credo'" (1899), he commented as follows on a resolution about the trade-union movement, written by Marx and adopted by the Geneva Congress of the International Brotherhood of Workers (the First International) in 1866:

> The resolution . . . correctly points out the significance of the economic struggle, *warning both socialists and workers*, on the one hand, against *overrating it* (a tendency noticeable among British workers at that time) and, on the other, against *underrating it* (which was noticeable among the French and the Germans, especially the Lassallians).[1]

Lenin then related the resolution's arguments for a positive approach to trade unions; but in the passage I have quoted, with its "on the one hand" and "on the other," it was not the Congress or Marx who were speaking but only Lenin himself. The Marx of the sixties would not have warned anyone against overrating the economic struggle. He saw trade unions as the workers' main weapon and in fact attached greater value to them than to the political organizations. This was historically

---

[1] Lenin, *Sochineniia* (4th ed.), IV, 158 (italics added).

justified: even in Germany, at the time the only country with more or less significant political workers' organizations, two socialist organizations (Lassalle's followers and Eisenach's) were fighting each other, groping their way to a truly socialist policy; in other countries the socialist movement was barely out of the embryonic stage. Only in trade unions, especially in England, did Marx see a promise of the growth of a genuinely proletarian movement with ever larger aims.[2]

The fear of overrating the economic struggle and the labor organizations that served it received its "theoretical consecration" in *What Is To Be Done?*:

> The history of all countries bears witness that by its own efforts alone the working class can develop only a trade-unionist consciousness, that is, realize the need to unite in unions, to fight employers, to press the government to enact laws the workers need, and so on. The socialist doctrine, on the other hand, has developed out of the philosophical, historical, economic theories evolved by the intelligentsia, the educated members of the propertied classes. By their social position, Marx and Engels themselves, the founders of modern scientific socialism, belonged to the bourgeois intelligentsia. In Russia, likewise, *the theoretical doctrine of Social-Democracy emerged quite independently of the spontaneous growth of the labor movement; it emerged as a natural and inevitable result of the thought processes of the revolutionary socialist intelligentsia.*[3]

Lenin concluded: "Since the working masses cannot possibly develop an independent ideology, the only question is, Will it be a bourgeois or a socialist ideology? . . . The spontaneous development of the labor movement leads to its subordination to bourgeois ideology. . . ."

---

[2] See my book *Lénine et le mouvement syndical* (Paris: Editions "Nouveau Prométhée," 1935), pp. 16–17. In so freely interpreting the resolution of the 1866 Geneva Congress and putting—unconsciously perhaps—his own thoughts into it, Lenin must have been influenced by the views he had formed while translating Sidney and Beatrice Webb's *Industrial Democracy*. (The translation, by Vladimir Il'in—that is, Lenin—came out in Petersburg as *Teoriia i praktika angliiskogo trèdiunionizma*, Vol. I in 1900, Vol. II in 1901.) Vanguards of the international labor movement in the middle of the nineteenth century, the English trade unions had largely lost this role by the end of the century, when the movement had made great strides in most European countries. But it was these "old" trade unions that apparently remained Lenin's idea of the movement in general. The "new" trade-unionism, with far broader economic and political aims, which emerged early in the new century and became the foundation of the British Labour Party, seems to have interested him little. The immense bibliography of the second and third editions of Lenin's *Sochineniia* contains not one major work on the subject that came out after the Webbs'.

[3] Lenin, *Sochineniia*, V, 347–48 (italics added).

What, then, was the task of Social-Democracy? It was to *"divert"* the movement from its spontaneous tendency and to "draw it under the wing of revolutionary Social-Democracy."[4]

The thesis is not really argued but merely repeated over and over. Lenin himself finally noticed this:

> But why, the reader may ask, should a spontaneous movement, a movement along the line of least resistance, lead to the dominance of bourgeois ideology? For the simple reason that bourgeois ideology is much older in origin than socialist ideology, is more thoroughly elaborated, and disposes of immeasurably greater means of dissemination.[5]

Aware, perhaps, of the weakness of this reasoning, Lenin sought the backing of Karl Kautsky. He quoted Kautsky's comments (in 1901) on the draft of a new program of the Austrian Social-Democrats:

> The draft states: "The more capitalist development multiplies the proletariat, the more the latter is compelled and enabled to fight capitalism. The proletariat comes to realize" the possibility of, and the need for, socialism. In this sense, socialist consciousness would be an inevitable, direct result of the proletariat's class struggle. But that is wholly untrue. . . . Modern socialist consciousness can emerge only on the basis of profound scientific knowledge. . . . And the carrier of that knowledge is not the proletariat but the *bourgeois intelligentsia* [K. K.'s italics]: modern socialism, too, was born in the heads of individual members of that stratum and communicated by them to outstandingly intelligent proletarians, who in turn carry it into the proletariat's class struggle where conditions permit. Thus socialist consciousness is something brought in from the outside (*von Aussen Hineingetragenes*), not something spontaneously arising from the proletariat's class struggle. . . .[6]

Evidently fearing that this might be misconstrued to mean that socialist thought evolved independently of the actual labor movement—just as was done later by Lenin—Kautsky corrected his formulation and elaborated his views at the Austrian Social-Democratic Congress in the fall of 1901:

> True, the labor movement cannot by itself generate Social-Democratic thought. The labor movement generates the socialist instinct; it generates in the proletariat the desire for socialism because the proletarian becomes increasingly aware that on his own, as an individual, he cannot

---

[4] *Ibid.*, pp. 355–56.
[5] *Ibid.*, p. 357.
[6] *Ibid.*, p. 355.

achieve the ownership of the means of production. But the theoretical understanding needed to change this instinct into clear consciousness has not come from proletarian circles because the proletariat lacks the requisite conditions for scientific work. This conviction was born in the heads of bourgeois scholars scrupulous and objective enough not to be blinded by the needs of the bourgeoisie. . . . From the union of the labor movement with socialist theory, there emerged new, Social-Democratic ways of thinking, and in the course of their development not only workers learned from socialist theoreticians but socialist theoreticians learned from workers.[7]

Without examining the assumption that only a *bourgeois* intelligentsia can work out a socialist ideology and that the working class cannot produce its own socialist theorists, I want to point out the basic difference between Kautsky's and Lenin's conceptions. According to Kautsky, the proletariat develops a socialist *instinct*, which makes it receptive to socialist theory. According to Lenin, the proletariat develops merely the desire to fight capitalism *within the framework and on the home ground of bourgeois society*; socialist consciousness has to be brought in *entirely* from without, *against* the proletariat's spontaneous tendency to duck "under the wing of the bourgeoisie." Lenin's conception later played an enormous role in shaping the psychology of Bolshevik "professional revolutionaries." It cleared the ground for the inner change in Bolshevism, for its gradual transformation from left-wing Social-Democracy into a totalitarian system under the colors of state socialism.

It would be a mistake to think that Lenin developed these views without an inner struggle against the Social-Democrat in himself. There are signs of it in *What Is To Be Done?* In the section "Organizations of Workers and Organizations of Revolutionaries" he referred to trade unions with unexpected sympathy:

> Workers' organizations for the economic struggle must be trade-union organizations. Every Social-Democratic workman must support and actively work in these organizations as much as he can. That is true. But it is not at all in our interest to insist that only Social-Democrats can be members of "trade" unions: this would limit the extent of our influence over the masses. Let any worker who understands the need to unite for fighting employers and the government be a member of a trade union. The very aim of trade unions would be unattainable if they did not unite all those who are capable of even the most elementary understanding,

---

[7] Quoted in G. V. Plekhanov's "Rabochii klass i sotsialdemokraticheskaia intelligentsiia" (*Iskra*, Nos. 70 and 71), in *Sochineniia*, XIII, 129.

[that is,] if [they] were not very *broad* organizations. And the broader they are, the greater will be our influence over them, an influence resulting not merely from the "spontaneous" development of the economic struggle but deliberately, directly exerted over their comrades by the socialist members of these unions. . . .[8]

Lenin did not absolutely rule out working even with the legal labor organizations that had just appeared, mainly under the aegis of the Okhrana. His realistic approach to them is expressed in the long quotation from *What Is To Be Done?* on pages 287–88 in this book. Let me repeat just a few lines of it here:

We can and must tell the Zubatovs and the Ozerovs: Do your best, gentlemen, do your best! Inasmuch as you are setting a snare for workers . . . we shall take care of unmasking you. Inasmuch as you are taking a real step forward . . . we shall say: Much obliged, pray go on! . . . Any increase [of scope for the workers] will be useful to us and speed the emergence of the kind of legal societies in which *provocateurs* will not be catching socialists but socialists will be catching converts.[9]

This is hard to reconcile with the basic conception of *What Is To Be Done?* And it is significant that the part of Lenin's theory that concerned "spontaneity and consciousness" and dragging the proletariat "under the wing of revolutionary Social-Democracy" became instantly popular with the Bolsheviks, whereas the part about making use of any "increase of scope for the workers" was almost immediately forgotten. The first apparently answered some inner need of Bolshevism; the second was a foreign body in the Bolshevik system of views.

I believe that Lenin realized that his words might lead his readers farther than he intended. In *What Is To Be Done?* he remarked:

We have purposely chosen this angular formulation, we are purposely speaking in stark and cutting terms—not from any desire to talk in paradoxes but in order to "nudge" the Economists onto the tasks they are impardonably neglecting [and to make them see] the difference between trade-unionist and Social-Democratic policies, which they are refusing to understand.[10]

At the Second Party Congress the following year Lenin went so far as to say that "the Economists had bent the pole one way; to straighten

---

[8] Lenin, *Sochineniia*, V, 423.
[9] *Ibid.*, p. 425.
[10] *Ibid.*, p. 392.

it out, it was necessary to bend it the other way, and that is what I did."[11] Yet, when he reissued *What Is To Be Done?* in 1907 in the collection *Twelve Years* (*Dvenadtsat' let*) he made minor changes but left intact the important passages I have quoted. And it was the most obnoxious formulations that were incorporated in the rigid permanent canons of Bolshevism.

---

[11] *Ibid.*, VI, 446.

The Myth of the "Liberationist" Origin of the Petersburg Soviet of Workers' Deputies

P. N. Miliukov's *Reminiscences* contain the following amazing lines on the Petersburg Soviet:

> Few are aware that the Soviet of Workers' Deputies owed its very existence to the Union of Liberation and its Petersburg group, not to Trotsky and the Mensheviks, who claimed to have been its creators. Like the "banquets" idea and the idea of the Union of Unions, the idea of the Soviet of Workers' Deputies had been put forward and carried out by the Liberationists, after "Red Sunday." For this they made use of the Shidlovskii Commission appointed by the government to investigate the needs and demands of the workers. One of the workers' deputies who got into this Commission, Khrustalev, passed his mandate to the *intelligent* Nosar'. "Intelligentsia" speeches began to resound in the Commission. The officials noticed at once that "revolutionaries had gained control of the deputies"—the Commission was disbanded and Nosar' exiled from Petersburg. But the Liberationists brought him back and hid him. Some of the unmolested deputies to the Commission formed a "soviet," and by the spring of 1905 had increased its membership to fifty or sixty. In this form the Soviet of Workers' Deputies existed until October, meeting at the illegal printing press of the Union of Liberation or at the homes of members of the "Large Group." The first appeal to factory workers to convoke a new soviet was printed at this press. At the same time Nosar' came out of hiding—he had been hiding in an empty railroad car and sleeping at Liberationists' homes—and became the

chairman of the Soviet, at the Free Economic Society, where the Liberationists had long since ensconced themselves as masters.[1]

Miliukov apparently took this from E. D. Kuskova, who had written:

> The October days of 1905. Bustle, clamor, demonstrations, collections for the "armed uprising." . . . For about three months before that, [we] had been working with Grigorii Stepanovich Khrustalev in the workers' union. A "liquidationist," as the expression was. A "moderate," favoring "constitutional forms" of work. . . . Berated "excesses," "demagoguery." Illegal, however; had been sent out of Petersburg. Evidently for this very moderation.
>
> And all of a sudden—October. [He was] transformed, unrecognizable. Sat in a railroad car on the sidelines of Nikolaevskii railroad, sending out proclamations to the factories: Elect a Soviet of Workers' Deputies! A piquant historical detail: this proclamation was printed at the press of our Union of Liberation. At the time, in October, it was the only surviving illegal press: those of the SR's and the S-D's had just been demolished by the police. I remember how these leaflets, about convoking the first Soviet of Workers' Deputies, were dried at my apartment. . . . Wet, uncut. . . . Sometimes Khrustalev, still apparently illegal, came to spend the night.[2]

Kuskova's memory is failing her in this story, written over twenty years later. Everything about it is wrong: that Khrustalev sent out the appeals, that they were printed at the Liberationists' press, dried at her apartment, and so on.

Khrustalev himself wrote a brief history of the Soviet,[3] in which he says that the Soviet had been formed on October 13 on the initiative of the Menshevik Group and that he appeared in it only at its second meeting, October 14, as a deputy from the Printers' Union.[4] He does not mention that the Union of Liberation had anything to do with the emergence of the Soviet. Nor is it true that the leaflets were printed at the Liberationists' press. The appeal "To All Men and Women Workers" was found in police archives and reprinted in full in one of the early collections of the Leningrad Istpart.[5] It has the heading "Russian Social-Democratic Labor Party," and below it, "Proletarians of All

---

[1] P. N. Miliukov, *Vospominaniia (1859–1917)* (New York: Chekhov Publishing House, 1955), I, 342–43.

[2] E. D. Kuskova, "Otkrytki (Iz tetradki vospominanii)," *Sovremennye Zapiski* (Paris), XXV (1925), 419.

[3] G. Khrustalev-Nosar', "Istoriia Soveta Rabochikh Deputatov (do 26-go noiabria 1905 goda)," in *Istoriia Soveta Rabochikh Deputatov g. S.-Peterburga* (Petersburg, 1906), pp. 45–169.

[4] *Ibid.*, p. 65.

[5] *1905 god v Peterburge*, Vol. I: *Sotsialdemokraticheskie listovki* (Leningrad-Moscow: Istpart, 1925), pp. 315–16.

Countries, Unite!"; it is signed "Soviet of Deputies of Petersburg Factories and Plants"; at the bottom, after the signature, it has "Published by the Petersburg Group of the RSDRP." Even supposing that both the heading and the last line were mistakes, they would have been corrected if the Liberationists had printed the appeal and could not have appeared in the first place if they, and not the Mensheviks, had initiated the Soviet.

Kuskova's remark that the leaflets were dried and cut at her home is equally preposterous. They could have been dried there only if they had also been printed there; and they would have been cut only if they had been printed on both sides of the sheet—a procedure generally avoided in underground work and unnecessary in this case since the text is quite short, less than one page of an average-size book. Furthermore, the leaflets were not printed but mimeographed, judging by the editors' description of the copy in the Istpart collection.

Miliukov is even more astray. He speaks of a "soviet" comprising fifty or sixty former deputies to the Shidlovskii Commission and functioning from spring to October, 1905. There is absolutely no mention of such a soviet in the numerous writings on former deputies to the Shidlovskii Commission. That such a soviet should have met at an illegal printing press is utterly impossible. I shall take up only one more of Miliukov's many errors: that the Soviet met at the Free Economic Society, a stronghold of the Liberationists. Actually the first three meetings, on October 13, 14, and 15, took place at the Technological Institute. Only when the institutions of higher learning were closed on October 16, did the Soviet meet at the Free Economic Society—for its fourth session, on October 17.[6]

This would suffice to close the subject, if it weren't for the rumors about the Liberationists' active role that were current in Petersburg in the fall of 1905. In rightist circles it was believed that the Union of Unions had organized the Soviet. Surprisingly, even the Okhrana thought so. Reporting to the Department of Police on the strike movement, the chief of the Okhrana, General A. V. Gerasimov, wrote on November 2:

> The main initiative and the organizational work in the said strikes belong to the Union of Unions; in order to achieve maximum influence over the workers, through whom strikes are in effect carried out, [the Union of Unions] immediately set out to create a new organization that could impose its decisions on the workers, on condition of co-operating with the unions and the revolutionary factions.
> This organization is the "Soviet of Workers' Deputies," formed with

---

[6] Khrustalev-Nosar', "Istoriia Soveta Rabochikh Deputatov . . . ," p. 76.

the direct participation of the local Social-Democratic factions, which took a sympathetic view of the idea of the Union of Unions."[7]

And further on: "The activity of the Soviet is entirely under the influence of [the revolutionary organizations], that is, mainly under the influence of the Union of Unions."

In another report, on November 4, Gerasimov wrote: "A new dangerous organization has appeared on the scene, created under the influence of the Union of Unions and styling itself 'Soviet of Workers' Deputies.' "[8] As late as November 22, a document about bringing G. S. Khrustalev in for questioning stated: "During the political general strike, organized and begun on the initiative of a group of a revolutionary character calling itself the Union of Unions, there appeared in Petersburg a new very serious organization which took the name of Soviet of Workers' Deputies."[9]

These notions were abandoned once the officials had studied the materials pertaining to the trial of the Petersburg Soviet. There is no reference to the Union of Unions in the indictment, which reads, in part:

> In October, 1905, among persons participating in the labor disorders occurring in Petersburg at the time, there emerged the idea of organizing a special workers' committee which would take over the unification and direction of the labor movement. This committee, according to the plans of its organizers, was to be formed of elected workers' deputies. . . .[10]

It may be interesting to check our data against the writings of members of the enemy camp, the officials of the Okhrana. Such books exist: General Gerasimov's memoirs, in German,[11] and a history of Social-Democracy in Russia, with special stress on 1905, by General A. I. Spiridovich of the Palace Okhrana. Regrettably, Gerasimov does not discuss the origins of the Petersburg Soviet; Spiridovich does:

> During the stormy days of the October strike, thanks to the initiative and agitation of Social-Democrat Mensheviks, there came into being in St. Petersburg the "All-City Soviet of Workers' Deputies of the City of Petersburg," whose prototype as a revolutionary collective had been given by *Iskra* as early as its No. 101.[12]

---

[7] *1905 god v Peterburge*, Vol. II: *Sovet Rabochikh Deputatov* (Leningrad-Moscow: Istpart, 1925), p. 102.

[8] *Ibid.*, p. 120.

[9] *Ibid.*, p. 121.

[10] *Protsess Soveta Rabochikh Deputatov. Podrobnyi otchet s obvinitel'nym aktom, rechami podsudimykh i pr.* (Petersburg: Mir, 1906).

[11] Alexander Gerassimoff [Gerasimov], *Der Kampf gegen die erste russische Revolution. Erinnerungen* (Frauenfeld-Leipzig: Huber & Co., 1934).

[12] General A. I. Spiridovich, *Istoriia bol'shevizma v Rossii. Ot vozniknoveniia do zakhvata vlasti. 1883–1903–1917* (Paris, 1922), p. 107.

The Ivanovo-Voznesensk Sobranie Upolnomochennykh:
Myth and Reality

I have already spoken in chapter iii of the Ivanovo-Voznesensk textile strike which began on May 12, 1905, the day after a meeting of workers and the Party organization. From the article "Talka," a reliable account by A. E. Nozdrin, an engraver, chairman of the workers' *Sobranie Upolnomochennykh* ("Assembly of Delegates") during the strike,[1] we learn the following facts: The meeting of May 11 had drawn up the workers' demands (p. 84); on May 13 about forty thousand strikers gathered in front of the city's Administration Building; after some speeches on needs and demands, the list of demands was given to the senior factory inspector, Svirskii; on May 14, at another mass meeting in Administration Square,

> at the height of the speeches, Svirskii appeared in front of the speakers' platform and asked to be heard, to confirm . . . that he had handed our demands to the manufacturers. From him we learned that the manufacturers were unwilling to satisfy all our demands but did not refuse to negotiate with us; they considered, however, that it was technically

---

[1] A. E. Nozdrin, "Talka. Revoliutsionnye puti Ivanovo-Voznesenskikh tkachei v 1905 godu," in *1905 god v Ivanovo-Voznesenskom raione*, ed. O. A. Varentsova *et al.* (Ivanovo-Voznesensk, 1925), pp. 82–143. In 1905 Nozdrin was middle-aged, having been born in 1862 (*Krasnyi Arkhiv*, 1935, No. 2/3, p. 128). He was a non-party man, as was the secretary of the *Sobranie Upolnomochennykh*, I. D. Dobrovol'skii (*1905 god v Ivanovo-Voznesenskom raione*, p. 349). Two more secretaries were elected a few days later: N. P. Grachev and A. F. Sukhovskii (F. Samoilov, *Pervyi Sovet Rabochikh Deputatov* [Moscow, 1931], pp. 37–38). These two also were non-party men (*1905 god v Ivanovo-Voznesenskom raione*, p. 349).

impossible to negotiate with the entire mass [of workers]—negotiations could begin only with elected representatives, and at each mill separately; [Svirskii], too, recommended this as the best way to settle the conflict.

From the same tribune the governor himself agreed to this and guaranteed complete immunity to the elected representatives.

The negotiations with the governor and with Svirskii were in the nature of a rather correct exchange, and the crowd listened closely to what both its friends and its adversaries had to say. . . .

The offer to negotiate through elected representatives . . . was found acceptable; we took it as a partial concession to one of our main demands: "A permanent elective commission of workers and management in equal number to establish internal regulations and resolve all misunderstandings between workers and management."

Once we had interpreted this as a concession . . . it no longer sufficed us: we decided to broaden the proposed form of negotiations for the duration of the strike . . . and asked Svirskii to tell the manufacturers that we agreed only to a general meeting of workers' representatives and management representatives and refused to negotiate at each mill separately. [Pp. 89–90.][2]

On May 15 the strikers again gathered in the square. The inspector repeated that negotiations could be conducted only for each concern separately and that the delegates' immunity was guaranteed, and said that elections could be held at the mills or wherever the workers wished. Nozdrin writes:

At a signal from the platform, "Comrades, divide by mills and elect delegates," elections began right there in the square, but for reasons of secrecy we decided to move them to the boulevard, blocking ourselves off from curious onlookers. On the boulevard we again divided by mills; the boulevard benches served as speakers' platforms.

Only the mutual-aid society of mill engravers did not hold elections on the boulevard; the engravers elected three delegates. [Nozdrin was one.—S. S.]

The delegates met on the same day at the Meshchanskaia Uprava building—their own choice (p. 95). Svirskii opened the meeting but "considering it awkward to preside over the conference because of his role of mediator . . . proposed that a chairman be elected" (p. 96). This was done.

On May 17, at the suggestion of the chief of police, the daily mass

---

[2] See also Samoilov's story quoted in n. 9 to chapter iii. It shows that the Bolshevik Group, far from initiating it, was quite unprepared for the idea of electing a strike committee to conduct negotiations, let alone a soviet of workers' deputies.

meetings were moved out of town, to the bank of the river Talka, where the delegates also met, though they still used the Meshchanskaia Uprava for official occasions. Several times the factory inspector came to the meetings on the Talka.

The negotiations—through the inspector and directly with representatives of the management of separate factories—were laborious and frustrating. The mill owners would not yield, the attitude of the police and the governor was hardening. Additional troops were brought in. On May 27 the Meshchanskaia Uprava was closed to the delegates (p. 116). On June 3, Cossacks dispersed a meeting on the Talka; many workers were beaten up or wounded; a score or more were arrested, Nozdrin among them. The strikers in turn began to indulge in "excesses" (cutting telephone and telegraph wires, setting fire to one mill). The mood was becoming ugly, and the authorities backed down. The chief of police responsible for the brutalities of June 3 resigned on June 9. On June 12 all the prisoners were released (p. 127). Meetings on the Talka resumed, but the negotiations made little headway. A few manufacturers agreed to partial concessions and the workers returned to work, but at most mills the strikers held firm. Most owners had left for Moscow with their families. The hungry workers began to despair. A few suburban summer homes of mill owners were set on fire; here and there a grocery store was looted. Reprisals were intensified. On June 27 a strikers' meeting on the Talka decided to resume work on July 1, "to replenish our strength and then renew the fight for our rights and demands presented to the manufacturers at the beginning of the strike" (pp. 132–33).

The *Sobranie Upolnomochennykh* disbanded. The literature differs on the exact date. Podvoiskii writes that on June 25, after a new refusal of demands, "the Soviet of Workers' Deputies [*sic*] laid down its mandate, announcing at the meeting that it would no longer answer for the consequences."[3] Gorin writes that "after another sacking of grocery stores, the Soviet on June 24 was forced to lay down its mandate."[4] Samoilov disagrees with Podvoiskii:

> The Soviet never divested itself of its powers. That time, because the strikers' especial resentment threatened to overflow in the most unforeseen excesses, the Soviet sent the authorities a paper signed by all its members, informing them that it could not be responsible for possible excesses, in view of the extreme stubbornness of the manufacturers.[5]

---

[3] Podvoiskii, *Pervyi Sovet Rabochikh Deputatov* . . . , p. 9.

[4] P. Gorin, *Ocherki po istorii Sovetov Rabochikh Deputatov v 1905 godu* (Moscow, 1925), p. 8.

[5] F. Samoilov, "Pervyi Sovet Rabochikh Deputatov v 1905 godu," *Proletarskaia Revoliutsiia*, 1925, No. 4, p. 131.

Nozdrin relates that he was still negotiating with the chief of police on June 26, and that on the same day a meeting of the delegates decided to call a general strikers' meeting for the twenty-seventh (p. 132). This was the meeting that decided to end the strike. Nozdrin's account gives no further mention of the activity of the *Sobranie Upolnomochennykh*—it had ceased.

Almost all Bolshevik authors who wrote on Ivanovo-Voznesensk after Podvoiskii's "discovery" called the *Sobranie Upolnomochennykh* "Soviet of Workers' Deputies." Yet in 1905 neither the *Sobranie Upolnomochennykh* itself nor anyone else called it that. A number of letters about the Ivanovo strike were published in Geneva in *Proletarii*,[6] and several more, seized in transit, were later found in police archives.[7] Not one of them refers to a "soviet of workers' deputies."

How far the local Bolsheviks were from the idea of turning the *Sobranie Upolnomochennykh* into a soviet of workers' deputies is graphically confirmed by the fact that all the leaflets issued during the strike were signed, not by the workers' representatives, but by the Ivanovo-Voznesensk Group of the Northern Committees of the RSDRP (later, the Ivanovo-Voznesensk Committee of the RSDRP). The Group's leaflet of May 23 began: "To keep all comrades informed on the progress of the strike, the Ivanovo-Voznesensk Social-Democratic Group has decided to issue daily bulletins."[8]

Under the circumstances, to maintain that the Ivanovo-Voznesensk strike committee (the *Sobranie Upolnomochennykh*) was an organization of the same type as the future Soviets of Workers' Deputies is to clash with reality and with one's own integrity. A striking example of such a clash is the following pronouncement of the Bolshevik Party historian N. N. Baturin:

> The first, typical model of all later soviets of workers' deputies was the Ivanovo-Voznesensk Soviet, which was formed in mid-May, 1905, and existed for two and a half months [?], that is, longer than any other Soviet. At present it is especially fitting to remember this remarkable organization of the Ivanovo-Voznesensk textile workers, particularly since it did not receive due recognition either at the time (in 1905) or later and was actually little known.[9]

---

[6] In Nos. 4, 5, 9, 10, and 13.

[7] S. Shesternin, "K 30-letiiu Ivanovo-Voznesenskoi vseobshchei stachki," *Krasnyi Arkhiv*, 1935, No. 2/3, pp. 127–37.

[8] Samoilov, *Po sledam minuvshego*, p. 80.

[9] N. N. Baturin, *Bor'ba za sovety, kak organy proletarskoi diktatury* (Leningrad: Priboi, 1925), quoted from N. N. Baturin, *Sochineniia*, ed. A. I. Elizarova, M. S. Ol'minskii, and M. A. Savel'ev (Moscow-Leningrad), p. 190.

The Moscow Soviet of Workers' Deputies: Myth and Reality

Communist historians often draw invidious comparisons between the avant-garde Moscow Soviet of Workers' Deputies and the laggard Petersburg Soviet. In the *Short Course* (1938) we read:

> The Petersburg Soviet of Workers' Deputies, as the soviet of the main industrial and revolutionary center of Russia, of the capital of the Russian empire, was to have played a decisive role in the Revolution of 1905. However, it proved unequal to its tasks, because of its poor Menshevik leadership. . . .
>
> The Moscow Soviet of Workers' Deputies played an entirely different role in the Revolution. The Moscow Soviet followed a revolutionary policy from the first days of its existence. The leadership of the Moscow Soviet was in the hands of the Bolsheviks.[1]

The same contrast is drawn in the new *History of the CPSU* (1959):

> The Petersburg Soviet, led by the Mensheviks, did not fulfil its main role—did not become an organ of armed uprising and of the struggle to overthrow autocracy. The Bolshevik-led Moscow Soviet and the sector soviets in Moscow played an outstanding role in the Revolution.[2]

Professor G. D. Kostomarov, a recent historian of the Moscow Soviet of 1905, has taken great pains to prove that the Bolsheviks had

---

[1] *Istoriia Vsesoiuznoi Kommunisticheskoi Partii (bol'shevikov). Kratkii kurs* (Moscow: Gospolitizdat, 1938), p. 76.

[2] *Istoriia Kommunisticheskoi Partii Sovetskogo Soiuza* (Moscow: Gospolitizdat, 1959), p. 98.

favored the idea of soviets from the start. But in that case they would have initiated the Moscow Soviet in September/October, at the peak of the strike movement—it is a matter of record that they were more influential with the Moscow workers than the Mensheviks were at the time. Official histories have difficulty explaining why the Soviet was formed so late that its first meeting took place only on November 21 or 22.[3]

In the labor movement of 1905, Moscow lagged behind not only Petersburg but many provincial cities for a number of reasons. A report of the Moscow Committee, apparently of late summer, 1905, with a remark in Lenin's hand, "A most instructive report from one of the model organizations of our Party," diagnoses these reasons as follows:

> The Moscow proletariat has not had the educating and organizing experience of open struggle, even on an economic basis. Even the titanic strike movement that engulfed all Russia this year only sideswiped Moscow. The young organization has not had time to establish its influence over the broad masses firmly enough for its voice to be listened to and its appeals followed. One has to take advantage of the rare instances of spontaneous upsurge. The scattering, and mixed character, of the factories hamper unification; partial strikes often pass unnoticed by workers in the same industry but at different plants. The workers are a mixed lot; the textile industry, in which relations often are still patriarchal, predominates. Most advanced are the workers in the machine industry, but they are lost in the general mass. The body of organized workers is not yet such that we could say that clear-cut Social-Democrats predominate among them—most were caught up in the movement only recently, have not yet got their bearings in questions of program, let alone of tactics. . . .[4]

---

[3] The date of the Moscow Soviet's first meeting remains uncertain—which is in itself a sign of its minor role in the events of 1905. S. Chernomordik (P. Larionov) in his introductory article to *Izvestiia Moskovskogo Soveta rabochikh deputatov, 1905 g.* (Moscow: Istpart, 1925), p. 5, gives the date as November 22. When this article was included in the collection of his articles *1905 god v Moskve* (Moscow: Istpart, 1925), he added the note: "Now there is documentary proof that the first meeting of the Moscow SWD took place on November 21" (p. 67). Most later works have November 21, but November 22 also appears—for example, in the collection of documents and materials published by Akademiia Nauk SSSR, *Revoliutsiia 1905–1907 gg. v Rossii*, in the volume entitled *Vysshii pod"em revoliutsii 1905–1907 gg. Vooruzhennye vosstaniia. Noiabr'-dekabr' 1905 goda*, Part I, ed. A. L. Sidorova, G. M. Derenkovskii, G. D. Kostomarov, G. N. Kuziukov, and A. M. Pankratova (Moscow, 1955), p. 581 (with a reference to *Novaia Zhizn*, November 24). Yet the same Kostomarov gives November 21 in *Moskovskii Sovet rabochikh deputatov 1905 goda* (Moscow: Moskovskii Rabochii, 1948), p. 24; and so does Pankratova in *Pervaia russkaia revoliutsiia 1905–1907 gg.* (2d ed.; Moscow, 1951), p. 154.

[4] Quoted by V. I. Orlov, with a reference to Arkhiv Istparta, in his foreword to the collection *1905. Bol'shevistskie proklamatsii i listovki po Moskve i Moskovskoi*

With the rise of the strike movement, the workers naturally felt the need for a directing and co-ordinating elective organ. The seed thrown by the Menshevik leaflet "Prepare for the Struggle, Elect Deputies!"[5] fell on fertile soil. P. N. Kolokol'nikov, the foremost Menshevik party worker in Moscow in those days, tells us:

> Agitation for factory representation began in August, with the leaflet "Organize, Comrades, Elect Deputies!" [This is undoubtedly the above-mentioned leaflet "Gotov'tes' K bor'be, vybiraite deputatov!"—S. S.] The leaflet was distributed in large quantity. The agitation connected with the rising wave of strikes found a ready soil. Not only were deputies elected at the striking factories; deputies of the same kind of factories united into soviets of deputies.
>
> The first such soviet was that of the ribbon weavers. . . . Ribbon weaving is a more skilled profession than ordinary weaving, and a ribbon man cannot instantly be replaced with an untrained weaver. In August the Moscow ribbon factories were struck. . . . That was when the soviet of deputies of ribbon factories came into being, with the late Isuv's closest participation. . . .
>
> The soviet of deputies of the ribbon factories did not become widely known, unlike the soviet of deputies of the printing presses, organized during the famous general strike of workers in the printing trade, in the second half of September. There was unrest among the printers as early as August. In September partial strikes began. The illegal union of printers combined them into a general strike and took the initiative in organizing a soviet of deputies. The strike began September 20. . . . The mood was mounting. So as not to lose leadership in the movement, the union organized a soviet of deputies. The soviet met openly, with

gubernii, pod obshchei redaktsiei M. N. Pokrovskogo (Moscow-Leningrad, 1926), pp. v–vii. Orlov, on p. 3, tentatively places the report in early August, 1905, but on p. 242 it is placed "toward the fall 1905." It is clear that it was not written before the end of the summer ("Spring and summer were spent on . . ."), yet before the upsurge of September—that is, it must have been written in the first half of September.

The backwardness of the Moscow labor movement until the late summer of 1905 is also mentioned by M. I. Vasil'ev-Iuzhin (quoted in P. Gorin, *Ocherki po istorii Sovetov Rabochikh Deputatov v 1905 godu* [Moscow, 1925], p. 207) and by Breslav (quoted in *Bol'shevistskie listovki . . .*, p. 3). A striking confirmation is the Moscow Committee's leaflet of July, 1905, "Ko vsem moskovskim rabochim i rabotnitsam," which begins: "'Among the Moscow workers all is well,' police *ataman* Trepov reports to the ministers with a broad grin. Gleefully the ministers and their underlings rub their hands dripping with the blood of the working people of Petersburg and the Caucasus, Lodz, Odessa, Ivanovo-Voznesensk—wherever the worker has risen to the holy struggle. 'In our Moscow it's quiet,' snicker the police sleuths happily . . ." and so on. (*Listovki moskovskikh bol'shevikov v period pervoi russkoi revoliutsii* [Moscow: Istpart, 1955], p. 226.)

[5] *Iskra*, No. 111, September 24, noted the appearance of this leaflet in the section "Partiinaia pressa."

the city governor's knowledge but without police present. . . . Chistov presided; Sher reported on talks with the management. . . . A similar soviet was formed by joiners during the strike at furniture factories; it was headed by the Bolshevik Nikolaev.[6]

N. S. Nikolaev, the only Bolshevik among the men who came to the fore through their activity in the Moscow soviets, had risen from the ranks and was a man of no consequence in the Party organization. The other party workers mentioned—Iosif Andreevich Isuv, Nikolai Ivanovich Chistov (president of the illegal Printers' Union), and Vasilii Vladimirovich Sher—were all prominent Mensheviks.

Iskra published a Moscow correspondent's report of September 25 that "a meeting of the Group and of sector centers" had outlined plans for organizing the movement, such as "inviting [the workers] to elect deputies and establishing contact among deputies."[7] On the same day, a meeting of printers' deputies declared itself the soviet for the printing trade.[8] Soon the idea of an all-city soviet was born. Kolokol'nikov writes:

> In late September, on the Mensheviks' initiative, attempts were made to link together organizationally the deputies of separate factories and branches of industry. General meetings of deputies took place at the Museum of Assistance to Labor on October 2 and 4. At the first there were thirty-two representatives from five trades; at the second, twenty-eight from six trades—the overwhelming majority Social-Democrats. Represented were the printers, joiners, metal workers, tobacco workers, ribbon weavers. Chistov presided over the meetings. The meetings began with reports on the progress of the strike movement. The first meeting declared it necessary to "combine the deputies by trade and then into a general soviet of workers of all Moscow.[9]

At that time the railroad workers' movement had already begun; it soon led to a nationwide railroad strike and culminated in the general strike of October. The railroad strike brought forth a new organ—the

---

[6] P. Kolokol'nikov [K. Dmitriev], "Otryvki iz vospominanii," in *Materialy po istorii professional'nogo dvizheniia v Rossii*, II (Moscow: Istprof VTsSPS, 1924), 227.

[7] *Iskra*, No. 112, October 8, 1905.

[8] The resolution of the general meeting of printers' deputies on September 25 recognized the need to establish a permanent soviet of deputies from printing presses "for the duration of the strike," but it also declared: "Until a better organization of printers is established, the soviet of deputies must remain after the strike, too, to maintain regular contact among the printing presses, to check that both sides fulfil the decisions made, and to convoke separate or general meetings as the need arises." The resolution is printed in *Listovki moskovskikh bol'shevikov* . . . (1955), pp. 265–67.

[9] Kolokol'nikov, "Otryvki iz vospominanii" (1924), p. 229.

Moscow Strike Committee. This somewhat delayed the creation of the Soviet of Workers' Deputies:

The Strike Committee became the leading organ of the October strike. Originally it had been formed by railroad people, apparently members of the local center of the railroad union, which belonged to the Union of Unions and consisted almost entirely of qualified employees, [having] nothing in common with railroad workers and low-level employees. According to the plan of its organizers, the Strike Committee was to include only representatives of political parties and professional-political unions. The origin of the Committee and its composition, which predetermined its political platform and tactics, could not satisfy Social-Democracy. But [the latter] did not consider it possible to break up an already established center at the peak of the battle, preferring to join it and fight from within for its democratization and proletarianization, by [introducing] representatives from striking railroads and factories. . . .

Representatives of striking workers were thus introduced into the Strike Committee, largely under the pressure of the Social-Democrats. At the same time, however, there also [appeared] more and more representatives of the bourgeois-democratic intelligentsia, as more new groups were drawn into the general strike. . . . Clearly a committee so mixed in composition and in political outlook was not our dish. Therefore, while temporarily remaining in the Strike Committee, we took steps to create instead, or side by side with it, an organ representing the working masses, to direct their fighting actions. The Soviet of Workers' Deputies, whose foundation had been laid at the conferences of representatives of five trades on October 2 and 4, was to be that organ. Nor did work in this direction cease during the October strike. On-the-spot agitation for electing deputies continued. About October 10, at the Surveyors' [Institute], a large Menshevik Party meeting of workers was held, with a lecture on organizing a soviet of workers' deputies. Finally on October 15 a third meeting of deputies from striking factories was called, at the Technical School. The meeting was well attended and lively. It agreed on the need to organize an all-city soviet. . . . As a first step . . . several meetings by branches of industry—one of them textile workers—were scheduled for October 18 at the Technical School to unite the striking factories and draft their common demands. Unlike the meetings of October 2 and 4, which only workers who were Party members had attended, the meeting of October 15 attracted many non-Party deputies.[10]

---

[10] P. Kolokol'nikov, "Otryvki iz vospominanii," in *Materialy po istorii professional'nogo dizheniia v Rossii* (Moscow, 1925), III, 216–17. At about the same time the Moscow Menshevik Group issued its appeal of October 14, "K bor'be!": "The struggle is flaring up. Like a fire, the general strike is engulfing all Russia. Higher and higher rises the new wave of the people's outrage. It grows in its mighty, tempestuous progress. It seizes city after city, sweeping everything before it.

The Manifesto of October 17, N. E. Bauman's assassination in Moscow on October 18, and the resulting tension delayed the creation of a Moscow soviet. Perhaps the Federative Council, formed on October 18, also had something to do with the delay. It restricted the Mensheviks' independence; and persuading the Bolsheviks to co-operate proved impossible. Kolokol'nikov wrote of these trying weeks:

> The preparatory work for organizing a Moscow soviet of workers' deputies dragged on for a long time. One of the main snags was the Bolshevik Committee's uncertain stand on organizing a soviet. At last . . . on November 21, at the Studiia theatre on Povarskaia, the first conference of the Soviet took place, under the chairmanship of the printer N. I. Chistov.[11]

The Mensheviks' role in the prehistory of the Moscow Soviet is clear from the preceding pages. We can judge of the Bolsheviks' role from their leaflets, published in several editions. The rising strike movement in September naturally attracted the attention of the Bolshevik organization, which responded to the printers' strike with two leaflets: "To the Men and Women Workers of the Printing Press of the Sytin Co.,"[12] issued by the City sector of the Moscow Committee, and "To All Men and Women Workers of Moscow,"[13] issued by the Moscow Committee. Neither mentioned electing deputies or even contained the word "deputies." What organizational ideas the first leaflet contained are expressed in the following lines:

> Array yourselves, comrades, under the red banner of Social-Democracy, which alone is defending your interests. Organize, comrades, then the

---

Perhaps this wave will be that ninth wave that will overwhelm the rotten edifice of tsarism, wipe the shame and the curse of our motherland, tsarist autocracy, off the face of the earth. On to the battle for freedom, comrades! Moscow, the heart of Russia, must become—is becoming—the heart of the nationwide uprising. . . ."

And so on. There follow some political and economic demands, and then: "For the sake of these demands, lay down your work. Hold meetings. At every factory and plant, discuss the situation. Draw up the special individual demands and the common demands of the whole working class. Elect deputies to lead the strike. The deputies will organize the scattered workers. . . . Let the deputies of all factories combine into a *general soviet of deputies* of all Moscow. Such a general soviet of deputies will unite the whole Moscow proletariat and give it the cohesion and organization it needs to fight all its enemies—the bourgeoisie as well as autocracy. . . ." The appeal ends with the slogans "Hail to the general strike! Hail to the armed uprising!" (*1905. Bol'shevistskie proklamatsii i listovki* . . . , pp. 441–43.) This appeal is discussed in more detail further on.

[11] Kolokol'nikov, "Otryvki iz vospominanii" (1925), p. 221.

[12] *Listovki moskovskikh bol'shevikov* . . . (1955), Item 130, pp. 280–81.

[13] *Ibid.*, Item 118, pp. 256–57.

entire working class will merge into one united family, attack its enemy, autocracy, and smash the bloodstained throne.

The second leaflet, issued a few days later, when the strike had spread and the idea of a soviet was in the air, did not mention deputies either and ended with these words:

> From torpor to strike, from strike to armed uprising, from uprising to victory—that is our path, the path of the working class. So take heart, comrades, forge ahead, to battle for the people's liberation! Down with autocracy! Long live the Russian Social-Democratic Labor Party!

In other words, the Party and nothing but the Party. The same attitude prevailed throughout the general strike. Several Moscow Committee leaflets of that period have been preserved: "To the Population," appealing for support of the strike; "To All Workers"; "To All Moscow Workers";[14] and an untitled leaflet.[15] The first does not discuss organization; the second urges the workers to arm and organize armed squads [*druzhiny*] at their factories, which would then "fuse into one national militia"; the third, very short, gives vent to feelings of outrage ("the blood of striking workers has crimsoned the streets of Moscow") and calls for a broader strike; the fourth appeals, "Unite more closely into a single army, a single Social-Democratic Labor Party." None mentions the Soviet, whereas all emphasize strengthening the Party organization. The hostility to the whole idea of soviets was so great that even the *Biulleten'*, which the Moscow Committee put out from late September until the end of the general strike,[16] never acknowledged the soviets that had emerged in several branches of industry or mentioned the meetings of deputies of October 2 and 4.

There was no immediate change even when the Federative Council of the Moscow Committee and of the Moscow Group was formed on October 18 and drew up the joint demands of both organizations. A

---

[14] *Ibid.*, Items 140, 151, 153.

[15] *Listovki bol'shevistskikh organizatsii v pervoi russkoi revoliutsii 1905–1907 gg.*, II, 98–100. This leaflet, present in the three-volume edition of Moscow leaflets, is not included in the 1955 edition (see n. 4)—perhaps because it contains the demand to withdraw troops from Moscow. This demand was repeated in the Federative Council's leaflet (*ibid.*, p. 112–14), which is also excluded from the 1955 edition.

[16] *Biulleten'*, No. 1, giving particulars of the events of July 20–31, came out already in early August (see *Listovki moskovskikh bol'shevikov* . . . [1955], Item 109, pp. 235–39); *Biulleten'*, No. 2, dealt with the events of September 26; thereafter it came out regularly. Its last issue, No. 12, described the events of October 17–19 (see *Listovki moskovskikh bol'shevikov* . . . [1955], Items 120, 125, 126, 133, 134, 136, 144, 146, 147, and 149).

leaflet signed by both the Bolshevik Committee and the Menshevik Group urged: "Organize, comrades, close your ranks, array yourselves under our clean proletarian banners! Unite in a single Social-Democratic Party and prepare for the decisive battle."[17] This leaflet is significant in its stress on a *single* party, an increasingly popular idea at the time. There is still no mention of the soviets.

Only in November, in a leaflet issued by the Federative Council, "On the Congress of Zemstvo and Municipal Leaders"[18] (it opened on November 6), was the Soviet of Workers' Deputies first mentioned in a document committing the Moscow Committee. The leaflet appealed in the name of the Soviet to all organized workers to "elect representatives to announce to the Zemstvo Congress the unswerving will of the Moscow proletariat." Actually the Soviet did not yet exist: two more weeks passed before it held its first conference; but apparently the Bolsheviks' resistance had been broken.

Below I shall try to analyze why the Moscow Soviet was so much less effective than the Petersburg Soviet, but first I want to quote from the reminiscences of some Bolsheviks active in the events of 1905. In the middle twenties, M. I. Vasil'ev-Iuzhin described the origin of the Moscow Soviet:[19]

> The idea of creating a soviet of workers' deputies in Moscow emerged in the Moscow proletariat in September or early October, 1905, when the general strike flared up in Moscow that later spread all over Russia. At the height of the strike the Moscow Social-Democrats issued an appeal entitled "On to the Struggle!" I shall quote it here in full as an exceptionally vivid document indicating the stand of our Party organization on a number of basic questions posed by events at the time.[20]

There followed the text of the leaflet discussed in note 4. It had been issued by the Menshevik Group, not the Moscow Committee ("our organization"). Vasil'ev-Iuzhin, it is true, did not remember the leaflet and quoted it from an article (in the collection *The December Uprising in Moscow in 1905* [*Dekabr'skoe vosstanie v Moskve v 1905 godu*] [Moscow, 1920]), whose author "unfortunately did not indicate" which of the Moscow organizations had issued the appeal. But from "its spirit, its content, its stand" Vasil'ev-Iuzhin knew it was Bolshevik:

---

17 *Listovki moskovskikh bol'shevikov* . . . (1955), Item 155, pp. 330–31.

18 *Ibid.*, Item 159, pp. 339–40.

19 M. I. Vasil'ev-Iuzhin, "Moskovskii Sovet rabochikh deputatov v 1905 godu," *Proletarskaia Revoliutsiia*, April and May, 1925. This article was also published separately in 1925.

20 *Proletarskaia Revoliutsiia*, April, 1925, pp. 84–85.

It is even possible that it had been written by me, for I wrote or edited most of the proclamations, resolutions, and other such documents of the Moscow Committee at the time and later also of the Federative Committee and the Soviet of Workers' Deputies. The style . . . also seems like mine. . . . Regrettably, this proclamation was no longer on hand at the Central Archives, where Comrade Maksakov says he found it. My efforts to find it elsewhere—at the Istpart, the Museum of the Revolution, and so on—also proved futile.[21]

This story was demolished right away. The leaflet in question was published in the 1926 edition of Bolshevik leaflets with the editors' comment that it had been found in the archives of the Moscow Okhrana and that "Comrade Vasil'ev-Iuzhin erroneously ascribes [it] to the Bolshevik organization. See his booklet *The Moscow Soviet of Workers' Deputies in 1905* [*Moskovskii Sovet Rabochikh Deputatov v 1905 g.*], p. 10."[22] This should have settled the matter, but oddly enough Vasil'ev-Iuzhin's discovery was taken up in 1927 by such a relatively objective writer as Nevskii, who spoke of "an extremely interesting document, known to everyone in Moscow but of course thoroughly forgotten, and only recently brought to light from archives" —the leaflet published by Vasil'ev-Iuzhin.[23]

This appeal "On to the Struggle!" is a truly remarkable document. There is nothing incredible in the assumption that already the events of September, 1905, had made the Moscow Bolsheviks draw on the experiences of Ivanovo-Voznesensk, and of Kostroma, and of the Moscow printers, and . . . the entire earlier movement.

In short, "the idea of a soviet was in the air already in September, and the Bolshevik organization formulated it."

Nevskii may have been honestly mistaken. His work appeared a year later than the *Bolshevik Leaflets,* but it could have gone to press earlier. However, other official historians continued to present Vasil'ev-Iuzhin's attractive fantasy as incontrovertible proof of early Bolshevik initiative in creating the Moscow Soviet. Kostomarov, the editor of the 1955 collection of 1905 Moscow Bolshevik leaflets, included in it the leaflet "On to the Struggle!" (with the title *V bor'be* instead of *K bor'be!*)[24], adding the Moscow Committee's signature to it and even quot-

---

[21] *Ibid.*, p. 85.

[22] *Bols'shevistskie listovki* . . . , p. 441.

[23] V. Nevskii, "Sovety v 1905 godu," in *1905. Istoriia revoliutsionnogo dvizheniia v otdel'nykh ocherkakh,* ed. M. N. Pokrovskii (Moscow-Leningrad, 1927), III, 25.

[24] *Listovki moskovskikh bol'shevikov* . . . (1955), Item 141, pp. 303–4.

ing it in his foreword.[25] Yet he must have thoroughly studied the 1926 edition, in which the origin of the leaflet is documented. He writes that "the originals of the leaflets published here are kept at Tsentral'nyi Gosudarstvennyi istoricheskii arkhiv, at the library of Institut Marksa-Engel'sa-Stalina pri TsK KPSS, and at Institut istorii partii MK i MGK KPSS. References to sources are given after each document."[26] References are indeed given for 251 documents out of a total of 252. The exception is leaflet 141, the one we are discussing. Here we read: "See *Leaflets of Moscow Bolsheviks in 1905* (Moskovskii Rabochii, 1941), pp. 215–16"—a very poor substitute for an archival reference.

The claim of the leaflet's Bolshevik authorship was definitely dropped only after the Twentieth Party Congress, when an attempt was made to put some limits to the distortion of history. The leaflet is not included in the three-volume collection *Leaflets of Bolshevik Organizations during the First Russian Revolution* (1956). And in a more recent article on the Soviets of 1905 we read:

> For a long time the leaflet "On to the Struggle!" was mistakenly ascribed to the Bolsheviks. At present it has been ascertained that [it] was issued by the Moscow Group of the RSDRP (see *Arkheograficheskii Ezhegodnik for* [1957], published by AN SSSR, 1958, p. 198; and TsGIAM, collection of illegal publications, No. 8270).[27]

Vasil'ev-Iuzhin must have found it difficult to explain to the reader —and to himself—why the Soviet was not formed soon after the leaflet's appearance. He took the bull by the horns:

> Why didn't we earlier, during the strike, carry out our original intention to organize a soviet of workers' deputies?
>
> At first we were too busy with other things. The strike was going on in a very concerted fashion. Our cadres of professional revolutionaries, small at the time, were up to their necks in work. Even the Committee could meet only sporadically, for short periods, and had to form an executive commission of two or three of its members as the organ of leadership. Besides, the Party was rapidly gaining enormous authority and popularity in the eyes of the broad masses, and it seemed to us that it would be able to lead the proletariat's political struggle directly,

---

[25] *Ibid.*, p. 13.

[26] *Ibid.*, p. 15.

[27] V. E. Tsys', "Obrazovanie Sovetov rabochikh deputatov v 1905 godu i otnoshenie k nim bol'shevikov i men'shevikov (Tsentral'no-promyshlennyi raion Rossii)," in the collection of articles *Voprosy istorii KPSS* (Moscow: Akademiia obshchestvennykh nauk pri TsK KPSS, 1959), p. 306.

without help from ancillary organizations, especially non-partisan ones.[28]

This is mildly put but basically correct. The Moscow Committee did believe that the Party organization of professional revolutionaries could gather all the threads of the movement in its hands, and it did dislike the idea of "non-partisan organizations." The implication is clear that "we" therefore impeded the creation of a soviet.

As their leaflets show, the Bolsheviks for a long time simply ignored the masses' unmistakable wish for a soviet. Also quite revealing in this respect are the writings of two members of the Moscow Committee. One of them is M. Liadov, who came to Moscow on October 13 after escaping from the Baku jail and for two months played a notable role in the Committee (in December he, Shantser-Marat, and Vasil'ev-Iuzhin were the *troika* intrusted with the top-level leadership of the movement). In his reminiscences, written in the middle twenties, he first mentions the Soviet only in December: until then the problem did not exist for him.[29] The other is S. Chernomordik, secretary of the Moscow Committee in 1905 (from August). His long article "1905 in Moscow" mentions the Soviet only at the end, in connection with its meeting of December 4, after the arrest of the Petersburg Soviet.[30] In the article "The Moscow SWD," he writes:

> The Moscow Soviet was not a leadership organ of the revolutionary Moscow proletariat but a fighting organ through which the Bolsheviks implemented their political influence over, and guidance of, the proletarian masses. The Moscow Soviet was also a kind of conductor of the political influence of Social-Democracy into the masses. Thus there was no need for the Soviet to have any special directing or business organs, such as an executive committee. The Party organizations fulfilled [these] functions, while the Soviet had only a moral importance and a political one insofar as it unified the broad non-partisan proletarian masses.[31]

Chernomordik probably did not realize that his formulation reduced to zero the Soviet's importance as an organ of the broad masses—and what an indictment this was of the Bolshevik policy

---

[28] *Proletarskaia Revoliutsiia*, April, 1925, p. 89.

[29] M. Liadov, *Iz zhizni partii v 1903–1907 gg.* (*Vospominaniia*) (Moscow: Kom. Universitet im. Ia. M. Sverdlova, 1926).

[30] S. Chernomordik [P. Larionov], "Piatyi god v Moskve," in the eponymous collection of his articles published by Istpart (Moscow, 1925), pp. 7–46.

[31] S. Chernomordik, "Moskovskii SRD," in *Piatyi god v Moskve* (Moscow, 1925). This article was first published as an introduction to another book (see n. 3 to this appendix).

toward the Soviet; but he did render the Moscow Committee's idea of the Soviet's tasks and nature. Vasil'ev-Iuzhin expresses this idea rather well in his article "The Moscow Soviet of Workers' Deputies" in the Moscow *Bor'ba* of December 1, 1905:

> The purpose of the Soviet of Workers' Deputies is to assist in the unification and leadership of the proletariat's political and economic struggle. Such organizations are necessary where Social-Democracy, the proletariat's only reliable leader, has not had time to encompass the broad masses in its orderly organization when the revolution begins. They are powerful helpers of the Party.[32]

Here the idea is still cast in more or less diplomatic terms. It was expressed more bluntly at the Conference of (Bolshevik) Northern Committees in Moscow on November 21 to 23: "The Soviet of Workers' Deputies must be the Party's technical apparatus for carrying the RSDRP's political leadership to the masses."[33] A technical apparatus attached to the Party—that was all the Moscow Bolsheviks wanted the Soviet to be.

To round out the picture, let us see how modern Bolshevik historians describe the origin of the Moscow Soviet of 1905. The eyewitnesses who wrote in the twenties on the whole respected the facts as they remembered them; if they falsified history it was by suppressing those that clashed with the Party line. History was groomed Bolshevik style but retained some elements of truth. The "creative" historians brought up on the *Short Course* in the Stalin era indulge in tendentious fiction. Under their pens the myth assumes an existence independent of reality.

G. Kostomarov's little book on the Moscow Soviet[34] has been until recently standard reading for young historians. Its basic thesis is that the Moscow Bolsheviks advanced the idea of soviets as early as August, 1905, and remained faithful to it:

> In August, 1905, the Moscow Committee of the Party, drawing on the experience of the formation of a soviet in Ivanovo-Voznesensk, issued a special leaflet urging the Moscow workers to elect deputies to soviets at all factories and plants. The Moscow Committee's appeal met with the warmest sympathy of the masses.[35]

---

[32] This article by Vasil'ev-Iuzhin is also reprinted in an appendix to his work on the Moscow Soviet of 1905; see *Proletarskaia Revoliutsiia*, May, 1925, pp. 130–31.

[33] See n. 50 to chapter iv.

[34] G. Kostomarov, *Moskovskii Sovet rabochikh deputatov v 1905 godu* (151 pp.; Moscow: Moskovskii Rabochii, 1948); and the 2d edition (200 pp.; Moscow, 1955). I used the first edition, not having been able to obtain the second.

[35] *Ibid.*, pp. 18–19.

Did "the Ivanovo-Voznesensk experience" really prompt the Moscow Committee to call for elections to a Moscow soviet? Let us look at the Bolshevik leaflets assembled by the same Kostomarov. The only leaflet to which his words could possibly apply is the already mentioned "To All Men and Women Workers of Moscow" issued in July. It begins with a lampoon of the Moscow workers' apathy (see n. 4). Then it asks: "Nearby, the Ivanovo-Voznesensk [workers] have been struggling for a month and a half with spirit, tenacity, courage. Heroes still exist, the fighters are countless. What about us, comrades?" The "appeal" part of the leaflet says:

> Gather in workshops and factories, discuss the burning needs. Now is the time to eradicate the vilest abuses, sweep out the worst stooges of the bosses. But no separate talks with the bosses. The workers have common needs; the same yoke weighs them down.
>
> Let us combine the main demands of the whole working class of Moscow and pledge mutual support to the end. One for all, all for one.[36]

This is a far cry from urging the workers to form a soviet. And in the latter half of September, when the workers really faced the problem of creating soviets, the Moscow Committee, as we have seen, not only failed to support the movement but tried in several leaflets to deflect it into strengthening the Party organization instead. Ignoring these leaflets, Kostomarov states that in early October "the Bolshevik Moscow Committee addressed to all laboring people an appeal that played a major role in the creation of the Moscow Soviet"—and quotes at length from the Menshevik leaflet "On to the Struggle!" Kostomarov continues:

> The workers and laboring people of Moscow met this fiery appeal of the Bolsheviks with exceptional enthusiasm. With the greatest willingness, they went forth to struggle under the leadership of our Party.
>
> The struggle to create an all-Moscow soviet of workers' deputies was growing broader and broader.
>
> The liberal bourgeoisie in alliance with the Mensheviks formed a "Strike Committee" to offset the burgeoning Soviet of Workers' Deputies. At the beginning of the political strike of October there were thus two diametrically opposed organs leading the proletariat's strike struggle in Moscow. From the outset of their activities, a tense struggle developed between them. The Bolsheviks exposed the counterrevolutionary nature of the Strike Committee and made every effort to counterbalance it by organizing sector soviets and an all-Moscow soviet of workers' deputies.

---

[36] *Listovki moskovskikh bol'shevikov* . . . (1955), pp. 228–29.

The Mensheviks, donning the mask of "representatives" of the workers' interests, tried to obscure the counterrevolutionary nature of the Strike Committee and hampered the creation of soviets in every way.[37]

No sources are given for any of this, with one exception: quoting the leaflet "On to the Struggle!" Kostomarov refers the reader to the 1941 edition of the collection of Bolshevik Moscow leaflets. Anyone who has followed the *documented* data I have presented will see Professor Kostomarov's work for the mythmaking it is. He goes on in the same vein:

> At the Bolsheviks' insistence, a meeting of the Soviet of Workers' Deputies of Moscow's five main industries took place on October 2. . . . On October 4, a second meeting of the Soviet of Workers' Deputies of five industries took place. . . . After the conferences of October 2 and 4 the question arose of formally organizing an all-Moscow soviet and convoking its first plenum.
>
> On October 10 this question was debated at a crowded Bolshevik meeting. The Moscow Mensheviks also discussed this question at the same time. . . . They naturally became enemies of the emerging Soviet and made every effort to obstruct its formal organization.[38]

This unbelievable distortion of the Soviet's beginnings fittingly culminates in the following analysis of the Soviet's weakness:

> The Mensheviks' double-dealing tactics severely hampered the work of the Moscow Soviet. Because of the sabotage of the Mensheviks and SR's, the Soviet could not complete a number of organizational measures. Thanks to the Mensheviks it proved impossible, for instance, to elect a permanent chairman of the Soviet. As a result, the functions of chairman at important meetings were often performed by random people. For the same reason, the Soviet failed to develop the minimal necessary technical apparatus and did not even have permanent premises. Nor were the proper measures taken to provide it with a material base of its own. . . .[39]

After the Twentieth Party Congress, Kostomarov's book was severely criticized (by Z. M. Bograd) in *Voprosy Istorii*:

> [He] patently diverges from the true course of history. . . .G. Kostomarov's antihistorical attempts to embellish history instead of recording it truthfully harm rather than help the creative study of the rich experience of the Revolution of 1905–7; [they] often turn into shallow glorification and hallelujahs.[40]

---

[37] Kostomarov, *Moskovskii Sovet rabochikh deputatov* . . ., pp. 19–20.
[38] *Ibid.*, pp. 20–22.
[39] *Ibid.*, p. 30.
[40] *Voprosy Istorii*, March, 1956, p. 158.

Of course the reviewer does not mention that the Mensheviks' role had also been distorted; but this crushing analysis of Kostomarov's work made other historians more cautious.

There have been no new editions of Kostomarov's book. But in 1959 the Academy of Social Sciences published a study by V. E. Tsys'[41] which revives the myth in a new variant. Tsys' admits that "the printers' strike was directed by the Menshevik union of Moscow printers, which in August had declared its solidarity with the Moscow Group of the RSDRP,"[42] and that the Mensheviks had a good deal to do with the emergence of various soviets in late September and early October. But he contends that they tried to keep the movement within the bounds of the economic struggle, whereas the Bolsheviks, with exemplary energy, preached the need to prepare for "the decisive battle between the revolutionary forces and the forces of autocracy."

> When the workers in the printing trade, despite the Menshevik leaders of their union, openly began to support the Bolsheviks' political line in the revolution, the leaders of the union, just as the nationwide political strike was in the making, attempted to turn the printers' soviet into a trade-union organization.[43]

And when the deputies of five trades called upon the Moscow workers to form an all-Moscow soviet, and the idea received "wide support,"

> the Mensheviks could not openly oppose the workers' desire to unite in an all-city soviet, but, making use of their influence and of the less conscious deputies' support, they tried to give the Soviet a narrowly trade-union character. . . . All this shows that although the Mensheviks formally "assisted" in creating soviets of workers' deputies, they wanted to turn them into narrow trade-union organizations.[44]

The leaflet "On to the Struggle!," whose Menshevik origin was now admitted, also received a new interpretation:

> Only when the development of the strike struggle had almost brought the working class to open armed action against autocracy, and the proletariat's victory had become a realistic prospect, were the Mensheviks forced, in the leaflet "On to the Struggle!" of October 14, to advance the slogan of an all-Moscow soviet of workers' deputies and an armed uprising.
>
> All this, however, was only the usual Menshevik line of adapting to the rise of the labor movement. . . . The fear of being jettisoned by the

---

[41] V. E. Tsys', "Obrazovanie Sovetov rabochikh deputatov . . . ," pp. 271–334.
[42] *Ibid.*, p. 294.
[43] *Ibid.*, p. 298.
[44] *Ibid.*, p. 299.

movement forced the Mensheviks to recognize formally the slogans of uprising and of creating an all-city soviet.[45]

Not so the Bolsheviks! Tsys', it is true, does not assert that they actually called for a soviet before or during the strike; but he does say that they tried hard to overcome the Mensheviks' influence and to combine the strikes into a general political strike that would lead to a nationwide strike and to an armed uprising;[46] and that

> right after the Strike Committee had announced the end of the strike [that is, about October 20.—S. S.] the Bolsheviks left it and began the struggle for an all-Moscow soviet of workers' deputies in which the entire revolutionary working class of Moscow would be represented.[47]

This is pure invention. No wonder the author gives no sources for his assertion that the Bolsheviks called for a Moscow soviet "right after" the strike, though the rest of his study abounds in references.

The story goes on in the same way: the Bolsheviks displayed great energy, carried high the banner of revolution; the Moscow Soviet resulted from their efforts; the Mensheviks wanted the workers to concentrate on the economic struggle and hampered the creation of a soviet which might become the center of the political struggle. Even the late emergence of the Soviet was due to Menshevik interference with Bolshevik plans:

> That there was some delay in the creation of an all-Moscow soviet was largely due to the disruptive activity of the Mensheviks, to their policy of adapting the organizations that the working class was creating to the struggle for economic concessions. Trying to get the workers on their side, they played on the backward sentiments of the most downtrodden part of the working class not yet fully aware of the need to conduct a political struggle against autocracy.[48]

It would be redundant to refute these statements.

---

[45] *Ibid.*, pp. 305–6.
[46] *Ibid.*, pp. 300–301.
[47] *Ibid.*, p. 304.
[48] *Ibid.*, p. 310.

Index